INTERNATIONAL MONITORING OF PLEBISCITES, REFERENDA AND NATIONAL ELECTIONS

International Studies in Human Rights

VOLUME 32

The titles published in this series are listed at the end of this volume

INTERNATIONAL MONITORING OF PLEBISCITES, REFERENDA AND NATIONAL ELECTIONS

Self-determination and Transition to Democracy

Yves Beigbeder

MARTINUS NIJHOFF PUBLISHERS
DORDRECHT / BOSTON / LONDON

Library of Congress Cataloging-in-Publication Data

Beigbeder, Yves.
International monitoring of plebiscites, referenda and national elections : self-determination and transition to democracy / Yves Beigbeder.
p. cm. -- (International studies of human rights ; v. 32)
Includes index.
ISBN 0-7923-2563-X (alk. paper)
1. Plebiscite. 2. Referendum. 3. Self-determination, National. 4. Election monitoring. I. Title. II. Series: International studies in human rights ; v. 32.
JX4054.B43 1994
341.2'9--dc20 93-39167

ISBN 0-7923-2563-X

Published by Martinus Nijhoff Publishers,
P.O. Box 163, 3300 AD Dordrecht, The Netherlands.

Sold and distributed in the U.S.A. and Canada
by Kluwer Academic Publishers,
101 Philip Drive, Norwell, MA 02061, U.S.A.

In all other countries, sold and distributed
by Kluwer Academic Publishers Group,
P.O. Box 322, 3300 AH Dordrecht, The Netherlands.

Printed on acid-free paper

To Pauline and Mathieu

TABLE OF CONTENTS

ACKNOWLEDGEMENTS

I wish to thank all the organizations' representatives who have given some of their time – some of whom have usefully reviewed part of my text – and have helped me to obtain relevant information and documentation. In particular, my thanks are extended to representatives of the following organizations:

- in Atlanta, where my research started, the Carter Center,
- in Washington, D.C., the Organization of American States' Unit for the Promotion of Democracy, the International Human Rights Law Group, the National Endowment for Democracy, the National Democratic Institute for International Affairs, the International Republican Institute, the International Foundation for Electoral Systems,
- in London, the Commonwealth Secretariat,
- in Strasbourg, the Council of Europe's European Commission for Democracy through Law, and Parliamentary Assembly,
- in Warsaw, the Office for Democratic Institutions and Human Rights of the Conference on Security and Cooperation in Europe,
- in Paris, the International Federation of Human Rights,
- in Geneva, the European Community's Documentation Office, the International Commission of Jurists, the Inter-Parliamentary Union.

A special thanks is addressed to the ever-helpful and patient staff of the United Nations Library in Geneva.

The editing skills and willing assistance of Mandy Eggleston are, again, as for previous books in English, gratefully acknowledged.

Finally, my wife's long-tried patience and support have helped the completion of this work.

The author has written this book in a personal capacity: the views and assessments are his own responsibility – they do not necessarily represent the views of, nor commit in any way, the organizations he is associated with.

FOREWORD

The international monitoring of elections has become a prominent feature of post Cold War international relations. With the end of the Cold War, trends towards democratization in Eastern Europe, and superpower agreements resulting in the resolution of regional conflicts in Africa, Central America and Asia have resulted in the holding of presidential, parliamentary and local elections in countries with no or little tradition in Western style democracy.

The proliferation of elections since the late 1980s has brought to prominence the legitimizing of this process through international observation. Election monitors have regularly been dispatched by international organizations such as the United Nations, the Commonwealth, the Organization of American States and the Conference on Security and Cooperation in Europe to monitor the "freedom and fairness" of elections. In addition, observers from non-governmental organizations added their weight to legitimizing the idea of democracy in the host countries concerned.

In his very timely and in many regards innovative book, the author rightly asks himself whether international observers can effectively help in a country's transition to democracy, and whether Western countries would force ill-prepared countries into a ritual of democracy without substance.

These are fundamental questions which have to be addressed by all contemporaries. The author courageously and successfully attempts to give us a broad overview of monitoring plebiscites and referenda for self-determination as well as elections in the search of a new post Cold War political order. In particular, he situates the notions of self-determination and democracy in their historical and political context before analyzing the monitoring of plebiscites by the international community from the days of the League of Nations.

The experience by the United Nations in monitoring plebiscites and elections features prominently in the study. But the author also examines in detail initiatives by other intergovernmental organizations such as the Organization of American States, the Commonwealth and various European organizations. In addition, an entire chapter is devoted to "Election assistance and monitoring by non-governmental organizations". NGOs, because of their often close contact with the electorate, can meaningfully complement international monitoring by intergovernmental organizations.

This book does not have the pretence to repeat the mistakes of the Cold War era and give us ready made answers. But it has the great merit to allow the reader to acquire a well-informed awareness and have a welcome general view of international election monitoring. For the author tells us convincingly that "elections are the building block of all democracy: no elections, no democracy".

RONALD DREYER
International Election Observer – Research Fellow, Graduate Institute of International Studies (Geneva)

August 1993

INTRODUCTION

> Ballots are the rightful and peaceful successors to bullets.
> Abraham Lincoln
> Message to Congress, July 7, 1861

International organizations and government representatives have monitored plebiscites, referenda and elections in trust and other dependent territories or sovereign countries since the First World War.

International monitoring of such processes was intended to give a guarantee to the populations of the territories or countries and to the international community that the people had been able to exercise freely their right to self-determination – the free choice of the population of a territory to join, or not, an existing state, – the right of a colony to become an independent and sovereign State, – or the right of the people of a country to choose freely their political regime, their political and social institutions and their political leaders through free, genuine and periodical elections.

The independence, expertise and international composition of the monitoring teams is to guarantee their impartiality with regard to the ruling authorities, the competing factions or parties, and the value of their assessment of the electoral process and its results.

International monitoring, by focusing international attention on an electoral process, may deter manipulation or fraud by a government, armed forces or electoral authorities, – it shows international solidarity with the population concerned and gives international support for the electoral process and for democracy. International observers are expected to report publicly and honestly on the extent to which political, electoral, and more generally, human rights, are respected in a particular country.

The recent expansion of international monitoring of national elections is directly related to the spectacular political and economic changes which have occurred since 1988, the end of the Cold War, the apparent triumph of Western values over the Communist ideology, and the peoples' rejection, in many countries, of totalitarian or authoritarian governments: these changes amplified a new wave of democratic expansion which started in the 1970s.

The "Third Wave of Democratic Expansion"

In its 1992 Annual Survey, Freedom House reported that, out of the 183 nations evaluated by the survey, 91 had democratic systems, 15 of which were considered in the "Partly free" category; another 35 governments were in varying degrees of a transition to a more open and pluralistic system. Once major competitors to liberal democracy, Communist states had been reduced to six, and traditional monarchies to twelve; military regimes numbered eighteen. Of all the surveyed nations, 38 remained one- or dominant-party political systems – in 57 of the 126 countries that were either democratic or in transition to democracy, military, para-military and security forces played a significant political role. Out of a world population of 5.37 billion people, 25% lived in countries categorized as "Free", 43% in "Partly Free", and 32% in "Not Free societies".

Over the last decade, Freedom House has recorded 28 successful democratic transitions around the world, the largest wave of liberalization in the history of mankind.

There were 44 democracies in 1972, 56 in 1980 and 91 in 1992.

In its 1992 Human Development Report, the U.N. Development Programme (UNDP) made an attempt to construct a political freedom index. On the basis of the data collected for 104 countries representing 92% of the world's population, the analysis showed that about a third had high political freedom, another third had reasonable political freedom, and the remaining third modest to low political freedom.[1]

Huntington[2] has identified several cycles or waves in the evolution of modern democracy: from 1820 to 1920, the first democratic "long" wave spread from the United States to Northern and Western Europe, some British dominions and a few countries in Latin America; a reverse undemocratic wave, from 1920 to 1945, which affected Germany, Italy, Austria, Poland, the Baltic States, Spain, Portugal, Greece, Argentina, Brazil and Japan; a third wave, from 1945 to 1962, when democracy expanded as a consequence of the U.S. imposition of democracy on West Germany, Austria, Italy, Japan and South Korea, combined with decolonization during which many newly independent countries adopted the political forms of the imperial powers; a second reverse wave (1960–1975), in which military coups and revolutions reduced the number of democracies from 36 to 30; and finally, the period from 1975 to the present, which Huntington characterizes as the "third wave" of democratic expansion.

While this "third wave" is clearly a global phenomenon, which, since 1989, followed the demise of the Communist ideology and global ambitions, the form, scope and intensity of the democratic processes and advances differ from Europe to Latin America to Asia to Africa. A few selected examples follow.

Central and Eastern Europe

After more than four dark and dangerous decades of Cold War, on 9 November 1989, the Berlin wall fell and most of the peoples of Central and Eastern Europe progressively regained their free political choice and freedoms. Through the first free elections held since they were submitted to the dictatorship of the Communist Party, under the military threat of the USSR, the people rejected Socialism under its imposed political and economic forms.

In April 1989, a Round Table decided to break the monopoly of the Communist Party to the election of the Polish Diet: 35% of representatives of the non-Communist opposition were allowed to be elected. Independent economic and cultural associations were authorized, including the Solidarity union and a students' association, but political associations or parties were not, yet, authorized. On 18 June, Solidarity won 161 seats at the Diet (35%) and 99 of the 100 seats of the newly created Senate. In September, the new Polish government included only four Communist members out of 20. In November–December 1990, Lech Walesa was elected President by 73% of the votes.

In June 1989, the Hungarian Communist party and nine opposition groups agreed to negotiate a transition towards a pluralist democracy. In September, the ex-Communist Party, renamed Socialist Party, revoked the concept and practice of the "dictatorship of the proletariat" and "democratic centralism". The first free legislative elections organized since World War II were held in March–April 1990: out of 386 elected representatives, 165 belonged to the Democratic Forum (MDF) and 92 to the Alliance of Free Democrats.

In October 1989, the newly appointed East German Chief of government announced that secret, free, democratic and pluralist elections would soon be organized. In November, Chancellor Helmut Kohl proposed a reunification plan and free elections. The first free elections organized in East Germany since 1933 gave 40.9% of the votes to the Christian Democrats. On 3 October 1990, the Federal Republic of Germany and the German Democratic Republic were reunified.

In November 1989, in Prague, "Civic Forum", led by Vaclav Havel, organized impressive manifestations demanding democratic reforms. The newly formed government included 10 non-Communists out of 21 members. In June 1990, Civic Forum won the legislative elections, the first free elections since World War II: Civil Forum with 46.6% of the votes, while the Communist Party obtained only 13.6% of the votes.

In Romania, in December 1989, following violent manifestations and the execution of Nicolae Ceaucescu and his wife, a Front of National Salvation, led by Communist or ex-Communist leaders, announced that free legislative elections would be held. These were held in May 1990, giving 66% of the votes to the Front. Later elections, held on 27 September 1992, gave a less impressive relative majority to the Front: 28.3% of the vote for the Senate, and 27.7% for the Chamber of

Deputies. Electoral fraud was alleged by the opposition Democratic Convention and some non-governmental organizations' observers.

In January 1990, the Bulgarian National Assembly abolished Article I of the Constitution which affirmed the "leading role" of the Communist Party. The first free elections since World War II gave 47.15% of the votes to the Socialist Party (ex-Communist Party). In October 1991, the Union of Democratic Forces (UDF) led the Socialist Party with 110 of the 240 seats, vs. 106 to the latter. On 8 November, the UDF leader formed a minority government, without any Communist minister for the first time since 1944.

In June 1991, the Albanian Communist government resigned after a three-week general strike. A new coalition government was formed, with non-Communist members. The Albanian Democratic Party won the March 1992 general elections, sealing the end of Communism in this country.[3]

More or less advanced democratization in Central and Eastern Europe was accompanied or followed by ethnic strife and the dislocation, in 1991 and 1992, of the former Soviet "Empire", Yugoslavia and Czechoslovakia into separate independent States.

Democratization in Central and Eastern Europe, following the defeat of the Communist ideology, the bankruptcy of Socialism as an economic panacea and the downfall of the "other" Great Power, drew world attention, – in part because "totalitarian" states, unlike "authoritarian" ones, were deemed incapable of an evolution towards democracy and liberalism, – in part, because popular unarmed insurrections succeeded in overthrowing powerful governments and entrenched political and economic regimes, – and, in part, because these events were widely publicized and reported by written and audiovisual media.

Latin America

Unrelated to de-communization, several Latin American countries preceded Central and Eastern European countries in democratic advances, in spite of their turbulent politics: for instance, in the past 48 years, Central America and Panama have had 105 changes of President – 30 through coups and 55 through elections. Military governments ruled in Chile from 1973 to 1989, in Paraguay from 1954 to 1989, in Argentina from 1976 to 1983, in Uruguay from 1973 to 1984, in Ecuador until 1979, in Peru from 1969 to 1980, in Brazil from 1964 to 1985.[4]

As related by Pastor,[5]

> The decision by General President Ernesto Geisel gradually to open the Brazilian political system – the abertura – was a model adopted by other military governments. The process was controlled by the military, but it led step-by-step toward wider elections for more positions until January 1985 when an opposition leader was elected president in an electoral college vote.

In 1978, power was transferred peacefully from the president to the leader of the opposition party in the Dominican Republic for the first time in a century. In April 1979, a social democratic leader was elected president in Ecuador, and despite reservations by the military, he was inaugurated in August. In May 1980, Fernando Belaunde, who had been overthrown by the Peruvian military 12 years before, won the presidental election and took power.

Honduras ended a phase of military regimes and began its democratization in 1982. Some threats of a military coup d'état appeared in 1992.

Democracy was restored to Argentina in 1983 after her defeat in the Falklands/Malvinas war. Democracy was forcefully re-established by U.S. military interventions in Grenada (October 1983) and in Panama (December 1989). In March 1990, Chile continued its democratic transition by the installation of the civilian government of President Patricio Aylwin.

On 7 August 1987, the Presidents of the five Central American nations signed the Guatemala Procedure, also known as Esquipulas II. In part, the Presidents undertook to launch a process of democratization in their countries, to promote a national dialogue, to decree a national amnesty, to bring about a genuine cease-fire, and to promote the holding of free, pluralistic and fair elections. The Presidents also agreed that they would invite the U.N. and the Organization of American States (OAS) to send international observers to verify the various electoral processes.

Elections took place in Nicaragua in February 1990 under the observation of a U.N. and an OAS mission: in all, 2,578 foreign observers from 278 organizations, as well as 1,500 journalists, observed or monitored the electoral process, which saw the victory of the candidate of the opposition to the Sandinistas (see Chapter 6).

The fragility of democratic transition was, however, demonstrated by the military overthrow, on 29 September 1991, of President Jean-Bertrand Aristide, who had been legitimately elected in internationally supervised elections in December 1990 (see Chapter 6).

Another disturbing sign of a possible reversal to past authoritarian practices was the "auto-golpe" (a self-administered coup) committed by President Alberto Fujimori of Peru in April 1992, with the support of the armed forces, in dissolving the national legislature, placing prominent lawmakers, opposition leaders and journalists under arrest, suspending civil liberties and sending armored vehicles in the streets.

A more encouraging signal was given by the leaders of Spain, Portugal and 17 Latin American countries at the second Ibero-American summit meeting held in Madrid: in a declaration signed on 24 July 1992, they clearly favoured "representative democracy" and respect for human rights, in a rebuff to Cuba's regime. In a reference to the recent constitutional coup in Peru and the failed military coup in Venezuela, the declaration denounced the use of force to solve problems and rejected any attempt to change the democratic order in the nations concerned.[6]

Asia

In Asia, democratic Australia, New Zealand, Japan, India, South Korea and the Philippines are still facing the last remaining Communist giant, China, accompanied by North Korea and Vietnam, and surrounded by authoritarian governments, generally controlled by their armed forces, prompt to repress democratic movements.

Most of the latter governments maintain that economic development deserves a higher priority than human rights, opposition political parties and independent trade unions and a free press. Such assertions may be based on the Confucian tradition which values human community and order more highly than individual rights. However, improved social and economic welfare is causing popular demands for more democracy and individual freedoms, for instance in Thailand, Myanmar (Burma) and Indonesia.

Thailand has been ruled by the military for six decades through a coalition in Parliament. In May 1992, popular manifestations against the appointment of General Suchinda Krapayoon as Prime Minister were brutally repressed by the army. The appointment by King Bhumibol, on 21 May, of Anand Panyarachun as Prime Minister restored civil peace, at least temporarily. In parliamentary elections held in September 1992, an alliance of four pro-democracy parties, called "angels", won by a small margin (185 out of 360 seats), thus rebuking the pro-military parties, known as "devils".[7]

Myanmar is under military rule since 1962, when General Ne Win toppled in a coup U Nu, the first civilian Prime Minister since independence was proclaimed in 1948. The military have stopped all political opposition through strict press censorship, arbitrary arrests or exiles, the replacement of civilian by military tribunals, torture of political prisoners. Pro-democracy demonstrations were repressed by the army in August 1988 (hundreds of deaths). In May 1990, legislative elections saw the victory of the National League for Democracy, but the military kept the power: the League's leader, Aung San Suu Kyi, 1991 Nobel Prize winner was placed under house arrest and the People's Assembly was not allowed to meet. On 17 December 1991, the U.N. General Assembly censured the government of Myanmar for the "grave human rights situation in the country" and urged it to allow all citizens to participate freely in the political process.[8]

Following manifestations in January and March 1990, the Parliament of Mongolia abolished the "leading role" of the Communist Party. However, in the first free elections held since 1920, on 29 July 1990, the Communist Party, in power since 1924, retained 345 seats out of 430 at the National Assembly: opposition parties gained 37 seats. In June 1991, a U.N. Mission gave advice on including human rights clauses in drafting a new constitution.

Also following manifestations for democratic reform in April 1990, King Birendra I authorized the formation of political parties in Nepal, which had been prohibited since 1960. The first multi-party elections since 1959 were held in May 1991.[9]

The U.N. plan for Cambodia, approved by the U.N. Security Council in February 1992, is the most ambitious peace-making and election-monitoring operation to be carried out by the international organization in a sovereign country: its purpose is to re-establish its real independence, to restore civil peace and to introduce a democratically elected constituent assembly (see Chapter 7). However, the implementation of the plan was frustrated by the non-cooperation of the Khmer Rouge and the results of the U.N.-organized elections have been contested by the Government party.

Africa

In Africa (South of the Sahara), the movement towards democracy has made some progress in recent years under the external pressure of foreign donors and the internal pressures of opposition leaders and the people, tired of arbitrary government, corruption and declining living standards and aroused by the success of the political changes in Central and Eastern Europe.

After independence, most African countries dismantled the multi-party political systems and the democratic institutions (separation of powers, freely elected representatives, independent Parliament and justice, individual guarantees etc.) which they had inherited from their colonial past. They were replaced by either repressive one-party systems, ruled by anti-colonial leaders who led their country to independence and remained in power indefinitely as "President for life", or by recurrent military dictatorships: in the period 17 April 1958 to 7 October 1986, there were 71 coups d'état and 118 attempted coups in African countries. In Zambia, before his fall, President Kenneth Kaunda devised "one-party participatory democracy", a contradiction in terms. Some of the rulers, like Uganda's Amin Dada, the "Emperor" Bokassa (Central African Republic) ruled by terror and massacres of their own population.[10]

After decades of political and economic mismanagement, African governments leaders could no longer blame the former colonial powers. After the collapse of Communism in Europe, they could no longer play East against West for political and financial support.

President Mitterand, in his address at the Franco-African summit in La Baule in June 1989, linked French aid to African countries to democratic and human rights advances. He said that France would go on giving help, but

> This traditional aid will be more tepid for regimes that behave in an authoritarian manner, without accepting the evolution toward democracy, and more enthusiastic for those who take this step bravely and go as far as they can.

In 1990, Britain's Foreign Secretary, Douglas Hurd, said:

> Countries which tend towards pluralism, public accountability, respect for the rule of law, human rights and market principles should be encouraged.

> Governments which persist with repressive policies, corrupt management and wasteful, discredited economic systems should not expect us to support their folly with scarce aid resources which could be used better elsewhere.

The U.S. State Department also announced in 1990 that aid to its friends in Africa would be conditioned on progress toward democracy. At the Commonwealth summit in 1991, the British Prime Minister formally encouraged, for the first time, democratic progress in Africa.[11]

African leaders, at least rhetorically, followed suit: on 6 July 1991, the heads of state and governments of the ECOWAS countries (Economic Community of West African States) signed the "Abuja Declaration", pledging themselves to promote democracy in the subregion on the basis of political pluralism and respect for fundamental human rights, including respect for freedom of thought, conscience, association and religion. On 28 May 1992, in the first Pan-African Conference on Democracy and the Management of Transition in Africa, the African political leaders adopted the "Dakar Declaration" which commits them to lead Africa from the one-party system to multi-party democracy.

The organizer of the conference, the Senegalese Minister of State, Maître Abdoulaye Wade, recalled that only in four African countries, opposition had taken power as a result of elections: Benin, Cape Verde, Sao Tome and Principe and Zambia; more than 40 countries still had not achieved full transition. The Carter Center considers that nine African countries have reached the democratic stage. In addition to the four mentioned above, the Carter Center includes Botswana, the Gambia, Mauritius, Namibia, Senegal.[12]

The democratic transition, in many African countries, will be an uphill struggle: for instance, in mid-1992, the Government of Côte d'Ivoire, under the leadership of President Felix Houphouet-Boigny (in power since 1960), had jailed 75 pro-democracy protestors, – five members of the opposition had been arrested in Equatorial Guinea, although opposition parties had been legalized, – an opposition leader had been shot in Togo. On the positive side, contested elections have been held in 11 African countries in the five years prior to 1992, and contested elections were being planned in 12 countries.[13]

Japan's White Paper of 7 October 1992 also announced its intention to "moralize" its foreign aid ($11.03 billion in 1991) by taking into account the respect of human rights in recipient countries, as well as their expenses in armaments, in order to play an active role in the promotion of democracy, human rights, peace and development. Tokyo would revise its aid policy in case of grave violations of democracy and human rights, excessive military expenses or of evolutions "unacceptable by the international community".[14]

The issue of the relations between democracy and Islam will be reviewed in Chapter 2.

Democracy and Intergovernmental Organizations

Are intergovernmental organizations (IGOs) "democratic"?

In the sense of "internal democracy", this would require that all member states be "equal" in participation and in decision-making.

The present U.N. Secretary-General, B. Boutros-Ghali has recalled that internal democracy requires

> the fullest consultation, participation and engagement of all States, large and small, in the work of the Organization. All organs of the U.N. must be accorded, and play, their full and proper role so that the trust of all nations and peoples will be retained and deserved.[15]

This book will not consider this aspect of democracy, but, rather, whether IGOs have been, or are now explicitly and actively concerned with the democratic nature of their member states' government, institutions and practices.

Although Woodrow Wilson wanted to create a "club of democratic nations", on the premises that democracies are inherently peaceful, members of the League of Nations did not need to show any democratic credentials to be admitted. Membership in the U.N. is open to "all peace-loving states which accept the obligations" of the Charter: undemocratic states were admitted without investigation. The East/West conflict, the ideological confrontation between Western liberal values and institutions and the Socialist concept of one-party "peoples' democracies", the U.N. interest in achieving and maintaining universality, prevented the organization from assuming an overt pro-democracy stand until the late 1980s. Even then, the traditional conflict between national sovereignty and international intervention in such fields as human rights, humanitarian intervention, and, more recently, electoral monitoring of national elections, have occasionally hampered a full recognition of Western democratic values in the U.N. context.

For instance, the Declaration adopted on 31 January 1992 by the political leaders of the 15 governments on the Security Council avoided any firm commitment to promote democracy. The Western members of the Council wanted the Declaration to recognize that democracy and respect for human rights will contribute to a more peaceful world, but China, India and Third World states resisted such an endorsement by arguing that by so doing the U.N. would involve itself in the domestic affairs of other countries in violation of Article 2.7 of the U.N. Charter. The final text only stated that

> Rapid progress has been made, in many regions of the world, towards democracy and responsive forms of government, as well as towards achieving the Purposes set out in the Charter.

The Council members also noted

> that U.N. peace-keeping tasks have increased and broadened considerably in recent years. Election monitoring, human rights verification and the repatriation of refugees have in the settlement of some regional conflicts, at the request or with the agreement of the parties concerned, been integral parts of the Security Council's effort to maintain international peace and security. They welcome these developments.[16]

Boutros-Ghali was more forthcoming in his first statements following his election: he clearly linked democracy to peace and security, and to development.

In his statement of 3 December 1991 to the General Assembly, he said that the fourth basic issue confronting the international community was:

> *Fourthly*, I wish to stress the United Nations role in strengthening the fundamental freedoms and democratic institutions which constitute an essential and indispensible stage in the economic and social development of nations. If there is no development without democracy, there can also be no democracy without development.[17]

In his "Agenda for Peace" of 17 June 1992,[18] he added:

> There is an obvious connection between democratic practices – such as the rule of law and transparency in decision-making – and the achievement of true peace and security in any new and stable political order. These elements of good governance need to be promoted at all levels of international and national political communities.

He cautioned: democracy is not a magic potion – and U.N. activities to promote democracy must not become a means of intervention in the internal affairs of Member States.[19]

In 1992, the Directors-General of UNESCO and ILO also openly embraced democracy. Federico Mayor said that UNESCO could make original contributions to the development of human rights in a rapidly evolving world:

> No one could doubt the intimate links between human rights and democracy. Only democracy could provide the framework within which minority cultures could find full expression, within which intercultural dialogue could take place.[20]

Michel Hansenne said that the spectacular change in the world's political climate gives the ILO a historic opening to promote democracy universally. However, he warned that democracy can hardly survive without a healthy economy which will make true social progress possible: ILO would not advocate a return to "wild capitalism". He added that political freedoms must be accompanied by economic and social rights.[21]

The U.N. Development Programme (UNDP) report published in 1991 included, for the first time, the "Human Freedom Index" mentioned above. The Index was based on the *World Human Rights Guide* compiled by Charles Humana, and covered 88 countries in 1985. On the basis of international human rights texts, the Index used 40 criteria for judging freedom. The UNDP Administrator William H. Draper emphasized that the report was

> about human freedom where the creative energies of the people are unleashed to generate economic and social opportunities for themselves and for their societies.

The report also said that the basic objective of human development is to enlarge the range of people's choice to make development more democratic and participatory. Each individual should have the opportunity to participate fully in community decisions and to enjoy human, economic and political freedoms.

The Group of 77 charged that the Index was an attempt to impose Western values on the Third World and demanded that it be suppressed in the future.

As an intergovernmental organization, UNDP submitted to these pressures. No "Human Freedom Index" was published in the 1992 Report: "further research" was to be undertaken on a "universally acceptable" political freedom index, an impossible mission. In particular, the future index would have to take into account the response of governments to various allegations of human rights violations. In fact, in view of its political implications, the construction and publication of such an index should best be left to independent, non-governmental, research organizations.[22]

Kenneth K.S. Dadzie, Secretary-General of UNCTAD, also spoke for democracy and freedom at the Eighth U.N. Conference on Trade and Development held in Cartagena in February 1992:

> The sound of freedom reverberated throughout the world. There might be different perceptions of freedom, but what mattered was the acceptance of democratic rules and understandings which permitted nations and people, weak and strong, to share a common house in mutual respect and solidarity.[23]

Michel Camdessus, Managing Director of the International Monetary Fund, warned that if democracy was to stay stable, it needed the firm foundation of an economy which was sound and showed progress: if the leadership became complacent, or gave way to demands of populism, there was a risk that a vicious cycle of demagoguery and economic instability would lay the ground for the return of dictatorial regimes.[24]

Lewis T. Preston, the World Bank President, also had a cautious attitude. While he agreed that "good governance" was very important to the development process, he said that the Bank does not, nor can it, interfere in a country's internal political affairs: it does not advise on the kinds of political structures that countries ought to have.[25] IMF and World Bank critics would not admit that these organizations have, or have had, a neutral influence on politics in developing countries.

Outside the U.N. system, regional organizations have recognized or promoted democracy in words or in action.

The Council of Europe, since its creation in 1949, has been a credible and durable bastion for pluralist democracy and human rights: as an exclusive "club of democracies", it has established the first and the best regional system of international judiciary protection of human rights.

In December 1949, the Development Assistance Committee of the Organization for Economic Cooperation and Development (OECD) adopted a Policy Statement on Development Cooperation in the 1990s, in which it recognized the existence of a vital connection, now more widely appreciated, between open, democratic and accountable political systems, individual rights and the effective and equitable operation of economic systems.[26]

Other regional organizations, like the U.N. at the global level, have opted for regional "universality", i.e. the participation of all countries of the region without concern for the democratic or non-democratic nature of their institutions and practices.[27]

For instance, while the OAS Charter declares

> that representative democracy is an indispensable condition for the stability, peace and development of the region

as seen above, democracy is only progressing slowly among the OAS members, with a few reversions to undemocratic situations.

Furthermore, the OAS declared purpose "to promote and consolidate representative democracy" is restricted by its declared "due respect for the principle of nonintervention".[28]

The Will of the People

Article 21 of the Universal Declaration of Human Rights adopted by the U.N. General Assembly on 10 December 1948 establishes, among other rights, everyone's right to take part in the government of his country, directly or through freely chosen representatives and affirms that

> The will of the people shall be the basis of the authority of government; this will shall be expressed in periodic and genuine elections which shall be by universal and equal suffrage and shall be by secret vote or by equivalent free voting procedures.

As early as 1948, the U.N. member states thus acknowledged, when they adopted the Declaration, that countries' governance should be based on democratic principles and practices in order to be legitimate. "Periodic and free elections by universal and equal suffrage and by secret vote" were the basic elements of the formula by which democracy was installed or renewed.

In old and stable democracies, the formula is applied in accordance with well-established and generally respected constitutional, legal and administrative rules and regulations. Flaws, deviations, frauds are usually prevented, or reported through independent institutions and the counterpowers to government authorities: an independent electoral council, judiciary control and sanctions, opposition political parties, voluntary associations, the medias.

The decision of the population of a colonial territory to create a sovereign and independent state, or to join another state, through a self-determination referendum or plebiscite may be challenged if its organization is entirely left to the colonial power. Elections organized in an authoritarian or totalitarian country in transition to democracy may be challenged if only controlled by the government authorities and ruling party.

In both instances, in order to demonstrate that such processes are genuinely free, the authorities in charge have found it useful, or have been requested or persuaded, to have recourse to basic or supplementary international election monitoring by IGOs, other governments' representatives, and NGO's, besides allowing full coverage by international media.

In 1935, an International Commission of the League of Nations organized the plebiscite in the Saar on union with Germany or France. The U.N. monitored decolonisation plebiscites and elections in the 1950s and 1960s mainly in Africa. The Commonwealth sent election observers in the 1960s in British Guiana, Mauritius, Gibraltar, and in 1980, in Zimbabwe and Uganda. The OAS has sent election observers to Latin American countries since 1966.

In 1989–1990, the U.N. Transition Assistance Group's military and civilian contingents supervised the transition of Namibia from colonial status to national sovereignty and monitored the preparation for and holding of free and fair elections for a Constituent Assembly. U.N. and OAS Observers verified the electoral process in Nicaragua in 1989–1990, the first time the U.N. had monitored an election in a sovereign country. Another U.N. Observer Group, together with hundreds of other international observers verified the Haitian elections held in December 1989. The U.N. Mission for the Referendum in Western Sahara is monitoring the cease-fire since September 1991 and is mandated to monitor the voting by the Western Saharan people either for independence of the territory or for its integration into Morocco, a self-determination exercise. The U.N. Plan for Cambodia includes the organization of elections by the Organization: the U.N. Transitional Authority in Cambodia (UNTAC) has been deployed in 1992 and elections for a constituent assembly were held in May 1993. Another U.N. Mission has verified and observed the Angolan elections held on 29 and 30 September 1992.

In his statement to the Twenty-eighth Assembly of Heads of State or Government of the OAS, on 29 June 1992, the U.N. Secretary-General said, "Today, promoting democracy and strengthening democratic institutions is an essential aim of the United Nations".[29]

U.N. activities in this field include election monitoring, and also expert advice and assistance on democratic elections, constitutional law, drafting national legislation on election processes and human rights and training of legal and other public officials. In June 1992, the U.N. was involved in preparing or carrying out electoral assistance missions in over 14 African countries.

NGOs, including the U.S. National Endowment for Democracy, the Council of Freely Elected Heads of Government, the International Human Rights Law Group, the International Federation of Human Rights, Freedom House, the International Foundation for Electoral Systems and many others, have played an active role in election monitoring: their independent status allows them to intervene more quickly, to be more outspoken and, if need be, more critical than IGOs and government representatives.

In countries subjected to civil war or in emergent or unstable democracies, the verdict of the polls is the only universally accepted test of legitimacy. As stated by the former Prime Minister of Pakistan, Benazir Bhutto:

> Elections must not only be fair, they must also be seen to be fair. The presence of observers, therefore, is a deterrent to fraud. The observers' report can help legitimize an election in an emerging democracy. It is harder to steal an election if the whole world is watching.

However, elections, even if they are internationally monitored, do not transform overnight a former Communist state or a military dictatorship into a mature, peaceful and pluralist democracy, no more than democracy can bring instant development, wealth and happiness to its deprived citizens. Democracy is a fragile plant, and the democratic process can be reversed.

Still, free and periodical elections are an essential prerequisite to the creation and maintenance of democracy, which is itself a prerequisite to the legal and enforceable protection of human rights.

The "Democratic Entitlement"

The current democratic wave and the increasing demand for international monitoring of elections in sovereign countries raise various issues.

International monitoring of self-determination in colonial territories has generally been accepted by most countries, albeit more enthusiastically by Third World countries than by colonial powers. However, some Third World countries determined to annex a neighboring colonial territory did not allow a U.N.-monitored plebiscite or referendum to take place: for instance, India and Kashmir, Indonesia and West Irian. The present attitude of Morocco with regard to the planned U.N.-monitored referendum in Western Sahara casts doubts on its real intentions. Should the world community have insisted, should it insist now, that the internationally approved self-determination process proceed notwithstanding those countries' ill- will?

International monitoring of national elections has raised the traditional objection of national sovereignty: the U.N. should not intervene "in matters which are essentially within the domestic jurisdiction of any state" (Art. 2.7 of the U.N. Charter). Even though no such monitoring has taken place without the formal request or consent of the national authorities concerned, a minority of U.N. member states has expressed its reticence, if not its frank opposition, to this unexpected and unwelcome extension of the U.N. role into uncharted waters.

Some government representatives have presented, and resented, these new activities as another imposition of Western values on their traditional culture and society. Is democracy a political objective to be reached by all nations and applied by standard practices, – or are democratic values and practices to be adapted to the stage of political, economic and cultural development of each country? Are countries free to "take" from the democratic kit what they can absorb and accept, and "leave" what is abhorrent to their mores or premature in their present state of development?

The Chinese and Indian leaders present at the Security Council Summit Meeting of Heads of State and Government on 31 January 1992 presented the latter view:

> The people and governments of the various countries are entitled to adopt the social system and ideology of their own choice in the light of their national conditions.[30]

Governments have a choice, but how can the "people" choose when they cannot express their opinion in free referenda or in free and periodical elections?

Like the debate on a "right to international humanitarian intervention",[31] some critics have labelled international election monitoring as an unwanted interference into the internal affairs of poor and weak developing countries, an interference from which rich and powerful states are protected. It is relevant to note that, in April 1992, the representatives of the 12 member states of the European Community told the U.N. Special Committee on Peace-keeping Operations that, with the consent of the states concerned, the U.N. should encourage the holding of democratic elections by sending civilian observers.[32]

Thomas M. Franck has recently referred to the two radical propositions contained in the U.S. Declaration of Independence [33]: the "democratic entitlement", the proposition that governments derive their just powers from the consent of the governed, – the second proposition is that a nation earns "separate and equal station" in the community of states by demonstrating "a decent respect to the opinions of mankind", which Franck calls the "legitimating power of the community of nations":

> Both textually and in practice, the international system is moving toward a clearly designated democratic entitlement, with national governance validated by international standards and systematic monitoring of compliance.

The final question is whether the "democratic entitlement" will continue to expand in more and more countries, and whether the legitimating power of the community of nations will become a universally accepted international process. Will the "third wave" of democratic expansion endure and grow, in spite of all the political, ethnic and military turbulences, the economic disparities, the cultural, religious and social differences?

Will the voice of all the "peoples of the United Nations" be finally allowed to be heard?

Plan of the book

The first chapter is a general introduction to the concepts of self-determination and democracy, and their foundation on such electoral processes as plebiscites, referenda and elections.

Chapter 2 presents several examples of rejection of democratic values and practices, rejection based on ideologies – Socialism (Marxism-Leninism), Fascism and Nazism, – religion – Islam, – or political/military autocracy: their common stand is the rejection of representative democracy based on free and periodical elections.

Chapter 3 reviews the self-determination plebiscites entrusted to the League of Nations.

Chapters 4 through 7 examine the role of the U.N. in monitoring self-determination electoral processes, then its increasing involvement in organizing or observing elections in sovereign countries, as part of peace-keeping operations.

Election assistance and monitoring by the Organization of American States, the Commonwealth and European intergovernmental organizations are reviewed in Chapter 8.

Chapter 9 refers to election assistance and monitoring by non-governmental organizations.

Following a Conclusion, a few samples of election observation guidance and forms are reproduced in Annexes.

A final word about terminology. "Monitoring" is used as a generic term to include either the organization and conduct of an electoral process, or its supervision and verification, or more frequently, its observation and assessment.[34] An "electoral process" is used as a generic term to include plebiscites, referenda and elections, with their common basis: the free and organized expression of the will of the people.

Notes

1. Freedom House is an independent research center on human rights, based in New York, which publishes every year, since the early 1970s, a "Comparative Survey of Freedom" rating all countries on "political rights" and "civil liberties". Its last publication is *Freedom in the World – Political Rights and Civil Liberties – 1991–1992*, by Freedom House, New York, 1992. See also *Human Development Report 1992*, UNDP, New York, p. 32.
2. Samuel P. Huntington, "Democracy's Third Wave", *Journal of Democracy* 2 (Spring 1991): 12–34.
3. A summary of these events is found in *Chronologie des relations internationales depuis 1945*, Charles Zorgbibe, PUF, Paris, 1991. For the 1992 Romanian elections, see the *International Herald Tribune*, 9 Oct. 1992.

4. *Le Monde*, 22 July 1992.
5. *Democracy in the Americas – Stopping the Pendulum*, Robert A. Pastor, Ed., Holmes and Meier, New York/London, 1989, pp. 6–7.
6. *International Herald Tribune*, 25–26 July 1992.
7. *International Herald Tribune*, 20, 25 May and 12 June 1992, *Newsweek*, 8 June and 28 Sept. 1992.
8. U.N. General Assembly Resol. 46/132, – U.N. *Press Release* HR/3055 of 4 March 1992, *International Herald Tribune*, 31 March 1992, *Le Monde*, 25 April 1992, *Newsweek*, 8 June 1992.
9. See note 3.
10. *Trimestre du Monde*, 1/1992, p. 137, *The Economist*, 22 Feb. 1992.
11. *Trimestre du Monde*, 1/1992, *The Economist*, 22 Feb. 1992, *International Herald Tribune*, 18 May 1992.
12. *West Africa*, 4–10 Nov. 1991, 1–7 June 1992, *Le Monde*, 30 May 1992, *Africa Demos*, Vol. II, No. 2, February 1992.
13. *The Economist*, 22 Feb. 1992, *Le Monde*, 8 July 1992, *West Africa*, 12 July 1992.
14. *Le Monde*, 8 Oct. 1992.
15. *An Agenda for Peace, Preventive diplomacy, peace-making and peace-keeping*, Report of the Secretary-General pursuant to the statement adopted by the Summit Meeting of the Security Council on 31 January 1992, U.N. Doc. A/47/277-S/24111 of 17 June 1992, para 82.
16. U.N. Security Council Doc. S/23500, *International Herald Tribune*, 31 Jan. 1992, Paul Lewis, "Security Council split on rights and arms issues".
17. U.N. Doc. SI/30/91, 16 Dec. 1991.
18. *An Agenda for Peace*, op. cit., para. 59.
19. U.N. *Press Release* SI/30/91 of 16 Dec. 1991.
20. U.N. *Press Release* HR/3044 of 25 Feb. 1992.
21. ILO Press No. 13–92 and ILO Report "Democratisation and the ILO", Report of the Director-General (Part I), 1992, and "ILO Information", Aug. 1992.
22. *Human Development Report 1991*, 1992, UNDP, *–U.N. Observer and International Report*, Aug. 1991.
23. *Press Release* UNCTAD VIII/3 of 10 Feb. 1992.
24. *Press Release* UNCTAD VIII/8 of 12 Feb. 1992.
25. *Finance and Development*, June 1992, p. 4.
26. OECD: Policy Statement on Development Cooperation in the 1990s: Meeting of Aid Ministers and Heads of Aid Agencies, 4–5 December 1989 (Paris, 1990), p. 5.
27. The suspension of Cuba from participation in the OAS was justified by its Communist regime – Communism was declared incompatible with the principles of the OAS – and not on the grounds of not being a democracy; otherwise, many other Latin-American countries should also have been suspended from participation in the OAS.
28. OAS Charter Preamble and Art. 2 b.
29. U.N. *Press Release* SG/SM/1342 of 29 June 1992.
30. Security Council Doc. S/23500.
31. *The Role and Status of International Humanitarian Volunteers and Organizations – The Right and Duty to Humanitarian Assistance*, Yves Beigbeder, Kluwer/M. Nijhoff, 1991, Ch. 11 and Postscript.
32. U.N. *Press Release* DH/1129 of 28 Apr. 1992.
33. "The Emerging Right to Democratic Governance", *American Journal of International Law*, Vol. 86, Jan. 1992, No. 1, pp. 46 and 91.
34. For instance, the U.N. has defined six basic operational concepts for its electoral assistance: a) organization and conduct of elections; b) supervision; c) verification; d) following the electoral process; e) providing coordination and support to the activities of international observers affiliated with other organizations; and f) technical assistance. See U.N. Doc. A/47/668/Add.1 of 24 Nov. 1992, "Guidelines for Member States considering the formulation of requests for electoral assistance".

CHAPTER 1

SELF-DETERMINATION AND DEMOCRACY

External self-determination enables the population of a territory to decide freely whether to join, or not, an existing state, or whether it will become an independent and sovereign state. Internal self-determination enables the people of a country to choose their political system, their political, economic and social institutions and their political leaders, or to make important constitutional or political decisions. Both external and internal self-determination imply a democratic process, i.e. a free and clear choice by the population of the territory or country through a plebiscite, referendum, or through elections.

Self-determination

One of the purposes of the U.N., as formulated in its Charter, is:[1]

> To develop friendly relations among nations based on respect for the principle of equal rights and self-determination of peoples, and to take other appropriate measures to strengthen universal peace.

Self-determination is again mentioned in other Articles of the U.N. Charter (Art. 73.b and 76.b), but with specific reference to non-self-governing territories: self-determination has been widely used under U.N. auspices or with U.N. support to initiate and complete the decolonization process.

The right to the free determination of peoples had been proclaimed by the French Revolution, but Lenin was the first, in his writings of 1915 and 1916, to promote this concept at the international level. His purpose was ideological: free determination was only a means to achieve socialism, the liberation of oppressed peoples would contribute to the realization of the socialist revolution in the world. The principle was to apply to colonies and semi-colonial countries, like China, Persia, Turkey as well as to countries of Central and Eastern Europe (Austria, the Balkans and Russia).[2]

Woodrow Wilson, in his Fourteen Points of 18 January 1918, proposed a different, non-revolutionary version of self-determination, based on the liberal principle of nationalities of the 19th century and the democratic principle according to which governments must be controlled by the will and vote of their peoples. While Lenin called mainly for "external" democracy, in order to free oppressed peoples, Wilson wanted both external and internal democracy. In his view, the realization of the ideals of self-determination and democracy would minimize conflicts in international relations. Wilson wanted to remodel a few existing states, using the criterion of respect of nationalities, without challenging the colonial powers, except those defeated in World War I.

After World War II and the adoption of the U.N. Charter, different attitudes were adopted by different groups of member states regarding self-determination:

- the Socialist group followed Lenin's lead by considering that self-determination was essentially an anti-colonialist weapon to free peoples subjected to colonial domination, as well as such racist regimes as that in South Africa. Internal self-determination meant the right of the people to "choose" a socialist regime;
- Third World countries agreed with the Socialist group concerning anti-colonialism and anti-racism. They added the struggle against all forms of neo-colonialism, and, on the insistence of Arab countries, the support for the self-determination of such oppressed people as the Palestinians. In view of the many existing or potential ethnic and tribal conflicts in a number of developing countries, they toned down or even excluded the right of minorities or nationalities to secede from recognized states, as demonstrated by the Biafra Civil War;
- the Western group supported self-determination as the right of all peoples to choose freely a political regime or a government of their choice: they considered self-determination as the fundamental criterion of democratic legitimacy of governments. Colonial powers among the Western group had initially opposed, or tried to delay, self-determination processes in their colonial territories.

International Plebiscites and Referenda

These may be defined as the consultation of a people by means of a vote as to its wishes on an important public question.

The direct vote of all electors of a state may be, under the name of a plebiscite or referendum, a normal constitutional instrument of internal legislation, as, for example, in the Swiss Confederation and Swiss Cantons, and in some states of the U.S. In other cases, constitutional referenda have sanctioned new constitutions or fundamental constitutional changes, as, for instance, the referendum held in France on 28 September 1958 by which the Constitution of the Fifth Republic was approved. Such a process is then part of the legal consultation and participation rights of the population of a country.

International plebiscites or referenda differ from these internal processes in that they are organized and conducted on the basis of international agreements, whether of a bilateral or multilateral character, or that, even without international agreements, they concern the international "fate" of a territory, its independence as a sovereign state or its annexation by a sovereign state.

International plebiscites took place well before the self-determination and democratic concepts and entitlements were defined and proclaimed.

Plebiscites took place during the French Revolution as a way to conciliate annexations with the doctrine of renunciation to territorial conquests. With the development of the principle of nationalities, the Italian unification (1860–1870) was carried out in the name of the will of the people and by plebiscites. Savoy and Nice were annexed to France by the Treaty of Turin of 24 March 1860, sanctioned by two plebiscites in April.

The 1919 Peace Treaties required that plebiscites be carried out only in some cases, but not as an absolute principle.

For instance, plebiscites were carried out in High-Silesia on 20 March 1921 and in Saarland on 13 January 1935. However, neither the restitution of Alsace-Lorraine to France, the annexation of Southern Tyrol and Fiume by Italy, the attribution of Bessarabia to Romania nor other transfers of sovereignty decisions were subjected to plebiscites.

Only one plebiscite was to be carried out under the Peace Treaties of 1947. It was not required by the Italian Peace Treaty, but by the French Constitution of 1946, which stipulated that "no transfer, no exchange, no adjunction of territory is valid without the consent of the population concerned". Held on 12 October 1947, it confirmed the integration of Tenda-Briga to France. At France's invitation, neutral observers were invited to the territory to oversee the correctness of the plebiscite.[3]

Plebiscites and referenda organized under the auspices of the League of Nations will be reviewed in Chapter 3; those organized under U.N. auspices will be reviewed in Chapters 5, 6 and 7.

Democracy

What is democracy? Huntington[4] said that democracy has a useful meaning only when it is defined in institutional terms, and not in terms of its purposes: the key institution in a democracy is the selection of leaders through periodical, competitive elections. Gastil adds that freedom

> requires that a people has a proven right to change their government through their politically equal votes, and that they are free to organize and propagandize for the purpose of achieving these changes.

Democracy's main tenet is therefore that government shall rest on the consent of the governed, that consent, or dissent, being expressed at free and periodical elections. Modern democracy also requires a fair system of representation to guarantee the sovereignty of the people. In a few countries, representative democracy through elections is complemented, but not replaced, by referenda, a process of direct democracy.

Origins of Democracy

Modern democracy has a debt to Greece and Rome, to the slow development of the British unwritten Constitution, to the American and French Revolutions, their Constitutions and Bills of Rights, and to various political writers.

Greek democracy applied to the city state, a small area with a small population: the Greek citizen was actually and in person a soldier, a judge and a member of the governing assembly. Under this direct democracy, no representation of the electors was needed. Slaves did not belong to the democratic circle. To Greek philosophers like Plato and Aristotle, there was no opposition between the individual and the state: the test of good citizenship was observance of the laws. Both thinkers emphasized the importance of political education in order to preserve the state from anarchy, the result of uncontrolled democracy. Plato's solution, as outlined in the *Republic*, lay in an aristocracy of political intellect, a body of "Guardians" qualified to rule through a rigid system of training. Aristotle sought escape from the tyranny of the mob in the "Polity", a type of middle-class government.

The Romans initially introduced a system of checks and balances through three elements of government: the monarchical element, transferred from the original kings, manifested itself in the office of the two Consuls, elected annually, each with the right to veto the other, – the aristocratic element was embodied in the Senate, an Assembly with, at one time, great legislative powers, – the democratic element existed in the meetings of the people, besides the election of the Consuls. The Roman system was essentially that of a direct democracy, suitable to small city-states but not to an expanding Empire: it ended as despotism.

The evolution of Britain's political government from royal despotism to constitutionalism and then democracy can be traced back to the Magna Carta, the Charter granted by King John in 1215, recognizing the rights and privileges of the barons, church and freemen, – the Petition of Right of 1628, – and to Statutes like "Habeas Corpus" (1679) and the Act of Settlement (1701) which secured, on the one hand, the immunity of the citizen from false imprisonment, and, on the other, the immunity of the judge from royal interference. Through the Revolution of 1688–1689, power was effectively transferred from the king to the "King in Parliament". The statutes then passed, the Bill of Rights and the Mutiny Act gave Parliament control of the Army. Parliament had a general legislative supervision, while the executive function was left in the hands of the king and his ministers. The Rule of Law, meaning the equality of all citizens before the law, was transferred to the colonies.

As noted by Strong,[5] by the second half of the 18th century, Britain was a constitutional, though not a democratic, state. By conventional growth and by a series of statutes her three organs of government, legislative, executive and judicial, were properly constituted and related in such a manner as to ensure the absence of tyranny. The principle of representation was deeply rooted in this system, but no ideas of franchise extension had yet come to be accepted as practical politics. Nevertheless, in the middle of the 18th century, Britain was the only constitutional state in the world.

This political system became a model described and admired by political writers, as well as a model for the later political development of other states.

Montesquieu's *De l'esprit des lois* (1748) is recalled mainly for his support for the separation of legislative, executive and judicial powers, on the British model:[6]

> So that one cannot abuse of power, it is necessary that, through practical arrangements, power stops power.

He also pleaded for "moderate" governments, the rule of law and the election of their representatives by the people:

> Political freedom is only found in moderate governments, – liberty is the right to do what the law permits, – the people chooses its representatives by their vote.

Rousseau's *Social Contract* (1762) developed the revolutionary political theory, inspired by John Locke and Hugo Grotius, that a ruler could only derive his powers from a social contract with his subjects, which imposed obligations on him as well as granting him rights. According to Rousseau, the will of the sovereign could only be the "general will" of the people. The social contract theory had already been upheld by the Huguenots in France and the Netherlanders under Spanish rule, the former suffering from religious intolerance and the latter from political tyranny. By 1581, a group of the Netherlands subjects of King Philip II of Spain, assembled in their States-General had already asserted

> that God did not create the subjects for the benefit of the Prince, to do his bidding in all things whether godly or ungodly, right or wrong, and to serve him as slaves, but the Prince for the benefit of the subjects, without which he is no Prince.[7]

Rousseau felt that real (direct) democracy only suited small states, aristocratic elective government suited those of middle size, and monarchy great ones: however,

> Were there a people of gods, their government would be democratic. So perfect a government is not for men.

Rousseau also made the important point that the history, character, habits, religion, economic base and education of the people must be taken into account before setting up any machinery in a specific country. No rules or means apply universally.[8]

Democratic governments are deemed to promote equality, individual rights, justice, human welfare, and to support even the pursuit of happiness. Thomas Jefferson wrote, in 1812, that

> the only orthodox object of the institution of government is to secure the greatest degree of happiness possible to the general mass of those associated under it.[9]

In fact these lofty goals can be those, in words at least, of all types of governments, from the democratic to the totalitarian.

Immanuel Kant has argued in his "Perpetual Peace" (1795) that democratic republics would form a "pacific federation" excluding the use of force among its members in an enduring and stable way, with the following three arguments:

- First, democracies identify other republics as just, because they are governed by the rule of law, the respect for human rights and the consent of their citizens. As a result, democratic norms of internal decision-making, the peaceful search for compromise among equals, are transferred to the international arena;
- Secondly, liberal republics respect international law on the basis of compatible core values;
- Thirdly, Kant argued that trading states are unlikely to go to war, since the "spirit of commerce" is incompatible with the use of force.

Once established, democracies lead to peaceful relations, because democratic government is controlled by the citizens and therefore it will not enter into violent conflict which may subject the citizens to bloodshed and war. In Kant's words:

> If the consent of the citizens is required in order to decide that war should be declared... nothing is more natural than that they would be very cautious in commencing such a poor game, decreeing for themselves all the calamities of war. Among the latter would be: having to fight, having to pay the costs of war from their own resources, having painfully to repair the devastation war leaves behind, and, to fill up the measures of evil, load themselves with heavy national debt that would embitter peace itself and that can never be liquidated on account of constant wars in the future.

Schumpeter supported the notion of peaceful democracies on a similar basis. He argues that imperialist expansion and war benefits only a minority of profiteers, arms-producers and members of the military establishment.

Fukuyama has recently adopted the same theme: war was the product of the zero-sum strivings of aristocracy and totalitarianism. As all nations turn toward the positive-sum spirals of democratic capitalism and world trade expands at a pace of 14% a year, he asserts that war will disappear.[10]

Toward the end of the 18th century, the writers' themes and claims were translated into political declarations and charters and new types of governments.

The American War of Independence ended with the creation of the U.S.A., founded upon a Constitution, promulgated in 1787. The Constitution embodies the principles enunciated in the Declaration of Independence (1776), which states:

> that all men are created equal; that they are endowed by their Creator with certain inalienable rights, that among these are Life, Liberty, and the Pursuit of Happiness; that to secure these rights, governments are instituted among men,

> deriving their just powers from the consent of the governed; that, whenever any form of government becomes destructive of these ends, it is the right of the people to alter or abolish it, and to institute a new government, laying its foundations on such principles, and organising its powers in such form, as to them shall seem more likely to effect their safety and happiness.

The Bill of Rights was added to the U.S. Constitution in 1791.

The principles of equality, human rights, government by consent of the governed, right of the people to reject a government "destructive" of these principles were now part of the basic political charter which had founded a sovereign state.

At the beginning of the French Revolution, the National Assembly of 1789 drew up the "Declaration of the Rights of Man and of Citizen", which affirmed the dogmas of the contractual origin of the state, the sovereignty of the people, and individual rights, as seen by the following extracts:

> Men are born free and equal in rights... The aim of every political association is the preservation of the practical and imprescriptible rights of man. These rights are liberty, property, security and resistance to oppression... Sovereignty resides exclusively in the nation... The nation has the imprescriptible right to change its constitution.[11]

Whatever its excesses, the French Revolution became a symbol of political freedom and a challenge to every constituted government which did not recognize and embody the sovereignty of the people.

Not a lover of the French Revolution, Tocqueville's political model was the American democracy, as Montesquieu's had been Britain's moderate government. Besides the American constitutional allocation of rights and responsibilities to federal and state authorities, he believed that the strength of the American political system was the tradition, which had developed in an unplanned way, of local self government and groups of persons working in private associations to pursue their common interests. He felt that the absence of these strong group affiliations, intermediate between the levels of the family and the state, and intermediaries between individuals and the state, for example in France where they had been systematically destroyed by the Revolution, was a primary cause of political instability.[12]

Democratic Requirements

There are old and new democracies, countries in transition to democracy, democracies in danger, democracies reversing to autocracies of various types. What are the conditions required in order to establish or maintain a democratic government?

Skidmore[13] has identified five internal factors which may strengthen democracy: – the need for consensus on the rules of the democratic game: no democracy can survive if the contenders for power are not prepared to accept the outcome of such democratic processes as elections, court decisions and parliamentary votes; – the need for a strong political party system: strong political parties are an all-important vehicle for channelling power and fixing government responsibility; – the need for economic growth, in order to deliver the welfare that the electorates expect; – the need for a democratic military; – and the need for social reform.

The need for consensus on democracy applies primarily to the country's elites: the genuine democratic beliefs of the political, military, economic, intellectual and religious leaders. It also applies to the majority of the population and its determination to defend liberty, if necessary, at all costs: the strength of a democracy is only as great as the will of the people to uphold it.

Huntington[14] has identified five major (external) factors which have contributed significantly to the occurrence and the timing of third-wave transitions to democracy:

1. The deepening legitimacy problems of authoritarian regimes in a world where democratic values were widely accepted, the consequent dependence of these regimes on successful performance, and their inability to maintain "performance legitimacy" due to economic (and sometimes military) failure.
2. The unprecedented global economic growth of the 1960s, which raised living standards, increased education, and greatly expanded the urban middle class in many countries.
3. A striking shift in the doctrine and activities of the Catholic Church, manifested in the Second Vatican Council of 1963–65 and the transformation of national Catholic churches from defenders of the status quo to opponents of authoritarianism.
4. Changes in the policies of external actors, most notably the European Community, the United States, and the Soviet Union.
5. "Snowballing", or the demonstration effect of transitions earlier in the third wave in stimulating and providing models for subsequent efforts at democratization.

Dahl characterizes working (as opposed to ideal) democracy as a system that ensures that the actions of government are in relatively close correspondence with the wishes of relatively many of its citizens for a long period of time. He demonstrates that for such a state of affairs to hold at least eight institutional guarantees must be present:

- freedom to form and join organizations,
- freedom of expression,
- the right to vote,
- eligibility for public office,
- the right of political leaders to compete for support and votes,
- alternative sources of information,
- free and fair elections,
- institutions for making government policies depend on votes and other expressions of preference.

The absence of any of these guarantees casts serious doubt on the authenticity of a regime's credentials.[15]

Democratic Government and Human Rights

Democratic government, or political constitutionalism, is based first on the recognized existence of a sovereign state, defined by Woodrow Wilson as "a people organized for law within a definite territory". Law is binding and enforceable within the state territory. Its source may be the written or unwritten constitution, laws enacted by the legislature, regulations prescribed by the government or government agencies, case-law, or custom. An unwritten or written constitution determines to which organs, bodies or agencies the various government functions are entrusted, how these organs are set up and organized, for what duration, what power they have, how this power is to be organized, what are the rights of the governed. Some written constitutions include a Bill of Rights of the citizens. A system of checks and balances limits the authority of government organs, themselves organically separated but functionally related: the classical separation of powers includes an executive (government and administration), a legislature with the ultimate power to make laws, and an independent judiciary, concerned with the application of the law in individual cases and the infliction of penalties on those who infringe the law or state regulations. The central importance of law-making and its democratic character demand that the members of the legislature be elected periodically by the "sovereign" (in the Swiss terminology), i.e. by the people, the government then representing the elected majority in the legislature.

Democracy is rooted in the traditional individual human rights and freedoms, labelled as "formal human rights" by Communist ideology in contrast with its alleged "real" democracy of social and economic rights. Western democracy's emphasis on the individual, based on a Judeo-Christian tradition, separates it from both authoritarian and totalitarian regimes for which the citizen has mainly duties toward the all-powerful, all-encompassing and all-benevolent state. The liberal concept of the state stresses more the civil society, whereby individual and groups take initiatives on all aspects of social and economic life, while the state is left to a supplementary or subsidiary position.

Such fundamental, formal human rights are those contained in the Universal Declaration of Human Rights and the International Covenant on Civil and Political Rights, such as: equal rights of men and women, right to life, prohibition of torture, cruel, inhuman or degrading treatment or punishment, prohibition of slavery, right to liberty and security of person, no arbitrary arrest or detention, right to a prompt trial, liberty of movement and freedom to choose one's residence, right to leave any country, including one's own, equality before the courts, presumption of innocence, no retroactivity of criminal law, freedom of thought, conscience and religion, right to hold opinions without interference, right of peaceful assembly, freedom of association, equal protection of the law, protection of minorities, right to education, etc.

These rights and freedoms provide the essential civil protection of the individual against the potentially excessive and/or arbitrary power of the state, its institutions and its officials. Article 25 of the Covenant prescribes precisely the political rights of citizens:

Every citizen shall have the right and the opportunity . . .
a) To take part in the conduct of public affairs, directly or through freely chosen representatives;
b) To vote and to be elected at genuine periodic elections which shall be by universal and equal suffrage and shall be by secret ballot, guaranteeing the free expression of the will of the electors;
c) To have access, on general terms of equality, to public service in his country.

These political rights require the essential freedoms of speech, publication, assembly and association, freedom of the media (press, radio, television), freedom to dissent and contest, the right to have and express different opinions, the right to have access to different views, the right to create political parties and the right (but not the obligation) to join them, the right to vote freely for a chosen party or candidate, without government or administrative coercion or pressures, without fear of legal or physical threats or punishment, by the public authorities, the police, the military or parastatal forces, or foreign occupation forces.

Freedom House's annual "Comparative Survey of Freedom" has two dimensions: political rights and civil liberties. It defines political rights as rights to participate meaningfully in the political process, the right of all adults to vote and compete for public office, and for elected representatives to have a decisive vote on public policies. Civil liberties are rights to free expression, to organize or demonstrate, as well as rights to a degree of autonomy such as is provided by freedom of religion, education, travel, and other personal rights. Freedom House rates political rights and civil liberties on seven-point scales, from the least free or least democratic to the most free or most democratic, by comparing countries. Its checklist for freedom ratings is shown in Table 1.1.

Democratic Elections

In short, a political system is democratic to the extent that the rulers, the decision-makers, are under effective popular control, which in practice means that democratic rulers are chosen, or rejected through periodically held elections. While candidates for election may stand for more or less precise policies (electoral platforms), voters do not generally decide directly on specific policies when voting for a party or a candidate: their elected representatives will make such decisions over the forthcoming months or years of their mandate. Exceptions are "direct democracy" as applied on the agora in Athens or in a few Swiss cantons, or referenda whereby citizens accept or reject a specific public decision, a process which may be initiated by the government on an optional or obligatory basis, or by a set minimum number of citizens.

Table 1.1. Freedom House Checklist for Freedom Ratings

Political Rights

1. Chief authority recently elected by a meaningful process
2. Legislature recently elected by a meaningful process
   Alternatives for (1) and (2):
   a. no choice and possibility of rejection
   b. no choice but some possibility of rejection
   c. government or single-party selected candidates
   d. choice possible only among government-approved candidates
   e. relatively open choices possible only in local elections
   f. open choice possible within a restricted range
   g. relatively open choices possible in all elections
3. Fair election laws, campaigning opportunities, polling and tabulation
4. Fair reflection of voter preference in distribution of power
   – parliament, for example, has effective power
5. Multiple political parties
   – only dominant party allowed effective opportunity
   – open to rise and fall of competing parties
6. Recent shifts in power through elections
7. Significant opposition vote
8. Free of military or foreign control
9. Major group or groups denied reasonable self-determination
10. Decentralized political power
11. Informal consensus; de facto opposition power

Civil Liberties

12. Media/literature free of political censorship
    a. press independent of government
    b. broadcast independent of government
13. Open public discussion
14. Freedom of assembly and demonstration
15. Freedom of political or quasi-political organization
16. Nondiscriminatory rule of law in politically relevant cases
    a. independent judiciary
    b. security forces respect individuals
17. Free from unjustified terror or imprisonment
    a. free from imprisonment or exile for reasons of conscience
    b. free from torture
    c. free from terror by groups not opposed to the system
    d. free from government-organized terror
18. Free trade unions, peasant organizations, or equivalent
19. Free businesses or cooperatives
20. Free professional or other private organizations
21. Free religious institutions
22. Personal social rights: including those to property, internal and external travel, choice of residence, marriage and family
23. Socio-economic rights, including freedom from dependency on landlords, bosses, union leaders, or bureaucrats
24. Freedom from gross socioeconomic inequality
25. Freedom from gross government indifference or corruption

Source: R.D. Gastil, Freedom House, 1988, pp. 9 and 10.

Another principle of democracy is that of political equality of voting citizens: all adult citizens, men and women, are entitled to vote, each voter has one vote and each vote should count equally, without weighting. The corollary of this principle is that the number of representatives should, in principle, be directly proportional to the number of votes cast for them, so that all parties and nuances of political opinion are represented. While proportional representation responds to requirements of fairness and clarity, its unadulterated application has, in some countries, led to a lack of a clear majority in parliament through a proliferation of small parties: this has caused political instability through changing coalitions, as well as a reluctance to tackle pressing problems and to take difficult decisions, as in the French Fourth Republic. The U.K. and the U.S. have a system of single-member constituencies, which, in spite of its anomalies, has the positive effect of reinforcing the two-party tradition and of avoiding the need for coalition, or minority governments. There is no "best" democratic representative system: it has to be adapted to the country's culture and traditions, while recalling that the "raison d'être" of a legislature is not only to reflect the opinion of the country, but also to establish and maintain good government.

Voting must be free, without coercion or intimidation of the voters. Secret ballot must be guaranteed and enforced. Polling and tabulation of the votes must be controlled by independent officers, representatives of the political parties in competition and independent observers, including media reporters.

There must be more than one candidate for each position, and candidates must be free to stand for election outside the main, dominating party or parties, not deterred by legal or other obstacles. All candidates and their parties must be free to publicize their programmes, criticize their opponents or the government, in the press and in other media, to hold meetings, on an equal basis with other candidates and parties. The free, open and legal creation and development of political parties, within the human rights principles of "freedom of association" and "freedom of expression", is an essential part of the democratic process: it enables different opinions and proposals to be expressed publicly, it enables citizens to join and support the group which closely expresses their own views and claims, and to vote for the party representatives. An open and legitimate opposition provides a peaceful opportunity for a change in policies and government.

Free elections enable the effective choice of representatives to take place, i.e. to ensure the popular control of decision-makers at election time. The result of the elections (confirmation of the party in power, or change to a new majority or coalition) needs to be accepted by those in power, all political parties and the outvoted citizens – as well as by other powers such as the military – subject to control that the electoral process has been fair.

Elected representatives are then responsible to take policy decisions during the term of their mandate, within limits set by the written or unwritten constitution. Decision-making in the legislatures is by simple or qualified majority voting: minorities in the legislature are bound to accept such decisions, subject to proper discussions and hearings before votes are taken. Minority views should be heard and respected, even if eventually rejected.

As summarized by Mayo,[16] the full role of elections must be considered from several viewpoints:

a) From the point of view of the individual voter, elections are the means by which he takes his share in political power by voting for the representative of his choice.
b) By means of elections the voters collectively bring the decision-makers under popular control, a control that is ever present in the minds of representatives because any part of their behaviour in office (or in the case of aspiring candidates, out of office) may affect their chances at the next election.
c) The election is also an authorization granted to representatives to make decisions – to govern within the scope of a policy platform, if there is one, subject to the sanction of the next election. The election result invests representatives and decisions with legitimacy. In short, the government which is produced and invested with legitimacy is the chief social purpose of the whole electoral process.

To these points, we can add that elections establish or expand an area of freedom together with the principle of accountability: following a well-planned and well-supervised electoral process, the elected representatives and the government remain under the control of the people (the voters and their parties, free associations, trade unions, the media – assisted or informed by foreign observers), who can insist on an improvement of the rulers' performance, a correction of government policies, and an expansion of democracy over resisting sectors of the society, such as the military or the economic elite.

Mayo has also identified the specific values of a democratic system:[17]

- the peaceful, institutionalized, voluntary adjustment of disputes;
- ensuring peaceful change in a changing society;
- the orderly succession of rulers;
- the minimum of coercion;
- diversity of beliefs and action, the value of open channels and liberties;
- the attainment of justice through public vocal pressures and political compromise;
- the freedoms found in a democracy.

Transition to Democracy

There is no short-cut to democracy, as the political evolution in the former USSR, Eastern European countries and Yugoslavia has shown.

Even "mature" Western democracies have had authoritarian lapses in the recent past: De Gaulle's return to power in 1958 formally respected the French Constitution's rules, but was in fact triggered and implemented under the threat of an army intervention related to the Algerian Liberation War.

Even old democracies have their problems: in Churchill's well-known aphorism, "Democracy is the worst form of government except all those other forms that have been tried from time to time."

John F. Kennedy recognized that a democracy is the most difficult kind of government to operate. George Bernard Shaw wrote that "democracy substitutes election by the incompetent many for appointment by the corrupt few." [18]

In democracy, as in other political systems, leaders may be or become corrupted, they may abuse their legitimate powers, adopt pork-barrel, electoralist decisions, prevaricate, avoid urgent or important decisions, renege on electoral promises; political parties may abuse a dominant position, impose appointments by patronage or nepotism, pervert the electoral process. Leaders may be incompetent, they may neglect their public duties. Non-elected lobbies may apply an excessive influence on leaders.

However, democracy, unlike other political systems, has its built-in corrective measures and sanctions: errors or faults are publicized through free media, faults or crimes may be judged and sanctioned by an independent judiciary, and recall or non-re-election will provide political sanction.

In spite of these corrections, part of the "sovereign" people in some democracies, perhaps not fully aware of the alternatives, have withdrawn from the electoral process: for instance, a low turnout of eligible voters is found in Switzerland and in the U.S. Their reasons may be contempt for "politics", for corrupt politicians, a feeling that their elected representatives ignore their real claims (unemployment, criminality, immigration etc.) and are only interested in their own political career, and that the vote is a useless "fraud": in the words of the students during the 1968 French "cultural revolution", "elections = treason", or "trap for the fools". But if no elections are held, how can the people's opinions be publicly expressed, and how do citizens choose or reject political programmes and leaders?

The distrust or rejection of traditional democratic practices is one of the reasons for the creation of far-right or neo-fascist, sometimes hidden as "non-political", candidates or parties trying to build on real discontent or imagined grievances. Far-left groups have often adopted similar views about the "corruption" of representative democracy and the need for a violent revolution by a minority of activists, in the name of the oppressed proletariat.

In many developing countries, democratic roots are shallow: as noted by Diamond,[19] many of these new "democracies" have initiated only the rudiments of democratic institutions:

> Elected executives lack effective control over the military and may need to weigh actions against the threat of a coup. Legislatures are weak, poorly financed, and understaffed. Legal systems lack the training, resources, and authority to protect human rights and due process. Political parties lack organization, resources, meaningful ties to interest groups and grassroots constituencies, and the political skill and experience to govern effectively. Also missing,

> typically, is the cultural and civic infrastructure of democracy: a strong commitment to democracy widely shared among elites and citizens, a variety of democratic associations and interest groups autonomous from the state, and an independent, pluralistic mass media.

The U.N. Committee on Information has recently stressed the importance of a free, pluralistic and independent press. For the U.N. Secretary-General, the press has a crucial role to play in promoting the spread of democracy: it can give voice to the ideas and opinions of a broad cross-section of society.[20]

Can true democracy exist without a relatively widespread enjoyment of basic economic security, education and health? In other words, is development a precondition for democracy, or, is democracy a precondition for development?

Development is not clearly nor necessarily based on democracy, as exemplified by the modernization of Chile accomplished under the Pinochet regime, or the economic successes of the South-east-Asian "tigers". On the other hand, the economic failures or decline of Socialist countries and of African dictatorships seem to support the economic liberalism postulate that economic progress and growth need the freedom of individual entrepreneurship, the freedom to create new products and new firms, free competition, without state planning, state monopolies, excessive state regulation and control.

Barsh[21] believes that democracy does not appear to "cause" growth, but that economic differentiation creates demands for democratic participation, which governments must then meet in the interests of further economic growth and political stability. Democracy is neither a "quick-fix" for development problems, nor a substitute for resources. On the long run, however, democracy and development can become mutually reinforcing.

Chinese leaders, who encourage economic liberalization and repress political and individual freedoms, are likely to be faced again with democratic demands, in the same way as the creation of an educated middle class, in part a product of economic growth, as in Thailand, creates conflicts between democratic claims and rigid, and often corrupt, military regimes.

An Indian representative to the U.N. Preparatory Committee of the 1993 World Conference on Human Rights said that democracy, freedom and tolerance were necessary for human rights, but did not guarantee their enjoyment. There were hundreds of millions of people who were so crushed by the burden of poverty that they had little time or inclination to worry about other human rights. In his view, the Conference should emphasize that development, without which democracy would "whither away", should be the central global concern so that the weakest and the poorest were enabled to enjoy human rights.

Can democracy take root and prosper in African countries afflicted by the "seven plagues", in the words of the U.N. Secretary-General, plagues which affect the whole continent: commodity prices and debt, – drought and desertification, – food shortages and famine, – epidemics and pandemics which, like AIDS, affect the youngest and fittest, – overpopulation of the cities and often of the countryside, – the locust peril, – and, last but not least, war and migration.[22]

Development and democracy must progress hand in hand: a number of African countries have shown that democratization can proceed even under dramatic economic circumstances. As stated in Resolution 46/143 of the U.N. General Assembly adopted on 17 December 1991, development requires an integrated approach taking into account such areas as population, health, nutrition, water, sanitation, housing, communications, education and training, as well as the need to create more opportunities for employment, in an environment which guarantees opportunities for political freedom, popular participation, respect for human rights, justice and equity, all of which are essential for enhancing human capacities to meet the challenge of development.

Democracy (political freedom) and human rights are now formally and internationally acknowledged as essential requirements leading to development.

International Monitoring of Plebiscites, Referenda and Elections: Nature and Purposes

The purposes of international plebiscites and referenda are different from those of elections although they all imply a consultation in which the population of a certain area expresses its wishes by means of a ballot. In the former cases, these wishes usually concern a particular proposition (for instance, independence or integration into another country), while in the second case, the ballots serve to elect candidates to public positions, such as members of a constituent assembly (for instance in Namibia), members of parliament, a president.

Such operations may be planned and carried out internally, by the political (or military) powers ruling the country or territory, without intervention, guidance or observation by foreigners, thus giving a relatively free hand to the electoral organizers, subject to national constitutional, legislative and administrative regulations and political constraints. However, in contentious or controversial cases, when the rulers' reputation for fairness and respect of basic freedoms is questionable, in countries where the population has never before been allowed to express its views freely, in countries in transition towards democracy, when other countries' interests may be at stake, in militarily occupied territories, the presence of foreign observers may be formally authorized, or even requested, by the country's authorities so that the fairness of the electoral process may be assessed by independent and neutral persons. If the assessment is positive, the observers' report will serve as an international stamp of approval of the process, thus publicly and internationally legitimized for internal and external purposes.

Even without formal authorization from the country's authorities, journalists routinely investigate and report on political and electoral conditions, and on a specific, significant, electoral process in most countries. Political scientists and other researchers have also studied elections in various countries and visited such countries during the election process.

On a bilateral (government to government) basis, diplomatic staff traditionally observe and report to their home ministry on political and electoral developments in their country of assignment: however, their reports remain normally confidential to the Foreign Affairs Ministry of the diplomatic envoys.

Still on a bilateral basis, in recent years, official delegations from other countries have been invited to observe controversial or transition elections by the country's authorities where the electoral process was taking place. For instance, in 1982, 17 countries were represented by official observer missions in El Salvador.[23] Here again, the main addressee of the missions' report is the government organizing the mission, although some reports may be made public. Reports by missions from well-established democracies have a particular value for those who have organized the electoral process, and their impact on international public opinion may be important. On the other hand, their assessments and reports only represent the views of one country, with that country's own political, social and cultural background and attitudes.

On a multilateral basis, a number of intergovernmental organizations (IGOs) have sponsored such missions, including the United Nations (U.N.), the Organization of American States (OAS), the Commonwealth, the Council of Europe. IGO missions, requested or approved by the recipient country, are either authorized by the IGO's governing body or by the head of its secretariat. They are normally composed of persons of different nationalities, and therefore not suspect of partiality for or against a particular country or party, its political regime and traditions. IGO missions give formal international legitimacy to the observed electoral process, with the weight that organizations of states may have: the world community of nations (the U.N.), or a regional group (the OAS). On the other hand, IGOs may be tempted to pay too much respect to diplomatic courtesies: heads of IGO secretariats are, themselves, subject to election and re-election, and are sensitive to governmental pressures: hence, it is essential that IGO missions be composed of renowned, independent personalities, competent in electoral processes and conversant with the recipient country's history, politics and language, and that missions' reports not be subject to internal censorship, or other internal or external pressures.

Many non-governmental organizations (NGOs) send observers to monitor elections, many of which are based in the U.S., some in the U.K., Germany, Canada, Switzerland or France. Some are human rights groups, some are linked to national parliaments and/or political parties or to trade unions, some have religious affiliations. In principle, by definition, NGOs should be independent from governments and from intergovernmental organizations: they have more freedom of action, investigation and expression than government and IGO representatives, they are closer to the people, or to segments of the population friendly to their beliefs or concerns: they can be more outspoken, more critical than government or IGO observers. On the other hand, NGOs' financial resources are usually more limited than those of governments and IGOs, thus limiting their operational capacity – and their assessments may be criticized for representing particular constituencies or being biased by national, political or cultural prejudices. Some NGOs may send a mission in order to provide a credible counter-assessment to the likely opinions of official or unofficial delegations.

According to one of Garber's "Guidelines for International Election Observing",[24] an election observer mission may be sent to ensure that an independent, impartial and objective report evaluating the electoral process in a particular country is prepared; to encourage participation in the electoral process by undertaking to report any significant manipulation of the electoral process; and/or to assist in ensuring the integrity of the electoral process. A further justification might be to evaluate the general human rights situation of a country, which may bear upon the legitimacy of the electoral process.

The general objective of an international election observer mission is to demonstrate by its presence, activities and reporting international support for democracy in a particular country. Its presence may assist in preventing electoral fraud and manipulation, by the implicit threat of negative reporting. The mission's evaluation will also publicly legitimate (or not) the electoral process, or the genuineness of the expression of popular will in a particular territory or country.

More precisely, the goal of the mission is essentially to assess and report on an electoral process, including electoral laws and regulations, announcement of the referendum, plebiscite or election, registration of voters and candidates, logistics, the political education campaign, the political campaign, the election day balloting procedures and the way they were observed, the counting of the votes and the proclamation of the results.

The role of the international mission and its duration may vary.

An IGO may be authorized to organize and implement a plebiscite or referendum in a colonial country, prior to independence: in such a case, the IGO has the right to design or alter the electoral laws and procedures, appoint electoral officials, conduct the electoral process, announce the results, while the administering authorities play only a passive role.

In most cases, the administering authorities of a colonial territory or the government of a sovereign state remain in charge of the electoral process, subject to decisions (for instance, of the U.N. Security Council) or recommendations (for instance, of the U.N. General Assembly) of the IGO's governing bodies. Basically, as in the case of Namibia, the general scenario of the electoral process was based on U.N. Security Council's resolutions, while the South African authorities administered the preparation and implementation of the elections. Changes in electoral procedures were the result of negotiations between the South African authorities and the U.N. Representative of the Secretary-General.

Missions to sovereign countries are generally observation missions, sometimes preceded by assessment missions, and complemented by technical assistance and training. As an exception, the U.N. was entrusted, among other tasks, with the organization and management of the whole electoral process in Cambodia, from the registration of voters to the announcement of results.

IGO and NGO representatives may be able or requested to advise, and make suggestions to the government officials concerned on electoral legislation and procedures, on technical and practical arrangements, on equal access to the media, on registration, voting and ballot-counting.

In all cases, observers' missions will report on the conduct and results of the electoral process. Their report will evaluate the electoral process, praise and criticize, and offer suggestions for future improvements. In some cases, the final report may condemn the electoral process and propose its annulment.

Mission Planning and Management

An IGO electoral observer mission can only be sent to a sovereign state at the latter's request, or with its consent. Similarly, an IGO mission may only be sent to a colonial country at the request or with the consent of the administering authority.

Additionally, the mission, its mandate and its financing are generally authorized by the IGO governing body or bodies.

In theory, the IGO may not necessarily agree to all requests for election monitoring. Before doing so, it may consider, as recommended by Amato for the U.N.:[25]

- whether the election can serve a useful purpose for the concerned population;
- whether the quality of the territory's electoral laws and arrangements are adequate to ensure a free and fair expression of the popular will;
- whether the member states of the organization are in agreement as to the election's significance.

In practice, political considerations will prevail: the IGO secretariat may not have the political free-hand to reject a request by a member state, and even less a request by the governing body, except perhaps on financial grounds.

For NGOs, Garber has listed the following factors to be considered before determining whether to send a mission:[26]

- has there been a request for observers from the host country;
- has the NGO been monitoring political developments in the host country for a period of time;
- does the election represent a transition in power from a colonial or non-democratic government;
- have there been prior instances of fraud or manipulation in the electoral process of the host country;
- is there a debate surrounding the legitimacy of the election;
- and is the election occurring in a country where there have been serious allegations of human rights violations?

For IGOs, either confirmation letters are exchanged or formal agreements are negotiated and approved by the IGO and the host country in order to determine the status and the mandate of the IGO observers. The process applied in the case of the OAS Electoral Observation Mission on the municipal elections in Paraguay in May and June 1991 is described hereafter.[27]

On 14 December 1990, the Government of Paraguay asked the OAS to send a mission to observe the municipal elections scheduled to be held on 26 May 1991. Following that request, two agreements were signed by the OAS General Secretariat and the Government of Paraguay. One concerned *The Privileges and Immunities of Observers of the Electoral Process in Paraguay*, and the other, between the Central Electoral Board, as the agency responsible for the organization, direction, inspection and holding of the elections, and the OAS, deals with *Electoral Observation Procedures*.

The Mission's Work Plan then targeted two basic objectives. The first was to observe and report on the electoral process in all its stages, using the National Constitution and the Electoral Code as a reference. The mission, consisting of 47 members, concentrated its activities on the conduct of the electoral campaign, including campaigning activities, the publicity media used, and the administrative and logistic organization of the polls. This included the appointment of election officials, production and distribution of the voters' rolls, distribution of documents and supplies, adoption of security measures, electoral training, and the balloting. Observers had interviews with party and electoral officials, monitored training sessions, attended campaign events and demonstrations, followed up on complaints, monitored news coverage by various media, and on voting day, observed the polls and the tallying of the votes.

NGOs do not negotiate formal agreements with host governments: if they have been invited to send an observer mission, they advise the host government of their acceptance – if they have not been invited to observe an election, they would normally notify the host government of their plan to send an observer mission. If agreeable to the NGO mission, the government would then facilitate meetings with electoral and other officials, and perhaps provide credentials. In cases when the host government is not expected to welcome such observation, an NGO may decide to send a mission without disclosing its purpose to the government.

The NGO sponsoring a mission should prepare its terms of reference which should be specific but also flexible.[28]

For instance, in September 1989, the Council of the Inter-Parliamentary Union, a Geneva-based NGO, decided to set up a mission to observe the elections scheduled for 7 to 11 November in Namibia. The mandate of the mission was

> to verify the legality of the elections, the non-falsification of electoral rolls and the free access of the population to all sources of information so that free and democratic elections may take place.

The members of the mission then defined their task, more precisely, as follows:

a) to ascertain that all Namibians entitled to vote were properly registered and that the electoral rolls were not tampered with;

b) to observe whether all those who registered were able to vote freely and that their ballots were properly and fairly counted; and
c) to enquire whether, during the electoral campaign and the election itself, information flowed freely to and from the people so as to ensure that they were able to vote under the best possible conditions.[29]

Some organizations provide their mission with a detailed list of questions to be considered and answered. For instance, the international observer delegation, sponsored by the U.S. National Republican Institute for International Affairs and the National Democratic Institute for International Affairs, which observed the May 7, 1989 elections in Panama was given precise terms of reference including a list of questions: extracts are given in Table 1.2.[30]

Table 1.2. National Democratic Institute for International Affairs – National Republican Institute for International Affairs

---

Terms of Reference (Extracts)

The National Republican and Democratic Institutes for International Affairs are organizing a sixty-person international delegation to observe the May 7, 1989 national and local elections in Panama. The delegation includes former heads of government, parliamentarians, political party leaders and election experts from across the democratic political spectrum: the U.S. component is bipartisan. . . .

This delegation's modest role is to reflect the consensus of the Panamanian people as they assess the May 7 elections. The delegation report will bear witness to that evaluation and will inform the international community about the nature of the electoral process and political developments in Panama . . .

Based on the Institutes' work in Panama during the past few months and, in particular, based on the findings of the advance team that visited Panama from April 3–10, 1989, the following are among the issues that appear most relevant for consideration by the delegation.

The political campaign

A. Were there any restrictions, *de facto* or *de jure*, that prevented the competing sides from conducting their respective campaigns in any region of the country?
B. Were there any arrests, detentions or killings of party leaders or other individuals during the campaign that appear politically motivated? Were there any exiles of political leaders during the campaign?
C. During the campaign, were candidates or voters intimidated into voting for a particular coalition, party or candidate by the armed forces, political parties or government officials? What was the response to such actions?
D. Was there evidence of illegal campaign practices by any of the participants? How did the authorities respond to these charges?
E. Was there evidence of government or military support for any of the coalitions, parties or candidates participating in the process?

Role of the media

A. Did the competing parties obtain adequate and relatively equal access to the media?
B. Did the government-controlled media provide adequate and balanced coverage of the political campaign?
C. Was the media censured during the campaign? Were journalists intimidated through arrests, detentions or the filing of charges during the campaign?

Administration of the elections

A. Did the Electoral Tribunal and the local electoral officials act, and were they perceived to have acted, in a non-partisan manner?

B. Were there adequate safeguards to prevent widespread fraud in the balloting process? Were voters able to cast a secret ballot? Was there any intimidation of voters by the military, local leaders or political parties on election day?

C. Was there evidence that prospective voters had been disenfranchised by arbitrarily removing them from the electoral registry or by assigning them to polling sites far from their homes? Was there evidence of multiple voting?

D. Were disputes in the counting process resolved in a non-partisan manner? Were there suspicious delays in the preparation or release of election returns?

E. Were there an adequate number of pollwatchers (*jurados*) designated by the accredited parties to cover all the polling sites? Were these pollwatchers permitted access to all polling sites and to the counting center?

The results

A. Were the official results reported in accordance with the Electoral Law? Were the results disseminated expeditiously?

B. Did the various Panamanian institutions recognize the results? If not, were challenges filed in accordance with the Electoral law?

C. Were the unofficial efforts to count the votes permitted? How did these unofficial efforts compare with the official results?

April 24, 1989

Source: "The May 7, 1989 Panamanian Elections", *International Delegation Report*, 1989, Appendix V.

The size of an observer mission varies from one person (Garber wisely recommends a minimum of two observers) to groups of any numbers, in relation to the size of the country to be monitored, the size of its population, the number of polling stations, the availability of qualified members and the financial resources provided for the operation.

The selection of observers will be based on various criteria: an international mission requires that its members have various nationalities. A U.N. mission will have observers from various continents, including industrialized and developing countries, while OAS mission observers will be selected mainly or only from member states of the regional organization. Observers should have qualifications, and if possible experience, in election supervision, including theoretical and practical knowledge of electoral laws and procedures, – political and/or legal training and experience, – knowledge of the host country, of its political, social and economic background, its electoral history and of its language, – participation in previous fact-finding missions, – ability to conduct a fact-finding investigation and to report factual findings. Observers should preferably have a professional or personal reputation for independence, impartiality and objectivity. If possible, one or several persons of international renown, former statesmen or high-level magistrates, should be included in the mission. It may also be useful to include members of different ethnic groups and of both sexes.[31]

The duration of the mission will depend, again, on several factors: the requirements of the host country, the capacity and interest of the sponsoring organization, its mandate, its competence, its human and financial resources.

A number of organizations may limit their observation to the actual election day or days.

Others may cover the entire electoral process, before, during and after election day. For instance, a typical international monitoring project conducted by the National Democratic Institute for International Affairs would include:

- one or more multinational pre-election missions to assess the campaign and the election system;
- a large-scale, high profile international delegation for election week led by one or more prominent international political figures;
- a post-election assessment mission;
- training programmes and the provision of technical assistance to domestic monitoring groups; and
- a staff presence in the country to work with local groups and to coordinate the project.[32]

In practice, the activities of a mission may be divided into three phases:[33]

- a pre-electoral period, during which the mission will assess the electoral law provisions, supervise their implementation and make recommendations for improving them. In judging the pre-electoral procedures, the mission will take into account the quality of the physical and administrative arrangements, the extent of political freedoms, the impartiality of the Election Commission (if any) and of the electoral officials, the awareness of the population as to the election's significance, the fairness of the campaign, the proper registration of voters and candidates;
- during the electoral phase, which includes the period from the actual casting of the ballots to the tabulation and proclamation of the results, the mission must ascertain that two criteria have been met: the ballot has been properly safeguarded so that each duly registered voter has been able to vote in complete freedom and only once, secondly, the tabulation and reporting of the results have been accurate;
- during the post-electoral period, the mission makes an overall assessment of the conduct and results of the election, based on the criteria set for the pre-electoral and electoral phases.

The mission report, once discussed and approved by its members, is then submitted to the body or organization which approved and organized the mission.

An IGO mission will normally submit its report to the head of the organization's secretariat, who will then circulate it to the organization's member states, including the host country, the member state which received the mission. Whether a draft of the text of the report is or is not reviewed by officials of the host country is a matter of discretion for the organization's secretariat. In principle, the mission's report should not be influenced by pressures either from the host country, from other member states or from the international secretariat: unless it is, and is seen as, an honest report by an independent group, the value of the electoral mission's assessment and recommendation will be diluted or lost.

An NGO mission will submit its report to its sponsoring organization or organizations: the sponsor will then decide as to the distribution of the report. NGO electoral observer mission reports are normally published by the NGO concerned.

Octavio Paz wrote that a country without free elections is "a country without a voice, without eyes, and without arms".[34]

While a free election alone does not make a democracy, there is no democracy without free and periodical elections. Elections are the pivotal, necessary, albeit not sufficient, mechanism to create a democratic state or to ensure that it remains one.

The organization of democratically run plebiscites, referenda and national elections responds to the insisting and expanding democratic demands of the people in more and more countries, who want to make freely their own decisions on national and international issues which affect them collectively and individually.

The international monitoring of such processes responds to the increasing interdependence of nations: the presence of competent and impartial international observers in the host country confirms or denies the legitimacy of the electoral process, while it also shows international support for democracy, respect for the populations' wishes and concerns and solidarity with other people's rights and freedoms.

Notes

1. United Nations *Charter*, Art. 1.2.
2. *La Charte des Nations Unies*, J.P. Cot and A. Pellet, Eds., Economica/Bruylant, 1985: see commentary on Art. 1.2 by A. Cassese, pp. 39–55.
3. *Droit international public*, Ch. Rousseau, Sirey, 1953, pp. 267–271.
4. Samuel P. Huntington, "The Modest Meaning of Democracy" in *Democracy in the Americas – Stopping the pendulum*, Robert A. Pastor, Ed., Holmes and Meier, 1989, pp. 11–28.
5. I am indebted to C.F. Strong, *Modern Political Constitutions*, Sigwick and Jackson Ltd., London, 1963, Chapter 2 for developments on Greece, Rome and the British democratic evolution. In Great Britain, even before the 1832 Reform Act, there were about 465,000 voters out of a total population of around 18 million. In the same period, there were only under 100,000 electors in France for a total population of about 26 million.
6. *De l'esprit des lois*, Montesquieu (1748), Classiques Larousse, Tome II, XI, 4, 5 and 6.
7. *The Lawful Rights of Mankind*, Paul Sieghart, Oxford University Press, 1986, p. 24.
8. Jean-Jacques Rousseau, *The Social Contract and Discourses*, Translated and Introd. by G.D.H. Cole, Revised and Augmented by J.H. Brumfitt and John C. Hall, Dent, London, 1990, Ch. 1, 2, 3, 4, 6, 7. See also, "The Theorem of Democracy" by Jacques Barzun, *Society*, 26: 3, Transaction Publ., 1989, p. 4.
9. Letter to F.A. Van Der Kemp, 22 March 1812, in *The International Thesaurus of Quotations*, R.T. Tripp, Penguin Books, 1970, p. 393 (393: 29).
10. "Why don't Democracies fight one another? Evaluating the Theory-Findings Feedback Loop", paper presented by Harvey Starr to the International Studies Association Meeting, March–April

1992, Atlanta, – Kant's quotation (1795) is in Reiss, Hans, Ed., *Kant's Political Writings*, Cambridge University Press, 1970, – re. Schumpeter, see Doyle, Michael W., "Liberalism and World Politics", *American Political Science Review*, Vol. 80, No. 4, p. 1153, – see also Georg Sorensen "The Ideas of Kant and Processes of Democratization: Consequences for Neo-Realist Thought", paper presented to the Inaugural Pan-European Conference in Heidelberg, 16–20 Sept. 1992, European Consortium for Political Research, – book review by George Gilder of Francis Fukuyama's *The End of History and the Last Man*, The Free Press, 1992, in *International Herald Tribune* of 15 Jan. 1992.

11. As quoted by Strong, op.cit., p. 38.
12. *On Democracy, Revolution and Society: Selected Writings*, Alexis de Tocqueville, – J. Stone and S. Mennell, Eds., University of Chicago Press, 1980, pp. 37, 38.
13. Thomas E. Skidmore, "The Future of Democracy", in *Democracy in the Americas*, op.cit.
14. Samuel P. Huntington, "Democracy's Third Wave" in *Journal of Democracy*, Spring 1991, p. 13.
15. Robert A. Dahl, *Polyarchy: Participation and Opposition*, Yale University Press, 1971.
16. H.B. Mayo, *An Introduction to Democratic Theory*, Oxford University Press, 1960, p. 73 (by permission of the Oxford University Press). See also the Introduction to *Electoral Systems – A World-Wide Comparative Study*, Inter-Parliamentary Union, Geneva, 1993.
17. Mayo, op.cit., p. 218–238.
18. Tripp, op.cit., pp. 146–147 (231: 7, 21, 49).
19. "Promoting Democracy" by Larry Diamond, in *Foreign Policy*, Summer 1992, p. 26.
20. U.N. *Press Releases* DH/1110 of 31 March 1992 and SG/SM/1328 of 5 May 1992.
21. R.L. Barsh, "Democratization and Development", in *Human Rights Quarterly*, Feb. 1992.
22. U.N. *Press Releases* HR/3074 of 7 April 1992 and SG/SM/1342 of 29 June 1992.
23. *Guidelines for International Election Observing*, Larry Garber, The International Human Rights Law Group, Washington, D.C., 1990, p. 3.
24. Ibid., p. 13.
25. "Elections under International Auspices, 1948–1970", Dennis John Amato, Unpublished dissertation, The Johns Hopkins University, Ph.D., 1971, microfilm, p. 22.
26. Garber, op.cit., p. 13.
27. OAS, Permanent Council, "Report of the Secretary General on the Observation of the Municipal Elections in Paraguay", Doc. OEA/Ser.G – CP/INF.3194/91 of 13 Nov. 1991.
28. Garber, op.cit., pp. 13–14.
29. Inter-Parliamentary Union "Report of the Mission to Observe the Elections in Namibia", Doc. CL/146/10-R.1 of 20 Dec. 1989.
30. National Republican and National Democratic Institutes for International Affairs, *The May 7, 1989 Panamanian Elections*, International Delegation Report, 1989, p. 73.
31. Garber, op.cit., p. 14.
32. National Democratic Institute for International Affairs, "NDI's Approach to International Election Assistance" (undated leaflet).
33. Amato, op.cit., pp. 32–33.
34. As quoted by Jimmy Carter in his Foreword to *Democracy in the Americas – Stopping the Pendulum*, R.A. Pastor, Ed., Holmes and Meier, 1989.

CHAPTER 2

THE REJECTION OF DEMOCRACY

The road to universal democracy is not a one-way road: there have been and there will be many roadblocks and deviations for countries in transition to democracy.

The democratic ideology and practices have taken centuries to develop in the Western countries: the evolution had to weaken and then defeat despots, absolute monarchs and emperors, military rulers, religious imperialism.

Similar opposition to democracy is currently found in a number of countries: those ruled by dictators, military rulers, who have taken power as anti-colonialist leaders, or by force and terror, and intend to keep it against all popular demands. Their motivation may not be particularly ideological, but nationalistic and populist: they might reinforce their hold on power through calls on patriotism, military ventures, xenophobia, maintenance of the unity of the country vs. tribal division, protection against external economic pressures, claims of efficiency and achievements.

On the other hand, ideological opposition to Western democratic values has been unequivocally affirmed, in this century, by marxism-leninism and fascism-nazism: both ideologies have been applied in specific countries, both aspired to expand to other countries and either replace "bourgeois" democracy or become the dominant political and economic system in newly independent countries. Both ideologies have been defeated and discredited, although a few countries still have Communist governments, and there are fascist-nazi minority groups in a number of Western countries.

While fascism-nazism totally rejected democracy by the leadership principle, a one-party system and, for nazism, blatant racism, the Bolshevik Revolution intended to create a new type of democracy, ensuring the workers' leadership through the dictatorship of the proletariat and collectivism. It inspired immense devotion and hopes for a new, equal and fair society, hopes which were destroyed by the revelations of Stalin's terror regime and methods, and the failure of socialism in the economic field. The "democratic revolution" initiated reluctantly by Gorbachev ended with the end of the Soviet Empire, the break-up of the USSR and the democratization of most Central and Eastern European countries.

Relations between state and religion, after centuries of struggles, have been settled progressively in Christian democratic countries by an imposed, or agreed separation of functions, leaving only religious (or sometimes, educational or welfare) functions to established religions. State power is then not to be interfered with by religious authorities, who can still express their views and influence public authorities and public opinion within legal limits.

Traditional Islam, in theocratic states, claims to assume both state authority and to rule civil society. In the views of most Western observers, the strict interpretation and implementation of the Islamic dogma tends to prevent any evolution towards democracy.

The various types of totalitarian or authoritarian regimes have a common point: they reject, in various degrees, modern political rights and civil liberties. The rejection of democracy implies the rejection of political pluralism, of the electoral process, or of a fair electoral process, and of representative government. Dissent is treason and elections, if held, are the object of manipulation or coercion, in distrust of the people's voice and wisdom. The holding, or not, of free, genuine and periodical elections remains as the key criterion in order to distinguish between democracies and non-democracies.

Socialist States: People's Democracies

Socialist states introduced a new concept of democracy and a non-democratic (in the traditional sense) method to ensure that "socialism" gained and retained power without having to resort to free and periodical elections, nor to accept their verdict.

In the words of Soviet authors, the 1917 Revolution brought with it a totally new type of state – the Soviet socialist state. This state became a "pure dictatorship" for the exploiter classes – the bourgeoisie and the landowners – and a real democracy for the working people who had been previously barred from political participation. With the victory of socialism, the state of the dictatorship of the proletariat became a political organization of the whole people under the leadership of the working class. Lenin said that "the Soviets are the highest form of popular rule".[1]

Although the Bolsheviks were the smallest of the Russian socialist parties, they used the October 1917 Revolution to gain full power and to establish a single-party claiming to represent the workers and peasants of Russia.[2]

When elections to a constituent assembly, held in November 1917, only gave a quarter of the votes to the Bolsheviks, the assembly was dissolved by a decree of the Central Executive Committee of the Soviets, which the Bolsheviks dominated. The *Pravda* of 26 December 1917 had said that the elections gave no clear indication of the "real voice" of the masses. Shortly afterwards, the Third Congress of Soviets declared itself the supreme authority and approved the government's action in dissolving the constituent assembly. Lenin had declared that the Soviet Republic represented not only a higher form of democratic institutions (in comparison with the middle-class republic and the constituent assembly), but it was also the sole form which rendered possible the "least painful transition to socialism".

On 14 June 1918, the Central Executive Committee outlawed the opposition. Its resolution stated:

> The representatives of the Social Revolutionary Party (the right wing and the centre) are excluded, and at the same time all Soviets of Workers', Soldiers', Peasants' and Cossacks' Deputies are recommended to expel from their midst all representatives of this faction.

Karl Marx and Friedrich Engels had foreseen that the transition from capitalism to socialism would involve the seizure of state power by the proletariat, in order to "win the battle of democracy".

According to Marx and Engels, the often quoted experience of the Paris Commune of 1871 provided the first opportunity to see how the working class might organize society following a successful seizure of power. Unlike representative parliamentary government, Marx saw the Commune as a form of popular and truly egalitarian democracy that would enable the proletariat to rule.

Karl Kautsky had argued that the transition to socialism, in the more advanced capitalist countries could and should take place in a democratic manner following the electoral victory of a mass-based socialist country. He thought that this parliamentary road to socialism would quickly lead to a revolutionary break with capitalism and the rapid construction of socialism within one or two decades, with a minimum of coercion.

Rosa Luxembourg rejected Kautsky's conception of the parliamentary road to socialism, but disagreed with Lenin and Trotsky on the need for an authoritarian party dictatorship during the transition to socialism. She contended that freedom only for the supporters of the socialist government and the members of the revolutionary party amounted to no freedom at all. She stated forcefully the case for unrestricted freedom of the press, the right to assembly, general elections, during the transition to socialism.

Lenin disagreed: dictatorship and coercion were necessary because of both the continuing resistance of the bourgeoisie, and the external and civil wars which socialist revolutions generate. A dictatorship of the proletariat (then a minority in Russia) meant a minority imposing its will on the majority. As it had done in making the Revolution, the Party must act in the name of the proletariat.

In *The Defence of Terrorism*, published in 1920, Trotsky rejected parliamentary democracy, equality before the law and civil laws as bourgeois frauds, and argued that the class war could be fought and won only by force, not by votes. To reject terror was to reject socialism.

In 1920, Kautsky wrote that, starting out with the idea of establishing the dictatorship of the proletariat the Bolshevist regime was bound to become the dictatorship of the party within the proletariat.

Socialist Elections

Socialist elections do not reserve any surprises: the selected candidate of the Communist Party is elected, without unnecessary or illegal competition, by close to 100% of the voters.

The first Soviet Constitution of 1918, applicable to Russia but used as a model in other Soviet Republics, had established legal electoral discriminations: in principle, there was universal suffrage, for men and women, but those who "exploited" other people's work, the clergy, former police officials etc. were disfranchised, – workers (one representative for 25,000 inhabitants in the cities) were advantaged in relation to peasants (one representative for 125,000 inhabitants in the country). At all elections, the representatives were elected by a show of hands, not by secret ballot. The 1924 Constitution, applicable to all the Soviet Republics, maintained similar discriminations. Voters could only vote for one list of communist and no-party candidates.

The 1936 Constitution introduced universal, equal and direct suffrage with secret ballot.[3] It suppressed the previous exclusion of citizens alleged to be "exploiters" or other sinners, and established an equal representation of city and country dwellers. Still, the one-party and one-list system remained, any opposition being treated as dissidence or treason.

All citizens who had reached the age of 18, irrespective of race, nationality, sex, religion, education, domicile, social origin, property status, or past political activity had the right to vote in the election of deputies, except for those legally certified insane.

Every Soviet citizen of 18 or more was eligible for election to a local Soviet, – at 21, for election to the Supreme Soviet of a Union or Autonomous Republic, – at 23, for election to the Supreme Soviet of the USSR. In practice, the quasi totality of eligible voters used their voting rights: in the 1937 election to the Supreme Soviet, 96.8% voted, – in 1966, 99.94%.

The right to nominate candidates was granted to mass organizations and societies, including the Communist Party, trade unions, co-operative and youth organizations, cultural societies, as well as general meetings of industrial and office workers or enterprises and institutions, servicemen of separate military units, general meetings of farmers at collective farms and villages, and workers at state farms.

In practice, as all these organizations were controlled by the Communist Party, the Party kept full control on these nominations, and only one candidate was registered in each constituency.

The official reply to critics of the "one candidate only" elections was the claim that the nominated candidates represented the entire population. All the candidates were nominated on behalf of the single bloc of Communists and non-Party people, this bloc uniting the entire population. The Communists and the non-Party people did not stand separately in the elections, but all together in close alliance and in a united front. They had a common political platform and the same candidates. Even though the Soviet electoral law did not prohibit the registration of several candidates in each constituency, this right was not availed of, because

> in the USSR there neither are nor can be any contending social forces or groups fighting for dominant positions in representative bodies during elections.[4]

To critics of the "one-party" system, the official answer was:

> Is not the existence of several parties in society the sign of true, genuine democracy? We Soviet people give a clear and unequivocal answer: no, it is not. The democratic or anti-democratic nature of public life, of a state, of a government's policy, is determined not by the number of parties but by the substance of the policy of this state, of these parties – by whether this or that policy is carried out in the interests of its overwhelming majority, or in the interests of its minority.[5]

In fact, the Soviet political system denied most accepted political rights: a single party, one party-selected candidate only in each constituency, the prohibition of multiple political parties and candidates, the prohibition of any public discussion of and campaigning for, political options and policies other than those of the socialist dogma as applied by the Communist Party, the *a priori* rejection of any opposition to socialism as practised in the Soviet Union: basically, the effective lack of choice of political options.

In its 1987–1988 report, Freedom House noted:[6]

> Political Rights. The Soviet Union is ruled by parallel party and governmental systems: the party system is dominant. Elections are held for both systems, but in neither is it possible for the rank and file to determine policy. Candidacy and voting are closely controlled, and the resulting assemblies do not seriously question the policies developed by party leaders ... the all-embracing party structure renders local power minimal.
>
> Civil Liberties. The media are totally owned by the government or party and are, in addition, regularly censured. Major deviations from the party line are found primarily in unofficial underground publications. Arrest and exile have silenced nearly all dissident criticism ... political prisoners are present both in jails and insane asylums ... Since the Bolshevik Revolution there has never been an acquittal in a major political trial. Insofar as private rights, such as those in religion, education, or choice of education, exist, they are de facto rights that may be denied at any time. Travel within and outside of the USSR is highly controlled ... Other rights, such as those to organize independent labor unions, are strictly denied.

The violations of human rights resulting from the imposition of closed one-party political systems in Socialist countries have been denounced by Kruschev in his 1956 report and have been confirmed by the opening of secret archives in the USSR and satellite countries following the collapse of Communism in those countries in the years 1989–1991. According to Maier, the Stalinist repression was responsible for approximately 20 million Soviet victims, human losses due to forced dekulakization and deportation. According to Ellenstein, the number of violent deaths caused by civil wars, famine, repression in the USSR from 1914 to 1953 may be estimated at 55 million.[7]

On 26 March 1989, voters rejected 32 of 160 regional First Secretaries of the Communist Party, candidates to the elections to the new Soviet Congress of Peoples. Fifteen percent of the candidates were not members of the Party. A thousand constituencies had several candidates. In 1990, the first free elections took place in former Socialist countries, giving at last the voice to the people.

The Remaining Socialist States

The Chinese Revolution adopted the same themes as Lenin's. As stated by Mao:

> Our socialist democracy is democracy in the broadest sense such as is not to be found in any capitalist country. Our dictatorship is the people's democratic dictatorship led by the working class and based on the worker-peasant alliance. That is to say, democracy operates within the ranks of the people, while the working class, uniting with others enjoying civil rights, and in the first place with the peasantry, enforces dictatorship over the reactionary classes and elements of all those who resist socialist transformation and oppose socialist construction. By civil rights, we mean, politically, the rights of freedom and democracy.[8]

China is a one-party communist state under the collective leadership of the Politburo. A National People's Congress is indirectly elected within Party guidelines. The mass media remain closely controlled tools to mobilize the population. Unarmed pro-democracy student protests were violently suppressed in June 1989, followed by arrests, summary trials, long sentences or executions. There are unknown thousands of political prisoners.

According to Amnesty International, Tibetans peacefully protesting Chinese rule are routinely jailed for weeks, months and even years without charges being filed. Protesters have been shot and killed and prisoners systematically tortured, some to death.

In June 1992, China demanded that members of a party favoring democracy should be banned from Hong Kong's executive body. The British colony is scheduled to revert to China in 1997.

China has supported the Khmer Rouge's brutal rule in Cambodia, whose leaders are responsible for the killing of one to two million of their own citizens, from April 1975 to January 1979, when Vietnamese forces replaced the Khmer Rouge by another, more classical, Communist government.

Economic liberalization (a "socialist market economy") in China may trigger new popular demands for democratic reform. However, China's Communist Party maintains that there is no alternative to party rule. In October 1992, the Party Chairman, Jiang Zemin, said:

> The goal is to build a socialist democracy suited to Chinese conditions and absolutely not a Western, multi-party, parliamentary system.[9]

The Democratic People's Republic of Korea (North Korea) is a hard-line Communist dictatorship in which the organs and assemblies are only a facade for Party or individual rule. The communism and Marxism on which the governing system is alleged to be based, seems to have been replaced by Marshal Kim Il Sung's personal ideology. National elections allow no choice. Individual civil liberties are non-existent: unofficial reports suggest that imprisonment is used extensively to curtail rights to freedom of expression and association guaranteed under the International Covenant on Civil and Political Rights, to which the Republic acceded in 1981.[10] Possible policy changes may occur on account of North Korea's increasing economic difficulties, following the loss of Soviet support.

Vietnam is also a traditional Communist dictatorship with the pretence of parliamentary democracy. Actual power is in the hands of the Party, dominated by a small group at the top. Civil liberties are practically non-existent. As noted by Neher,[11] Vietnam has no history of democracy. Its traditions are Confucianist, stressing hierarchy and order, and, more recently Communist, emphasizing the unquestioned supremacy of the Party. Vietnamese leaders have been shocked by the demise of Communist governments in Europe and the rise of democracy in the world.

From the Vietnamese perspective, Western democracy represents all that their leaders have rejected: unstable regimes led by self-serving bourgeois leaders against the interests of the masses. They believe that Vietnam is not ready for democracy: the strong leadership of the Party is necessary to assure the nation's stability and progress.

Although opposition parties or groups are not allowed, in the November 1989 local-level elections, candidates were allowed to campaign with competing platforms. Economic problems and the need for foreign capitalist investments and ventures may cause demands for political reforms and individual freedoms.

Cuba is the last Communist bastion in Latin America after the February 1990 elections in Nicaragua which unseated the Sandinistas. Cuba remains a one-party Communist state based on the Soviet model, although real power lies with the "Lider Maximo", Fidel Castro. No free elections have been held since Castro took power in 1959. Popular elections at the municipal level are closely supervised. Provincial and national assemblies are elected by municipalities but can be recalled by popular vote. Political opponents are excluded from nomination by law or by Party decisions. No debate is allowed on major political, economic or social issues. Once elected, the assemblies do not oppose the Party decisions. Individual freedoms are severely restricted.

Late in 1991, Castro described multi-party democracy as "multiporqueria" (multi-piggishness). On December 28 1991, at a session of Cuba's one-party National Assembly, he described it as an instrument of imperialism.

The revision to the Cuban Constitution approved on 12 July 1992 by the National Assembly and a law of 29 October 1992 granted some "democratic" concessions, while reinforcing Castro's own powers. The Assembly approved the principle of direct universal suffrage, by secret ballots, for the election of its members: however, the one-party system remains, as opposition parties will still be unable to have their candidates placed on lists of "authorized" candidates. In July 1992, Luis Pita Santos, founder of the Cuban Association for the Defence of Political Rights was jailed for five years for "illicit association, contempt and clandestine printing". Before trial, he was held in a psychiatric hospital, in the Soviet fashion.[12]

In January 1992, the former mayor of Dresden, Wolfgang Berghofer, admitted that he had rigged election results on the orders of his Communist superiors in East Berlin: he is accused of cutting the opposition's electoral results in Dresden from 12% to 2.5% in the May 1989 local elections. His lawyer said that "you cannot distort what is already falsified", as in the totalitarian Communist system, elections were only fictitious exercises in support of the regime.[13]

Indeed, one-party and one-candidate elections, where no opposition views or candidates are allowed, are fictitious: their outcome only represents what the political power wanted them to represent: total "popular" support to Socialism.

Other Communist-Inspired Movements

Soviet or Chinese (Maoist) communism, or their ideological deviations or distortions, have inspired a number of clandestine revolutionary parties or groups who have used violence to try to overthrow the legitimate government, the established order, and assume power: they have thus rejected "bourgeois" representative democracy and its electoral processes.

Besides the European far-left terrorism of the now (hopefully) defunct German and Italian Red Brigades and French "Action directe", the "Partido Communista del Peru – Sendero Luminoso", founded by Abimael Guzman in 1970, began armed insurgency in 1980.

The Party has been waging a nationwide campaign of attacks on government property, on communications and electricity network, on state-run cooperative farms and on private businesses. Its "bureaucracy of terror" has carried out numerous killings, mostly of civilians, some after torture and mutilation. The Party has boycotted elections and threatened to murder prospective candidates and voters.

The Peruvian government has stated that the fanatic group is responsible for the death of more than 25,000 persons in political violence, and for at least $22 billion in economic damage. The Party, calling itself the "Fourth Sword of Communism", after Marx, Lenin and Mao, lost its leader on 12 September 1992 when Guzman was captured by government forces. He was sentenced to life imprisonment on 7 October 1992.

Another violent Communist group is the marxist-leninist Workers Party of Kurdistan (PKK), whose 10,000 armed militants are fighting the Turkish government and army in order to obtain Kurdish independence. This rebellion is officially estimated to have killed a total of about 5,000 people since 1984 – soldiers, policemen, guerrillas and civilians – more than a third of whom in 1992.[14]

Fascism and Nazism

> Democracy represents the disbelief in all great men and all elite societies: everybody is everybody's equal.
>
> Nietzsche[15]

Neither Fascism nor Nazism made any pretence of creating a "new type of democracy": they openly rejected the sovereignty of the people, parliamentary representative democracy, free elections, equality and Christian values.

They created totalitarian one-leader, one-party systems, stirred up an aggressive nationalism backed by strong military forces, destroyed most political rights and civil liberties, prevented any opposition through terror tactics, blamed all sins and corruption on such scapegoats as the Jews, the foreigners, the bolsheviks, the capitalists, the cosmopolitans. Their power was based on totalitarian control of the civil society by the secret police, party officials and informers, sanctioned by imprisonment, torture and death in concentration camps.

They came to power through a combination of street terror tactics, threats and pressures on the political establishment, followed by more or less regular elections.

Their progress was encouraged by the fear of an expanding Bolshevism, following the 1917 Revolution, the economic crisis and consequent unemployment and poverty, a violent social climate, the incapacity of democratic parties to understand the danger and to create effective alliances.

Fascism and Nazism lost state power following the defeat of the Third Reich and Italy in the Second World War, but, after a period of total official rejection, their ideology has reappeared in democratic countries in minority political parties or small, violent groups, and in the writings and teaching of revisionist "historians".

With common traits, Fascism and Nazism have their own history and ideological characteristics.

Fascism

The Italian "National Fascist Party" was created in November 1921 by Benito Mussolini.

Mussolini, the founder of Italian fascism, was originally a Socialist, a revolutionary and a Republican: he became a national socialist (although socialism was an international movement), a corporatist, and a royalist linked with the middle classes.

In the May general elections of 1921, only 35 Fascist deputies were elected out of a total of 520. Leaving aside the electoral process, Benito Mussolini, the "Duce", and his "black shirts" practised intimidation and terror tactics as a means to control the population and the legal authorities. Faced with the "March on Rome" of October 1922, in order to avoid civil war, King Victor-Emmanuel III asked Mussolini to form a government.

Mussolini suppressed the freedom of the press and obtained full powers from the Chamber of Deputies and the Senate, under a threat of dissolution.

The elections held in 1924 were, according to Francesco Nitti,[16] more in the nature of government nominations: 356 Fascist deputies were elected, out of a total of 535. They were the last relatively free elections in Fascist Italy.

A totalitarian regime was progressively introduced: all non-Fascist political parties, trade unions and other social and cultural associations were suppressed. The Fascist Grand Council became the only effective organ of government. A law of September 1928 reduced elections to a parody: voters could only vote yes or no to candidates on a single list established first by Fascist trade and employers' unions, and then by the Grand Council.

Mussolini thus effectively destroyed the democratic structure, and by a series of measures, replaced it by the Corporate State, based on what he called National Syndicalism. In 1939, the Chamber of Deputies was replaced by the Chamber of Fascios and Corporations.[17]

Mussolini had established a total dictatorship over the country.

In April 1939, Mussolini invaded Albania.

In June 1940, Italy joined Germany in the war against France and the U.K. In July 1943, the King divested Mussolini of all his powers, with the support of the Grand Council, and placed him under house arrest. In September, German troops rescued Mussolini and established him as head of a puppet Republic in northern Italy. Also in September, the Italian Army capitulated. Mussolini was executed by Italian partisans on 28 April 1945.

The Fascist wave, with different national characteristics, had spread in other European countries:

- in May 1926, Jozef Pilsudski established a dictatorship in Poland which maintained only the forms of a parliamentary democracy;
- in Portugal, also in 1926, a military coup took power, which led to the dictatorship of Antonio de Oliveira Salazar in 1928. Salazar's regime was more an authoritarian right-wing regime than a fascist one. His "New State" was a conservative Catholic corporatist regime which shunned every type of radicalism, including fascism;
- the Spanish Civil War (1936–1939) was won by General Francisco Franco, El Caudillo. Franco imposed on Spain a Fascist regime, although no Falangist can-

didate had been elected in the last parliamentary elections of 1936. Adopting the ideology of the Falange, he organized Spain from a "broad totalitarian approach by means of all national institutions guaranteeing its totality, unity and continuity". All political opposition was outlawed and suppressed, the economy was organized into corporatist structures and trade unions were replaced by a "Syndical Organization", led by active Falangists, to which all workers were obliged to belong. More a conservative general than a revolutionary fascist, he did not declare war against the Allies during World War II, and relied increasingly on the Army, the Church, the landowners, and at the end of his "reign", the royalists;

- in Yugoslavia, in January 1929, King Alexander dissolved the Parliament, suspended the Constitution and established a dictatorial regime;
- dictatorial regimes were also established in the Baltic countries;
- in defeated France, in June 1940, Marshall Petain obtained full powers from the Chamber of Deputies and Senate and appointed himself Chief of an authoritarian, semi-fascist and anti-semitic "Etat français", promoting a "National Revolution" and collaboration with Nazi Germany. De Gaulle re-established a democratic Republic after France's liberation;
- in the Western hemisphere, Colonel Juan Peron established a fascist-corporatist state in Argentina between 1943 and 1955, under the name of "justicialismo". Presented as a third solution between capitalism and socialism, Peronism was a populist dictatorship which ruined the economy and suppressed free labour unions.

Following World War II, Italy, and later Portugal and Spain, joined the democratic group. Yugoslavia and the Baltic countries came under Communist rule.

Nazism, a distinctive racist branch grafted on the Fascist tree, will be reviewed later.

Fascist ideology

As Fascism took different characteristics in different countries, and as it evolved with the times, its ideological foundation is difficult to identify, except by a multi-dimensional typological definition, such as that given by Linz[18]:

> We define fascism as hypernationalist, often panationalist, anti-parliamentary, anti-liberal, anti-communist, populist and therefore anti-proletarian, partly anti-capitalist and anti-bourgeois, anti-clerical, or at least, non-clerical movement, with the aim of social integration through a single party and corporative representation not always equally emphasized; with a distinctive style and rhetoric, it relied on activist cadres ready for violent action combined with electoral participation to gain power with totalitarian goals by a combination of legal and violent tactics. The ideology and above all the rhetoric appeals for the incorporation of a national culture tradition selectively in the new synthesis in response to new social classes, new social and economic problems, and with new organiza-

> tional conceptions of mobilization and participation, differentiate them from conservative parties. The appeal based on emotion, myth, idealism, and action on the basis of a vitalistic philosophy is initially directed at those least integrated in the class structure – youth, students, demobilized officers – to constitute a self-appointed élite and later to all those disadvantageously affected by social change and political and economic crisis against the social system . . .
>
> Hypernationalism is reflected in a deep-seated hostility to all organizations and movements that can be conceived as international in character – that is communism, even socialism, international finance capitalism, the Catholic Church, or at least the Vatican, freemasonry, the League of Nations, pacifism, and the Jews, even in those movements that are not initially anti-Semitic and even less racist.

For fascism, society is the end, individuals the means: individual rights are only recognized insofar as they are implied in the rights of the State. The authority of the State is absolute, and the State power is held in the hands of the Leader. Fascism extolled the values of the group, of the collectivity, of unity of the people and unanimism: it fought against anything which tended to divide or differentiate, or which stood for diversity or pluralism: liberalism, democracy, parliamentarism, multiparty system, the division in social classes, the class struggle. In the words of Sternhell, the people's "unity finds its most perfect expression in the quasi-sacred figure of the leader".[19]

Ebenstein and Fogelman[20] have listed seven basic elements of the fascist outlook, which are summarized hereunder, to which our own comments are added:

1. Distrust of reason, or rationality, stressing the sentimental, the fanatical and the dogmatic: the empire, the leader and his assertions and ambitions are taboo issues which are not discussed critically: "Mussolini is always right". Fascism was also an anti-intellectual reaction against the rationality of democracy. It was a new religion in opposition with the banality of the bourgeois life, the materialism of capitalism and the platitude of liberal democracy.
2. Fascism rejects the Jewish-Christian-Greek concept of equality and opposes it with the concept of inequality, based on strength: men are superior to women, soldiers to civilians, party members to non-party members, one's own nation to others, the strong to the weak, the victors in war to the vanquished.
3. Fascism stresses violence and lies and repression of political opponents, as threatening deterrents to the rest of the population.
4. Government by a self-appointed elite group, a small minority of the population, qualified not particularly by birth, education, social standing, or professional or civic achievements, but selected by the leader as his close associates and supporters who have helped him to come and remain in power, – in opposition to the "democratic fallacy" that people are capable of governing themselves and that elections are an appropriate method for the selection of leaders. Political pluralism and parties are to be abolished, as well as representation by conflicting factions.

The fascist "leadership principle" expresses the extreme form of the elite concept: the leader is infallible, endowed with mystical gifts and insights. He uses innovative propaganda, slogans, radio and public appeals, mass meetings, ubiquitous photographs and portraits of the leader, in order to promote the "cult" of his personality, obtain total adhesion and popular support to his themes and programmes, and suppress any dissent as treasonable.

5. Fascism is totalitarian: it employs authority and violence in all social relations, whether political or not, in order to control all phases of human life.
6. Nationalism, imperialism imply that the elite nation is superior to others and is entitled to rule them. Early Italian fascism concentrated on the ambition to revive the ancient Roman Empire and was relatively free from racism. In 1938, Mussolini announced that the Italians were a pure and superior race, but did not follow Hitler's extreme racist theories and consequent mass extermination of the "inferior races".
7. Opposition to international law and order, or war is the logical outcome of fascist beliefs in inequality, violence, elitism, racism and imperialism. In the words of Mussolini

> War alone brings up to their highest tension all human energies and puts the stamp of nobility upon the peoples who have the courage to meet it.

Fascist regimes reject the international principles of peaceful settlement of international disputes, international cooperation and organization, equality of countries, national sovereignty and refuse to abide by the requirements of the Covenant of the League of Nations. Mussolini conquered Ethiopia in 1935–1936, in spite of the ineffective collective security sanctions edicted by the League, which Italy left in 1937.

The corporate state applied fascist principles of organization and control to the economy. The fascist economy is subdivided into state-controlled associations of capital and labour, and each association has a monopoly in its trade and occupation. Thus, the one-party state is the ultimate arbiter of conflicts between capital and labour.

Nazism

After a failed putsch in November 1923, Hitler came to power on 30 January 1933 as Chancellor, at the request of President Hindenburg. He then used his position and circumstances to install progressively a nazi dictatorship. Following the Reichstag fire, on the night of 29 February, Göring ordered the arrest of all Communist deputies and leading officials, the closing of their offices and a ban on all their publications. The next day, Hitler secured another emergency decree signed by the President, "For the Protection of People and State: to guard against Communist acts of violence endangering the state". Its Article 1 suspended until further notice the seven sections of the constitution guaranteeing the fundamental rights of the citizen[21]:

> Thus restrictions on personal liberty, on the right of free expression of opinion, including freedom of the press, on the right of association and assembly, and violations of the privacy of postal, telegraphic and telephonic communications, and warrants for house-searches, orders for confiscations as well as restrictions on property rights are permissible beyond the legal limits otherwise prescribed.

The number of arrests made by the regular police in Prussia during March and April was estimated at 25,000. This hastily improvised emergency decree served to provide the legal basis for the Nazi police state for the 12 years of the Third Reich.

The following elections, held on 5 March 1933, gave 43.9% of the votes to the Nazis. However, the Nazi Party used anti-constitutional means to obtain this result: besides the street terror tactics, opposition parties were deprived of their means of propaganda during the election campaign; early in March 1933, the activities of the Communists, the Social Democrats and the Catholic Center Party were curbed, while all the resources of the State official broadcasting and other communications were placed at the full disposal of the National Socialist government.

On 24 March, the new Reichstag gave Hitler, the "Führer", full powers. On 19 August 1934, a plebiscite confirmed, by 90% of the votes, the assumption by Hitler of the functions of Chief of State in addition to those of Chancellor.

Individual and public freedoms were abolished: freedom of the press, freedom of public meetings, independence of the courts: the judges were instructed by Göring that they must act as representatives, as trustees of the National Socialist Party, as Party and State are one. Loewenstein noted that, in 1935, nearly 100,000 people were in concentration camps, while 186,000 people had been sterilized.[22]

In March 1938, Hitler annexed Austria; Czechoslovakia followed, in 1938–1939. German (and Soviet) troops invaded Poland in September 1939, which triggered the French and British declarations of war against Germany. After its victory on the Western front, Germany invaded the USSR in June 1941, repeating Napoleon's mistake.

On 1st May 1945, Hitler committed suicide in his Berlin bunker and on 8 May, Germany capitulated without conditions.

Nazi Ideology

Nazism was based on the same principles as fascism, but added exacerbated racism to those.

Nazism was openly nationalist and conservative in character. Hitler exalted national unity over class-based politics. He was for the traditional authoritarian values of will, discipline, order, hierarchy. He was against modernism, marxism, and democracy. For him, the parliamentary system suffered from four vices: the principle of the majority, politics founded on interest and pluralism, democracy as a form of the power of capital, and the expression of decadence and weakness.

> Democracy is the victory of the most vulgar, the worst, the weakest and above all of the coward, the irresponsible ... the masses are composed only of medioc-

rities. One hundred blindmen do not give sight, one thousand cowards do not create a hero, a hundred thousand parliamentarians do not create a statesman... a people submitted to the principle of the majority is doomed to disaster... the parliamentary principle of majorities goes against the aristocratic principle of nature.[23]

Hitler denounced the venality of the parliamentarian representatives, their dependence on the lobbies. He was proud of having defeated democracy on its own terms, through democracy.

The "führerprincip" was the basis of the party: Hitler's authority derived, not from his office, nor from any form of election, but from his charismatic gifts as a leader. All power was concentrated in the hands of the leader, unencumbered by any constitutional or parliamentary control, nor any legalistic, ethical or humanitarian considerations.

The Nazi state embraced all forces of the country, it embraced "the human beings, body, soul and spirit" and all their activities, whatever they may be: the National Socialists represent the State and represent, at the same time, the Party, so Party and State are one.

In order to preserve the people's "racial value",[24] the state had to defend the people against contamination by three poisons, each of which Hitler identified with the Jews. These are: – internationalism, – pacifism and – egalitarianism, democracy and majority rule, which are hostile to individual creativity and leadership.

Hitler divided mankind into three categories: the founders of culture (the Aryans), the bearers of culture (the Japanese, as an example), and the destroyers of culture, the Jews. The mythical figure of "the Jew" was to Hitler the source of the racial contamination and social decomposition which undermined Aryan supremacy.

As the highest or purest remnant of the Aryan race, the Germanic people, the "master race", was entitled to dominate, enslave or even exterminate the inferior races or peoples, such as the Jews, the Gypsies, the Slavs.

The total loss of life among the European nations in the Second World War has been estimated at 40 million. The consequences of Nazism's racist propaganda and action, the planned extermination of all European Jews, have been estimated at between 5.6 and 6.9 million Jews put to death in 1939–1945.[25] In addition, more than half a million Gypsies and political opponents have also been exterminated on Nazi orders.

In the words of Bullock,[26]

Nazism and Fascism glorified will, authority, power and war. Their validity depended on success: neither could survive defeats as total as those which overtook Hitler and Mussolini.

The United Nations' Repeated Condemnation of Fascism and Nazism

As recalled in a 1981 Resolution of the U.N. General Assembly (Resol. 36/162),

> the United Nations emerged from the struggle against nazism, fascism, aggression and foreign occupation, (which had caused) the suffering, destruction and death of millions of victims . . .

In the Atlantic Charter of 14 August 1941, Roosevelt and Churchill had already stated that

> after the final destruction of the Nazi tyranny, they hope to see established a peace which will afford to all nations the means of dwelling in safety within their own boundaries, and which will afford assurance that all the men in all the lands may live out their lives in freedom from fear and want.

In the 1942 "Declaration by United Nations", the signatory governments were

> convinced that complete victory over their enemies is essential to defend life, liberty, independence and religious freedom, and to preserve human rights and justice in their own lands as well as in other lands, and that they are now engaged in a common struggle against savage and brutal forces seeking to subjugate the world.[27]

On 11 December 1946, the General Assembly affirmed the principles of international law recognized by the Charter of the Nürnberg Tribunal and the judgment of the Tribunal (Resol. 95 (I)), and, on 9 December 1948, the Assembly approved the Convention on the Prevention and Punishment of the Crime of Genocide (Resol. 260 A (III)).

Then, starting in 1967, a succession of resolutions condemned

> any ideology, including nazism, which is based on racial intolerance and terror as a gross violation of human rights and fundamental freedoms and of the purposes and principles of the Charter of the United Nations;

and called upon all States to take immediate and effective measures against such manifestations of nazism and racial intolerance.[28]

While the first resolutions condemned such ideology on the grounds that it had caused war, that it may "embitter" relations between peoples and groups (an understatement), that it may jeopardize world peace and the security of peoples, the resolution adopted on 18 December 1971 by the General Assembly made an explicit reference to democracy as an effective "vaccine" against nazism and racial discrimination (Resol. 2839 (XXVI):

> *firmly convinced* that the best bulwark against nazism and racial discrimination is the establishment and maintenance of democratic institutions, that the existence of genuine political, social and economic democracy is an effective

vaccine and an equally effective antidote against the formation or development of Nazi movements and that a political system which is based on freedom and effective participation by the people in the conduct of public affairs, and under which economic and social conditions are such as to ensure a decent standard of living for the population, makes it impossible for fascism, nazism or other ideologies based on terror to succeed.

The 1985 resolution expressed "deep alarm" at the existence of groups and organizations which propagate totalitarian ideologies and practices, including Nazi, Fascist and neo-Fascist ones (Resol. 40/148).

Resurgence of Fascism and Nazism

In August 1992, the U.N. Human Rights Sub-Commission on Prevention of Discrimination and Protection of Minorities expressed concern about the alarming growth of new forms of xenophobia, racist propaganda and violence in recent years.[29]

Neither racism nor anti-semitism were invented by Hitler: anti-semitism is at least as old as Christianity, and the French prophet of racism, Gobineau, published his "Essai sur l'inégalité des races humaines" in 1853–1855.

The American Ku Klux Klan was racist vs. the blacks in the 19th century: it was organized to frighten blacks from using their newly won franchise after the Civil War. In the 20th century, the Klan broadened its intolerance by attacks against the Jews, the Catholics and other groups who were not white, Anglo-Saxon and Protestant. It has recently provided neo-Nazi propaganda to German extreme-rightist groups.

The South African policy of apartheid, now rescinded, segregated the racial groups, African, Asian, Coloured and White. The African majority was denied voting rights and its civil rights were strictly limited. The ultimate political power was reserved for the "superior" race, the White.

After a period of forced discretion following World War II, political parties and groups advocating more or less openly fascist or nazi themes were formed in Western Europe. They are openly nationalistic, xenophobic, they are encouraging anti-immigration protests and sometimes organizing physical attacks against immigrants, they are supporting and publicizing the revisionist "historians" theses which deny the nazi genocide and suggest that the Holocaust is a Jewish invention. They denounce the corrupt politicians, they reject capitalism, communism, European integration, atlanticism, modernism, they exalt a nostalgia for patriotic tradition and the nazi or fascist authoritarian order. They are more or less openly anti-semitic.

In Italy, the neo-fascist "Movimento Sociale Italiano" (MSI) was created in 1946. Its best electoral score, together with the monarchists, was 9% of the votes at the 1972 legislative elections. It obtained 7% of the votes at the 1988 legislatives. In 1964 and 1970, putsches attempted, but failed, to overthrow the young Italian Republic. More radical groups, such as "Ordine Nuovo" and "Avanguardia

Nazionale" promoted revolutionary terrorism, on parallel, albeit ideologically opposed, lines to the Red Brigades. Between 1969 and 1975, "black" terrorism was responsible for dozens of deaths and hundreds of wounded people. In August 1980, the terrorist organization "Third Positionist Nuclei Armati Rivoluzionari" (NAR) bombed Bologna railway station, killing 86 people. MSI members were suspected by the Italian police to have taken part in the bombing of the Naples-Milan train in 1984, in which 15 people were killed.

In Germany, the strongest far-right party, the "Republikaner", was founded in 1983 by Franz Schönhuber, a former Waffen-SS officer. Its candidates obtained 7.5% of votes in the elections to the West Berlin house of representatives in January 1989. Also in 1989, it won 7.1% of the votes to the European Parliament elections. It had 10.9% of the votes in the elections to the Baden-Wurttemberg state parliament in April 1992. Other far-right parties are the anti-foreigner German People's Union and the German Alternative.

In August 1992, violence by neo-Nazi groups against foreign refugees in Rostock, a city in former East Germany, has raised international concern in view of Germany's past.

According to the German Federal Office for the Protection of the Constitution, extreme-right movements had 40,000 members in the whole of Germany in 1991: among those members, 4,400 (3,000 of whom are in the ex-German Democratic Republic), belong to movements openly referring to nazism and advocating violence against immigrants. "Skinheads" comprise 4,200 of those violent neo-Nazis. Violent actions against foreigners rose from 270 in 1990 to 1,500 in 1991.[30]

Jörg Haider's Freedom Party won 22.6% of the vote and 23 seats in Vienna's 100-seat assembly in the November 1991 elections, compared to 8 seats in 1987 and 2 seats in 1983. His party won 33 seats in the Austrian Parliament, with 16.6% of the votes in the 1990 general elections. Haider's public statements combine racism, xenophobia and anti-parliamentarism.[31]

Although the country of human rights, France had violent rightist political parties between the two World Wars and a tradition of anti-semitism. The Vichy government promulgated a discriminatory Status of the Jews in October 1940 and was responsible for the deportation of 76,000 Jews to Nazi Germany. Jean-Marie Le Pen's National Front obtained 13% of the votes in regional elections held in March 1992. The Front's message is nationalistic, anti-foreign, anti-European integration, anti-immigrant and racist. Its weekly publication is both anti-Arab and anti-semitic, it calls for the repatriation of immigrants and claims that the gas chambers were a mere "detail" of the Second World War. Since 1984, the National Front has held ten seats in the European Parliament and is the major party in the Technical Group of the European Right.

A nazi street force, the French and European National Party has links with other right-wing terrorist groups, especially in Italy.

Other far-right groups In Western Europe include the Belgian Vlaams Blok, the Danish National Socialist Bund, the Swiss National Socialist Party etc.

In Hungary, Istvan Csurka, vice-President and ultra-nationalist ideologist of the ruling Hungarian Democratic Forum (MDF) published a virulent pamphlet on 20 August 1992, containing openly anti-semitic allegations, recalling the nazi slogans of an "international Jewish conspiracy" and the financial influence of the "liberal-bourgeois Jewry". The official reaction to such blatant racism was feeble.

At the European level, the European Social Movement (MSE) and the more activist New European Order (NOE) were founded in 1951. The MSE died in 1960, while the NOE, sited in Lausanne, still survives as a racist, anti-communist, anti-capitalist, anti-judeo-American and revisionist organization.

The World Union of National-Socialists (WUNS) was founded in 1962 by the British Colin Jordan with the support of Lincoln Rockwell, chief of the American Nazi Party, who then became "World Führer". Other international nazi or racist groups include the NSDAP/AO (Nazi party abroad) and the Northern League.[32]

These extreme-right political parties and groups only represent a relatively small electoral minority of European countries' populations, although their verbal, and sometimes physical, violence is potentially dangerous. However, the democratic institutions of West European countries appear strong enough to act as "vaccine" and "antidotes" to the neo-fascist and neo-nazi ideologies, provided that democratic governments, parties, associations and citizens remain actively vigilant: in particular, organized mob violence must be prevented or severely sanctioned.

Islam and Democracy

Is Islam compatible with democracy? Do Islamic nations apply recognized democratic principles and practices, or has Islam invented its own type of democracy?

In view of the diversity of the political regimes practised by Islamic countries, republican or monarchist, secular or religious, testing, or not, multi-partyism and elections, with apparent or discreet military support, some having been colonized, and therefore influenced by different European countries (the U.K., France, the Netherlands), it is not possible to give a simple, unique and factual answer to these questions. Furthermore, there is also a diversity of religious and ideological interpretations and religious practices in Muslim societies which belies the assumption that Islam is monolithic.

In popular Western opinion, Islam has acquired a very negative notoriety: repressive regimes, non-elected leaders, limited political rights and civil liberties, intolerance towards the "infidels", no independent justice, no due process, barbaric condemnations (Salman Rushdie's death sentence for his alleged blasphemy, mutilation of limbs, the stoning of adulterers), terrorism carried out or supported by states, liberation movements or religious groups, the taking of hostages, official sex discrimination, as well as anti-Western rhetoric.

These characteristics have mostly been attributed to the Islamist fundamentalists who believe, like the traditionalists and the quietists, that Islam is simultaneously the religion, the way of life and the form of government. On the other hand, liberal Moslems believe that some form of separation between Islam and politics is desirable and possible, and try to conciliate Islam with modernity.

The 1979 Iranian revolution, a fundamentalist victory, was clearly in opposition to the fundamental principles of democracy. Its rulers do not tolerate any real opposition (Islamic or non-Islamic): political opponents are routinely jailed or executed, while dissidents charge that Iran's foreign agents continue to murder overseas exiles, such as the Shah's last Prime Minister, Shahpur Bakhtiar, killed in France in August 1991.

On the other hand, Iran's Constitution makes reference to both divine and popular sovereignty. Political participation (but without right to dissent) is stressed in articles of the Constitution which affirm that the people should participate "in determining their political, economic, social and cultural destiny" (Principle 3), which provide for a popularly elected national Consultative Assembly (Principle 62) and for periodic referenda on issues that are submitted "directly to the people for a judgment" (Principle 59). In an homage to democracy, the Constitution noted that the government of the Republic had been endorsed by the Iranian nation by an affirmative vote of 98.2% of the majority of eligible voters[33]: this percentage was unfortunately typical of voting in totalitarian countries.

Although Iran is a party to the International Covenant on Civil and Political Rights, it was condemned in December 1988 by the U.N. General Assembly for the "numerous and detailed allegations of grave human rights violations" referred to in the U.N. Special Representative's report, concerning the right to life, the right to freedom from torture or cruel, inhuman or degrading treatment or punishment, the right to liberty and security of person, the right to a fair trial and the right to freedom of thought, conscience and religion, the continued harrassment and discrimination against the Baha'is, a renewed wave of executions in July-September 1988, "irregularities" in the treatment of political prisoners etc. (Resol. 43/137).

In August 1992, the U.N. Subcommission on Prevention of Discrimination and Protection of Minorities adopted a resolution endorsing the urgent call by the Special Representative to the Government of Iran to comply with human rights standards. It condemned Iran's continuing grave violations of human rights, especially: the use of excessive force to suppress anti-government demonstrations, including summary executions and arbitrary arrests; executions, systematic torture and maltreatment of political prisoners; stoning, torture and degrading treatment of citizens, especially women, in public; renewed persecution of religious minorities and summary killings of Baha'is and suppression of freedom of thought, expression and association. The Subcommission requested the Special Representative, in his next report to the General Assembly and the Commission on Human Rights, to include information on executions, arrests and measures to suppress political opposition, including the formation of special paramilitary units, and any further information of the assassination of Professor Kazem Rajavi.

The Iranian representative rejected these allegations and accusations as unfounded.

In October 1992, expert members of the U.N. Human Rights Committee examined Iran's fulfilment of the obligations assumed under the International Covenant on Civil and Political Rights. Among their major concerns were the broad range of crimes for which a person could be condemned to death, including for example adultery, the fact that 884 executions had taken place the previous year alone, forms of punishment such as amputations of limbs and stoning to death or throwing persons off high buildings, and extraordinary swift justice, in one case requiring only 24 hours between arrest and execution. Speakers noted that all such practices cast doubt on Iran's compliance with the Covenant.[34]

In Sudan, where an Islamic fundamentalist regime took power in 1989, human rights organizations have condemned the authorities for the torture of political prisoners, the training of terrorists and the degrading treatment of citizens. The Constitution has been suspended, political parties dissolved, the press is suppressed and the judiciary under political control. A journalist has described fundamentalist Sudan as a "thoroughgoing police state". The war against the predominant Christian and animist South has caused a million deaths and close to 2 million refugees. Relief agencies are refused access to the refugees' camps, and generally to Southern areas. The Sudanese regime leader, Hassan al-Turabi, recently announced that Islam is a wave of history which will come through evolution or revolution.[35]

In most other Islamic countries, traditionalist or modernist, governments have banned fundamentalist parties or groups and fight against their influence.

Are there any principles, or standards, which may lead Islamic nations towards democracy, or which raise obstacles to this evolution?

Basic Principles of an Islamic State

A Convention of the 'Ulama representing all the schools of Islamic thought, held on 21–24 January 1951 in Karachi issued an agreed statement on the "Basic Principles of an Islamic State": although the Islamic State is by definition a theocracy, these principles do not exclude some democratic processes related mainly to "consultation". The principles are relatively liberal, with some exceptions, and support the principle of elections, the separation of government powers, as well as citizens' rights. A few extracts follow[36]:

> The Constitution of an Islamic State shall comprehend the following basic principles: –
>
> 1. Ultimate sovereignty over all Nature and all Law vests in Allah, the Lord of the universe, alone.
> 2. The law of the land shall be based on the Qu'ran and the Sunnah, and no law shall be enacted nor any administrative order issued, in contravention of the Qu'ran and the Sunnah.

3. The State shall be based not on geographical, racial, linguistic or any other materialistic concepts, but on the principles and ideals of Islamic ideology

. . .

6. It shall be the responsibility of the Government to guarantee the basic necessities of life, i.e., food, clothing, housing, medical relief and education to all citizens without distinction of race or religion, who might temporarily or permanently be incapable of earning their livelihood due to unemployment, sickness or other reason.

Citizens' Rights

7. The citizens shall be entitled to all the rights conferred upon them by the Islamic law, i.e., they shall be assured, within the limits of the law, of full security of life, property and honour, freedom of religion and belief, freedom of worship, freedom of person, freedom of expression, freedom of movement, freedom of association, freedom of occupation, equality of opportunity and the right to benefit from public services.
8. No citizen shall, at any time, be deprived of these rights, except under the law; and none shall be awarded any punishment on any charge without being given full opportunity of defence and without the decision of a court of law

. . .

10. The non-Muslim citizens of the State shall have within the limits of the law, complete freedom of religion and worship, mode of life, culture and religious education. They shall be entitled to have all their matters concerning Personal Law administered in accordance with their own religious code, usages and customs.
11. . . . non-Muslim citizens . . . shall be entitled equally with the Muslim citizens to the rights of citizenship as enunciated in paragraph 7 above.
12. The Head of State shall always be a male Muslim in whose piety, learning and soundness of judgement the people or their elected representatives have confidence.
13. The responsibility for the administration of the State shall primarily vest in the Head of the State, although he may delegate any part of his powers to any individual or body.

Governance of the State

14. The Head of the State shall function not in an autocratic but in a consultative (Sura'i) manner, i.e., he will discharge his duties in consultation with persons holding responsible positions in the Government and with the elected representatives of the people

. . .

16. The body empowered to elect the Head of the State shall also have the power to remove him by a majority of votes . . .

18. All citizens, whether members of the Government, officials or private persons, shall be subject to the same laws and the jurisdiction of the same courts.
19. The judiciary shall be separate from and independent of the executive, so that it may not be influenced by the executive in the discharge of its duties.

The same document, under "Fundamentals of an Islamic Constitution", stresses that all collective affairs are performed by mutual consultation:

> As regards the mode of consultation, it has been very wisely left to the discretion of Muslims. Islam does not prescribe any definite form for the formation of the consultative body or bodies for the simple reason that it is a universal religion meant for all times. It does not, therefore, lay down whether the people should be consulted directly or through their accredited representatives; whether the representative should be elected in general elections or through electoral colleges; whether consultative body should have one house or two houses; etc.
>
> ...
>
> The consultation should be free, impartial and genuine
>
> ...
>
> ...the Islamic Constitution must devise such a system of election as may enable the whole community to give their verdict without any tinge of fear, favour or fraud.

Democratic Reform Prospects

In most Islamic states, sovereignty is not vested in the people, but in Allah: political parties may be formed and may propagate their views provided that those views do not run counter to the Islamic ideology on which the state is based, i.e. the shari'a.[37] Anti-Islamic parties and propaganda are therefore excluded, in violation of the freedoms of opinion, association and expression. The dogmatic religious texts, beliefs and required practices, which are inseparable from the Islamic State's governance, do not provide the basic elements of political freedom and individual liberties.

The first written constitution of Saudi Arabia, since the country was founded in 1932, was promulgated by King Fahd in March 1992. It creates a Consultative Council (Majlis al-Shura) which will have the right to initiate laws and review foreign and domestic policies: its 60 members will not be elected, but chosen by the King. The King may disband the Council and appoint a new one at his will. The decrees also grant governors and local assemblies in Saudi Arabia's 12 provinces extensive autonomy in deciding priorities on spending and development plans. They stress the right to privacy and forbid government authorities from arresting, spying and violating basic human rights without cause.

Following these modest reforms, King Fahd said, also in March 1992, that democracy was incompatible with Islam, because it was not suited to society in Saudi Arabia and other traditional societies in the Gulf, as these societies are based on Islam. The King said:

> Islam is our social, political and economic system and Islamic law is its own comprehensive constitution . . . comprising social justice, economic justice, the judiciary, everything . . . The democratic system prevailing in the world does not suit us in this region.[38]

Kuwait's Constitution is the only one among the Gulf monarchies to stipulate that "sovereignty resides in the people". However, the last Assembly had been dissolved by the government in 1986 for a "wrong use of democracy". New elections to the National Assembly were held on 5 October 1992: however, electoral franchise was still limited to the 80,000 male Kuwaitis whose families have been citizens since 1920, or 12% of the population. The seven groups of the Islamic and democratic opposition campaigned separately. Some of the issues which will be raised by the new Assembly will be the extension of the franchise and women's vote.[39]

Libya's Gadhafi wrote in his "Green Book" that elections lead to a dictatorial system (the rule of the majority) and that parliaments are deceitful representations of the people, – he also rejects political parties, referenda. He has set up popular committees (Basic People's Conferences) and the General People's Congress, a non-elected Parliament, bodies which are supposed to replace the government and all other state functions as well as the law.[40]

Algeria introduced political pluralism following anti-government riots in October 1988. In the June 1990 municipal elections, the first multi-party elections since independence in 1962, the "Front Islamique du Salut" (FIS), a fundamentalist party, won 54% of the votes, while the National Liberation Front (FLN) (the ruling party) only obtained 34%. The FIS obtained 49% in the first round of general elections in December 1991. The government, with the support of the army, cancelled the second round, not willing to allow the FIS to use democratic elections in order to create a non-democratic Islamic state. Ali Benhadj, a prominent FIS leader, had been quoted as saying: "Democracy is apostasy (or atheism)".[41]

On 5 July 1992, the Jordanian Parliament adopted a law legalizing multi-partyism, on the condition that parties ensured total financial transparency.[42]

On 4 September 1992, a revision of the Moroccan constitution was adopted by referendum by 99.98% of the voters. It provides for an independent Constitution Council and an Economic and Social Council. The Parliament will have the right to create inquiry commissions. The King, however, said that he would not give up his large powers, as these are in part governmental and in part religious: he would not become a constitutional monarch.[43]

Secularization and Democratization: The Turkish Case

Although modern Turkey is far from being a model democracy, its political evolution is an interesting example of an Islamic nation becoming a secular State, and evolving from a one-party system to a multiple party democracy, evolution interrupted by military interventions.

For hundreds of years, Islam had been a pillar of the Ottoman Empire, and the Sultans exercised both temporal and religious power. Ninety-eight percent of Turkey's population are Islamic believers.

In 1923, Mustafa Kemal, later called Atatürk, founded the Republican People's Party (RPP), which exercised power in a one-party system. There was no separation between party and government: the party was the government. The RPP was politically democratic and populist, in favour of a secular state, and economically statist. As from 1919, Kemal had directed a military response against the dismemberment of the Ottoman Empire. His objective was to create a new Turkey as a nationalist, modern and secular republic, based on a strong army.[44]

The Kemalist Constitution of 30 April 1924 abolished the discredited institutions of the Sultanate and the Caliphate and the Turkish State was declared a Republic.

In 1925, polygamy was abolished and religious orders suppressed.

Initially, Islam was retained as the state religion: this was abolished in 1928. Sovereignty was given unconditionally to the Nation, and the Grand National Assembly became the sole rightful representative of the nation, exercising sovereignty in its name. Legislative authority and executive power were concentrated in the Assembly, which exercised its legislative authority directly, and its executive authority through the person of the President of the Republic elected by it, and through a Council of Ministers chosen by the President.

The Assembly was to be composed of representatives elected by the Nation: every Turk, woman or man, who had completed his twenty-second year, was entitled to vote in these elections.

The Constitution was amended on 5 February 1937: it defined the Turkish State as Republican, Nationalist, Populist, Statist, Secularist and Revolutionary. The RPP had adopted in 1935 six "fundamental and unchanging principles" which explained some of these terms. In particular, populism meant an absolute equality before the law without any privileges for any individual, family, class or community. Kemalism rejected the marxist concept of class conflict: the Republic was a community divided into various professions according to the requirements of the division of labour for the individual and social life of the Turkish people.

As to the "secularist" principle:

> As the conception of religion is a matter of conscience, the Party considers it to be one of the chief factors of the success of our nation in contemporary progress, to separate ideas of religion from politics, and from the affairs of the world and of the State.

Even after the death of Atatürk in November 1938, secularism was recognized by the ruling elites as a requirement for westernization and modernization.

In 1945, the introduction of multi-party politics made religion a political factor in the competition of parties for votes. In the 1960s, Islam was considered as an antidote against communism.

In 1952, Adnan Menderes, one of the leaders of the Democratic Party, then in power, wrote:

> The Turkish people are Muslims and will remain Muslims. No one has the right in this country to violate the freedom of conscience ... This country cannot tolerate the turning of so sacred an institution as religion into the instrument exploited by the dregs of society and political pedlars ... Just as dragging the army into politics is a serious crime, so is trying to make a sacred institution like religion the vehicle and instrument of various aims, interests and political disputes.[45]

In 1953, the "Law to Protect the Freedom of Conscience" was passed to prevent religion from being used for political ends.

In 1960, a military regime took over from the Democratic Party, headed by a National Unity Committee. The Committee, in spite of its full commitment to Kemalism, realized that Islam was a vital ingredient in the Turkish character. As noted by Ahmad,[46] since it was counter-productive and harmful to adopt a hostile attitude towards religion, it would be wiser for the state to retain control so that it could not be exploited by the "narrow-minded" and the reactionaries. At the same time, the State could keep reforming Islam so as to make it serve social change in Turkey.

In October 1965, the Justice Party camed to power: Inönü then warned the government that religious fanaticism was as dangerous for Turkey as communism.

The army intervened in 1971 and in 1980 and a new Constitution was adopted in 1982, which reinforced the powers of the executive and abridged some freedoms.

A member of the Council of Europe, Turkey is trying to continue its democratisation, which has been hampered by military coups, the violent Kurdish separatism and its economic problems. The separation of religion and state imposed by Atatürk seems to have taken roots in this Islamic country, thus lifting a possible obstacle to further democratisation and to modernisation.

Obstacles to Democratization

The rejection of Western values by the Islamic fundamentalists, but also by many Moslem populations, is an obstacle to accepting an evolution towards democratic principles and practices.

Western values are equated with corruption, materialism and immorality. Resentment against the Western colonialists which "enslaved" their nations was revived during the 1956 Suez crisis, and more recently, during the Coalition war against Iraq. The condemnations and sanctions ordered against Iraq and Libya by the Western-dominated Security Council have added to this resentment and compounded the Arab humiliation. They see the Western leaders apply double standards: their political and moral exigencies of democracy and human rights only apply to others. Some of the Arab leaders are perceived as Western stooges. Modernisation has only brought unemployment, more misery and more inequality.

In a reaction of pride, Islamic peoples recall that Islam brought civilization to the Occident. They believe that everything is in the Qu'ran and Sunnah: Islam is the best religion.

The divine and immutable sovereignty of the sacred texts is incompatible with the principle of popular sovereignty. Islamic unanimism rejects the rule of the majority, the competition of multiple political parties, the existence of a "loyal" opposition, the acceptance of a peaceful change from theocracy to democracy.

The fact that fundamentalist and traditional countries' leaders are both religious and political leaders consolidates and legitimates their power, while it de-legitimizes political dissenters and challengers.

There is a lack of sense of national unity in some Islamic countries. As a result, ethnic, tribal or family allegiances dominate any sense of loyalty to the broader entity.

Other obstacles are not specific to Islamic countries: they include the influence of the military establishment on politics, the traditional or modernist rulers' taste for power and its privileges, and their refusal to become constitutional monarchs, or to cede or share power as a result of democratic referenda or elections.

Bedjaoui[47] wrote recently:

> Islam is also required today to realize its passage towards renewal within its authenticity, care being taken that it does not get out of hand. If Islam maintains economic and political relationships within the "sacred" domain, society cannot be modernized. By definition the "sacred" excludes any contestation, any discussion, therefore any participation. The "sacred" imposes duties: it does not promote rights. Citizenship, i.e. the fact of belonging to a political community, freedom of choice, and quite simply freedom, the power of decision, in brief the practice of democracy, cannot blossom. The key to Islam's renewal, to progress and development, is in the distinction between man's relationship with God, which is part of the "sacred", and political and economic relationships between men which belong to the secular domain and must be withdrawn from the "sacred". I do not see any other way.

Authoritarian Regimes

Dictatorships are of all times: their roots are not necessarily ideological or religious – the attraction of power and the enjoyment of its privileges are a sufficient motivation for the ambitious, the visionary, the nationalists, the demagogues, those who also want wealth, those who want to be adulated and feared.

Leaders have taken power by force with the support of the military, or following popular plebiscites (with one candidate only) or one-party elections. They have then remained in power for indefinite periods, without allowing any electoral challenge, or under well-controlled elections. Some of them have anointed themselves as "President-for-life", somewhat imprudently, or even as "Emperor" of a short-lived Empire.

Such dictatorships or authoritarian, non-democratic regimes cannot survive without military support, threats of and actual violence, and periodical repression. They imply a curtailment of political rights and civil liberties. The lack of institutional and popular control, the dependence of the legislative and the judiciary on the self-appointed executive, the permanent monopoly of one man and/or one party to the supreme national power produce abuses, corruption, passivity of the governed and a lack of preparation for peaceful change and political transition. Violence will often follow the fall of the tyrant.

When Soviet communism appeared as a military and ideological threat, Western countries often supported authoritarian regimes with weapons, military support, financial subsidies and credits, open or covert political support.

Western support weakened or disappeared with the fading of the "Red Danger" and the dislocation of the "Evil Empire": Western governments then tied their economic and financial aid to commitments of political democratization and economic liberalization. The U.S. and other Western donors applied pressures in order to entice reluctant presidents or other civil and military leaders to respect freedom of association (multi-partyism), freedom of political reunion and campaigning, periodical and free elections. Also required were the creation or strengthening of representative assemblies with real political power, separation of power between the executive, the legislative and the judiciary, and the independence of the latter two.

The reluctance of ruling leaders to accept some or all of these democratic requirements is not necessarily related to such ideologies as socialism or fascism, or to religious constraints, or to their sincere belief that they have been "chosen" to save their country, that they are the only capable statesmen, that their work is not yet completed. Rare are the political leaders who will gracefully, or willingly, give up power and its attributes: the power to rule over a country, to appoint officials, to have authority over the leaders and institutions in all sectors of the country's life, to take important decisions which may affect the civic, economic, social, cultural, religious rights of its population, to have easy access to the nation's resources, including official or illicit financial benefits, is like a drug to which all its users, small or big, become addicted.

Examples of the practices of two authoritarian governments, and of their resistance to accept a democratic transition, follow.

According to Freedom House[48]:

> Indonesia is a controlled parliamentary democracy under military direction. Recent parliamentary elections allowed some competition but severely restricted opposition campaigning and organization. The number and character of opposition parties are carefully controlled, parties must refrain from criticizing each other, candidates of both government and opposition require government approval, and the opposition is not allowed to organize in rural areas. All parties must accept the broad outline of state policy and the state ideology. All civil servants are expected to vote for the government. In any event parliament does not have a great deal of power ... Military officers are included in most legislatures and play a major role in the economy as managers of both public and army corporations ... All newspapers are subject to fairly close government supervision ... radio and television are government controlled ... freedom of assembly is restricted ... The Indonesian bureaucracy has an unenviable reputation for arbitrariness and corruption ... the judiciary is not independent ...

President Suharto came to power in 1965 as the General who put down a coup against then President Sukarno that was blamed on the Communists: the repression is alleged to have caused approximately 500,000 deaths. There have been five parliamentary elections since then, to elect 400 of its members, while 100 seats are undemocratically reserved for appointed military members. The three political groups authorized to contest the parliamentary elections are the government-backed Golkar, the Indonesian Democratic Party (PDI) and the Moslem-oriented United Development Party (PPP). The 1992 elections gave 67.3% of the vote to Golkar (73% in 1987), 17.5% to PPP and 15.2% to PDI. The elections were peaceful and orderly, although the latter two parties complained that restrictions on political organizing and campaigning prevented them from matching Golkar, which is backed by the 4 million member bureaucracy and local officials in the villages. The President is chosen a year after the elections by a special assembly composed of members of the Parliament and additional government nominees. The real power is in the hands of the President and the Army.

In May 1992, Suharto made an apparent democratic concession: he let it be known that he would revoke a decree that gave him sweeping powers to rule the country when he first came to power. Parliament would also be given more authority. This information was released after the clash of armed Thai troops and pro-democracy demonstrators in Bangkok a few days before.

Whether the President and the army will allow a real democratization is still unclear.[49]

Other reluctant leaders are found on other continents: in Africa Kenyan President Daniel arap Moi is another classical example of the use of delaying tactics against a transition to democracy, in the fear of losing power.

Moi has practised, like a number of other African leaders, "patrimonialism", which Nguema has defined as a traditional type of social structure in which the chief or ruler maintains authority through his officials, army, etc. who were retained by him and whose loyalty is to him personally. Another common feature of African politics is the phenomenon of "tribalization" of the State, which implies that the majority of economic development projects are channelled towards the native province of the head of State, where, in case of elections, he is assured of strong support.[50]

Moi has been in power in Kenya since the death of Jomo Kenyatta in 1978. His governing system has gradually eliminated all forms of political accountability, by dismantling the British colonial heritage of separation of powers: both Parliament and the judiciary have become subservient to the President.

After defeating a 1982 coup attempt, the legislature under the control of the Kenya African National Union (KANU) passed a law that made Kenya a one-party state. Only members of the party could run for office, and political opponents were excluded, jailed or expelled. Opposition statements were either ignored or declared treasonous. Selection of top party and national leaders was by acclamation. Rights of assembly, organization and demonstration were severely limited. Corruption has been rampant among Moi's close supporters.

During the Commonwealth Heads of Governments Meeting held in Harare in October 1991, Moi told journalists that he needed just another five years to prepare his people for multi-party democracy. He argued that the West took a thousand years to build its civic institutions, and that Africa should be given time to do the same.

Moi had previously denounced multi-party democracy as an invitation to tribalism, hooliganism, banditry and treason.

In November 1991, Western donors, in discussing aid for Kenya during a World Bank meeting, called for early implementation of political reform "to reinforce the benefits of economic structural change": this meant "greater pluralism, respect for human rights and firm action to deal with corruption".

Responding to this pressure, Moi reluctantly agreed to multi-partyism in December 1991. General pluralist elections were held on 29 December 1992: unexpectedly, the President's party, KANU, won a majority in Parliament with 95 seats against 88 for a divided opposition. In spite of allegations of fraud and in spite of the continuation of Moi's hold on power, these elections, the first multi-party elections in 26 years, are an encouraging step in a transition to democracy, thanks to the election of an opposition in Parliament.[51]

However, Moi's continued resistance to institutional and political change, comparable to that of Zaire's President Mobutu Sese Seko, is likely to increase the risks of violence in the unavoidable transition of their countries towards democracy.

Notes

1. *Soviet Socialist Democracy*, B. Bayanov, Y. Umansky, M. Shafir, Progress Publishers, Moscow, 1968, pp. 68, 71, 73. Lenin's quotation is in *Lenin, Collected Works*, 5th Russian Ed., Vol. 36, p. 535.

2. These initial remarks are based on Alan Bullock's *Hitler and Stalin – Parallel Lives*, HarperCollins, 1991, pp. 65, 66, 102 (by permission of HarperCollins Publishers, London and McClelland and Stewart, Toronto), – and on Richard L. Harris' *Marxism, Socialism and Democracy in Latin America*, Westview Press, 1992, pp. 7, 11–12, 14–15, 122 (with permission of Westview Press, Boulder, Colorado). See also Karl Kautsky' *The Dictatorship of the Proletariat*, The National Labour Press, 1919, pp. 68, 69, 84.
3. See Bayanov et al., op.cit., pp. 81–91.
4. Ibid., p. 90.
5. *The Soviet Crucible: Soviet Government in Theory and Practice*, S. Hendel Ed., New York, 1958, pp. 335–336.
6. Raymond D. Gastil, *Freedom in the World – Political Rights and Civil Liberties – 1987–1988*, Freedom House, New York, 1988, pp. 400–402.
7. Charles Maier's estimate is in Note 7, p. 1125, from *The Unmasterable Past*, Cambridge, Mass., 1988, – Jean Ellenstein's estimate is from *D'une Russie à l'autre – Vie et mort de l'URSS*, Messidor/Ed. Sociales, Paris, 1992, as reported in *Le Monde*, 2 Oct. 1992.
8. Quoted by Harris, op.cit., p. 35.
9. *U.N. Observer and International Report*, July 1992, *International Herald Tribune*, 19 June and 13 Oct. 1992.
10. See Gastil, op.cit., pp. 337–338, and *Amnesty International Report 1990*, p. 141.
11. Clark D. Neher, "Democratization in Southeast Asia", in *Asian Affairs – An American Review*, 18/3, Fall 1991, pp. 141–144.
12. Gastil, op.cit., p. 298–299, *Le Monde*, 14 July and 31 Oct. 1992.
13. *International Herald Tribune*, 8 Jan. 1992, *Le Monde*, 9 Jan. 1992.
14. *Newsweek*, 28 Sept. 1992, *Le Monde*, 15 Sept, 9 Oct. 1992, *The Economist*, 10 Oct. 1992.
15. Nietzsche, *The Will to Power*, 1888, 752, Tr. A.M. Ludovici.
16. F. Nitti, *Bolshevism, Fascism and Democracy*, George Allen and Unwin, London, 1927, p. 81.
17. C.F. Strong, *Modern Political Constitutions*, Sidgwick and Jackson Ltd., London, 1963, p. 48.
18. Juan J. Linz, "Comparative Study of Fascism", in *Fascism: A Reader's Guide*, Walter Laqueur Ed., Penguin Books, 1979, pp. 25–26.
19. Zeev Sternhell, "Fascist Ideology", in Laqueur, op.cit., p. 368.
20. William Ebenstein and Edwin Fogelman, *Today's Isms – Communism, Fascism, Capitalism, Socialism*, 9th Ed., Prentice-Hall, 1985, pp. 107–115.
21. Bullock, op.cit., pp. 345–346.
22. "The Totalitarian State in Germany and the Individual", Prince Hubertus Lowenstein, in *The Annals of the American Academy of Political and Social Science*, Vol. 180, July 1935, pp. 26–28.
23. Marlis Steinert, *Hitler*, Fayard, Paris, 1991, pp. 208–209. Translated from the French by the author.
24. Bullock, op.cit., p. 160.
25. Ibid., pp. 157–158 and Appendices 2 and 3.
26. Ibid., p. 1070.
27 *Everyone's U.N.*, 1979, p. 3.
28. See U.N. General Assembly Resol. 2331 (XXII), 1967–2438 (XXIII), 1968–2545 (XXIV), 1969, –2713 (XXV), 1970–2839 (XXVI), 1971–34/24, 1979–35/200, 1980–36/162, 1981–37/179, 1982 –38/99, 1983–39/114, 1984– 40/148, 1985–41/160, 1986–43/150, 1988.
29. U.N. *Press Release* HR/3135 of 11 Aug. 1992. However, few speakers in the Sub-Commission agreed on measures which could be used to combat these phenomena. For Italy and Germany, see Anne-Marie Duranton-Crabol, *L'Europe de l'Extrême Droite – De 1945 à nos jours*, Ed. Complexe, Bruxelles, 1991. See also "The Far Right in Europe: a Guide (Campaign against racism and facism)" in *Race and Class*, Institute of Race Relations, Vol. 32, No. 3, Jan. – March 1991.
30. *Le Monde*, 29 Aug. 1992, *International Herald Tribune*, 30 July, 26 Aug., 7 Sept. 1992, *The Economist*, 10 Oct. 1992.
31. *Newsweek*, 27 Apr. 1992, *Le Monde*, 24 Sept. 1992.

32. *Time*, 6 Apr. 1992, *Newsweek*, 27 Apr., 28 Sept. 1992, – see also Duranton-Crabol, op.cit.
33. "Democratization and Islam", John L. Esposito and James P. Piscatori, in *Middle East Journal*, Summer 1991, Vol. 45, No. 3, p. 437.
34. U.N. *Press Release* HR/3162, 27 Aug. 1992 (morning), HR/3215 of 30 Oct. 1992 (afternoon).
35. *Time* and *Newsweek*, 15 June 1992.
36. *Concept of Islamic State*, Islamic Council of Europe, London, 1979, pp. 8–9, 22–23.
37. *The Principles of State and Government in Islam*, Mohammad Asad, Dar Al-Andalus, Gibraltar, 1980, pp. 20, 60–61.
38. *International Herald Tribune*, 2 and 31 March 1992, *Middle East International*, 29 May 1992.
39. *International Herald Tribune*, 6–7 June 1992, *Newsweek*, 21 Sept. 1992, *Le Monde*, 6 Oct. 1992.
40. *Le livre vert*, Moammar El-Kadhafi, Cujas, Paris, 1976.
41. Esposito, op.cit., *The Economist*, 14 Apr. 1992, *Time*, 15 June 1992.
42. *Le Monde*, 11 July 1992.
43. *Le Monde*, 2, 7 Sept, 1992.
44. Developments in Turkey are mainly based on Feroz Ahmad's *The Turkish Experiment in Democracy – 1950–1975*, The Royal Institute of International Affairs, C. Hurst and Co., London, 1977, Ch. I and XIII. See also *Atatürk and Turkey of Republican Era*, Union of Chambers of Commerce of Turkey, 1981, and *Histoire de la Turquie*, Robert Mantran, PUF, Paris, 1988, p. 118.
45. Ahmad, op.cit., p. 369.
46. Ibid., p. 375.
47. Mohammed Bedjaoui, Judge at the International Court of Justice, in *Aspects du système des Nations Unies dans le cadre de l'idée d'un nouvel ordre mondial*, Colloque des 22–23 nov. 1991, Institut d'Etudes politiques d'Aix-en-Provence, Pedone, Paris, p. 119. Translated from the French by the author.
48. Gastil, op.cit., pp. 327–329.
49. *International Herald Tribune*, 25 May, 9, 11, 15 June, 4 Sept. 1992, – *Le Nouveau Quotidien*, 10 June 1992.
50. See U.N. Human Rights booklet "African Seminar on International Human Rights Standards and the Administration of Justice – Cairo (Egypt), 8–12 July 1991, p. 28. Isaac Nguema is a member of the African Commission on Human and Peoples' Rights.
51. *West Africa*, 4–10 Nov. 1991, 25–31 May 1992, *Africa Demos*, Feb. 1992, – *The Economist*, 22 Feb. and 14 Nov. 1992, *Le Monde, 9 Jan. 1993.*

CHAPTER 3

THE LEAGUE OF NATIONS, DEMOCRACY AND PLEBISCITES

The creation of the League of Nations was the first concrete attempt to create a universal organization with the purpose of promoting international cooperation and achieving peace and security. It was due to the efforts of such private groups as The League to Enforce Peace in the U.S. and the League of Nations Society in the U.K. and to the determination of a few statesmen, including the British Lord Robert Cecil, the French Léon Bourgeois and, as the principal actor, the U.S. President, Woodrow Wilson. The senseless destructions, the human, material and financial losses, the atrocities, the nationalistic passions and hates caused by the four long and bloody years of the First World War were a powerful incitement to politicians and private groups and citizens to make it the "last war" through a world organization of peace and cooperation.

Wilson was the main promoter of the future League. He gave public support to the concept of the League as early as 1916. In his address of 2 April 1917, invoking a formal Congressional declaration of war upon Germany, he asserted the national purpose of fighting

> for a universal dominion of right by such a concert of free peoples as shall bring peace and safety to all nations and make the world itself at last free.[1]

He served as Chairman of the committee which formulated the Covenant of the League, dominated by himself, the British Lord Robert Cecil and South African Jan Christiaan Smuts.

Wilson's views were based on nineteenth century philosophy of political liberalism, and in particular on democracy, nationalism and self-determination. He expected these values and concepts to be translated at the international level through the Covenant.

Following Kant's thesis, he believed that world peace could be established only by a compact among democratically governed nations. His assumption was that democracies, in contrast to autocracies, are inherently peaceful.

The League: A Club of Democratic Nations?

Wilson originally considered that only democracies would be admitted to the League:

> Only the free peoples of the world can join the League of Nations. No nation is admitted to the League of Nations that cannot show that it has the institutions which we call free. No autocratic government can come into its membership, no government which is not controlled by the will and vote of its people. Nobody is admitted except the self-governing nations, because it was the instinctive judgment of every man who sat around that board that only a nation whose government was its servant and not its master could be trusted to preserve the peace of the world. It is a league of free independent peoples all over the world and when that great arrangement is consummated there is not going to be a ruler in the world that does not take his advice from his people . . . The people of this world – not merely the people of America, for they did the job long ago – have determined that there shall be no more autocratic governments. The Hapsburgs and the Hohenzollerns are permanently out of business. They are out of date because this Great War with its triumphal issue, marks a new day in the history of the world.
>
> It (The Covenant) provides for the destruction of autocratic power as an instrument of international control, admitting only self-governing nations to the League of Nations. No nation is admitted to the League of Nations whose people do not control its government.[2]
>
> No autocratic government could be trusted to keep faith within it, or observe its covenants. It must be a League of Honour. Intrigue would eat its vitals away; the plottings of inner circles who could plan what they would and render account to no one would be a corruption seated at its very heart. Only free people can hold their purpose and their honour steady to a common end and prefer the interests of mankind to any narrow interest of their own.[3]

Private associations, such as the British League of Nations Union shared the same view: the League should be a League of peoples, not a League of Kings and Emperors – and as nations must have some measure of self-government to enable them to enter into covenants of peace, it must be a League of Free Nations.[4]

The final text of the Covenant does not state that only "democratic" states will be admitted to the League. The only conditions for admission (in addition to the original and named members), were, under Article 1.2:

- the applicant must be a "fully self-governing State, Dominion or colony";
- its admission must be agreed to by two-thirds of the Assembly;
- the applicant must give effective guarantees of its sincere intention to observe its international obligations, and accept such regulations as may be prescribed by the League in regard to its military, naval and air forces and armaments.

According to Walters,[5] there are reasons for thinking that in Wilson's mind the word "self-governing" was intended to mean "possessing democratic institutions", although this point was not made clear during the meetings of the Committee which drafted the Covenant. The proper sense of the word "self-governing", as also of the French translation "qui se gouverne librement", is: free to make its own decisions, i.e. not forced to act under the instructions of another State, i.e. a fully sovereign State. It does not imply that its government should be democratic.

In practice, the word was always understood in the sense of a requirement for external sovereignty. Contrary to Wilson's original views and wishes, the Assembly did not make a democratic Constitution one of the conditions of a state's admission; nor was it ever proposed that the loss of democratic credentials could be the basis for the expulsion of any Member. For instance, the admission of the USSR in 1934 was certainly not based on its democratic credentials. Its expulsion from the League, in 1939, was caused by its aggression on Finland, and not on the undemocratic nature of its internal institutions and practices. The withdrawals from the League of Japan and Germany in 1933, from Italy in 1937 and from Spain in 1939, were not due principally to their non-democratic political regime, but to their rejection of the League's international obligations.

It seems that Wilson realized himself that the democratic requirement could not be applied: in a meeting with Dr. Isaiah Bowman on 10 December 1918, Wilson made the point that he was in favor of letting states have a wide area of liberty in which to play with reference to their form of government.[6]

Limiting the League to democracies only would have severely limited the potential number of member states, further to the absence of the biggest democracy, the U.S.A. Secondly, the creation of a "Club of (real) democracies" might have encouraged the formation of a counter-group of countries rejected from League membership: this would have prevented any hope of one universal organization, and would have further weakened the League. The Comintern (the Communist International) almost played this role: Lenin saw the Comintern, founded in 1919, as a counter-organization to the League: in his view, which was overturned in 1934, the aims of the Comintern and the League were mutually exclusive.[7]

Finally, the problem of defining and applying democratic criteria would have had to be faced: except for a list of democracies published in 1924, surveys based on democratic indices have only been prepared by researchers since the 1960s. Even if these had been available, it is unlikely that government representatives in the League's Assembly would have agreed to reject specific countries for being "undemocratic", and thus not belonging to the "civilized" family of nations, for diplomatic, political, cultural or other reasons.[8]

Although the League never grouped all existing states, and lost 16 member states between 1919 and 1939, the principle of universality of membership prevailed over democratic criterions for admission.

Self-determination through Plebiscites

The French Revolution initiated a few plebiscites in relation with France's annexation of Comtat-Venaissin and Avignon (1791), Savoy, Mulhouse, Hainaut and Rhineland (1792) in an effort to conciliate its alleged renunciation to territorial conquests and the wishes of the inhabitants of the territories concerned.

The doctrine of national self-determination is based on that of people's sovereignty. To the philosophers of the French Revolution, the right of conquest, one of the divine rights of monarchs, was incompatible with the right of peoples to choose their own rulers. To assert that a conqueror could retain his domination over the inhabitants of a conquered territory against their will was to deny the doctrine of popular sovereignty and to change free men back to slaves. In order to harmonize foreign relations policies with these principles, the doctrine of no annexation without consultation of the inhabitants was formulated, a doctrine indeed revolutionary for Europe. A decree adopted on 22 May 1790 by the Constituent Assembly had an article by which the French nation definitely renounced all wars of conquest.

This solemn and definite commitment was short-lived.

Political expediency, revolutionary expansionism and military necessity soon overcame the principle of consultation. Plebiscites were set aside by France as from 1795, and the Congress of Vienna of 1815 did not concern itself with self-determination and the consultation of populations.

This trend was reversed in the second half of the 19th century with the development of the principle of nationalities. The Italian unification process (1860–1870) was carried out in the name of the will of the peoples, by plebiscites by popular votes by manhood suffrage with no literacy qualification. Also in France, the annexation of Savoy and county of Nice, in accordance with the Treaty of Turin of 24 March 1860, was approved by two plebiscites in April 1860. The transfer of the Swedish island of Saint Bartholomew to France was sanctioned by a plebiscite (1877), as well as the separation of Norway from Sweden in 1905. The electoral qualifications in Norway in 1905 allowed all male citizens over 25 to vote, if not disqualified through indictment for crime or bankruptcy. Women were not given the vote until 1907.

The first electoral consultations under international monitoring were the General Elections organized in Moldavia and in Wallachia in 1857 under the supervision of a European Commission composed of French, British, Prussian, Russian, Austrian and Turkish representatives.

As noted by Sarah Wambaugh, for the first time in history, an international congress of great Powers, which had met to settle the future of a small, weak, and disunited people, postponed their action until they had ascertained the desire of the people themselves, and, as a further innovation, they agreed that this desire should be expressed by a vote taken under the supervision of an international commission.

The initiative to solve the question of these Danubian Principalities came from Russia in 1855. The Russian proposal and its modalities were incorporated in the

Treaty of Paris signed on 30 March 1856. The Treaty provided that the question of the organization of the Principalities of Moldavia and Wallachia, i.e. their union, should be settled by means of an assembly or "divan *ad hoc*" elected, by limited suffrage and indirect voting for delegates, divided into classes, in each principality under the joint supervision of the Porte and a European Commission. The first elections in Moldavia, on 19 July 1857 were invalidated on account of manipulation, "a parody of a vote", and had to be re-enacted on 10 September. Elections in Wallachia took place on 26 September. The union of the Principalities, despite conflicting policies and resistance of some of the Powers, was effective in 1859.

However, population consultation was not the rule: plebiscites were only rare exceptions to the general rule of arbitrary, forceful conquest or international political compromises, followed by annexation.

Annexations without consultation were more numerous than plebiscites and involved larger territories. For instance, the U.S.A. did not organize any plebiscite for the Louisiana Purchase (1803), the acquisition of Florida (1819), the annexation of Texas, New Mexico and California (1848), the purchase of Alaska (1867), the annexation of the Hawaii Islands (1897), Porto Rico and the Philippines (1898). The annexation by Prussia of Schleswig in 1867 took place without a promised plebiscite, and that of Alsace-Lorraine after France's defeat in 1871 was without popular consultation.[9]

Plebiscites under the Peace Treaties of 1919–1921

In his address to the U.S. Senate on 22 January 1917, President Wilson said:

> No peace can last, or ought to last, which does not recognize and accept the principle that governments derive all their just powers from the consent of the governed, and that no right anywhere exists to hand peoples about from sovereignty to sovereignty as if they were property.[10]

Already in 1916, he had said, before the "League to enforce Peace", that every people has a right to choose the sovereignty under which they shall live. As an influential leader, he was thus promoting both internal and external self-determination, i.e. the people's right to choose their political regime and leaders, and the people's right to decide their international status and fate.

In reality, the principle of external self-determination was applied only in a few exceptional cases by the victorious Allies of World War I, for whom secret treaties, strategic, political and economic interests, historic claims had more priority and importance than any genuine democratic concern for allowing the territories' inhabitants to express their wishes in free plebiscites. States preferred to make their decisions by conquest or by negotiation among the major Powers.

Contrary to Wilson's insistence on self-determination and transparency of international agreements,[11] secret treaties had been signed, in the period 1915–1917, between the U.K., France, Russia, Italy, Rumania which promised enemy territory to the future victors: Russia was to receive Constantinople, the Dardanelles, the Asiatic Bosphorus and other territories, – Italy was promised, in exchange for its entry into the war, the Tyrol south of the Brenner, Trieste, Gorizia, most of Istria, northern Dalmatia and the Dodecanese, – the U.K., Russia and France would divide among themselves Asia Minor, Syria and Mesopotamia, – Romania was promised Transylvania and parts of the Banat and of Bukowina, – Russia promised France Alsace-Lorraine, the Saar coal basin and the erection of the left bank of the Rhine into an autonomous state.[12]

These "promised" territorial allocations, even if they had to be later more openly discussed and decided upon during the Peace negotiations, had taken no account of the populations' interests or wishes.

In his speech, that of the Four Points, made before the U.S. Congress on 11 February 1918, Wilson made a clear statement on self-determination:

> National aspirations must be respected; peoples may now be dominated and governed only by their own consent. "Self-determination is not a mere phrase. It is an imperative principle of action, which statesmen will henceforth ignore at their peril... Second, that peoples and provinces are not to be bartered about from sovereignty to sovereignty as if they were mere chattels and pawns in a game.

On 4 July, he insisted on

> the settlement of every question, whether of territory, of sovereignty, of economic arrangement, or of political relationship, upon the basis of the free acceptance of that settlement by the people immediately concerned.[13]

The Peace Treaties of 1919 were far from applying these lofty principles, except in High Silesia and Saar, and other relatively minor cases.

The final text of the Treaty of Versailles provided that the frontier line of Germany with Denmark was to be fixed by plebiscite (Schleswig), three plebiscites were to determine the German-Polish frontier (Allenstein, Marienwerder, Upper Silesia), and the boundary between Germany and France between Lorraine and Luxembourg (the Saar) was to be fixed in 1935. In spite of Wilson's leadership in these matters, none of these plebiscites, except perhaps that in Marienwerder, had been proposed by the Americans.

Only one plebiscite (Klagenfurt) was contained in the Treaty of Saint-Germain, between the Allies and Austria, and none were provided in the Treaty of Neuilly. The Sopron plebiscite was not part of the Treaty of Trianon, but was decided upon later by the Venice Protocol of 13 October 1921.

The German request for a plebiscite in Alsace-Lorraine had been rejected by the Allies, on the grounds that these were evacuated territories reintegrated to France, and because of the useless and impractical character of a consultation: the will of the population was attested by the continuous protests since the provinces had been seized by Germany. If the population's will was so clear, one wonders why France did not take the small political risk to accept a plebiscite, while enjoying the benefit of honouring the democratic principle of self-determination. While French Socialists and British Labor were in favour of a plebiscite, the French government opposed it: in its view, to hold a plebiscite now would be to sanction the wrong done in 1871 by admitting the lawfulness of the aggression.

The German comments on the proposed conditions of peace of 29 May 1919 included the following statement concerning Alsace-Lorraine:

> When Germany in 1871, on the occasion of the reannexation of these territories, abstained from inquiring into the wishes of the population, she believed she was justified in doing so by the previous procedure of France and by the racial kinship of the population. Notwithstanding, it must be admitted that, according to the present general conceptions of right, an injustice was committed in 1871 by the failure to hold a plebiscite.

The proposal of a plebiscite in Austria was rejected by the Allies in 1919 as it probably would have resulted in a majority in favour of an early "Anschluss".[14]

Plebiscites were held under international auspices, as provided by the Peace Treaties, or by the Venice Protocol, for Sopron, as follows:
- Schleswig, 10 February and 14 March 1920;
- Allenstein and Marienwerder, 11 July 1920;
- Klagenfurt Basin, 10 October 1920;
- Upper Silesia, 20 March 1921;
- Sopron, 14–16 December 1921.

These plebiscites were monitored by International or Interallied Commissions, and not by the League.

The first plebiscite to be formally considered by the Peace Conference was that in North Schleswig, which had been in dispute between Denmark and Prussia since 1848 and for which a plebiscite had been promised in the Treaty of Prague in 1866. The Danish government requested that the German troops should be evacuated and the area placed under the authority of an international commission. These, and other requirements were included in Article 109 of the Treaty of Versailles, which began by affirming that "the frontier between Germany and Denmark shall be fixed in conformity with the wishes of the population".

The International Commission, which had temporary "general powers of administration", was to be composed of five members, from Norway, Sweden, Great Britain, France and the U.S.: the U.S. member declined to participate. The Commission was to take all steps which it thought proper to ensure the freedom, fairness, and secrecy of the vote. The right to vote was given to all persons, without distinction of sex, who had completed their twentieth year at the date of the coming into force of the Treaty, and were born in the plebiscite zone, or had been domiciled there since a date before 1 January 1900, or had been expelled by the German authorities without having retained their domicile there. The result would be determined by a majority of votes in one area, and by a majority of votes in each commune in the other area. The result would be immediately communicated by the Commission to the Principal Allied and Associated Powers and proclaimed. Another Commission would then trace the frontier line on the spot.

Similar processes were applied to the plebiscites in Allenstein, Marienwerder and Klagenfurt. International or Interallied Commissions were set up which, after the evacuation of German forces, were granted general powers of administration, including electoral arrangements required to ensure the freedom, fairness and secrecy of the vote. The results of the votes, together with appropriate recommendations, were then communicated by the Commissions to the Allied Powers for final decisions.

The plebiscite in Schleswig gave a majority for Denmark in the northern zone and for Germany in the southern zone. On 28 May 1920, the Conference of Ambassadors of the Principal Allied and Associated Powers decided in favour of the solution advocated in the majority report of the International Commission, i.e. that the frontier should follow the line between the two zones.

In spite of a Polish protest, the Conference of Ambassadors decided, on the basis of the results of the plebiscite in Allenstein, to assign three villages to Poland, leaving the remaining majority of villages to Germany. A majority also voted in favour of Germany in the Marienwerder plebiscite: five villages were given to Poland and the remainder of the area to Germany.

Following the plebiscite in the Klagenfurt Basin, the whole of the area was incorporated into Austria.

The plebiscite in Upper Silesia was the only concession granted by the Allies to Germany, at the insistence of Lloyd George who wished to make certain that the Germans would sign the Treaty and that British Labour would support it. This important coal basin and industrial area had been given to Poland in the draft Treaty of 7 May 1919, on the basis of the German language statistics which gave the Polish-speaking population as 65% of the whole.

The inhabitants of Upper Silesia were asked to indicate by a vote whether they wished to be attached to Germany or to Poland. The process was generally similar to those of the other plebiscites: evacuation of the German troops and designated officials, disbanding of military or semi-military organizations, placement of the plebiscite area under the authority of an International Commission of four members to be designated by France, the British Empire, Italy and the U.S.A. – the latter declined to participate. The area was then occupied by troops belonging to the Allied and Associated Powers. Eligibility to vote followed the standards set in the other plebiscites.

The Upper Silesia plebiscite took place on 20 March 1921: Germany had a global majority, but the results in the various communes were so entangled that the Allied Supreme Council transmitted the case to the Council of the League of Nations. The Council made decisions on the division of the territory between Poland and Germany in its recommendation of 12 October 1921, which included other measures intended to maintain the economic unity of the area, the settlement of disputes through arbitration and the protection of minorities.

The Treaty of Trianon, which came into effect between the Principal Allied and Associated Powers and Hungary on 26 July 1921, transferred the greater part of West Hungary (Burgenland), of which Sopron was the provincial capital, from Hungary to Austria. A Commission of Allied Generals was despatched to Sopron to supervise the transfer of territory, but disturbances occurred and the city of Sopron and the surrounding area remained under Hungarian control. By a Protocol signed in Venice on 13 October 1921, the foreign ministers of Austria and Hungary agreed that, eight days after the Commission of Allied Generals had decided that the country was in a state of complete tranquillity, a plebiscite would be held in Sopron and its neighbourhood. The Commission of Allied Generals was instructed by the Conference of Ambassadors to apply the Protocol. A Central Plebiscite Committee was created by the Commission: it was composed of three Allied officers, with two Austrians and two Hungarians serving in a consultative capacity, in charge of general arrangements and supervision of the eight Plebiscites Committees which were set up.

The Commission declared the area pacified on 3 December 1921. Allied troops took over the area from Hungarian troops and gendarmerie on 12 December. The voting took place on 14–16 December. In spite of an initial protest by Austria, the Conference of Ambassadors accepted the results of the plebiscite and ordered the transfer of the territory to Hungary. The transfer took place on 1 January 1922, and, on 20 February, Austria recognized the cession to Hungary.[15]

Plebiscites Entrusted to the League of Nations

The word "self-determination" is not found in the League's Covenant. A recognition of the principle of self-determination had been included in Wilson's first and second drafts of the Covenant concerning territorial readjustments. The third draft made those dependent not only on the people concerned but also on the states concerned. The final wording of Article X omitted all provision for territorial readjustments.[16] Only Article 22.4 makes a reference to "the wishes" of certain communities formerly belonging to the Turkish Empire which must be a "principal consideration" in the selection of the Mandatory, but does not elaborate on any modalities of this possible consultation, reserved for this specific category of communities.

Plebiscites were initially considered by the League twice, for the Aaland Islands and Vilna, but were not carried out. The Saar plebiscite, which had been included in the Treaty of Versailles, was actually organized and successfully carried out by the League.

In 1920, a dispute between Finland and Sweden over which country should own the Aaland Islands in the Baltic almost caused war between the two countries. The islands were part of Finland, but the islanders were Swedish and wanted to join Sweden. On the initiative of the British Government, the issue was referred to the Council of the League. The islanders wanted a plebiscite to decide their future, but Finland denied the League's right to intervene in a matter of internal jurisdiction. The Council affirmed its competence and set up a neutral commission to investigate the facts of the dispute on the spot. The commission advised that the Aalands should remain part of Finland, a decision announced by the Council in June 1921, reluctantly agreed to by Sweden. Finland also accepted the decision, and admitted that the League had a continuing concern to ensure that the rights of the Swedish-speaking minority were protected.[17]

In July 1920, Russia signed a peace treaty with the newly independent Lithuania, which recognized Vilna as the capital of Lithuania. The Poles then advanced towards Vilna, in pursuit of the fleeing Russian troops, and laid claim to the city: there were, then, more Poles than Lithuanians in Vilna. The Poles accused the Lithuanians of helping the Russians and called upon the Council of the League to act to prevent war between themselves and the Lithuanians. In September, the Council obtained an agreement on a ceasefire and a demarcation line between the armies of the two countries, which was to be safeguarded by a multinational military commission, an aborted forerunner to the U.N. peace-keeping operations. In October, the Poles broke their agreement and seized Vilna.

The Council proposed on 28 October 1920 that a plebiscite should be held in the city and surrounding territory of Vilna to settle the dispute over sovereignty between the two countries. Unlike the votes in the Paris Treaties, this plebiscite was to be taken under the auspices of the League and under a truly international police force. Both countries accepted the proposal. The Council appointed an International Plebiscite Commission and the governments of Belgium, Denmark, France, Great Britain, Greece, Holland, Norway, Spain and Sweden agreed to contribute troops to the police force. However, in view of renewed fighting between the Poles and the Lithuanians, in March 1921, the Council voted to abandon the plebiscite in favor of direct negotiations between the two countries. It was only in December 1927 that the Council managed to get the two nations, both under dictatorial regimes, to accept an uneasy peace. In March 1938, Poland forced Lithuania to resume diplomatic relations under threat of immediate invasion.[18]

The Saar Plebiscite

After World War I, France had demanded that the Saar, a rich industrial area on her northeastern frontier, should become part of its territory as a compensation for the devastation inflicted by the German Army. Britain and the U.S.A. rejected this claim, but agreed that France should be given ownership of the coal mines and that the Saar should be placed under the government of the League, in the capacity of trustee, for the next 15 years, at the end of which the Saarlanders would be called upon to indicate the sovereignty under which they desired to be placed. A vote would take place by plebiscite on the three following alternatives: a) maintenance of the régime established by the Treaty (trusteeship of the League); b) union with France; c) union with Germany. All persons, without distinction of sex, more than 20 years old at the date of the voting, resident in the territory at the date of the signature of the Treaty, would have the right to vote. The other conditions, methods and the date of the voting were to be fixed by the Council of the League of Nations in such a way as to secure "the freedom, secrecy and trustworthiness of the voting".[19]

The Saar was thus placed under the government of an International Commission of five members (one French, one native inhabitant of the Saar Basin, not French, and three members belonging to three countries other than France or Germany – the Chairman, Geoffrey Knox, was British), from 1919 to 1935. The Governing Commission's rule was not democratic: the Saarlanders resented having to obey a government of foreigners.

Hitler came to power in Germany in January 1933. On 14 October, the day after Germany left the League, he broadcast a speech on foreign policy in which he proposed, *inter alia*, that France and Germany should decide directly among themselves the territorial attribution of the Saar and all the economic problems involved in the change of ownership of the coal mines, without plebiscite. The French insisted that the Saarlanders must be allowed to exercise the choice to which they were entitled under the Peace Treaty.

The Council of the League approved on 4 June 1934 the proposals of the Aloisi's Committee, which defined precisely who had the right to vote, how the voting lists should be established, what the electoral districts should be, and what methods should be used to determine the final result. A Plebiscite Commission of three members and one expert adviser was set up, with some 50 inspectors and sub-inspectors under its orders. A Supreme Plebiscite Tribunal and eight district tribunals were also created, composed of some 25 judges, deputy-judges, and officials. For the final vote, about 950 experienced officials were brought in from Switzerland, Holland and Luxembourg, so that a neutral chairman was in charge of every voting centre. Scandinavian countries also provided the necessary number of neutral, competent persons to staff these various international bodies.

On a British initiative, the first and last International Force in the service of the League was authorized by two resolutions of the Council of 8 and 11 December 1934 and promptly deployed in the Saar: 3,300 strong, the largest contingent and its Commander were British – Italy, Sweden and the Netherlands provided the Force's other contingents.

The plebiscite took place on 13 January 1935, "with perfect discipline and dignity". On 14 January, the ballot-boxes, guarded by detachments of the International Force, were carried to Saarbrücken, where 300 neutral tellers counted them.

Ninety percent of the electorate voted for reunion with Germany (477,119), 46,615 for maintaining the League trusteeship and only 2,124 for union with France.

Following France's acceptance of the results, the Council, in the presence of the Governing Commission and the Plebiscite Commission, decided that the territory would be united with Germany on 1 March 1935. The financial settlement of the former regime was carried out under the terms of the French-German agreements signed in Naples on 18 February 1935. As previously agreed, the Supreme Plebiscite Tribunal continued to function for one year in order to guarantee the inhabitants against reprisals or injustices on account of their attitude during the electoral campaign. After the vote, 8,000 persons left the Saar, of whom one-third were already refugees who had fled from the Nazi take-over and repression in Germany.

The results of the plebiscite were a success for Hitler, the enemy of the League and the main challenger of the Peace Treaties.

At the same time, the plebiscite itself was a political and operational success for the League, in implementing a commitment written in the Treaty of Versailles 35 years before. Signatory countries respected their word, including Germany, no longer a League member. All observers were impressed by the fairness and efficiency with which the plebiscite had been organized.

Sarah Wambaugh emphasized[20] that, while the Saar plebiscite was not perfect, it was a great improvement over previous votes. For the first time, the auspices were completely neutral, while the other post-war plebiscites had been controlled by the Allies:

> For the first time, the Plebiscite Commission was composed exclusively of citizens of states unquestionably neutral in the dispute, and the plebiscite was policed by an international force from completely neutral countries. For the first time the secrecy of the ballot was made absolute through the innovation of neutral chairmen of the voting bureaus and the counting of the ballots by neutrals only . . . the mere effect of the presence of the International Force enabled the Governing Commission to maintain order through a most difficult period without the necessity for its active intervention . . . The League achieved in the Saar an admirable record of success.

Eden wrote in his memoirs:

> The machinery in the Saar both before and during the plebiscite gave a glimpse of a supra-national salvation to a world which was imprisoning itself all the while more closely within the confines of the national state . . .[21]

Unfortunately, the success of this international operation had no pacifying effect on Hitler's plans: on the contrary, the Saarlanders' enthusiastic union with Germany comforted his views on the necessary role and expansion of a greater and dominating Germany.

Based on her experience as "expert adviser" of the Saar Plebiscite Commission, Sarah Wambaugh defined and listed the measures to be taken to secure a free and fair vote in an international plebiscite involving two states. Her list is shown in Table 3.1.

Table 3.1. Measures to be taken to secure a free and fair international plebiscite vote

1. The plebiscite must be held under the formal agreement of both parties.
2. The area must be neutralized and the agreement must clearly provide this.
3. On the signing of the agreement the area must be put at once under international control.
4. All troops of both parties must be evacuated at once.
5. A plebiscite commission of unquestioned neutrals, acceptable to both states, must be set up.
6. This commission must be supported by a police force of its own, however small.
7. The commission must have complete power over the administration of the area, itself taking the place of the highest officials.
8. It must have sufficient personnel to exercise this power effectively.
9. It must exercise this power for a sufficient time in advance of the vote to establish confidence that a change of sovereignty is possible.
10. It must remove the local key official and replace them with its own appointees approved by both parties.
11. It must set up an effective organization for supervision of all officials, using the local administrative divisions as the bases.
12. It must immediately reorganize the police.
13. It must immediately reorganize the judicial system, cutting off the local courts from the higher courts outside the area.
14. It must set up a plebiscite tribunal to have exclusive jurisdiction over all plebiscite offenses.
15. The regulations for registration and voting must allow sufficient time for all processes of registration.
16. They must provide adequate tests of identity of the applicants for registration.
17. They must provide adequate penalties.
18. The suffrage must include women as well as men; it should also include illiterates and prisoners.

Source: Plebiscites since the World War, Sarah Wambaugh, Carnegie Endowment for International Peace, Washington, D.C., 1933, p. 506 (with permission).

The Sanjak of Alexandretta

The Saar success was followed by an affront to a weakened League: the League was to organize elections in the Sanjak of Alexandretta in 1937–1938, but France and Turkey frustrated this plan.[22]

In 1936, the French Government reached an agreement with the Governments of Syria and the Lebanon, according to which the League mandates would last for three more years, following which both territories would become independent. The Sanjak, a district in northwestern Syria with a strong minority of Turkish population, would retain a special regime obtained by Turkey on their behalf in 1921.

Turkey claimed that the Sanjak should also become independent, while France was asking for the League Council's view of her duty as mandatory power.

In January 1937, the Council decided that the Sanjak should remain nominally part of Syria, but should enjoy almost total internal autonomy. In May, the Statute and the Fundamental Law of the Sanjak, as drafted by the Council, were ratified by both countries. The Fundamental Law was providing the Sanjak with its own legislative, executive and judicial institutions, including an Electoral Law. A permanent delegate of the Council was to reside on the spot in order to see that the Statute and the Fundamental Law were respected and to mediate, if necessary, between the Sanjak Government and the Government of Syria.

In implementation of the agreement, the Council of the League appointed an Electoral Commission in order to organize the election of the Sanjak Assembly. Its work was interrupted, in December 1937, at the request of Turkey, when it became clear that the electoral procedure would not ensure a Turkish majority. The Council agreed reluctantly to revise the Electoral Law, but a Turkish majority could not be obtained as long as an impartial body was there to supervise the proceedings.

The French authorities in the Sanjak, together with the Turks, made the work of the League's Commission impossible. In the dramatic pre-World War II period, the French wanted to keep their good relations with Turkey. On 26 June, the Commission suspended its work and returned to Geneva in indignation. A friendly French-Turkish organization replaced the neutral Commission: a Turkish majority in the Sanjak Assembly led to a Sanjak Government composed only of Turks. Turkish troops were stationed in Alexandretta and in June 1939, the Sanjak was annexed to Turkey under its Turkish name of the Hatay.

Neither the Council or the Mandates Commission of the League had been involved in these latter developments.

Assessment

In spite of Wilson's liberal convictions and wishes, the League of Nations was never a club of peaceful democratic nations. In spite of its ambitious objectives, the League was unable to establish a new, peaceful international order based on international law and justice.

In the unfortunate and decisive absence of the isolationist U.S.A., democracy was losing ground in Europe in the 1920s and 1930s, and nationalist, militaristic dictatorships were threatening and then destabilizing the fragile international order established by the Peace Treaties, an international order weakly defended by the remaining democracies, themselves divided if not opposed over the way to restrain Hitler's expansionist plans, or to try to appease him.

Wilson's own commitment to democracy and self-determination was not sanctioned nor confirmed by the other Allied Powers in the text of the Covenant.

A few plebiscites, with varying degrees of international monitoring, were inserted in the Peace Treaties – the more important ones being those of Upper Silesia and Saar.

However, plebiscites were only applied, restrictively, to a few European territories of nations defeated in World War I (but not to Alsace-Lorraine nor South Tyrol), and not to their colonies. Mandates were granted to the victors without any consultation of the territories' inhabitants. Colonial powers still applied the "spoils system", and had no intention to seek the views of the "natives" regarding their governance or international status, in their own colonial possessions or mandates.

In spite of these sobering considerations, the League's experiment, with all its deficiencies and weaknesses, has served as an institutional model, or anti-model, for the U.N. More specifically, the League's organization and monitoring of the Saar plebiscite, following a long period of international administration of the territory, has been a political and operational landmark and a real life test for the future role of international organizations in monitoring electoral processes. The use of nationals from neutral (not committed) countries in international plebiscite commissions and other bodies replaced the former victors' interallied commissions, thus giving a guarantee of political impartiality, reinforced by the creation of temporary, independent, international judiciary bodies. The formation and presence of an international force, composed of contingents of various neutral countries, served as a sketchy blueprint for the later U.N. peace-keeping or police forces deployed in the Sinai, in the Congo, in Namibia or Cambodia.

Neutrality and impartiality are the basic ingredients of such international operations. However, Walters noted[23]:

> An international body, whose corporate proceedings are subject to the scrutiny of all its Members, whether they be directly concerned or not with the question at issue, may have many faults: but that of deliberately favouring one side or the other is the fault of which it is least likely to be guilty. The real danger was not that it should be partial but that it should be inefficient.

The lesson is true also for the U.N. and all the other international organizations who engage in international monitoring of plebiscites and elections.

However, the crucial requirement for self-determination plebiscites or referenda is the political will or consent of the countries concerned, their conviction that populations should not be treated as "mere chattels and pawns in a game", but that their free vote should be the basis for territorial and sovereignty allocations.

Notes

1. Quoted by Inis L. Claude, Jr, in *Swords into Plowshares – The Problems and Progress of International Organization*, 4th Ed., Random House, p. 42, – from Ray S. Baker and William E. Dodd (Eds), *The Public Papers of Woodrow Wilson, War and Peace*, Harper, New York, (n.d.), I. 16.
2. *Woodrow Wilson's Case for the League of Nations*, Compiled with his approval by Hamilton Foley, Princeton University Press, 1923, pp. 64–65.
3. Quoted in *The League of Nations Union*, Series 2, Pamphlet No. 3, "The League of Free Nations", by G.A. McCurdy, M.P., London, 1919–1920.
4. Ibid.
5. F.P. Walters, *A History of the League of Nations*, Oxford University Press, 1952, p. 44.
6. See David Hunter Miller's *The Drafting of the Covenant*, G.P. Putnam's Sons, 1928. The reference was to the form of Poland's government: Wilson's words were that he was in favor of their having "any government they damned pleased."
7. Lord Robert Cecil, *A Great Experiment*, Jonathan Cape, London, 1941, p. 347, – Harold K.

Jacobson, *Networks of Interdependence – International Organizations and the Global Political System*, Knopf, New York, 2nd Ed., 1979, p. 70.

8. Raymond D. Gastil, *Freedom in the World – 1987–1988*, Freedom House, 1988, pp. 5–6, 27. Thomas Erskine Holland, in *The Elements of Jurisprudence*, published in 1900 (Clarendon Press) included in the family of nations a "charmed circle", the Christian nations of Europe and their off-shoots in America, the Ottoman Empire and Japan. Other states were not "normal international persons". The family of nations is "an aggregate of States which, as the result of their historical antecedents, have inherited a common civilization, and are at the same level of moral and political opinion".
9. See Charles Rousseau, *Droit international public*, Sirey, Paris, 1953, pp. 267–268, – and Sarah Wambaugh, *A Monograph on Plebiscites*, Oxford University Press, New York, 1920, pp. 2, 5 and Note 1, 11, 12, 101–116.
10. Quoted by Sarah Wambaugh in *Plebiscites since the World War*, Carnegie Endowment for International Peace, Washington, D.C., 1933, p. 5. (with permission).
11. The latter was inserted in Art. 18 of the Covenant, which states: "Every treaty or international engagement entered into hereafter by any Member of the League shall be forthwith registered with the Secretariat and shall, as soon as possible, be published by it. No such treaty or international engagement shall be binding until so registered."
12. Wambaugh, *Monograph*, op.cit., pp. 4 and 5. The texts of the secret treaties were published by the Soviet leaders in 1917– 1918.
13. Ibid., p. 11.
14. Ibid., pp. 14, 17, 20, 21, 37, and Rousseau, op.cit., 268–269. The German comments on Alsace-Lorraine are quoted in Wambaugh, *Plebiscites*, op.cit., p. 19, Note 3.
15. Rousseau, op.cit., p. 268. See also U.N. Doc.A/C.4/351 of 20 February 1957, "Plebiscites held since 1920 under the control or supervision of international organizations, Memorandum prepared by the Secretariat".
16. Wambaugh, *Monograph*, op.cit., pp. 40–241, Note 4.
17. George Scott, *The Rise and Fall of the League of Nations*, Macmillan, New York, 1973, p. 60.
18. Ibid., pp. 61–63, – Walters, op.cit., pp. 398–400, – Wambaugh, *Plebiscites*, op.cit., pp. 42–43.
19. Section IV of the Treaty of Versailles, 28 June 1919, Art. 45, 49, Annex, Art. 16 and 17, 27, 34.
20. Sarah Wambaugh, *The Saar Plebiscite*, Harvard University Press, 1940, pp. 317, 321.
21. Quoted by Scott, op.cit., p. 300, see also pp. 297–301, – Rousseau, op.cit., pp. 173–174, – Walters, op.cit., pp. 586–598.
22. This section is based on Walters, op.cit., pp. 742–745.
23. Ibid., p. 596.

CHAPTER 4

DEMOCRACY, SELF-DETERMINATION AND THE UNITED NATIONS

The United Nations has never been a "Club of democracies", no more than the League of Nations: admission requirements in the Charter do not include any democratic criteria.

On the other hand, the principle of self-determination is strongly affirmed in the U.N. Charter, in contrast with its absence in the Covenant. Many U.N. General Assembly resolutions have confirmed this principle which has served as a powerful instrument of pressure to encourage or force reluctant colonial powers to emancipate their dependent territories. More concretely, the U.N. has organized or monitored self-determination plebiscites or referendums in colonial territories, so that the populations concerned could express their will concerning the international status of their country or territory – union with another sovereign country, or independence as a sovereign country – upon being granted independence. The U.N. has also temporarily administered a few such territories as an interim authority before a transfer of sovereignty, or a plebiscite or referendum, or elections.

As previously mentioned, self-determination does not guarantee that internal democracy will prevail in a newly independent country, even though self-determination is achieved through a democratic process.

The U.N. concern for internal democracy was initially and formally limited by the respect due to national sovereignty and the Charter prohibition of any U.N. intervention in matters within the domestic jurisdiction of Member states: in fact, in the first 45 years of the U.N.'s life, the few existing democracies in the organization could not impose their democratic values and practices on the rest of the world. The evolution of the U.N. towards the acceptance of democratic principles as a universally recognized value and their active promotion was linked to the slow progress of the U.N. human rights programme: at the initiative of democratic countries' representatives, non-governmental organizations activists, and with the support of dedicated U.N. staff members, human rights legal instruments led the way to General Assembly Resolutions "Enhancing the Effectiveness of the Principle of Periodic and Genuine Elections", to technical assistance in legal and technical aspects of democratic elections, and finally to U.N. organizing and/or monitoring of democratic elections in sovereign countries. This uphill struggle still faces many ideological and practical obstacles and political adversaries, but the U.N., at last, has "turned democratic".

Member States' Admission Criteria to the United Nations

Membership to the U.N. was first granted to the 51 countries which took part in the San Francisco "United Nations Conference on International Organization", 25 April – 25 June 1945, or had previously signed the Declaration by United Nations of 1 January 1942, and which signed and ratified the Charter. Thereafter, membership was open

> to all other peace-loving states which accept the obligations contained in the present Charter and, in the judgment of the Organization, are able and willing to carry out these obligations.

Admission of these states is effected by a decision of the General Assembly upon the recommendation of the Security Council.

The International Court of Justice confirmed, in its Advisory Opinion of 28 May 1948, that the requisite conditions for admission are five in number: to be admitted to membership in the U.N., an applicant must

1. be a state;
2. be peace-loving;
3. accept the obligations of the Charter;
4. be able to carry out these obligations; and
5. be willing to do so.

The Court added that all these conditions are subject to the judgement of the Organization, i.e. the judgement of the Security Council and the General Assembly, and, in the last analysis, that of its member states. Consequently, a member called upon to pronounce itself by its vote, either in the Security Council or the General Assembly, on the admission of a state to membership in the U.N.

> is not juridically entitled to make its consent to the admission dependent on conditions not expressly provided by paragraph 1 of the said Article (Article 4).[1]

None of the conditions for admission imply that the applicants must show democratic credentials.

The Charter has been based on the concept of an extension of the wartime alliance into a peacetime organization. The "United" in United Nations came from the Atlantic Charter of 1941 and referred to nations united in war, not yet in peace. The ultimate decision-makers in the U.N. Security Council, its permanent members, were to be the leaders of the victorious military alliance. The Charter had been mainly negotiated between Franklin D. Roosevelt, its main inspirer, Winston Churchill and Stalin. Roosevelt died on 12 April 1945, a few days before the opening of the San Francisco Conference.

Contrary to Wilson's initial but inapplicable concept of creating a League of democratic nations, there is no evidence that either Roosevelt or Churchill had ever thought of such an impossible requirement for the U.N., which would have kept out of the organization their war ally, the USSR and other socialist States, as well as other States on other continents. Convinced that the lack of universality of the League's membership had contributed to its failure, the U.N. founders wanted the organization to be universal, to be a mirror of the real world, and to refrain from any political or moral judgement on the nature of States' internal political institutions, ideology and practices. The very general requirements of being a "peace-loving" state and acceptance of the Charter's obligations would open the door to practically all countries willing to join the organization.

The wartime Inter-allied Declaration of St. James Palace, in London, 12 June 1941, referred to the willing cooperation of "free peoples", not to the cooperation of "democracies". The Atlantic Charter of 14 August 1941 expressed the hope of peace for all nations, after the final destruction of the Nazi tyranny, and an assurance that all the men in all the lands may live out their lives in freedom from fear and want. The Declaration by United Nations of 1 January 1942 committed all signatories to employ their full resources against the enemies and not to make a separate armistice or peace with them. It went further: it linked the Allies' fight and expected victory to the defence of human rights:

> Being convinced that complete victory over their enemies is essential to defend life, liberty, independence and religious freedom, and to preserve human rights and justice in their own lands as well as in other lands, and that they are now engaged in a common struggle against savage and brutal forces seeking to subjugate the world, . . .

The Moscow Declaration of 30 October 1943 recognized the necessity of establishing at the earliest practicable date a general international organization, based on the principle of the sovereign equality of all peace-loving states, and open to membership by all such states. More detailed proposals for the creation of the U.N. were developed between the representatives of the USSR, the U.K. and the U.S.A. at the Dumbarton Oaks Conference, 21 August–28 September 1944, then between the representatives of China, the U.K. and the U.S.A., 29 September–7 October 1944, and finally at the Yalta Conference in February 1945.[2]

The principal objective of the new world organization was therefore the maintenance of peace and security, on the basis of universality of membership and national sovereignty. No qualitative selectivity of membership was envisaged, except as concerned the enemy (nazi, fascist) states.

The only indirect and veiled reference to popular sovereignty in the Charter is found in its Preamble, by the words "We the Peoples of the United Nations . . . ", words adapted from the first words of the U.S. Constitution ("We, the Peoples of the United States"), proposed by the U.S. delegation at the San Francisco Conference, and adopted only after a difficult debate.

The U.S. delegate justified the inclusion of these terms on the grounds that "they appeared to correspond to the democratic basis on which our new organization of peace and human welfare had been created after the long suffering of this war of peoples".

The Columbian delegate proposed to insert the following text in the Preamble:

> To proclaim that the principles of democracy and international solidarity and cooperation which are inscribed in the Atlantic Charter, constitute a minimum set of rules of conduct which every civilized state must observe and respect.

This text was rejected in Commission I by 17 votes against and 9 in favour.

Another proposal that member states should have democratic institutions was also rejected at the San Francisco Conference. Delegates felt that any attempt to evaluate the character and policies of governments would raise difficulties and might indeed be a breach of the principle of non-intervention in the domestic affairs of sovereign states.[3]

In practice, following the group admission of the first 51 states, considered to be all participants to the anti-Axis coalition during World War II, nine more states were admitted between 1946 and 1950. Only the enemy states, Germany, Italy and Japan, plus Franco's Spain, were originally excluded. Admission, during the Cold War, was the result of political bargaining between the U.S. and the USSR, starting with the "package deal" of 1955 (16 states admitted), without any judgment, on the part of the Security Council or General Assembly, as to the ability and willingness of applicant states to respect the Charter's obligations, and certainly not any inquiry and assessment of the nature of their political institutions.

The number of U.N. member states grew to 100 in 1960, 154 in 1980, 159 in 1984 and 183 in May 1993: universality is almost reached. Almost all countries, whatever their political regime, are members of the U.N. and may express, by votes and speeches, their national political, economic and social views on international issues.

Democratic countries belong to various groups in the U.N., and some of them also belong to regional specialized organizations, such as the Council of Europe and the European Community, to which only European democracies are admitted.

The global U.N. circle responds to different needs: in particular, the need for a global forum, the need for a dialogue, exchanges and possible rhetorical confrontation between different political, economic ideologies, different cultures and religious backgrounds. Excluding those countries which reject or violate democratic values and practices would be counter-productive to these aims.

The International Recognition of Self-determination

As a posthumous victory for Wilson, "self-determination" was formally inscribed in the U.N. Charter. Article 1.2 includes as one of the purposes of the U.N., "To develop friendly relations among nations based on respect for the principle of equal rights and self determination of peoples..."

Article 73 uses the more limited term of "self-government" in relation to non-self-governing territories, a "sacred trust" for U.N. members responsible for their administration, who should

> develop self-government, to take due account of the political aspirations of the peoples, and to assist them in the progressive development of their free political institutions...

Article 76 goes further, by referring to self-government *and* independence, but only for territories within the trusteeship system: one of its basic objectives is

> to promote the political, economic, social, and educational advancement of the inhabitants of the trust territories, and their progressive development towards self-government or independence as may be appropriate to the particular circumstances of each territory and its peoples and the freely expressed wishes of the peoples concerned...

In 1945, more than 750 million people – nearly a third of the world's population – lived in dependent territories. Roosevelt had hoped that the U.N. could be given special responsibilities, not only for taking over the League's mandated territories, but for exercising a watch over all dependent territories, and assisting their progress towards independence. Australia and the Philippines proposed, during the San Francisco Conference, that all dependent territories should be made trust territories, but did not pursue the idea. China and the USSR demanded that all dependent territories should eventually be led to independence, but this was resisted by the colonial countries, as well as by U.S. service departments.[4]

The Charter, as finally approved, represented a set of compromises between the declining colonial powers and an expanding anti-colonialism, promoted by former colonial possessions, with the strong support of Socialist countries, and with the encouragement of the U.S.A.

By 1960, anti-colonialist countries had become a majority in the U.N. General Assembly, which voted on 14 December the "Declaration on the Granting of Independence to Colonial Countries and Peoples" by a vote of 90–0, with nine abstentions cast mainly by colonial powers (Resol. 1514(XV)). The Declaration eliminated any distinction between trust territories and other dependent territories, and affirmed that immediate political freedom was a basic right for all peoples regardless of their stage of political, economic, social, or educational development: colonialism should therefore be brought to a speedy and unconditional end, and independence attained in accordance with the "freely expressed will and desire" of their peoples.

The Declaration states that the subjection of peoples to alien subjugation, domination and exploitation constitutes a denial of fundamental human rights, contrary to the Charter and an impediment to the promotion of world peace and cooperation, and that

> immediate steps should be taken, in Trust and Non-Self-Governing Territories or all other Territories which have not yet attained independence, to transfer all powers to the peoples of those territories, without any conditions or reservations, in accordance with their freely expressed will and desire, without any distinction as to race, creed or colour in order to enable them to enjoy complete independence and freedom.

The Declaration had been initiated by the Afro-Asian group, following an earlier initiative taken by the Soviet Union. The U.N. Declaration reflected the Bandung Declaration adopted in Indonesia by 27 African and Asian states in 1955.

Also in 1960, the General Assembly adopted a resolution setting forth the principles which should govern the General Assembly in determining whether a territory was or was not self-governing.

In 1961, the Assembly established a 17-member Special Committee – later enlarged to 24, then 25, but still called the "Special Committee of 24" – to examine the compliance of all States with the Declaration. It authorized the Committee to send visiting missions to the territories. The Committee also sent groups to supervise or observe the conduct of elections or popular consultations.

Since the adoption of the Declaration, the Assembly has repeatedly called upon all states to implement fully and faithfully all the relevant U.N. resolutions regarding the exercise of the right to self-determination and independence by peoples under colonial and foreign domination.[5]

Article 1 of the two International Covenants on Human Rights, adopted by the General Assembly in 1966, have confirmed the right of all peoples to self-determination, by virtue of which they freely determine their political status and freely pursue their economic, social and cultural development.

The Declaration on Principles of International Law concerning Friendly Relations and Cooperation among States in accordance with the Charter of the U.N., in Annex to resolution 2625 (XXV) of 24 October 1970, further enshrined the same principle.

On 11 December 1980, the General Assembly adopted resolution 35/118 as "Plan of Action for the Full Implementation of the Declaration on the Granting of Independence to Colonial Countries and Peoples". The Plan reaffirmed the right to self-determination, legitimized its exercise through armed struggle "against colonial and alien domination and racist régimes", directed the Special Committee to continue to send visiting missions to colonial territories, and

> to assist the General Assembly in making arrangements, in cooperation with the administering Powers, to secure a United Nations presence in the colonial territories to enable it to participate in the elaboration of the procedural arrangements for the implementation of the Declaration and to observe or supervise the final stages of the process of decolonization in those Territories.

Recent General Assembly resolutions have linked self-determination and human rights (Resol. 46/87–16 December 1991) and have reaffirmed the need for the

"Universal realization of the right of peoples to self-determination" (Resol. 47/83-16 December 1992).

While a number of these resolutions singled out South Africa and Israel, they overall gave strong and insistent verbal support to the decolonization wave, which influenced public opinion and governments, and gave hope and direct or indirect material and financial assistance to liberation movements.

The U.N. had a more concrete role in promoting the end of Western colonialism through the supervision or observation of popular consultations or elections in trust and other colonial territories, with the objective of ensuring that the people of a territory exercise their right to self-determination in complete freedom.

The authority for such missions was contained in resolutions of the General Assembly (e.g., in the cases of Togoland under British and French Administrations, Ruanda-Urundi, Western Samoa, the Cook Islands, or French Somaliland), the Security Council (e.g., Bahrein) or the Trusteeship Council (e.g., the many observation missions to the Trust Territory of the Pacific Islands). These resolutions, sometimes following a request by the Administering Authority, or a recommendation by a U.N. visiting mission, provided the legal basis for the U.N. physical involvement, and provided for the appointment of a Commissioner, or of a mission, and defined their mandates.

In such missions, the U.N. has asked, in principle, to be closely associated with all phases of the organization and conduct of popular consultations, which involved:

- review with the authorities of the legal and electoral framework, to ensure that it ensured complete freedom and impartiality;
- definition of a calendar for the various phases of the electoral process;
- setting up the system of voting;
- establishing the conditions for registration and registering voters;
- maintenance of law and order;
- implementation of a political education programme;
- monitoring of the political campaign;
- arrangements for polling day;
- provision of penalties for offences in connection with the vote;
- counting and tabulation of the vote;
- declaration of the results; and
- arrangements for appeals and review.

However, most of the early U.N. decolonization missions were small in size: the number of observers rarely exceeded 30. The small size of these missions (until the Namibia operation) severely limited the extent of the U.N. actual involvement in the planning and implementation of these popular consultations.

The list of plebiscites, referenda and elections held under the supervision or observation of the U.N. in Trust and Non-Self-Governing Territories, between 1956 and 1990, is shown in Table 4.1.

Table 4.1. Plebiscites, referenda and elections held under the supervision or observation of the United Nations in Trust and Non-Self-Governing Territories

Year	Territory
1956	Togoland unification and future Togoland under British administration: plebiscite supervision.
1958	Togoland under French administration: election supervision.
1959	British Cameroon (northern part): plebiscite supervision.
1961	British Cameroon (southern and northern parts): plebiscite supervision.
1961	Western Samoa: plebiscite supervision.
1961–1962	Ruanda-Urundi: election supervision (including referendum on the Mwami).
1963	Malaysia: inquiry on future of Sabah and Sarawak prior to establishment of Federation of Malaysia.
1965	Cook Islands: election supervision.
1967	Aden: election supervision (Mission was not permitted to achieve fulfilment of its mandate).
1968	Equatorial Guinea: referendum/election supervision.
1969	West Irian: act of self-determination.
1970	Bahrain: ascertain wishes of people of Bahrain.
1972	Papua New Guinea: election observation.
1974	Niue: referendum observation.
1974	Gilbert and Ellice Islands: referendum observation.
1975	Mariana Islands, Trust Territory of the Pacific Islands: plebiscite observation.
1977	French Somaliland: referendum/election observation.
1978	Trust Territory of the Pacific Islands: referendum.
1979	Marshall Islands, Trust Territory of the Pacific Islands: referendum.
1979	Palau, Trust Territory of the Pacific Islands: referendum.
1979	New Hebrides: election observation.
1980	Turks and Caicos Islands: election observation.
1983	Palau, Trust Territory of the Pacific Islands: plebiscite observation.
1983	Federated States of Micronesia, Trust Territory of the Pacific Islands: plebiscite observation.
1983	Marshall Islands, Trust Territory of the Pacific Islands: plebiscite observation.
1984	Cocos (Keeling) Islands: act of self-determination.
1986	Palau, Trust Territory of the Pacific Islands: plebiscite observation (February and December)
1987	Palau, Trust Territory of the Pacific Islands: plebiscite observation (June and August)
1989	Namibia: election supervision and control.
1990	Palau, Trust Territory of the Pacific Islands: plebiscite observation.

Source: U.N. Document A/46/609 of 19 November 1991, "Human Rights Questions: Human Rights Questions, including alternative approaches for improving the effective enjoyment of human rights and fundamental freedoms – Enhancing the effectiveness of the principle of periodic and genuine elections – Report of the Secretary-General", Annex.

The U.N. General Assembly has proclaimed the years 1990 to 2000 as the International Decade for the Eradication of Colonialism (Resol. 43/47 of 22 November 1988). As of September 1991, the U.N. considered that there were still 18 dependent Territories in which about 1.5 million people lived under some sort of foreign control: for a number of these territories, the administering countries contest that they constitute "colonies" whose status needs to be eradicated.[6]

Details on the U.N. role in observation or supervision of plebiscites, referenda and elections in dependent territories, necessarily limited to a few selected missions, will be given in Chapter 5. The Namibia operation is reviewed in Chapter 6.

United Nations Support for Internal Democracy

The universal respect for, and observance of, human rights and fundamental freedoms, is inscribed in several articles of the U.N. Charter, another considerable innovation and improvement over the League Covenant's very limited concern for the well-being and fair treatment of the native inhabitants of dependent territories, the "sacred trust of civilisation". These references to human rights were initially contained in the U.S. draft of the future U.N. Charter and met the objections of the Soviet and British representatives on the grounds that this might give the organization powers to intervene in the domestic affairs of member states and thus to violate national sovereignty: indeed, an accurate forecast of the impact of later human rights instruments. The U.S. insistence finally obtained the reluctant agreement of the other two powers, then of China, and the Organization's role in promoting the respect of human rights and fundamental freedoms was contained in the Dumbarton Oaks Proposals.

The Charter does not define in any specific terms the meaning of human rights and fundamental freedoms: there is no reference to political and civil rights. These were later included in the Universal Declaration of Human Rights, adopted by the General Assembly on 10 December 1948 (Resol. 217 A(III)). At the San Francisco Conference, proposals to embody in the Charter a "Declaration on the Essential Rights of Man" (as proposed by Panama), or a "Charter of the Rights of the Human Race" (Uruguay), were not examined for lack of time.[7]

The Universal Declaration's Article 21 is a democratic pronouncement:

1. Everyone has the right to take part in the government of his country, directly or through freely chosen representatives.
2. Everyone has the right of equal access to public service in his country.
3. The will of the people shall be the basis of the authority of government; this will shall be expressed in periodic and genuine elections which shall be by universal and equal suffrage and shall be held by secret vote or by equivalent free voting procedures.

Other articles endorse, *inter alia*, the freedom of opinion and expression, the freedom of peaceful assembly and association, some of the necessary requirements for the exercise of free elections.

Following the non-binding Declaration, further progress was achieved with the International Covenant on Civil and Political Rights, which recognizes the right of every citizen to take part in the conduct of public affairs, to vote and to be elected, and to have access, on general terms of equality, to public service in his country (Art. 25). The words" or by equivalent free voting procedures" in Article 21 of the Declaration do not appear in Article 25 of the Covenant, thus tightening this obligation of "universal and equal suffrage... by secret ballot" in "genuine periodic elections". The supervision of the implementation of the rights set out in the Covenant is entrusted to a Human Rights Committee, composed of 18 members serving in their personal capacity. Finally, the Optional Protocol to the Covenant enables the Human Rights Committee to receive and consider communications from individuals claiming to be victims of violations of any of the rights set forth in the Covenant. The Covenant and its Protocol were adopted by the General Assembly on 16 December 1966 (Resol. 2200 A (XXI)) and entered into force on 23 March 1976.

As of 8 September 1992, 113 countries were parties to the International Covenant on Civil and Political Rights and 66 to the Optional Protocol.[8]

While the U.N. General Assembly condemned nazism in a resolution of 1967 (see Chapter 2), it only endorsed the establishment and maintenance of democratic institutions, as the best bulwark against nazism and racial discrimination, in 1971 (Resol. 2839 (XXVI)).

U.N. General Assembly Resolutions "Enhancing the Effectiveness of the Principle of Periodic and Genuine Elections"

A more explicit support for democracy and democratic processes by the U.N. had to wait for the democratization wave of the late 1980s, so that a majority could be found in the General Assembly. Even then, the expressed interest and support of an intergovernmental organization, such as the U.N., in and for the democratic principle of periodic and genuine elections was opposed by those states who feared that this would develop into another unwanted international interference in countries' internal political systems, on the same lines as international human rights programmes and the alleged "right of international humanitarian intervention".[9]

A series of resolutions on "Enhancing the effectiveness of the principle of periodic and genuine elections" (the terms of the Universal Declaration of Human Rights) have been voted by the General Assembly since 1988.

The first resolution with this title was approved by the General Assembly without a vote on 8 December 1988 (43/157): while it condemned South Africa's apartheid, and thus the discriminatory white power over the black majority, the resolution did not focus exclusively on that situation. It stressed that periodic and genuine elections are necessary and indispensable to protect the rights and interests of the governed, and that determining the will of the people requires an electoral process which accommodates distinct alternatives, and that this process should provide an equal opportunity for all citizens to become candidates and put forward their political views, individually and in cooperation with others.

Since 1946, the General Assembly has year after year condemned South African racial discrimination and apartheid. The Security Council has termed apartheid abhorrent to the conscience of mankind, and all U.N. bodies concerned with racial discrimination and decolonization have denounced it. The innovation of the 1988 resolution was to link, for the first time, the condemnation of apartheid and the necessity of democratic elections. If universal franchise and periodic elections should be granted to the South African people, there is no reason why these rights and freedoms should not extend to all peoples.

While the resolution was adopted without a vote in the Third Committee and in the General Assembly, the delegate from Panama said, after the vote in the Third Committee, that in 1989, many Latin American states, including Panama, would be holding elections in accordance with their domestic legislation and the wishes of their peoples. It was vital for that process to be free of any outside interference which might prejudice the sovereignty of states.

The delegate from Mexico emphasized the same concern: there should be strict respect for the principles of non-intervention and self determination of peoples. The Commission on Human Rights should not have on its agenda an issue falling within the domestic competence of states: the Commission was not a supranational mechanism for the verification of electoral processes.

Expressing a complete misunderstanding of the intent of the adopted resolution, the delegate from Zambia said that the reference to "distinct alternatives" did not mean that states must adopt a multi-party system. Under its Constitution, Zambia was a "one-party participatory democracy" which had been established after experience of a multi-party system.[10]

Another "Enhancing" resolution was adopted without a vote by the General Assembly on 15 December 1989 (Resol. 44/146). However, it was adopted in the Third Committee only after its sponsors (most Western countries) had to accept the omission of "alternative" or "distinct alternatives", in other words, the elimination of pluralism from the electoral process and its outcome. This omission was regretfully admitted by the U.S. delegate in exchange for a broad agreement required for a long-term, cooperative task. The Dutch delegate said that the Third Committee was once again undermining individual human rights, as if the principle of periodic and genuine elections only applied to those countries whose national legislation provided for it.

Sponsored by Afghanistan, Angola, Cuba, Yemen, Iraq, Libya, Nicaragua, Tanzania, Viet Nam, Zambia and Zimbabwe, another rival resolution was adopted on the same date by a majority vote of 113, 23 against (including the U.S.A., Canada, Japan and the 12 members of the European Community) and 11 abstentions, entitled "Respect for the principles of national sovereignty and non-interference in the internal affairs of States in their electoral processes": the resolution stressed that all peoples have the right freely to determine, without external interference, their political status, and it appealed to all States to abstain from financing or supporting political parties or groups or from undermining the electoral process in any country. Recognizing that there is no single political system or single model for electoral processes equally suited to all nations and their peoples, and that political systems and electoral processes are subject to historical, political, cultural and religious factors, the resolution explicitly rejected the concept of the universality of democratic values and processes enshrined in the Universal Declaration of Human Rights and the International Covenant on Civil and Political Rights.

Although not a declared sponsor of that resolution, China was strongly behind it. Its delegate in the Third Committee said that every state had the right to choose its own electoral system, reflecting the will of the people. This choice was an internal affair and no foreign country had the right to arbitrarily criticize or attack it. Nor could any country justify the imposition of its own electoral system on other countries as a model. China was supported by such Latin American countries as Cuba, Nicaragua and Panama, and other Third World countries, fearful of any external political pressures or intervention in the name of democracy and human rights.[11]

In 1990, the "Enhancing" resolution, for the first time, affirmed the value of the electoral assistance provided by the U.N. at the request of member states, "in the context of full respect for their sovereignty", and believed that the international community should give serious consideration to ways in which the U.N. can respond to the member states' requests as they seek to promote and strengthen their electoral institutions and procedures (Resol. 45/150 of 18 December 1990, – recorded votes: 129–8–9).

In the Third Committee, the U.S. delegate said that recent experience in Namibia and Nicaragua had shown that U.N. support for elections could be instrumental in resolving difficult situations. The U.N. should strengthen its capacity to make electoral services available upon request and with full respect for the sovereignty of member states. The Organization could provide technical assistance to improve election procedures and offer electoral services as part of ongoing efforts to maintain peace and security.

The U.S. delegate suggested that the Secretary-General should implement the proposal put forward by President Bush during the general debate in the plenary that the U.N. should establish a special coordinator for electoral assistance to be assisted by an electoral commission of distinguished experts from around the world to meet the growing number of requests by states. These experts would act as the Secretary-General's special representatives during U.N. missions providing electoral assistance. U.N. electoral assistance would be made available on a case-by-case basis and a "prudent and frugal" approach should be maintained towards expenses of a general nature. Funding could be either on a voluntary basis or provided partially by regional organizations and by the member state requesting the assistance.

Not unexpectedly, the Chinese delegate disagreed with this position. The political and electoral system chosen by a country in accordance with its particular circumstances was a purely internal affair of a sovereign state. The U.N. had no mandate to interfere in the electoral practices of members states under the Charter.

The cases in which the U.N. had provided electoral monitoring related to decolonization and the settlement of crises threatening peace and security should not be confused with cases involving normal electoral practices in sovereign states. The establishment of permanent machinery to provide electoral assistance would undoubtedly exceed the Organization's mandate under the Charter.[12]

A parallel resolution on "Respect for the principles of national sovereignty and non-interference in the internal affairs of States in their electoral processes" was again voted at the initiative of Afghanistan, Cuba, Tanzania, Zambia and Zimbabwe (Resol. 45/151 of 18 December 1990, 111–29–11).

On 21 December 1990, the General Assembly adopted without a vote the "International Development Strategy for the Fourth U.N. Development Decade" which affirmed, *inter alia*, that human resources development, entrepreneurship and innovation, and the energetic application of science and technology, in a context of political freedom, respect for human rights, justice and equity, are all essential and relevant to growth and development. (Resol. 45/199).

Development and political freedom were again linked in a General Assembly resolution adopted on 17 December 1991 without a vote on "Developing human resources for development". The resolution emphasized the need for an environment guaranteeing opportunities for political freedom, popular participation, respect for human rights, justice and equity, as some of the essential elements to meet the challenge of development (Resol. 46/143).

The "Enhancing" resolution adopted in 1991 (Resol. 46/137 of 17 December 1991, – recorded votes: 134–4-13) affirmed, again, the value of the electoral assistance provided by the U.N. at the request of some member states, in the context of "full respect for their sovereignty". However, it affirmed that electoral verification by the U.N. should remain an exceptional activity of the Organization to be taken in well-defined circumstances, *inter alia*, primarily in situations with a clear international dimension. As a concrete step towards formally endorsing the U.N.'s growing role in this new international field of action, the resolution endorsed the Secretary-General's view that he should designate a senior official to act as a focal point in this area: this was no doubt inspired by President Bush's proposal to appoint a coordinator, but the "electoral commission of distinguished experts" which he had also proposed was not included in the resolution.

The resolution defined precisely the mandate of the senior official to be designated for these tasks, in addition to existing duties (in other words, no extra post was to be created): in order to ensure consistency in the handling of requests of member states organizing elections, he would assist the Secretary-General to coordinate and consider requests for electoral verification and to channel requests for electoral assistance to the appropriate office or programme, to ensure careful consideration of requests for electoral verification, to build on experience gained to develop an institutional memory, to develop and maintain a roster of international experts who could provide technical assistance as well as assist in the verification of electoral processes and to maintain contact with regional and other intergovernmental organizations to ensure appropriate working arrangements with them and the avoidance of duplication of efforts.

The Secretary-General was also requested to establish a voluntary trust fund for cases where the requesting member state was unable to finance, in whole or in part, the electoral verification mission.

Only Cuba, North Korea and Kenya voted against the resolution, while China (and a few other countries) abstained.

Again, in a somewhat schizophrenic approach, a majority of the same General Assembly voted on the same day the "rival", contradictory and superfluous resolution reaffirming the principles of national sovereignty and non-interference in the internal affairs of States in their electoral processes (Resol. 46/130 – recorded voting: 102–40–13).

Latin American countries still consider that their national sovereignty is their best protection, under U.N. auspices, against new unwanted interventions by the U.S.A., following a long history of overt or covert U.S. operations in their countries. These, and other developing countries, do not want Western countries to establish a new "colonialism" under the guise of converting them to democracy, and monitoring their elections.

In fact, according to the "Enhancing" resolutions, election monitoring by the U.N. can only take place, in sovereign states, at the request of the country's government, so that no violation by the U.N. of the sacrosanct principle of national sovereignty may arise.

The real fear of undemocratic countries' governments is that the precedents set by a number of U.N. missions of monitoring national elections may be used by political opponents to their regimes to request international supervision and verification of their electoral process. These countries' authorities might then be subjected to international pressure in the U.N. and in other instances to open their borders to international surveillance, and to international criticism if they refuse to do so.

The latest "Enhancing" Resolution, adopted by the General Assembly on 18 December 1992 (Resol. 47/138), commended the electoral assistance provided to Member States at their request by the Organization. It also welcomed the Secretary-General's decision to establish a focal point for electoral verification and electoral assistance, as well as an Electoral Assistance Unit within the Secretariat. It requested the Secretary-General to provide this Unit with adequate human and financial resources, and to reinforce the Centre for Human Rights through redeployment of resources and personnel, within existing resources (i.e. without additional costs). This Resolution was approved by 141 votes for, none against and 20 abstentions. The parallel counter-Resolution on "Respect for the principles of national sovereignty and non-interference in the internal affairs of States in their electoral processes" (Resol. 47/130) was also approved on 18 December 1992 by a recorded vote of 99–45–16.

U.N. Condemnation of Undemocratic Practices in Specific Countries

Since its creation, the U.N. has traditionally condemned in general racism and colonialism, and in particular such former colonialist countries as France and Portugal, South Africa for its apartheid policies, Israel for its violations of human rights of the Palestinian population in the occupied territories, and Pinochet's Chile for the violations of basic human rights and freedoms since the coup of 11 September 1973. More recently, the General Assembly's "deep concern" over continuing human rights violations has extended to other countries, including Afghanistan, El Salvador, Iran and Cuba. The Chinese repression of the June 1989 pro-democracy demonstrations was the object of a resolution of the U.N. Sub-Commission on Prevention of Discrimination and Protection of Minorities in August 1989.

These resolutions by U.N. bodies were concerned with the violation of human rights in general, but, until 1991, not with the specific respect of civil and political rights, nor with the open defence and promotion of democratic values and practices, except in relatively discreet and limited ways.

In the 1980s, the U.N. Human Rights Committee, established under article 28 of the International Covenant on Civil and Political Rights, has criticized specific governments for their violations of the Covenant, after considering individual communications submitted under article 5 of the Optional Protocol.

For instance, the authors of Communication No. R. 8/34, initially submitted on 30 May 1978 and reviewed by the Committee on 8 April 1981, were all candidates for elective office on the lists of certain political groups for the 1966 and 1971 elections in Uruguay. These groups (Marxist and Pro-Marxist political parties and groups) were later declared illegal through a decree issued in November 1973: Institutional Act No. 4 of 1 September 1976 deprived the authors of the communication of the right to engage in any activity of a political nature, including the right to vote for a term of 15 years.

The Government of Uruguay responded that it had temporarily derogated from some provisions of the Covenant relating to political parties, as it had a right to do so under article 4 of the Covenant. Nevertheless, it was the firm intention of the authorities to restore political life.

The Human Rights Committee found that the Government had not furnished full and comprehensive information on the exceptional circumstances which would have justified the declared state of emergency, thus legitimizing a departure from the normal legal régime prescribed by the Covenant. In addition, even on the assumption that a situation of emergency existed in Uruguay, the Committee did not see what grounds could be adduced to support the contention that, in order to restore peace and order, it was necessary to deprive all citizens, who as members of certain political groups had been candidates in the elections of 1966 and 1971, of any political right for a period as long as 15 years. This measure applied to everyone, without distinction as to whether he sought to promote his political opinions by peaceful means or by resorting to, or advocating the use of, violent means. The

Government had failed to show that the interdiction of any kind of political dissent was required in order to deal with the alleged emergency situation and pave the way back to political freedom.

The Committee, acting under article 5 (4) of the Optional Protocol, was of the view that, by prohibiting the authors of the communication from engaging in any kind of political activity for such a long period as 15 years, the State party had unreasonably restricted their rights under article 25 of the Covenant.

During the same session of the Human Rights Committee,[13] questions were asked of the representatives of Tanzania and Mali as to the compatibility of the one-party system applied in both countries, and the "democratic centralism" of Mali, and the rights and freedoms provided for in the Covenant. The representative from Mali replied that the single-party system had been chosen because of Mali's colonial history and in order to avoid the kind of "self-seeking practices" engaged in by large and small parties both in Africa and elsewhere. He said that the mass media were State-owned, but access to them was available to all citizens, – that, within the one-party system, individuals were necessarily given all political freedoms without any discrimination. Members of the Committee were clearly not convinced by these replies, and the representative from Mali promised to send a detailed supplementary report to the Committee. The representative of Tanzania only stated that she had followed the deliberations of the Committee "with interest" and assured the Committee that all relevant issues would be referred by her Government for study and for such action as might be necessary. Criticisms or questions asked by the Committee's members are published in the yearly reports of the Human Rights Committee, but are not widely publicized.

In 1991, the U.N. General Assembly adopted two resolutions, one concerning the situation in Myanmar (Resol. 46/132 of 17 December 1991) and the other one on the situation of democracy and human rights in Haiti. Both were caused by the action of undemocratic, military, self-appointed governments against the "will of the people": in both countries, the military annulled the clear results of legitimate elections, results which would have suppressed their own political power and privileges. In both cases, serious violations of human rights preceded and followed the military interventions.

Myanmar has been governed by a small military junta as a one-party "socialist" state since 1962: through the "Burmese Way to Socialism", under the rule of General Ne Win's Burmese Socialist Programme Party (BSPP), the once richest country in the region was progressively impoverished. Up to 40% of the national budget goes on military expenses. Massive, peaceful pro-democracy demonstrations in 1988 were smashed by the army, killing over 3,000 civilians. The State Law and Order Restoration Council (SLORC), led by two generals, was created in September 1988. It was to restore order, improve internal transportation and basic services, and hold multi-party elections.

Multi-party elections were held on 27 May 1990. The National League for Democracy (NLD) won 392 of the 485 seats contested, while the SLORC-sponsored National Unity Party, the successor to the BSPP, won only ten seats. The SLORC then nullified these results and took complete control of the country: the newly elected Assembly was never allowed to meet. Many of those elected have been placed either under house arrest or in jail, and several political parties have been banned. Dissident students and other activists have been tortured, and several political prisoners have died in jail. Public criticism of the régime is punishable by the death penalty, imprisonment, or hard labour. Martial law orders announced in 1989 permit military commanders to conduct summary trials and executions in military tribunals.

Both leaders of the NLD were sentenced to house arrest on 20 July 1989. Aung San Suu Kyi, the daughter of independence hero Aung San, rejected the government's offer of exile. She remains under house arrest, virtually incommunicado, saying that she will not leave the country until all political prisoners are freed and the SLORC puts a civilian government in place. In 1991, she received both the Nobel Peace Prize and the European Parliament's Sakharov human rights award in absentia.

At the 1990 session of the U.N. Commission on Human Rights, Myanmar was submitted, as well as other countries, to a confidential scrutiny of its "gross pattern of violations" of human rights, which led to the appointment of a special representative.

During the 45th General Assembly in 1990, a draft resolution criticizing Myanmar's grave human rights situation and calling for early improvement was blocked by China, Cuba, the Association of South East Asian Nations (ASEAN) and other developing countries. These countries feared setting an unwelcome precedent by addressing a country's electoral process and, for a few, to protect an important trading partner.

On 26 February 1991, the U.N. Human Rights Commission voted unanimously to condemn the Myanmar government for human rights abuses.

In July, ASEAN foreign ministers rejected a call by the U.S., the European Community and other Western nations to apply joint pressure on Myanmar to restore democracy and improve human rights.

On 17 December 1991, the General Assembly adopted without a vote a resolution entitled "Situation in Myanmar". The resolution quoted the statement in the Universal Declaration of Human Rights: "the will of the people shall be the basis of the authority of government". In an indirect appeal, it welcomed the Secretary-General's statement on the award of the Nobel Peace Prize to Aung San Suu Kyi and his repeated appeals for her early release from house arrest. The General Assembly then

1. (took) note of the assurances of the Government of Myanmar to take firm steps towards the establishment of a democratic State and (looked) forward to the early implementation of this commitment;
2. (expressed) its concern at the information on the grave human rights situation and (stressed) the need for an early improvement of this situation;

3. (urged) the Government of Myanmar to allow all citizens to participate freely in the political process in accordance with the principles of the Universal Declaration of Human Rights;
4. (decided) to continue its consideration of this question at its forty-seventh session.

However, the price of consensus in the adoption of the resolution was the deletion of a specific phrase expressing the Assembly's concern at the "continued deprivation of liberty of a number of democratically elected political leaders". Describing the last-minute deletion of this phrase as "regrettable", France announced that it, along with eight other European countries wished to withdraw co-sponsorship of the resolution.

In March 1992, the Commission on Human Rights decided that the situation of human rights in Myanmar would from now on be discussed in open session, and no longer in the confidential "1503" procedure.

The Commission adopted by consensus a resolution deploring the fact that the Government, despite the assurances given at various times that it would take firm steps towards the establishment of a democratic State, had not to this day fulfilled those commitments. The Commission expressed its concern at the seriousness of the human rights situation in Myanmar and, in particular, at the fact that a number of political leaders, including Aung San Suu Kyi and other leaders of the National League for Democracy, remained deprived of their liberty.

The Commission decided to nominate a Special Rapporteur for the purpose of establishing direct contacts with the Government and people of Myanmar, including political leaders deprived of their liberty, their families and lawyers, with a view to examining the situation of human rights in the country and following any progress made towards the transfer of power to a civilian Government and the drafting of a new Constitution, the lifting of restrictions on personal freedoms and the restoration of human rights.

The observer for Myanmar had previously said that the draft resolution being considered was totally unacceptable:

> It was lopsided, negative, and highly intrusive. It contained provisions which were based on unsubstantiated and politically motivated allegations emanating mainly from unsavoury anti-Government and anti-people elements.[14]

During the Forty-sixth session of the General Assembly, a resolution on "The situation of democracy and human rights in Haiti" (Resol. 46/7, adopted without a vote on 11 October 1991) strongly condemned

> both the attempted illegal replacement of the constitutional President of Haiti and the use of violence, military coercion and the violation of human rights in that country;
> (and affirmed) as unacceptable any entity resulting from that illegal situation . . .

In its preamble, the resolution expressed the "concern" of the General Assembly about the critical events which had brought about a sudden and violent interruption of the democratic process in Haiti, and asserted the importance of support from the international community for the development of democracy in Haiti. Details on the U.N.-monitored elections and military coup in Haiti will be given in Chapter 6.

During its forty-fourth session in August 1992, the Subcommission on Prevention of Discrimination and Protection of Minorities adopted several "pro-democracy" resolutions:

– In a resolution offering "Support for the restoration of democracy in Peru", the Subcommission deeply deplored the events (President Fujimori's assumption of dictatorial powers in April 1992) and expressed its most serious concern at the effect they were having on the operation of the institutional machinery of representative democracy in Peru and throughout the region. In July, the Human Rights Committee had pointed out that attempts to save democracy by killing it were destined to fail. The Committee urged the Peruvian Government to proceed quickly to hold the promised multi-party elections and to restore the rule of law and an independent judiciary which would protect the provisions of the Covenant.
– With regard to "Monitoring the transition to democracy in South Africa", the Subcommission recommended that a Special Rapporteur be appointed from among its members to report on the progress towards democracy, equality and social justice in South Africa.
– By a resolution on "Support for the recommendations of the Pan-African Conference on Democracy and Management of the Transition in Africa", the Subcommission took note of the deliberations of the Conference, held in Dakar from 25 to 28 May 1992, and attended by more than 200 political leaders from 42 African countries and by prominent figures from all parts of the world. It noted in particular the undertaking by participants to respect the fundamental principles of democracy and the recommendations of the Conference on measures to ensure the normal functioning of institutions such as a statute for opposition movements, definition of the role and status of the Army, and elections as the only means of access to power. The Subcommission strongly supported the Conference views stressing the interdependence of development and democracy, while reaffirming that development was not a prerequisite for building a democratic society or culture. It noted that the Conference had recommended the establishment of structures to remedy any dysfunctions in African democracies, including the establishment of a Pan-African transition monitoring mechanism and of an African mediation committee to settle political disputes and armed conflicts, under the aegis of the leaders of African political parties.

The Dakar Conference thus went much further than the African Charter on Human and Peoples' Rights. Its article 13.1 defines the citizen's political rights as

> the right to participate freely in the government of his country, either directly or through freely chosen representatives in accordance with the law.

The African Charter does not include the terms of the Universal Declaration of Human Rights regarding periodic and genuine elections, universal and equal suffrage, secret vote or equivalent free voting procedures.[15]

Criteria to be met Before Approval of a U.N. Mission of Electoral Assistance

Based on the Secretariat's experience, the Secretary-General defined, in 1992, as follows, the criteria which should be satisfied if an eventual mission for electoral verification is to be considered:[16]

a) Requests should pertain primarily to situations with a clear international dimension and which may relate to the maintenance of international peace and security;
b) U.N. monitoring should cover – geographically and chronologically – the entire electoral process, from the initial stages of registration through the elections themselves;
c) There should be a specific request from the Government concerned as well as broad public and political support for a U.N. role;
d) Approval of a specific mandate should be provided by the competent U.N. organ.

In 1991, the previous Secretary-General, while proposing these criteria, still considered it important for the U.N. to continue to use its discretion in deciding how to respond to requests and to decide on a case-by-case basis. The new Secretary-General also advocated greater flexibility in order for the U.N. to contribute most effectively to democratization processes. He felt that the criterion requiring government requests must always be fulfilled. For him, the experiences of Namibia, Nicaragua and Haiti showed clearly that a primary consequence of U.N. intervention is confidence-building. When a request is supported by a government and all involved parties, where elections constitute a potentially useful conflict resolution mechanism that may avert the possibility of armed confrontation and diminish the potential for more extensive intervention at a later stage, an early international presence may prevent later loss of life and the significant cost of a major operation, even if all criteria are not fulfilled.

The Haiti request did not meet the "international" criterion and was approved too late to allow the U.N. to cover the "entire electoral process": it was still approved by the General Assembly.

In the final analysis, the Security Council and the General Assembly may consider these criteria but are not bound by them: as sovereign political bodies, their decisive criteria will always be political.

Criteria may also differ according to the nature, type and duration of electoral assistance requested by a government. In his "Guidelines for Member States considering the formulation of requests for electoral assistance",[17] the U.N. Secretary-

General has recently defined six basic operational concepts for U.N. electoral assistance, with different degrees of U.N. involvement, and for which different criteria for consideration and approval by U.N. bodies may apply.

Types of U.N. Involvement in Electoral Assistance

In this document,[18] the Secretary-General has added two conditions to the criteria mentioned above. The first one re-affirms the universality of democratic principles, while the second refers to the desirability of operational coordination between observers' groups:

> While consideration must be given to particular local customs, circumstances and traditions, the basic legal framework for the electoral process must be in conformity with the relevant principles enunciated in fundamental international human rights agreements;
>
> In every type of operation, proper consideration will be given to the participation of other international, multilateral, regional, parliamentary or non-governmental organizations as well as Member States in sending observers orproviding technical or financial assistance to the electoral process. Efforts will be made to achieve adequate coordination and avoid duplication of efforts.

The Secretary-General then identified the following operational concepts: our own views are added.

A. Organization and Conduct of an Electoral Process. This complex type of operation implies that the U.N. assumes a role normally fulfilled by national election authorities: it may include the establishment of a system of laws, procedures and administrative measures necessary for the holding of a free and fair election, as well as the actual administration of the electoral process. These exceptional operations require a tailor-made design: no generally valid guidelines may be defined for them, except for the need for a considerable lead-time. The Cambodia and Western Sahara operations fall in this category.

B. Supervision of an Electoral Process. Supervision was frequently used in the context of decolonization operations, such as those in the British Cameroon, Rwanda-Urundi, Togo and Western Samoa, and recently in Namibia. In such operations, not only the results of the elections, but all steps of the process, in both its political and electoral aspects, require certification by the Special Representative of the Secretary-General to confirm the validity of certain crucial aspects. Such operations are not undertaken in an independent country.

The complexity of this type of operation requires that a preparatory mission visit the country to discuss with the authorities the specific terms of reference of the mission and the Status of Mission Agreement.

Terms of reference may vary from case to case, but will typically include the following points:

- the impartiality of the electoral authorities;
- the complete freedom of organization, movement, assembly and expression of political parties and alliances;
- the possibility of the parties to satisfy themselves as to the integrity of the electoral process by being present st all relevant stages through party observers;
- the fairness of access to State radio and television, both in terms of the timing and length of broadcast;
- the use of other public resources for political purposes;
- verification that election rolls are properly drawn, and that qualified voters are not denied identification and registration cards or the right to vote;
- reporting to the authorities on complaints, irregularities and interferences reported or observed, and, if necessary, requesting electoral authorities to resolve and rectify them;
- observing all activities related to the organization of the poll, the electoral campaign, the poll itself and the counting, computation and announcement of results.

C. Verification of an Electoral Process. Verification operations are conducted in a sovereign State at the request of its Government, such as in Nicaragua, Haiti, Angola and Mozambique, as well as some previous Trusteeship operations. The electoral process is organized and administered by a national organ, and the U.N. is asked to verify the freedom and fairness of specific aspects of the electoral process. A Special Representative is appointed, a Mission Agreement is prepared, and a network of observers is created. Rigorous statistical techniques, e.g., quick-counts and data banks of complaints, are utilized.

In our view, the terms of reference for such operations are very similar to those pertaining to "supervision" operations, the only real distinction being between missions to sovereign or non-sovereign countries.

Both supervision and verification activities may be part of broader missions with peace-keeping components, as in Angola and Mozambique.

D. Following an Electoral Process. In recent cases, the Secretary-General has asked the Resident Coordinator of the U.N. system in a country requesting observers to "follow the electoral process and report to him on its results". This approach is comparable to past "observation" missions where the Trusteeship Council sent small missions composed of representatives of Member States, who usually only spent a few days in the Territory.

This approach does not require detailed evaluation and public reporting on the freedom and fairness of the electoral process: no Mission Agreement is required, and the Resident Coordinator's reports are addressed exclusively to the Secretary-General. Additional staff support may be provided.

In our view, this activity has modest goals and only involves the U.N. in a limited way: no real supervision or verification, nor evaluation are carried out, – nor is there any public reporting, which is one of the main requirements and justification for international electoral observation and monitoring. The U.N. presence would only serve as a moral encouragement and support to a democratic transition.

E. Provision of Support to Other International Observers. This approach is used in cases where several countries and intergovernmental and/or non-governmental organizations have been invited by a Government to send observers for the electoral process and have agreed to do so. In this context, a more or less formalized structure, such as a Joint International Observer Group, may be created in order to provide both an umbrella and a common symbol, thus reinforcing the confidence-building effects of the international observer presence. An integrated and coordinated operation will also increase the efficiency and coverage of observation efforts. UNDP may provide a focal point for such coordination.

For example, UNDP provided logistical support for the April 1992 elections in Mali to observers from the Organization of African Unity, the Commission africaine des droits de l'homme et des peuples, the Ligue africaine des droits de l'homme, the Association des Juristes africains, among others. For the June 1992 elections in Ethiopia, UNDP provided support to a Joint International Observer Group composed of observers from several countries, volunteers from the international community in Addis Ababa, including the U.N. system. For the March 1992 elections in Albania, technical assistance provided by UNDP was coordinated with similar activities of the Warsaw Office of the Conference on Security and Cooperation in Europe (see Chapter 8) and with the Washington-based International Foundation for Electoral Systems (see Chapter 9).

The terms of agreement between the various organizations should preferably be recorded in a project document, providing for an advisory coordinating structure and a technical secretariat. It would also be useful for the Government to issue a Statement or a Code of Conduct for International Observers, stating their duties and privileges.

While such coordination is desirable, in our view it remains entirely dependent on the various observers' groups degree of willingness to cooperate. It is unlikely that countries' or NGOs' observers will accept the leadership of the U.N., or of another intergovernmental organization: in particular, NGOs' observers will wish to preserve their independence and autonomy of action, which is one of their strengths.

In any case, the proposed Joint International Observer Group would not issue any statement as to the free and fair character of the elections. Individual delegations which are part of the group would instead prepare their own reports under their own procedures in terms of contents and distribution.

F. Technical Assistance in Electoral Matters. Such activities may include the provision of analyses, advice, equipment or training to governmental institutions, either directly, or as part of major verification missions. Past technical assistance activities have included the establishment and maintenance of civic and electoral registers, electronic electoral data processing, legal and logistical assistance, civic and voter education, communications and vote-counting techonologies, public information, procurement of voting equipment and materials.

These activities are carried out by the U.N. Centre for Human Rights (Geneva), the UNDP Office of Project Services and the U.N. Division of Economic and Social Development (New York), or the U.N. Volunteers (Geneva).

Between 1 October 1991 and 30 September 1992, the U.N. received 31 requests for electoral assistance: of these, 12 related to technical assistance, 8 requested the sending of observers and 11 involved a combination of the two activities.

Management of U.N. Peace-keeping Operations

The U.N. operations in Namibia, in Angola (UNAVEM II), in Cambodia and in Western Sahara have been treated as U.N. "peace-keeping operations". While their ultimate purpose was to create conditions for holding a free and fair electoral process (elections or referendum), and to organize or monitor such a process, their mandate has included such traditional peace-keeping tasks as monitoring a ceasefire and disarming of parties in conflict. These forces have included both military and civilian components.

Peace-keeping missions are considered as "subsidiary organs" of the U.N., established pursuant to resolutions of the Security Council, or, exceptionally, of the General Assembly.

An operation authorized by the Security Council falls under its authority. The Secretary-General is responsible to the Council for the organization, conduct and direction of the operation, and he alone reports to the Council about it. The Secretary-General keeps the Security Council fully informed of developments relating to the functioning of the operation. All matters which may affect the nature or the continued effective functioning of the operation are referred to the Council for its decision.

The Secretary-General is assisted in these functions by the Office for Special Political Affairs – renamed the Office for Peace-keeping Operations in March 1992 – and the Field Operations Division at the U.N. headquarters in New York. Other assistance is given by the Military Adviser to the Secretary-General, the Legal Counsel, the Office of General Services, the Office of Programme Planning, Budget and Finance and the Office of Human Resources Management.

Coordination among the various units is entrusted to the Senior Planning and Monitoring Group on peace-keeping operations, established in January 1990. Task forces are appointed in U.N., New York, on specific operations being planned or implemented. They coordinate Headquarters directives to the Secretary-General's Special Representative in charge of a specific mission.

The Security Council resolution (or more exceptionally the General Assembly resolution) which authorizes an operation usually requests or authorizes the

Secretary-General to appoint a Special Representative as head of the U.N. operation in the field, with its military and civilian contingents. The Special Representative is responsible to the Secretary-General: he exercises authority over the operation within the mandate defined in the Security Council (or General Assembly) resolution(s). Diplomatic or serious operational problems may have to be referred by the Special Representative to the Secretary-General for decisions.[19]

Management of U.N. Electoral Assistance Activities
In accordance with General Assembly resolution 46/137, the Secretary-General designated, in 1992, Mr. James O.C. Jonah, Under-Secretary-General, Department of Political Affairs, as a focal point for electoral assistance activities. His functions are those detailed in the resolution, as mainly those of an assistant and adviser to the Secretary-General in this field and a coordinator.[20]

The "focal point" is assisted by a newly created Electoral Assistance Unit in the same Department, headed by Mr. Horacio Boneo with a small staff. All requests should be channelled through the Unit. The Unit will conduct fact-finding and evaluation missions and provide support for the initial stages of project development or major missions: however, when a mission becomes operational, implementation is the full responsibility of the relevant implementing organization. The Unit will develop a network of internal and external resources and build up an efficient information system.

Since the establishment of the Electoral Assistance Unit until April 1993, the U.N. has received 32 new requests for electoral assistance. In addition, the Unit has assisted in the establishment of electoral components of the missions to Angola and Cambodia. In total, since 1 April 1992, the U.N. has provided electoral assistance to 31 Member States – 24 from Africa, two from Asia, one from Eastern Europe and four from Latin America.[21]

A Task Force composed of representatives of relevant departments and organizations will meet periodically under the chairmanship of the focal point to exchange information and discuss coordination problems. Working arrangements are also established with the Department of Economic and Social Development of the Secretariat, the Centre of Human Rights and the UNDP.

UNDP Resident Coordinators are often involved in the initial contacts with Governments requesting electoral assistance. UNDP is also the primary source of financial support for technical assistance activities, including electoral activities, within the U.N. system.

The U.N. Centre for Human Rights in Geneva provides advisory and technical assistance in the legal and technical aspects of democratic elections as part of its programme of Advisory Services and Technical Assistance for Human Rights. The Centre, in consultation with the Government concerned, nominates experts in the various aspects of democratic elections whose mandate will be to review national legislation and the practical aspects of the organization of elections. These experts visit the country concerned for exchanges of views and experiences with those involved in the election process and make appropriate recommendations. Their mandate does not include involvement in the organization of the elections nor in supervising or observing how they actually take place.

Such electoral assistance has been provided between 1990 and 1992 to the Governments of Romania, Albania and Lesotho at their request.

For instance, the request for U.N. assistance from the Government of Lesotho related to the following matters, in preparation for the elections scheduled for 1992:

- advise and comment on the electoral law of the country;
- advise and assist on drafting of instructions to polling stations;
- advise and assist in drafting instructions to voters describing the steps involved in casting a valid vote;
- make various other suggestions on activities incidental to the holding of democratic elections which should be free and fair to all.

The last elections in Lesotho took place in January 1970. The country has been under military rule since 1986. The three-member U.N. expert team visited Lesotho in November–December 1991.

Another three-member U.N. team visited Romania in early April 1992: its members discussed the general principles and means of application of the legal and technical aspects of democratic elections with officials of the Government of Romania, members of the Parliamentary Committees drafting the new electoral laws, representation of political parties and others interested in these procedures.

In each case, the Centre draws upon the expertise of its staff, a collection of electoral laws from various jurisdictions, a roster of experts and a network of non-governmental organizations, to assist Governments in the highly technical undertaking of assuring the basic right of free and fair elections. The Centre's approach is pragmatic, within the framework of the relevant international standards.[22]

Summary

In contrast with the League of Nations, the U.N. has been actively involved in the decolonization movement, both through declarations, exhortations and condemnations, and actual monitoring of plebiscites, referenda and elections in trust and other dependent territories.

Even though most of the early U.N. missions were small in size and could not, in practice, apply a thorough legal and operational control over the electoral processes, the principle that self-determination should be monitored and legitimized by U.N. observation missions, representing the international community, constituted a significant extension of the role of the U.N. over that of the League, which had had a pioneering but limited role in this field: there was international confirmation that the "will of the people" should be the determining factor in major decisions affecting the international status of dependent countries or territories and the individual fate of their inhabitants. It was also affirmed that the international community had a responsibility in ensuring that the required consultation of the people was fair and genuine.

The role of the U.N. in monitoring elections in sovereign countries is an even more significant innovation insofar as it provides an explicit support given by the organization to the expanding need for democratic governance, not only in declarations and legal and technical assistance, but through field operations. While such operations had to be initially related to the general U.N. objective of maintaining international peace and security, they acquired their own legitimacy within the U.N. programme of promotion and respect for human rights and fundamental freedoms.

At last, the U.N. was becoming an influential actor in the "democratization wave" of the 1980s and 1990s.

Notes

1. Art. 3 and 4 of the U.N. Charter, and ICJ Advisory Opinion of 28 May 1948, "Conditions of admission of a State to membership of the U.N. (Art. 4 of the Charter), pp. 62 and 65.
2. *Everyone's U.N.*, U.N., New York, 9th Ed., 1979, pp. 2–6.
3. See UNCIO VI, pp. 44–45, 372–373, our translation from the French, – *La Charte des Nations Unies, Commentaire article par article*, J.P. Cot and A. Pellet, Eds., Economica/Bruylant, 1985, pp. 18–19, – *Charter of the U.N. – Commentary and Documents*, L.M. Goodrich, E. Hambro, A.P. Simons, Columbia University Press, 3rd Ed., 1969, p. 88.
4. *A History of the U.N.*, Vol. 1, Evan Luard, MacMillan, 1984, pp. 58–61. (with permission).
5. See for instance U.N. General Assembly Resol. 35/35, "Importance of the universal realization of the right of peoples to self-determination and of the speedy granting of independence to colonial countries and peoples for the effective guarantee and observance of human rights", 14 Nov. 1980. The resolution also refers to previous ,resolutions on the same subject, – Resol. 46/87 of 16 Dec. 1991.
6. For instance, the Falklands Islands and Gibraltar (U.K.), New Caledonia (France). See the U.N. Doc. "Teaching about Decolonization", 1992, pp. 21 and 27.
7. See the Charter's Preamble, 2nd para., Art. 1.3, 55.c., 62.2, –Luard, op.cit., pp. 32–33, – *La Charte*, op.cit., pp. 863–866, –UNCIO, IV, pp. 39–41, 374, –and U.N. Doc. *Human Rights, Fact Sheet No. 2*, Apr. 1988, p. 3.
8. See U.N. *Press Release* HR/3196 of 9 Oct. 1992, "Status of the International Human Rights Instruments" as of 8 Sept. 1992.
9. *The Role and Status of International Humanitarian Volunteers and Organizations – The Right and Duty to Humanitarian Assistance*, Yves Beigbeder, Nijhoff, 1991, Chapter 11.
10. U.N. Doc. A/C.3/43/SR.57 of 30 Nov. 1988.
11. U.N. Doc. A/C.3/44/SR.40, 41, 42, 50, 56 –A/C.3/44/L.59, L.60/Rev.1, Nov. 1989.
12. U.N. Doc. A/C.3/45/SR.38, 41, Nov. 1990. The "prudent and frugal" approach advocated by the U.S. delegate is worth noting, in view of the very "frugal" manner in which the U.S. meets its financial obligations to the U.N. budget.
13. See U.N. Doc. A/36/40, "Report of the Human Rights Committee", 1981, pp. 42, 45, 47, 50, 51, 53 and Annex XII.
14. U.N. Resol. 46/132, "Situation in Myanmar" of 17 Dec. 1991, –U.N. *Press Releases* HR/3054, 3 March 1992 (afternoon), and HR/3055, 4 March 1992 (morning), Commission on Human Rights Resol. 1992/58, –*The Interdependent*, Jan.–Feb. 1992, *International Herald Tribune*, 31 March

1992, *Newsweek*, 8 June 1992, *Freedom in the World, 1991–1992*, Freedom House, 1992, pp. 126–129.

15. U.N. *Press Releases* HR/3113 of 21 July 1992 (morning), HR/3164 of 28 Aug. 1992 and HR/3163 of 27 Aug. 1992, –Art. 21.3, Universal Declaration of Human Rights.
16. U.N.Doc. A/47/668 of 18 Nov. 1992, "Enhancing the effectiveness of the principle of periodic and genuine elections – Report of the Secretary-General", paras. 53–62. These criteria were also briefly mentioned in para. 79 of U.N. Doc. A/46/609 of 19 Nov. 1991 on the same Agenda item.
17. U.N. Doc. A/47/668/Add.1 of 24 Nov. 1992.
18. Ibid., paras. 2 and 3.
19. *The Blue Helmets – A Review of U.N. Peace-keeping*, U.N. 1990, pp. 405–408, and U.N. *Press Release*, SG/A/479 of 7 Feb. 1992. U.N. Doc. A/46/169 of 10 May 1991, "Secretariat Units dealing with peace-keeping operations – Report of the Secretary-General".
20. U.N. Doc. A/47/668 of 18 Nov. 1992, paras. 9–23.
21. U.N. *Press Release* GA/491 of 16 Apr. 1993, "Electoral Assistance Activities of United Nations System".
22. U.N. *Human Rights Newsletter*, Apr. July 1992, p. 11. –*Press Release* HR/2981 of 26 Nov. 1991, HR/3071 of 1 Apr. 1992.

CHAPTER 5

THE FIRST GENERATION OF UNITED NATIONS MONITORING OPERATIONS OF ELECTORAL PROCESSES

Shortly after its creation, the U.N. was requested to monitor electoral processes in divided countries (Korea and Germany) and in trust territories and non-self-governing countries generally in transition to independence.

The latter operations were part of the decolonization movement and had the following characteristics, as "first generation" monitoring missions:

1. The U.N. involvement was initially justified by the fact that some of the territories concerned were "Trust Territories", placed under its authority in accordance with Chapter XII of the Charter. Article 76.b specifically set as a basic objective of the trusteeship system the "progressive development" of the trust territories "towards self-government or independence" on the basis of the "freely expressed wishes of the peoples concerned". While the Charter does not explicitly grant a monitoring role to the U.N. with regard to the transition of a territory from trusteeship to independence, the responsibility of the General Assembly in the approval, alteration or amendment of the terms of trusteeship agreements under Article 85 of the Charter may be taken as an acceptable basis for such a role.

   In the 1960s, the U.N. extended its interest and involvement to all "non-self-governing" territories, under Chapter XI of the Charter.
2. The mandate given to the U.N. was generally to allow the inhabitants of a trust or non-self-governing territory to freely express their wishes as to the future of the territory, through the observation of a plebiscite, referendum, or through elections. These wishes were usually expressed in a vote for an option between independence of the territory as an independent country, or in joining a neighbouring independent country, – or an option between joining one or another independent country.
3. The monitoring mandate was granted either by the General Assembly, or by the Trusteeship Council, or by the Special Committee, or by the Security Council in case of a trust strategic territory, at these bodies' own initiative, or at the request of the territory's administering authority.

4. These operations were limited to trust and non-self-governing territories: they did not involve sovereign states.
5. The operations had a single objective, that of observing an electoral process and reporting the mission's findings to the authorizing U.N. body. They did not involve the establishment of democratic institutions nor of democratic governance in those territories.
6. The U.N. operations had a small size: the number of observers rarely exceeded 30. The size of the missions limited the scope and extent of the actual fulfilment of their observation tasks.
7. The first mission of this type took place in 1956 – the last one, in 1992.

The "second generation" operations have also included non-self-governing territories: Namibia and Western Sahara. However, these were, or were to be, relatively large and comprehensive operations, including both military and civilian components, as peace-keeping forces of a new type. In the case of Namibia, the U.N. mission played a significant role in the organization, planning, observation and verification of this process. The mission also included peace-keeping, disarmament measures, protection of human rights, and democratic nation-building. Under the U.N. plan for Western Sahara, the Special Representative of the U.N. Secretary-General should have sole and exclusive responsibility over the organization and conduct of the referendum, if and when it takes place.

However, as their main and striking innovation, the second-generation operations have included election monitoring in sovereign countries in transition to democracy.

Second-generation operations will be reviewed in Chapters 6 and 7.[1]

U.N. Election-Monitoring in Divided Countries: Korea and Germany

The division of these countries was a consequence of the ideological and military confrontation between East and West. In both cases, free elections were to be a prelude to unification. In both cases, the U.S. involved the U.N. in proposals to organize and monitor elections: these efforts were in part frustrated by the USSR in Korea, and totally rejected by the same country for Germany. The Cold War in Europe, and the approaching Korean War prevented any joint, cooperative attempt to give an independent and objective role to the U.N. in such sensitive political issues as the type of political regime which should be allowed to function in these countries. There was no possible compromise between the free choice of a Western type of democracy and the imposition of a Soviet-imposed "people's democracy".

Elections in Korea

During the Second World War, it had been agreed among the Allies that, after the defeat of Japan, Korea, a Japanese colony since 1907, would be restored to independence. The possibility of placing Korea under an international trusteeship had been proposed by Stalin in May 1945, but no agreement was reached.[2]

On 8 August 1945, the Soviet Union entered the war against Japan, and four days later, sent her troops into Northern Korea. It was then proposed by the United States, and accepted by the USSR, that the Japanese surrender should be accepted by Soviet forces in North Korea and by the United States in the South, these areas being divided North and South of the 38th parallel.

In December 1945, the Council of Allied Foreign Ministers, meeting in Moscow, agreed in principle to establish a "provisional Korean democratic government" for a united Korea. A joint commission was to be established, consisting of representatives of the United States and Soviet commands, to prepare proposals in consultation with democratic parties and organizations in Korea. Meanwhile, there would be a four-power trusteeship for the country, to be held by the United States, the Soviet Union, Britain and France.

Prolonged discussions only showed a total conflict of views, in particular about which groups and organizations within Korea were "democratic" and should be consulted about the constitutional system to be established. The Soviet Union held that any groups opposed to the Moscow Agreement and the trusteeship proposal had no right to be consulted.

The United States proposed that elections should be held separately in the two zones: representatives from each zone would then come together in numbers proportionate to population (the population of the South was twice that of the North) to establish a provisional government for a united Korea.

The Soviet Union wanted the provisional assembly to be appointed (not elected), with equal numbers from North and South, and with representatives only of those parties which fully supported the Moscow Agreement. Finally, the Soviet Union proposed that all U.S. and Soviet forces should be withdrawn by 1 January 1948, handing over to local authorities in each zone, so perpetuating the division of the country.

In September 1947, the United States brought the question to the U.N., as they did not wish the inability of the two powers to reach agreement to delay any further the "urgent and rightful claims of the Korean people to independence".

The Soviet delegate rejected the U.N. involvement: as a matter resulting directly from the war, the question was not one for the U.N. – then under Western domination – but for the victorious Allies.

The U.N. General Assembly adopted on 14 November 1947 a resolution (112(II)) which endorsed most of the U.S. proposals:

- a U.N. Temporary Commission on Korea (UNTCOK) was established to be present in Korea, to observe that the Korean representatives were in fact duly elected by the Korean people, with right to travel, observe and consult throughout Korea;[3]
- elections would be held not later than 31 March 1948 on the basis of adult suffrage and by secret ballot to choose representatives who would constitute a

National Assembly and establish a National Government of Korea. The number of representatives from each voting area or zone would be proportionate to the population. The elections would be under the observation of the Commission;
- armed forces of the occupying powers would be completely withdrawn as early as practicable and if possible within 90 days of the establishment of a Korean government.

The Soviet Union opposed this course of action: the Ukraine, one of the members of UNTCOK, refused to serve on the Commission. Radio Moscow and Radio Pyongyang began a carefully organized campaign of opposition and denunciation against UNTCOK. The Commission was denounced repeatedly as "a tool of American imperialism" and "the product of the mechanical majority" in the General Assembly.

The Commission's mandate was limited to observing and reporting on the elections to be undertaken by the authorities in the two territories. It had no legislative, judicial or administrative functions in Korea. It was not called upon to organize or conduct the elections.

In the South, the Commission was able to establish contact with the U.S. military government and the local Korean authorities, but it could not exercise any significant control or influence over the registration of voters, parties and over the electoral procedure.

In the North, the Commission was unable to obtain entry, let alone to influence the preparation and conduct of elections: no observation by the U.N. was carried out in that area.

In view of the lack of access to the North, some members of the Commission felt that its mission should be abandoned, as it would not lead to the unity of the country through the formation of a national government.

The Interim Committee, established to represent the U.N. General Assembly, with the same membership, decided on 26 February 1948 to adopt the view, strongly supported by the U.S.A. and the majority, that the Commission should implement its programme "in such parts of Korea as are accessible to the Commission", as a stage in the formation of a Korean government. This was in effect a commitment to the establishment of a separate authority in the South.

The Commission finally agreed to observe the elections in the South, scheduled for 10 May, provided it was satisfied that they would be held "in a free atmosphere, wherein the democratic rights of freedom of speech, press and assembly would be recognized and accepted".

Out of the eight members of the Commission, two opposed the decision to observe the elections in the South alone, and two more abstained.

During the elections, the Commission interviewed U.S. officials and Korean election officers and candidates, and travelled throughout the country. However, the total international staff of the Commission and the delegates at no time exceeded 60 persons, – the effective number of observers at any time did not exceed 30. This small team was engaged in observing the election in an area of about 40,000 square miles with a population of 20 million, a totally inadequate number of observers: in contrast, in the Saar plebiscite of 1935, there had been one observer to each 500 voters.

In the final observation period, the teams began their work on 7 May: they saw polling places being set up, had some contact with violence, watched police and other official behaviour, the activities of youth groups, observed the actual voting process and the disposition and counting of ballots. At the same time, similar observation was carried out by officers of the U.S. Army and by officials of the military government, who had sufficient manpower to place two observers into each of the 200 election districts.

In spite of important security measures, in the 10 days before the election, 323 persons, including 32 Korean policemen, were killed in various riots and raids. Radio Pyongyang at no time relented in its exhortations to violence and in its demands for an end to the election.[4]

On 10 May 1948, over seven million Koreans (72% of the registered voters) cast their ballots. The result was a victory for the right-wing parties, especially Syngman Rhee's National Association for the Rapid Realisation of Korean Independence and the Korean Democratic Party.

The Commission agreed to endorse the results of the election. It concluded that the results of the ballot of 10 May 1948 were

> a valid expression of the free will of the electorate in those parts of Korea which were accessible to the Commission and in which the inhabitants constitute approximately two-thirds the peoples of all Korea.

On 12 July, a constitution for the Republic of Korea was adopted, in theory covering the whole Korean peninsula and its accessory islands. Early in August, a South Korean government was officially established.

In the North, elections for a "Supreme People's Assembly" were held on 25 August, without U.N. observation. They included the "election" of delegates said to represent the South. On 7 September, a government was set up under the leadership of Kim Il Sung, also claiming to be the government of all Korea.

U.S. and Soviet forces started evacuating from Korea in September.

On the proposal of the United States, the General Assembly voted on 12 December 1948 resolution 195 (III) recognising the new South Korean government as

> a lawful government... based on elections which were a valid expression of free will of the electorate in that part of Korea and which were observed by the Temporary Commission; and that this is the only such Government of Korea.

Two other U.N. Commissions had electoral observation functions in South Korea. However, their main, impossible mandate was to promote the peaceful unification of Korea.

In 1949, the General Assembly created the U.N. Commission on Korea (UNCOK) to continue UNTCOK's work. UNCOK observed the South Korean elections of 30 May 1950 with a staff of only 18. Despite its limited size and resources, the Commission concluded that the election had been freely conducted and that the results were valid.

In 1950, the General Assembly created the U.N. Commission for the Unification and Rehabilitation of Korea (UNCURK). This Commission observed 13 South Korean elections and referenda in the period 1952–1969.[5]

At 1.30 p.m. on 25 June 1950, the South Korean Foreign Minister informed the U.N. Commission of a large scale attack by North Korean forces across the border.[6] The Korean War lasted until 27 July 1953, when an Armistice was signed. Korea remained, and still remains, a divided nation.

An Assessment

For Amato,[7] the real victor of the 1948 elections was the United States. The establishment of a government in South Korea allowed the U.S. to terminate an undesired military presence in South Korea and to withdraw its troops. In addition, UNTCOK served another American objective by giving international recognition to the "democratic" Republic of Korea while denying it to North Korea.

To this assessment, one may add that the Cold War prevented, then the Korean War froze, any serious attempt to unify the two Koreas through the holding of general elections in the whole territory. Clearly, the Soviet Union had no intention to allow free elections in North Korea, nor to authorize any international monitoring of such elections.

Even if the U.N. was in fact manipulated by the U.S. in observing elections only in South Korea, and in recognizing the Republic of Korea as the only legitimate, democratic government of Korea, the cancellation of the U.N. observation mission in South Korea, because the mission was not allowed in North Korea, would not have advanced the cause of democracy.

Politically and technically, the intergovernmental composition of the Commissions did not facilitate their work, in particular that of UNTCOK, whose members (countries' representatives) took different or opposing positions on important issues: political arguments and decisions should best be carried out at U.N. headquarters, leaving the international electoral observation group to focus on the operational problems. Such groups should preferably be composed of international civil servants and other impartial and neutral observers, and not of government representatives.

Also, technically, the small size of the Commissions limited their effectiveness and credibility.

Even if the Commission's influence in securing free elections in South Korea has been negligible or minimal, the creation by the U.N. of these bodies has retained a symbolic importance: the new Organization attempted to control, in one specific area, the implementation of the principle that

> The will of the people shall be the basis of the authority of government: this will shall be expressed in periodic and genuine elections . . .[8]

Investigating Conditions for Free Elections in Germany

Following the forced separation of Germany into two countries, the United States, Britain and France had been calling in their discussions with the Soviet Union for free elections throughout Germany as a means towards its reunification.[9]

At the 1951 General Assembly of the U.N., Britain and France proposed the setting up of a U.N. commission to examine whether conditions existed for the holding of free elections throughout Germany. The communist states opposed any discussion of the question as an intervention in domestic affairs. Also, as for Korea, they stressed that matters arising from the war were the responsibility of the victorious powers, and not of the U.N.

On 20 December, the General Assembly set up the "U.N. Commission to Investigate Conditions for Free Elections in Germany": it was to investigate conditions in both halves of Germany, to consider the constitutional provisions in force there, the freedom of political parties, and the organization of judiciary and police, and to report to the Secretary-General whether conditions for genuinely free and secret elections existed.

The communist states denounced this as a gross interference in domestic matters, and Poland refused to take part in the Commission, as she had been invited to do. On the other hand, the Western powers maintained that Germany was still under military occupation, and so had no sovereignty to violate. The proposal was designed, on the contrary, to promote the restoration of the German sovereignty.

The Commission decided that before it could undertake its principal task, it would first have to ascertain whether all the parties involved were willing to cooperate. The Commission proceeded to Germany in February 1952 and found that the Western Allies and the Federal Republic of Germany were willing to cooperate with the U.N. As predicted, the Commission was not given permission to travel in East Germany or East Berlin. The Soviet authorities and the authorities in East Germany refused to recognize the U.N. Commission and to accept its mandate: the Soviet Union had held that the only commission acceptable to it would be one composed of representatives of the four occupying powers. After further attempts, the Commission reported that it was unable to carry out the General Assembly mandate and therefore adjourned *sine die* in August 1952.

It had been clear to all that the Soviet Union would not permit an impartial body to determine whether conditions in one of its satellites were conducive to the holding of free and democratic elections.

In Luard's words,[10]

> The whole episode must really be regarded primarily as a propaganda exercise, designed to expose to the world the reluctance of the East German Government

to submit itself to free elections, and so to demonstrate its unrepresentative character.

This diplomatic exercise was not intended to become operational: the creation of the Commission was meant to focus world attention on the undemocratic nature of communist regimes.

No democratic consensus could possibly emerge in the U.N. during the Cold War.

Decolonization: The U.N. Role in Monitoring Self-determination Processes

The United Nations has been involved, or has involved itself, generally in promoting decolonization, and more directly by sending missions to monitor self-determination processes in trust and non-self-governing territories and to certify that such processes had been free and genuine, and represented the "will of the people".

Some of these missions achieved their main objective of ensuring that the inhabitants of a territory were allowed to make a genuine choice between clear options. Some only served to legitimize pre-determined options, as promoted by the strong anti-colonialist movement in the U.N., or as decided by influential or powerful states.

The objective of an early U.N. mission, which was to organize a self-determination plebiscite in Kashmir, remains unfulfilled.

The Frustrated Kashmir Plebiscite

Historical Background

In August 1947, India and Pakistan became independent dominions, in accordance with a scheme of partition provided by the Indian Independence Act of 1947. Under that scheme, the State of Jammu and Kashmir, an Indian princely state with a mainly Muslim population, was free to accede to India or Pakistan. The Hindu Maharajah of the State (referred to here as Kashmir) requested accession to India: the Indian Government (as voiced by Lord Mountbatten, its then constitutional head) accepted this request on the pledge that the question would be settled by reference to the people. When partition was to take place, Britain had decided that the destiny of states should be determined by their rulers rather than by their peoples.[11]

In January 1948, India complained to the Security Council that tribesmen and others, with Pakistan's support and participation, were invading Kashmir and that extensive fighting was taking place. Pakistan denied the charges and declared that Kashmir's accession to India was illegal.

On 20 January, the Security Council established a three-member U.N. Commission for India and Pakistan (UNCIP) to investigate the dispute and to exercise a mediatory influence (Resol. 39(1948)). On 21 April, the Council enlarged the membership of the Commission to five and instructed it to proceed at once to the subcontinent (Resol. 47(1948)). UNCIP was to place its good offices and mediation at the disposal of the two Governments. The Council also recommended various measures, including the use of observers, to stop the fighting and to create proper conditions for a free and impartial plebiscite. A plebiscite administrator would be appointed by the Secretary-General and would operate as an officer of the Kashmiri Government, when appropriate conditions had been restored in organizing a plebiscite. The plebiscite would be supervised by UNCIP.

India, however, announced that she refused to accept the Council's resolution and informed the Secretary-General that she would not be bound by it.

The UNCIP members arrived in the area in July 1948, and the next month, proposed a ceasefire and detailed arrangements for a truce and the holding of a plebiscite. Both sides accepted the proposals, with clarifications and understandings. The ceasefire came into effect on 1 January 1949 and a U.N. Military Observer Group in India and Pakistan (UNMOGIP) was set up to observe and report on the ceasefire.

In July 1949, military representatives of the two Governments signed the "Karachi Agreement" establishing a ceasefire line, to be verified mutually on the ground by local commanders on each side with the assistance of the U.N. military observers.

Early in 1949, Fleet Admiral Chester W. Nimitz, of the United States, had been appointed by the Secretary-General, in consultation with the two parties and with UNCIP, as U.N. Plebiscite Administrator.

Both India and Pakistan had then accepted the plebiscite proposal, but the Commission was unable to reach agreement with the parties on the terms of demilitarization of the State before a plebiscite could be held. Despite mediation by various U.N. representatives, differences between the parties remained.

In a press statement issued on 22 September 1949, UNCIP recalled that Security Council resolution 47(1948) of 21 April 1948 envisaged three related but distinct steps: a ceasefire, a truce period during which the withdrawal of forces would take place and, finally, consultations to establish the conditions by means of which the free will of the people of Kashmir would be expressed. The first objective had been achieved but, despite the Commission's efforts, no agreement could be secured on the other two.

UNCIP was terminated in March 1950: a U.N. representative was then appointed to exercise its powers and responsibilities.

In January 1957, the Security Council took up Pakistan's complaint that India had held a constituent assembly in Kashmir and drawn up a constitution that provided for the integration of Kashmir into India in violation of the earlier agreement for a plebiscite. In March 1957, India announced that it no longer accepted the principle of a plebiscite: the accession of Kashmir to India was a *fait accompli*.

Hostilities again broke out between the two countries in early August 1965. The Security Council called for a ceasefire, and the fighting was brought to an end in September 1965, with the assistance of UNMOGIP.

In January 1966, the Prime Minister of India and the President of Pakistan met in Tashkent, USSR, at the invitation of the Chairman of the Council of Ministers of the USSR. They announced their agreement that the withdrawal of all armed personnel of both sides to the positions held prior to 5 August 1965 should be completed by 25 February 1966 and that both sides should observe the ceasefire terms on the ceasefire line.

The 1971 civil war in East Pakistan culminated in Indian military invasion of that area in December and resulted in the creation of Bangladesh as an independent state. Fighting occurred also in Kashmir, but the war did not bring about any change in the situation in that region.

In December 1971, the Security Council adopted resolution 307(1971), by which it demanded that a durable ceasefire in all areas of conflict remain in effect until all armed forces had withdrawn to their respective territories and to positions which fully respected the ceasefire line in Kashmir supervised by UNMOGIP.

Following the adoption of this resolution, the representative of India stated that Kashmir was an integral part of India. The representative of Pakistan insisted that Kashmir was disputed territory whose status should be settled by agreement under the aegis of the Security Council.

In July 1972, India and Pakistan agreed in Simla, India, to define a line of control in Kashmir. However, India considered that, as a result of the war, the Karachi Agreement of 1949 had ceased to be operative and the mandate of UNMOGIP had lapsed: Pakistan rejected this view. The Secretary-General's position is that UNMOGIP can only be terminated by a decision of the Security Council.

The Current Position in Kashmir

In the absence of a political agreement, the Kashmir dispute festers: it could cause another war between India and Pakistan.

India persists in rejecting the plebiscite proposed by the Security Council in 1948 for Kashmir. In August 1992, in the first official talks between India and Pakistan in 20 years on their dispute over Kashmir, Pakistan restated its position that the fate of Kashmir should be decided by a plebiscite of its residents.

In Indian Kashmir, the four million inhabitants lived fairly peacefully until the 1980s. Then New Delhi revoked the autonomy which had been granted to a local leader. According to foreign diplomats in India and Pakistan, Pakistan began in 1989 to divert to Kashmir arms intended for the Afghan mujahedin, transforming a marginal rebellion into a guerrilla war. Among the major militant groups fighting against India's rule over Kashmir, two factions stand out: the largest and most popular faction is the Jammu Kashmir Liberation Front, which is fighting for an independent Kashmir, – the fundamentalist Hizbul mujahedin wants Kashmir to join Pakistan.

Launched in the summer of 1992, India's Operation Tiger is waging an aggressive offensive against the rebellion. The operation is using 400,000 Indian troops and police to man roadblocks and enforce a strict curfew in Kashmir. According to human rights groups, the security forces also conduct mass arrests, summary executions, reprisal killings against civilians and torture of detainees. An Indian official (the government chief information officer) has recently counseled moderation and said that torture was not part of Indian government policy. However, India's message is clear: there is no question that Kashmir could be separated from India through force or plebiscite. Giving in to the separatists in Kashmir would give hope and support to separatists in Punjab and other parts of India. India would break up, as the USSR and Yugoslavia have broken up, creating chaos and ethnic wars.

Estimates of the death toll vary: Pakistan counts 25,000 dead and 16,000 wounded in Kashmir from January 1990 to the end of 1992. India alleges that, in the same period, "terrorists" have killed 1,800 civilians and more than 400 security troops.

Under the principle of self-determination, the fate of Kashmir should be decided by its people: as proposed by Pakistan, they should be given the option of either remaining as an Indian State or joining Pakistan. However, they should also be offered the option of independence as a sovereign State, which may be favoured by many Kashmiris over the other two options.

In mid-1993, the 36 military observers of UNMOGIP were still deployed on both sides of the line of control and also along the border between Pakistan and Kashmir.[12]

U.N. Monitoring of Electoral Processes in Trust and Non-Self-Governing Territories

As discussed in Chapter 4, the U.N. has assumed an increasing role in promoting decolonization since the late 1950s and in the sixties. The U.N. General Assembly has first goaded willing or unwilling colonial countries into granting independence to their trust territories, and then to all colonial possessions. The landmark "Declaration on the Granting of Independence to Colonial Countries and Peoples", approved on 14 December 1960, proclaimed the necessity of bringing colonialism to a speedy and unconditional end. While it stated that all powers should be transferred to the peoples of these territories in accordance with their "freely expressed will and desire", precise methods for this transfer of powers were not identified.

In practice, and within the context of international anti-colonialism campaigns and pressures, a number of colonial possessions became independent by decision of the administering power, following, or not, discussions or negotiations with liberation movements' leaders, and/or armed rebellion, – in some cases, independence was declared on the basis of and following plebiscites, referenda or elections, – in some cases these electoral processes (plebiscites, referenda and elections) were monitored by the U.N. (and other organizations).

Among the Trust Territories, the Cameroons under French administration and Italian Somaliland under Italian administration became independent in 1960,

Tanganyika under British administration became independent in 1961, Nauru administered by Australia on behalf of a joint administering authority comprising Australia, New Zealand and the United Kingdom became independent in 1968, New Guinea under Australian administration became independent in 1975: the U.N. had no role in organizing or monitoring electoral processes in these territories as a prerequisite for their independence.

Similarly, many non-self-governing territories (non-trust territories) became independent without U.N. monitoring of electoral processes prior to independence: for instance, India and Pakistan in 1947, the Belgian Congo in 1960, Algeria in 1962, Guinea-Bissau in 1973.

U.N. monitoring of self-determination electoral processes was therefore not adopted, or accepted as a general rule, but only in specific cases. The reasons for non-requesting, or rejecting international monitoring was usually the wish of the administering authority to retain full power over the transition period to independence, to identify and legitimize the new leaders and control the emerging political processes.

A list of plebiscites, referenda and elections held under the supervision or observation of the U.N. in Trust and Non-Self-Governing Territories is in Table 4.1 (Chapter 4).

A few examples of electoral monitoring operations carried out by the U.N. in trust or non-self-governing territories follow, first in Africa, then in Asia.

African Territories

Trust Territories: The French and British Togolands – Self-determination through Plebiscite or Elections. The first trust territory to gain independence was British Togoland in 1957.

A former German colony, the territory was divided after World War I into two territories to be administered, one by Britain and one by France, under League of Nations mandates.

In 1946, France accepted to place her former League mandates under the U.N. Trusteeship System. However, the Brazzaville Conference, held in February 1944, had rejected any prospect of self-government for the French colonies, not even alluding to possible independence. As quoted by Amato,[13] the principle emerging from the Conference was the indivisibility (and the expected permanence) of the French Empire:

> The goals of the civilizing task carried out by France in her colonies reject any idea of autonomy, any possibility of evolution outside the structure of the French Empire; the eventual constitution, however distant, of self-government in the colonies is dismissed.

France's aim was therefore to maintain French Togoland and its other colonial possessions within the French Union (the former Empire), while Britain was generally more amenable to decolonization, as evidenced by her release of India. Britain had linked the future of her Togoland to the fate of the Gold Coast. Because of the small size, sparse population and poor resources of her part of Togoland, Britain had administered it as an integral part of the Gold Coast since 1920: London was therefore inclined to favor the amalgamation of her two territories into a single unit.

In June 1954, Britain informed the U.N. that the Gold Coast would soon be ready for independence. As Britain would no longer be able to administer her Togoland as part of Gold Coast, she suggested that British Togoland be allowed to become part of an independent Gold Coast, subject to a consultation of its inhabitants to ascertain their wishes concerning the territory's future. In December, the General Assembly requested the Trusteeship Council to dispatch a special mission to both Togolands to decide whether the inhabitants wanted separate independence, unification, integration with the Gold Coast or some other self-governing or independent arrangement (Resol. 860 (IX)).

Before the Mission's visit, the French National Assembly enacted a reform bill on 16 April 1955 expanding the powers of the French Togoland Territorial Assembly. The Assembly was dissolved and elections were held on the basis of direct but restricted suffrage: only 190,053 persons were allowed to vote out of a population of about one million. The elections resulted in a full victory for the two pro-French parties. However, the validity of the elections became subject to question, in view of evidence of electoral manipulation in favour of the victorious parties.

On 15 December 1955, the U.N. General Assembly passed a resolution calling for a U.N.-supervised plebiscite in British Togoland. The plebiscite was to be organized and conducted by the (British) Administering Authority in consultation with and under the supervision of a U.N. Plebiscite Commissioner, in order to ascertain the wishes of the inhabitants of British Togoland in regard to the union of their Territory with an independent Gold Coast or otherwise. Gold Coast was on the verge of independence. It also recommended that if France were to undertake a similar consultation, it should likewise take place under the auspices of the U.N. (Resol. 944 (X)).

On 9 May 1956, the U.N. supervised the plebiscite in British Togoland. The result showed a majority in favour of union with an independent Gold Coast.

In his report to the General Assembly of 5 September 1956, the U.N. Plebiscite Commissioner stated that the plebiscite had been held in an atmosphere of absolute freedom, impartiality and fairness. All eligible voters had had a chance to register and vote. The organization and conduct of the plebiscite had been excellent. Only minor irregularities had been recorded. He added that the (British) Plebiscite Administrator had conducted a fair plebiscite, and that the paramount element in the Plebiscite had been the high human quality, sense of responsibility, the dignity of the people of Togoland. The Plebiscite Administrator, in his report, expressed his profound gratitude to the U.N. Commissioner and his team, and acknowledged the exemplary degree of cooperation maintained between them and the Administering staff.[14]

The General Assembly approved the union and the Territory was united with the Gold Coast to form the new independent State of Ghana on 6 March 1957 (Resol. 1044 (XI)).

On 23 June 1956, the French National Assembly enacted a bill, known as "loi-cadre", which provided for the creation of an autonomous regime in French colonies or trust territories, including French Togoland. The loi-cadre was later seen as an important step in the evolution of French dependent territories towards self-government and ultimate independence. However, the choice offered to the inhabitants of those territories by referendum was not an option between independence, autonomy under the new French statute or continued trusteeship, but only the last two alternatives.

The referendum for French Togoland was scheduled for October 1956. The French government requested the Trusteeship Council to dispatch a mission to observe the referendum. The Council rejected this request, as the referendum did not offer the alternative of independence, and not to be subsequently confronted with a *fait accompli*. Non-administering members of the Council felt that France's principal aim was to terminate the trusteeship agreement without offering the Togoland people a meaningful choice concerning their future.

The referendum took place on 28 October 1956 with a participation of 77% of the electorate:. 72% of the voters endorsed the statute creating an autonomous regime.

On 23 January 1957, the U.N. General Assembly set up a Commission of six members in order to examine the "entire situation in the Territory": in a setback for France, the Assembly refused to endorse the outcome of the referendum and to terminate the trusteeship agreement, but it also called for new elections to the Togoland Legislative Assembly, thus challenging its representative character.

The U.N. Commission, which visited the territory in May and June 1957, was favorably impressed with the broad powers delegated to the Togoland government under the new statute. However, critics in the Trusteeship Council claimed that the statute had been approved by a Legislative Assembly which was unrepresentative and by an electorate which was not offered an alternative to self-government. In September 1957, the Council noted the intention of the Togoland Government to hold new elections before 1960, on the basis of direct universal suffrage for a new Legislative Assembly.

Then, in a surprise move, the Togolese government announced that it was prepared to hold new elections before the end of 1958 under U.N. auspices.

Discussions in the Fourth Committee in November 1957 raised issues of substance which are still controversial today.

Belgium challenged the right of the U.N. to observe elections in Togoland: this authority rested solely with the administering power. The British delegate noted that his government did not normally approve of U.N. observation of a general election. The Australian delegate felt that the procedure was highly unusual and that it should not be regarded as a precedent.

Such objections then expressed by colonialist countries, are now voiced by communist countries (China, Cuba), and Third World countries for reasons of a similar nature: formally, to protect States' national sovereignty, – in substance, to ensure that their political regime will not be subjected to international scrutiny and criticism.

On a purely technical basis, and leaving aside the U.N. observation issue, the British delegate rightly argued that, as a means towards self-determination, a general election was indeed a satisfactory instrument having many advantages over a plebiscite or referendum. While a plebiscite or referendum offered only a limited number of choices, a general election for an assembly permitted many points of view to be expressed. Furthermore, once the assembly was formed, it could work out the details concerning the country's future.[15]

On 29 November 1957, the General Assembly accepted the invitation of the Togoland government to make the necessary arrangements, in consultation with the administering authority, for the supervision of the elections by the U.N. The Assembly decided to elect a Commissioner who would supervise the elections to the Legislative Assembly, with the assistance of observers and staff, and would submit a report on the organization, conduct and results of the elections (Resol. 1182 (XII)).

Four factors hindered the U.N. mission in its performance:

- the mission arrived only two months before election day, an inadequate time to diagnose problems and propose solutions, and have improvements implemented;
- the small size of the mission: in addition to the Commissioner and a staff of 11 members, the mission was composed of 21 other U.N. secretariat personnel detailed by the Secretary-General to serve as observers. A much larger mission would have been necessary to observe more effectively elections in a territory with a population of more than one million;
- ill-adapted electoral laws;
- lack of cooperation of the Togoland government in improving election conditions.

Still, in spite of these difficulties, because of the U.N. presence, the revised electoral lists effectively represented a 39% change in the number of registrants over the original rolls.

The elections were held on 27 April 1958. The results showed an overwhelming victory for Mr. Olympio's nationalist party, a clear vote for independence. The Commissioner had concluded that in spite of defects and weaknesses,

> there is absolutely no doubt in my mind that the general outcome of the elections faithfully reflects the wishes of the people of Togoland as to their choice of representatives in the Chamber of Deputies.[16]

France and Togoland agreed in 1958 that Togoland would become independent on 27 April 1960, and that the trusteeship agreement should also be terminated at that time. This was endorsed by the Trusteeship Council in October 1958 and by the General Assembly in November (Resol. 1253 (XIII)).

A Non-self-governing Territory: Equatorial Guinea – Independence without Self-determination. Spain's colonial rights in Equatorial Guinea were recognized by the Convention of Paris in 1900. It was organized as a single colony in 1936 composed of the districts of Fernando Poo and Rio Muni, and administered by a Spanish Governor-General. Its population was estimated at 355,000 inhabitants.[17]

Like France, and other colonial countries, Spain was first totally opposed to the decolonization movement. In particular, it rejected any external intervention, such as those of the U.N., into its colonial affairs. Although it was admitted to the U.N. in 1955,

Spain refused, until 1960, even to transmit to the U.N.

> statistical and other information of a technical nature relating to economic, social, and educational conditions in the territories for which (it) was responsible

under Chapter XI of the U.N. Charter. Even less was Spain prepared to allow its dependent territories "to develop self-government", nor "to take due account of the political aspirations of the peoples" (Art. 73.b of the U.N. Charter).

Similar to the French policy of assimilation and integration into the metropolitan area, Spain terminated the territory's colonial status and converted the Fernando Poo and Rio Muni into two Spanish provinces. All Equatorial Guineans were granted Spanish nationality.

Spain's policy only changed in the early 1960s. Under international anti-colonialist pressures, it finally agreed late in 1960 to transmit information on its colonies to the U.N. Secretary-General. In August 1963, it offered the two provinces a degree of economic and administrative autonomy. A referendum in the colony approved the reform bill.

U.N. bodies used this opening to encourage and accelerate the expected decolonization process of Equatorial Guinea, even though the organization did not have the legitimate authority endowed to it by the Charter in relation to trust territories, i.e. in ensuring that administering Powers promote the development of such territories towards self-government or independence (Art. 76.b).

In September 1963, the U.N. Special Committee appealed to Spain to speed up the decolonization process. In 1964, the Committee affirmed the inalienable right of the people of Equatorial Guinea to "self-determination and independence" and called upon Spain to implement the 1960 Declaration as soon as possible. On 16 December 1965, the U.N. General Assembly reaffirmed the right of the people of Equatorial Guinea to self-determination and independence, but also

> *Request*(ed) the Administering Power to set the earliest possible date for independence after consulting the people on the basis of universal suffrage under the supervision of the United Nations. (Resol. 2067 (XX))

The proposed consultation under U.N. supervision, leading to independence, was now demanded by the U.N., instead of being requested by the administering power, thus showing the increased assurance and influence of the anti-colonialist voting bloc in the General Assembly.

In June 1966, the Special Committee received an invitation from Spain to visit the territory. The U.N. mission's report was very critical of Spanish colonial rule and of its electoral system which permitted only a small minority of the adult population to select government representatives. It also reported that Spain had severely curtailed political activities.

On 20 December 1966, the General Assembly noted the overwhelming desire of the Equatorial Guineans for complete independence not later than July 1968 and invited Spain to implement as soon as possible the following measures:

> 4...
> a) Removal of all restrictions on political activities and establishment of full democratic freedoms;
> b) Institution of an electoral system based on universal adult suffrage and the holding, before independence, of a general election for the whole Territory on the basis of a unified electoral roll;
> c) Transfer of effective power to the government resulting from the election;
> ...
> 9. *Request*(ed) the Secretary-General to take appropriate action in consultation with the administering Power and the Special Committee to ensure the presence of the United Nations in the Territory for the supervision of the preparations for and the holding of, the election envisaged in paragraph 4 (b) above and to participate in any other measures leading towards independence of the Territory. (Resol. 2230 (XXI))

As noted by Amato,[18] the terms of this resolution were striking. First, it stipulated what measures Spain was to take before an election was held in one of its non-self-governing territories. Secondly, the resolution assumed that the U.N. had the right to oversee not only the election itself but also the electoral preparations.

On 1 April 1968, the Special Committee adopted an even more striking resolution (U.N. Doc. A/AC.109/289), reaffirming the right of the people of Equatorial Guinea to independence, to be obtained by 15 July 1968, but omitting their right to self-determination: "...the question of accession to independence of Equatorial Guinea shall not be subject to any form of electoral consultation".

This extraordinary and undemocratic decision of the Committee was intended to ensure that no solution other than independence would be submitted to the people of the territory for *their* decision. As stated by the American delegate, ironically, the U.N. was denying the people of Equatorial Guinea the right to determine their own future by dictating to them their date of independence and by forbidding them to express their will on the question of a change in their political status.[19]

The resolution otherwise repeated the terms of the General Assembly resolution of December 1966 concerning the supervision by the U.N. of the preparations for, and the holding of, the general elections. To avoid a risk of partition, the resolution urged the administering Power to hold these elections on the basis of a single electoral roll for the whole territory.

A constitutional conference approved in June 1968 a constitution providing for the creation of a federal state with two autonomous provinces. After approval by the Spanish Cortes, the constitution would be put to a referendum in the territory on the basis of universal adult suffrage. Within two months of the referendum, general elections would be held to elect the president of the republic and the members of the national assembly.

In addition to the U.N. presence, Spain decided to appoint an independent electoral commission composed of two Spanish judges and four Guineans of "recognized impartiality and competence". The creation of this commission was to ensure the fairness of the electoral process to be carried out by the local colonial administration, in parallel with the U.N. observation mission: at the same time, it showed the good faith of the administering country.

On 6 August, the Secretary-General set up the "Mission for the Supervision of the Referendum and Elections in Equatorial Guinea". The Commission was composed of five members, from Niger (chairman), Chile, Iran, Syria and Tanzania, assisted by twenty members from the Secretariat in New York. Thirteen observers (also drawn from the U.N. Secretariat) were added to the mission for the elections which followed the referendum.

The mission's work suffered from several flaws and limitations:

- its terms of reference were never precisely defined (observation or supervision?), nor was there any clear agreement between Spain and the U.N. as to what its role was to be;
- its composition was politically unbalanced: four of its members were anti-colonialists who favoured the victory of the nationalist parties in the territory, even if they did not materially assist them. Their neutrality or impartiality could have been challenged;
- the arrival of the mission one day before the referendum could hardly enable it to adequately oversee and assess the outcome of this process;
- the mission's small size limited its ability to observe more than a limited number of polling stations.

The official results of the referendum, held on 11 August, showed overwhelming approval of the constitution.

The assessment of the U.N. mission on the conduct of the referendum was generally favorable: it felt that some problems which arose during the voting process were not of "such magnitude" as to question the results of the vote.

In preparation for the September elections, the mission urged Spain to rectify some deficiencies it had found in the election procedures.

The U.N. mission and its observers closely followed the election campaign which lasted from 11 to 20 September. They found that the campaign had been conducted in an orderly fashion without any reports of violence.

The election was held on 22 and 29 September. The mission's overall assessment of the election was highly favorable.

On 11 October, the General Assembly accepted the mission's findings and on 12 October, Equatorial Guinea acceded to independence.

Asian Territories

Western Samoa: A Consensus on Self-determination and Independence. A former "C" mandate of the League of Nations,[20] Western Samoa became a U.N. trust territory under New Zealand administration by Agreement approved by the General Assembly on 13 December 1946.

Although they recognized that the Agreement marked a considerable advance on the terms of the former mandate, many Samoan leaders were of the opinion that the territory should be granted immediate self-government, with New Zealand remaining in the role of adviser and protector. A petition to this effect was submitted to the Trusteeship Council in 1947, following which the Council sent U.N. missions in 1947, 1950, 1953 and 1959.[21]

The 1947 special mission and the 1950 Visiting Mission concluded that the Samoans were not yet ready for full self-government. The latter Mission suggested that an Executive Council be established in order to satisfy the Samoans' desire for increased participation in the executive branch of the Government: New Zealand implemented this proposal in 1952 with the establishment of the Executive Council, whose function was "to confer and advise the High Commissioner on the forming, determining and implementing of the policy of the Government of Western Samoa". Shortly before the arrival of the 1953 Visiting Mission, New Zealand proposed the creation of a Constitutional Convention, representative of all sections of the population. The 1959 Visiting Mission was informed that the New Zealand was prepared to approve a timetable for the attainment of self-government or independence by Western Samoa.

In its report, the 1959 Mission stressed the fact that it was a requirement of the U.N. that self-government or independence should be attained on terms and conditions which were in accordance with the freely expressed wishes of the people concerned. The Mission therefore felt that the General Assembly might regard a plebiscite as desirable.

In October 1960, the Legislative Assembly of Western Samoa ratified a constitution which provided self-government for the territory. Arguing that the provisions of Article 76 (b) of the U.N. Charter had now been met, New Zealand, the administering authority and the Prime Minister of Western Samoa requested that the trusteeship agreement be terminated on the territory's attainment of independence, scheduled for 1962.

Article 76 (b) refers to the progressive development of trust territories towards self-government or independence, and to the freely expressed wishes of the peoples. Accordingly, delegates to the U.N. General Assembly welcomed these developments but argued that the question of independence as well as the constitution itself should be submitted to the Samoan population for approval. Their apparently unnecessary insistence on a plebiscite stemmed mainly from the fact that the Legislative Assembly had been elected on the basis of restricted suffrage, and might not be fully representative of the Samoan people.

New Zealand and Western Samoan officials argued that a plebiscite was not necessary, as the Legislative Assembly was a representative body according to the customs of the Samoan people, and thus legitimate. However, they raised no objections to holding one if the General Assembly still considered it desirable.

The General Assembly then recommended, *inter alia*, on 18 December 1960:

> that the Administering Authority, in pursuance of Article 76 b of the Charter of the United Nations, take steps, in consultation with a United Nations Plebiscite Commissioner, to organize, under the supervision of the United Nations, a plebiscite in Western Samoa under New Zealand administration, in order to ascertain the wishes of the inhabitants of the Territory concerning their future;
>
> ... that ... the plebiscite should take place in the month of May 1961 and that the questions to be asked should be:
>
> 1. Do you agree with the Constitution adopted by the Constitutional Convention on 28 October 1960?
> 2. Do you agree that on 1 January 1962 Western Samoa should become an independent State on the basis of that Constitution?
>
> ... that the plebiscite should be conducted on the basis of universal suffrage with all adult citizens of Western Samoa being entitled to vote; (Resol. 1569 (XV))
>
> (and decided) to appoint a United Nations Plebiscite Commissioner for Western Samoa who shall exercise, on behalf of the General Assembly, all the necessary powers and functions of supervision, and who shall be assisted by observers and staff to be appointed by the Secretary-General in consultation with him.

The Commissioner was requested to submit to the Trusteeship Council a report on the organization, conduct and result of the plebiscite.

The Plebiscite Commissioner, Najmuddine Rifai, was assisted by five observers, six U.N. headquarters staff and one field service staff.

On the whole, the Commissioner was satisfied with the preparations for and the actual conduct of the elections. However, at the time of the U.N. mission's arrival, he found that the population was unaware of the issues involved in the election. The measures which he recommended to increase the population's awareness of those issues were quickly implemented by the authorities.

On 9 March 1961, the Western Samoan voters overwhelmingly approved the constitution (82.8%) and agreed to Western Samoa's accession to independence on 1 January 1962 on the basis of that constitution (78.7%). The U.N. Plebiscite Commissioner stated with satisfaction that "the plebiscite was fair and impartial".

On 18 October 1961, the U.N. General Assembly concurred with his findings and agreed to endorse the results: it resolved, in agreement with the Administering

Authority, that the Trusteeship Agreement would cease to be in force upon the accession of Western Samoa to independence on 1 January 1962. (Resol. 1626 (XVI)).

On 11 May 1961, the Prime Minister of New Zealand welcomed the outcome of this peaceful decolonization process:

> The overwhelming vote of the Samoan people in favour of their country becoming independent at the end of this year, represents the culmination of a long period of cooperation between Western Samoa, New Zealand and the United Nations designed to prepare Western Samoa to take its place in the international community as a sovereign independent State. All three parties can take pride in the result – New Zealand because it will see a country formerly administered by it become the first fully independent Polynesian state, and the United Nations because it will see the value of the Trusteeship System demonstrated once again. But the main credit must go to the leaders of the Samoan people who have over many years worked untiringly for the advancement of their country.[22]

West Irian: From Colonial to Indonesian Rule without Self-determination. The territory of West New Guinea (West Irian) had been a Dutch possession since 1828. When the Netherlands formally recognized the sovereign independence of Indonesia in 1949, the status of West Irian remained unresolved. It was agreed in the Charter of Transfer of Sovereignty concluded between the Netherlands and Indonesia at The Hague in November 1949, that the issue would be postponed for a year and that "the *status quo* of the presidency of New Guinea" would be "maintained under the Government of the Netherlands" in the meantime. The two countries interpreted these terms differently: the Netherlands considered that the *status quo* meant their continued sovereignty over West Irian. Indonesia interpreted the Dutch role to be strictly administrative, with the implication that West Irian would be incorporated into Indonesia after a year.[23]

The status of the territory was still being disputed when Indonesia brought the matter before the U.N. in 1954. Indonesia claimed that the territory rightfully belonged to it and should be freed from Dutch colonial rule. The Netherlands maintained that the 700,000 Papuans and Pygmies of West New Guinea were neither racially nor culturally related to the Indonesians and therefore should be allowed to decide their own future when they were ready to do so.

The future of the territory was discussed at the General Assembly's regular sessions from 1954 to 1957 and in 1961, but not resolved.

In 1961, the Netherlands announced that it was now ready to allow the inhabitants to decide their own future by plebiscite, and asked the U.N. to administer the territory long enough to organize and conduct the voting. This proposal was rejected by Indonesia, with the support of India, which, having decided to annex Goa, wanted no precedent for an impartial, U.N.-conducted plebiscite.

However, 13 African states proposed to the General Assembly, in November 1961, a draft resolution which emphasized the right of the people of New Guinea to self-determination. The Ambassador from Niger said:

> What has greatly surprised us in this dispute is that one of the parties is not asking for the opinion of the people of New Guinea... It is for the people of New Guinea themselves to say, in the present circumstances, who is entitled to claim sovereignty over their territory.

The African draft resolution was rejected, not reaching the required two-thirds majority. It was opposed by the Socialist countries, most of Asia and the Arab nations.[24]

In December 1961, Acting Secretary-General U Thant offered his good offices to resolve the dispute. Following a U.S. suggestion, he proposed that informal talks take place between the parties in the presence of former U.S. Ambassador Ellsworth Bunker, who would act as his representative.

Tension increased between the two countries: in 1962, Indonesia landed paratroops in the territory. In May, the Prime Minister of the Netherlands stated that his country's presence in West New Guinea was of a temporary nature and that his government was prepared to give its fullest cooperation to the Secretary-General's efforts to find an honest and just solution for the territory on the basis of Article 73 of the Charter – concerning responsibilities of administering Powers towards non-self-governing territories – and General Assembly resolutions on the question of colonialism.

An agreement was signed in New York by Indonesia and the Netherlands on 15 August 1962, following negotiations held under the chairmanship of U Thant, with Ambassador Bunker acting as a mediator.

The agreement, noted by the General Assembly on 21 September (Resol. 1752 (XVII)), provided for the administration of West New Guinea to be transferred by the Netherlands to a U.N. Temporary Executive Authority (UNTEA). Under the Secretary-General's jurisdiction, UNTEA would have full authority after 1 October 1962 to administer the territory, to maintain law and order, to protect the rights of the inhabitants and to ensure uninterrupted, normal services until 1 May 1963, when the administration of the territory was to be transferred to Indonesia. Besides these extraordinary executive and administrative responsibilities, the U.N. was also entrusted with a peace-keeping role through the creation of a U.N. Security Force. U Thant noted that for the first time in its history the U.N. would have temporary executive authority established by and under the jurisdiction of the Secretary-General over a vast territory. Unfortunately, the role of the U.N. in legitimizing the Indonesian undemocratic implementation of the Western Guineans "freedom of choice" was less to be praised.

Articles XVII through XXI of the agreement addressed the issue of self-determination. Article XVIII contained the following terms of reference[25]:

> Indonesia will make arrangements, with the assistance and participation of the U.N. Representative and his staff, to give the people of the territory an opportunity to exercise freedom of choice. Such arrangements will include
> a) Consultations (mushawarah) with the representative councils on procedures and appropriate methods to be followed for ascertaining the freely expressed will of the population.
> b) The determination of the actual date of the exercise of free choice within the period established by the present agreement.
> c) Formulation of the questions in such a way as to permit the inhabitants to decide (a) whether they wish to remain with Indonesia; or (b) whether they wish to sever their ties with Indonesia.
> d) The eligibility of all adults, male and female, not foreign nationals to participate in the act of self-determination to be carried out in accordance with international practice . . .

Neither the words "plebiscite" or "referendum" were part of the agreement, – the option of "severing ties with Indonesia" should have read "independence as a sovereign state".

On 1 May 1963, the UNTEA Administrator transferred full administrative control over the territory, then called West Irian, to the representative of the Indonesian Government. The Secretary-General announced that he was appointing six U.N. experts, under the supervision of Under-Secretary-General Narasimhan, to report at intervals of approximately six months in the implementation of Indonesia's obligation to consult the population on their ultimate political status.

In fact, the population's ultimate fate had been pre-determined: the Indonesian authorities ensured that the population would not wish to sever its ties with Indonesia. Instead of a plebiscite by universal and secret suffrage, the "free choice" was put, in public, to 1026 "specially selected" delegates, gathering between 14 July and 2 August 1969 in well-controlled "representative" councils who unanimously voted in favour of remaining with Indonesia.

The U.N. Representative's efforts to insert some democratic practices into the consultation were rebuffed: his request that all sectors of the population be allowed to participate freely in the consultation was dismissed as well as his more modest request that "one-man one vote" elections should be held at least in the urban centres.[26]

In spite of these affronts to the U.N. and to himself, the U.N. Representative reported[27] that within

> the limitations imposed by the geographical characteristics of the territory and the general political situation in the area, an act of free choice has taken place in West Irian in accordance with Indonesian practice, in which the representatives of the population have expressed their wish to remain with Indonesia.

The General Assembly acknowledged with appreciation the fulfilment by the Secretary-General and his representatives of the task entrusted to them under the

1962 agreement (Resol. 2504 (XXIV)). The Assembly rejected a Ghanaian proposal which would have required another, more democratic act of self-determination.

Power politics and anti-colonialism had prevailed over the principle of self-determination, with the blessing of a majority of states in the U.N. General Assembly.

Palau: The Last U.N. Trust Territory. Palau is the last remaining U.N. Trust Territory and the last of the former "Trust Territory of the Pacific Islands". Its population is estimated at approximately 16,000.

Formerly Spanish, then German colonies, the islands were granted to Japan, after World War I, as a "C" mandate from the League of Nations. After World War II, the group of 2,100 Pacific Islands with 140,000 inhabitants was granted to the United States as a former League mandate and as a territory "detached from enemy states as a result of the Second World War" under Article 77 (a) and (b) of the Charter, with the status of a strategic trusteeship, under Articles 82 and 83 of the Charter. Only this territory was declared as a strategic trusteeship, with the consequence that all functions performed by the General Assembly in approving regular trusteeship agreements and in exercising supervisory powers are exercised by the Security Council. The purpose of this arrangement was to give the U.S. a potential veto over any action considered adverse to its security interests. In practice, the Security Council never exercised its supervisory powers, although it annually received reports from the Trusteeship Council, as did the General Assembly for all other trust territories.[28]

The trusteeship agreement was approved by the Security Council on 2 April 1947. Collectively known as Micronesia, these islands and atolls form three major archipelagos: the Marianas, the Carolines and the Marshalls.

The Congress of Micronesia, elected on the basis of universal adult suffrage, was established in 1965. Subsequently, the Northern Marianas (the Mariana Islands except Guam, an unincorporated territory of the U.S.) was administered separately from the Carolines and Marshalls, which constitute the Federated States of Micronesia.

A Covenant to establish a Commonwealth of the Northern Mariana Islands in Political Union with the U.S. was signed on 15 February 1975. In a plebiscite observed by a U.N. Visiting Mission on 17 June 1975, the Covenant was approved by a majority of the voters.

Other entities of the Trust Territory, the Federated States of Micronesia – consisting of the islands of Yap, Truk, Pohnpei and Kosrae (within the Carolines) – and the Marshall Islands, have Compacts of Free Association with the U.S., approved in U.N.-observed plebiscites in 1983. The Northern Mariana Islands voted in 1975 to become a Commonwealth of the U.S.

The Compacts recognize the territories' authority in internal and foreign affairs, but grant defence and security responsibility to the U.S., and provide for U.S. economic assistance.[29]

By a resolution voted in December 1990 (Res/45/683), the Security Council, in the light of the entry into force of new status agreements for those three entities, determined that the objectives of the Trusteeship Agreement had been fully attained and decided that the Trusteeship Agreement with them was terminated. Palau remained as the only entity under the 1947 Trusteeship Agreement.

In Palau, six plebiscites have been held under U.N. supervision regarding the proposed Compact: in February 1983, September 1984, February and December 1986, and June and August 1987. In each, a majority supported the Compact, but fewer than the 75% required by the Palau Constitution: the 1979 Constitution (adopted by a 92% majority) forbids the "use, testing, storage or disposal of harmful substances such as nuclear, chemical, gas or biological weapons" and requires that this policy could only be changed by a 75% vote. The nuclear provision in the Constitution is in accordance with the South Pacific Nuclear-Free Zone Treaty.

The most recent referendum in February 1990, observed by a U.N. five-member visiting mission, yielded 60.8% in favour of the Compact. The mission was composed of representatives of China, Fiji, France, Papua New Guinea and the United Kingdom. Its terms of reference were to monitor the polling arrangements, casting of votes, closure of voting, ballot counting and the declaration of the voting results.[30]

The U.S. told the Trusteeship Council in 1983 that introducing nuclear weapons into Palau was "necessary if the United States is to meet its responsibilities for the defense of Palau". Palau is a potential site for a major U.S. naval base.

In March 1992, a Trusteeship Council Visiting Mission went to Palau to observe current conditions. The mission also discussed the final political status of Palau, which should be determined by the Security Council.[31]

The trusteeship agreement is certain to be terminated, but the future status of Palau is still uncertain: there is a clear popular majority for a Compact of Free Association with the U.S., with attendant economic benefits, but some apparent, understandable, resistance against the introduction of U.S. nuclear weapons in the territory. Unless the U.S. withdraw their exigencies, this resistance might finally result in a vote for independence of the territory.

An Assessment

Leaving aside the Cold War cases of Korea and Germany, the few examples of early U.N. monitoring of electoral processes in trust and non-self-governing territories given in this Chapter call for positive and negative comments.

On the positive side, the creation and intervention of U.N. missions have served as a symbolic and concrete support for decolonisation through peaceful, democratic electoral methods. While not mandated to establish democracies in newly independent countries, the U.N. and its missions, more than the League of Nations, have generally reinforced the principle of peoples' self-determination, with a few unfortunate cases of distortion or rejection of the principle. The U.N. missions have generally tried to improve the electoral processes, to provide better information to the future voters and to obtain voting by universal adult suffrage of both men and women, by secret ballot. U.N. resolutions have generally formulated the text itself of the questions to be posed in a plebiscite or referendum, thus ensuring that voters may choose among clear alternatives. The terms of reference of some missions have included monitoring of the electoral preparations, and not only observation of the voting process. Finally, the U.N. was authorized, or requested, to monitor elections in some of the territories, and not only self-determination plebiscites or referenda, thus preparing the ground for later election monitoring in sovereign countries.

On the negative side, the U.N. bodies (Trusteeship Council, Special Committee, General Assembly) and the U.N. Observation Missions have not always demonstrated their political impartiality in relation to self-determination issues and operations. Not surprisingly in view of the Third World majority in most U.N. organs during the decolonisation era, they often showed a definite bias against colonial Powers and in favour of developing countries, even when some of the latter openly perverted or rejected democratic self-determination processes. The obvious explanation of this bias is that the main objective and focus of U.N. activities in this field were to promote decolonisation, and that this exclusive political goal prevailed over theoretical or ethical considerations of self-determination and democracy.

While colonial countries originally rejected or opposed U.N. decolonisation resolutions and enterprises, while some of them tried to artificially "suppress the problem" by integration and assimilation programmes, they became progressively convinced that internal autonomy then independence of their colonial possessions were inescapable, and that cooperation with the U.N. was preferable to yearly confrontations in the General Assembly, without mentioning unrest or armed rebellion in their colonies.

When requested by the General Assembly or the Trusteeship Council to organize plebiscites, referenda or elections under U.N. observation, colonial countries generally accepted and facilitated such international monitoring. They accepted such requests even when they applied to non-self-governing territories, and not only to trust territories. Even when they thought that a plebiscite was not really necessary as a prerequisite to independence, as in the case of Western Samoa, New Zealand and Western Samoa raised no objection to holding one if the General Assembly still considered it desirable.

The U.N. appeared at times more concerned with its goal of decolonisation and its militant anti-Western colonialism than about the options of self-determination to be offered to the people: thus the Special Committee's undemocratic "decision" that the question of accession to independence of Equatorial Guinea "shall not" be subject to any form of electoral consultation.

The Trusteeship Council rejected the French request for U.N. observation of a referendum in Togoland, as the referendum did not offer the alternative of independence, and not to be confronted with a *fait accompli*. On the other hand, the General Assembly had no hesitation in authorizing U.N. observation of a fraudulous people's "consultation" in West Irian and in legitimizing its well-planned outcome, which gave no real "freedom of choice" between integration with Indonesia and independence. U.N. abstention in this case would have preserved the dignity of the organization, its member States and its Secretariat.

If self-determination is an internationally recognized principle, why does it not apply to the people of West Irian, East Timor, Tibet, Kashmir and other territories, as it has been applied to trust and other colonial territories?

Finally, these first U.N. missions revealed a characteristic trend of international election monitoring, which is still valid today: it is easier for international observers to approve the results of an electoral process than to reject them for unfair campaigning, electoral fraud or manipulation, lack of civil and political freedoms, pressures on candidates and voters, destruction of ballots etc. It is tempting to minimize such flaws, to consider that they are not of "such magnitude" as to affect the results, in the belief that it would be politically or practically impossible, or ill-advised to cancel the elections and start a new electoral process. The political, diplomatic, financial and other constraints surrounding an intergovernmental organization such as the U.N. tend to reinforce this temptation, while international observers belonging to non-governmental organizations should be in a stronger position to make independent, non-diplomatic assessments.

Politically, the success of U.N. observation missions in trust and non-self-governing territories has depended first on the international support given in the U.N. and to the U.N. in initiating such operations, – secondly, on the agreement, cooperation and good faith of the administering Power.

Technically, certain basic requirements need to be fulfilled: they were lacking in some of the early U.N. missions:

- the mission's terms of reference need to be clearly formulated by the authorizing body (Trusteeship Council, Special Committee or General Assembly), agreed to by the administering Power and communicated to all local officials;
- the mission's composition must be really international, and be seen as impartial, in the same way as U.N. peace-keeping forces have been constituted; the early missionary spirit of anti-colonialism is incompatible with the need to show impartiality and neutrality;
- the mission's size must be related to the size of the territory and of the population, unless a purely symbolic presence is required, or unless the U.N. mission may be supplemented by a sufficient number of other international observers from other organizations and governments;
- a mission needs to arrive in the territory well in advance of election (or plebiscite, or referendum) day: its members need time to meet the local officials, the electoral Commission if any, to familiarize themselves with the institutions, electoral law, procedures, territory and polling stations, – they need time to assess possible flaws and problems, make suggestions and see them applied; to

make arrangements for liaison and cooperation with other international observers;

– following the electoral process and announcement of the results, the mission's report must be carefully drafted and agreed, then forwarded to the authorizing authority.

Besides these political and operational requirements, which apply generally to all international observation missions, and not only to the now obsolete decolonization missions, the credibility of the U.N. and other international observers' mission relies essentially on the competence and independence of its members.

Notes

1. For a definition of first and second generation peace-keeping operations, in a broader context, see V.Y. Ghebali, "Le développement des opérations de maintien de la paix de l'ONU depuis la fin de la guerre froide" and comments by G. Abi-Saab in *Le Trimestre du Monde*, 1992/4, pp. 67–97.
2. This section is based on the following references: Evan Luard, *A History of the U.N.*, Vol. 1, Macmillan, 1984, pp. 229–239, (with permission) –Dennis J. Amato, "Elections under International Auspices – 1948–1970", unpublished dissertation, 1971, U.M.I. Dissertation Information Service, pp. 485–494, –Leon Gordenker, *The U.N. and the Peaceful Unification of Korea – The Politics of Field Operations, 1947–1950*, Nijhoff, 1959.
3. The Commission was to consist of representatives of Australia, Canada, China, El Salvador, France, India, Philippines, Syria, Ukraine.
4. Gordenker, op.cit., pp. 105–106.
5. Amato, op.cit., pp. 491–494.
6. Luard, op.cit., pp. 236–239.
7. Amato, op.cit., p. 490.
8. Universal Declaration of Human Rights, Art. 21.3.
9. Developments in this section are mainly based on Luard, op.cit., pp. 226–228, and Amato, op.cit., pp. 574–575.
10. Luard, op.cit., p. 228.
11. As references, see *Basic Facts about the U.N.*, U.N., 1989, pp. 64–67, – *The Blue Helmets – A Review of U.N. Peace-keeping*, U.N., 2nd Ed., 1990, pp. 155–171, –Luard, op.cit., pp. 278–294, – A. LeRoy Bennett, *International Organizations*, 3rd Ed., Prentice-Hall, 1984, pp. 114–117.
12. *New York Times*, Letters, 4 April 1992, – *International Herald Tribune*, 18 Aug. 1992, – *Newsweek*, 7 Dec. 1992, – *Le Monde*, 9 Dec. 1992. See also *International Herald Tribune* of 7 and 8 January 1993 for reports of a massacre of at least 40 people, 100 people wounded, setting houses and markets on fire by Indian paramilitary forces in the Kashmir town of Sopore, in revenge for an attack by anti-Indian militants. The Indian Government denies that human rights violations occur.
13. Amato, op.cit., p. 51. References for part of our text are summarized from Amato's Chapter III, "The Elections in French Togoland – 1958". See also, *Everyone's U.N.*, 1979, p. 278 and U.N. Doc. A/C.4/35. "B" mandates were especially former German colonies in Central Africa "at such a stage that the Mandatory must be responsible for the administration of the territory ..." – Art. 22.5 of the League's Covenant.
14. See U.N. Doc. T/1269 of 6 July 1956 and A/3173 of 5 Sept. 1956.
15. Amato, op.cit., p. 90.
16. Ibid., p. 132.
17. Ibid., Chap. VI.
18. Ibid., p. 325.

19. Ibid., p. 342.
20. "C" mandates were those "territories, such as South West Africa and certain of the South Pacific Islands, which owing to the sparseness of their population, or their small size, or their remoteness from the centres of civilization, or their geographical contiguity to the territory of the Mandatory, and other circumstances, can be best administered under the laws of the Mandatory as integral portions of its territory ...", – Art. 22.6 of the Covenant.
21. U.N. Doc. T/1564 of 23 June 1961, "Report of the U.N. Commissioner for the Supervision of the Plebiscite in Western Samoa", – Amato, op.cit., pp. 502–506, – see also *Everyone's U.N.*, p. 280.
22. U.N. Doc. T/1564, pp. 50–51.
23. This section is based on *The Blue Helmets*, op.cit., Chap. XII, – see also Amato, op.cit., pp. 565–570, – Bennett, *op.cit.*, pp. 162–163, – Thomas M. Franck, *Nation against Nation – What happened to the U.N. Dream and What the U.S. can do about it*, Oxford University Press, 1985, pp. 76–82.
24. Franck, op.cit., pp. 77–78.
25. Amato, op.cit., pp. 567–568, – *U.N. Treaty Series*, Vol. 437, 1962, p. 282.
26. Franck, op.cit., pp. 81–82.
27. U.N. Doc. A/7723, Annex I.
28. Bennett, op.cit., p. 332.
29. *Everyone's U.N.*, op.cit., pp. 281–282, – *U.N. Chronicle*, Sept. 1989, pp. 28–30, – *A Global Agenda – Issues before the 47th General Assembly of the U.N.*, J. Tessitore and S. Woolfson, U.N. Association of the U.S.A., 1992, University Press of America, p. 115.
30. U.N. *Press Release* DH/561 of 9 Jan. 1990. In a referendum held on 4 August 1987, a constitutional amendment was adopted allowing, in a subsequent referendum, the Compact to be approved by simple majority. In a U.N.-supervised referendum held on 21 August, the Compact was approved by 73.04% in favour: however, the Palau Supreme Court declared the 4 August referendum a nullity, thus reversing the decision of the 21 August referendum.
31. See U.N. Doc. T/RES/2194 (S-XXI) of 19 Dec. 1991, Resolution adopted by the Trusteeship Council, and "Report of the U.N. Visiting Mission to Palau, Trust Territory of the Pacific Islands, 1992", Trusteeship Council, OR:59th Session, May–June 1992, Suppl. No.1, T/1964.

CHAPTER 6

THE SECOND GENERATION: COMPLETED "PRO-DEMOCRACY" U.N. OPERATIONS

Ghebali has identified U.N. peace-keeping operations of a "second generation", as those initiated since 1989 with a broader mandate than traditional "peace-keeping", in the sense of freezing a conflict through an agreed ceasefire and separating the combatants, without attempting to resolve the dispute. "Second generation" operations have been concerned with "peace-building" and not only with peace-keeping: they have been entrusted with a broader, more active and more complex role in fulfilling such functions as nation-building, national reconciliation, internal democratisation and protection of humanitarian assistance.

For Abi-Saab, the second generation operations have extended their action vertically, towards essentially internal conflicts with some international implications, – and horizontally, to include all the range of the Charter's peace-maintenance strategy, in a broad sense. The military dimension of first generation peace-keeping operations is not necessarily predominant in second generation operations: their peace-building tasks include the improvement, through cooperation, of economic, social and cultural conditions, – and respect of human rights, in order to reach and possibly eradicate the deep roots of conflicts. Their tasks may also include the creation of conditions favouring political and social reconciliation and stability in a particular country. Finally, the success of some of these operations is dependent on the cooperation and support of not only governments, but also non-governmental entities such as liberation, rebel and legal or illegal opposition movements or groups.[1]

It should also be recalled that first or second generation peace-keeping forces did not have enforcement powers under Chapter VII of the U.N. Charter, until the Somalia precedent approved by the Security Council in March 1993 (Resol. 814).

In our more narrow field, U.N. observation missions of the first generation were only concerned with self-determination in trust and non-self-governing territories – they had no democratic mandate, except that of ensuring that the self-determination process was as free and fair as possible – they were relatively small operations with a limited number of observers and supporting staff.

U.N. electoral monitoring operations of the second generation are either a part of larger and more complex operations, with a broad mandate, or they are wholly focused on monitoring of national elections. Most of the operations, but not all, have been operationally and administratively modelled on the U.N. "peace-keeping forces" format, although their objectives and functions were different, with less, or no emphasis on military presence.

Two of these new operations, Namibia and Western Sahara, concern non-self-governing territories: however, the U.N. was not called into Namibia to observe a self-determination process, as independence had been decided decades before by U.N. bodies and the South West Africa People's Organization (SWAPO), the main liberation movement. The central objective of the U.N. operation was to create conditions for the holding of free and fair elections for a Constituent Assembly which would draw up a Constitution under which Namibia would proceed to independence as a free and sovereign State. Namibia was born as a democratic nation under U.N. auspices through a democratic process.

The U.N. Western Sahara operation is, or should be, a decolonisation and self-determination exercise in a former dependent territory. However, in contrast with "first generation" U.N. missions where the organization and conduct of plebiscites or referenda remained with the administering authorities, the Special Representative of the U.N. Secretary-General should have sole and exclusive responsibility over all matters relating to the self-determination referendum, including its organization and conduct. This operation, which is reviewed in Chapter 7, is meeting serious obstacles.

The other completed or on-going "second generation" operations contain the most striking innovation: they involve the U.N. in a matter which is "essentially within the domestic jurisdiction" of states, i.e. monitoring the planning, organization and conduct of national elections and assessing their fairness, in apparent contradiction with Art. 2.7 of the U.N. Charter. While such operations have only been carried out at the request of the State's authorities, their justification by relating such new U.N. activity to present or potential international security problems has appeared somewhat shallow: their real, proper justification is by reference to the promotion and encouragement of respect for human rights and for fundamental freedoms (Art. 1.3 of the Charter).

In this Chapter, we will review the following completed operations: Namibia, Nicaragua, Haiti and Angola. On-going operations in Western Sahara, Cambodia, El Salvador and Mozambique will be reviewed in the next Chapter.

However, mention will first be made of a small size, short U.N. mission sent by the U.N. Secretary-General to Panama in 1977, a discreet but extraordinary precedent in allowing the U.N. to observe an electoral process in a sovereign country.

The "Witnessing" Mission to Panama

On 13 September 1977, the U.N. Secretary-General received the following cable from General Omar Torrijos Herrera, head of the Government of the Republic of Panama:

On 23 October the Panamanian people will be going to the polls to vote on the new Panama Canal treaties. This will be a day of vital significance to the whole world. We invite you to come here or to appoint your representative to see how the people of Panama freely decide whether or not they approve of the new treaties. We hope that your representative will inform you and the international community of the freedom with which the Panamanians exercise their right to determine their destiny.

The Secretary-General accepted this invitation and appointed, on 11 October 1977, his Legal Counsel, Mr. Erik Suy, Under-Secretary-General, as his Special Representative whose mandate would be to witness how the people of Panama pronounced themselves upon the treaties between Panama and the U.S.A. signed at Washington, D.C. on 7 September 1977, the Carter-Torrijos Treaties. Mr. Suy was accompanied by six U.N. officials in his mission, which lasted from 19 October to 26 October.

The mission members observed pre-plebiscite campaigning, the voting itself in Panama City and a number of provinces, and the vote-counting.

In his report (Doc. A/32/424), the Special Representative stated that the mission was able to observe at first hand that the plebiscite proceeded calmly, in a very orderly fashion and with a full participation of the people. The atmosphere throughout the country was one of "sobriety and civil pride". In its visits to the polling stations, the mission was completely free to observe at all stages of the process. Having previously familiarized itself with the plebiscite law and regulations, the mission inspected the boxes and the ballot papers to ensure that they conformed with the regulations and observed the various stages of identification, inscription and fingerprinting of individual voters. The mission also observed the surrounding areas to identify possible attempts to influence voters in their decision.

The Special Representative reported that, thanks to the full cooperation and logistic support of the Panamanian authorities, he and his team were able to perform their functions in the best conditions and in total independence. It was his feeling that the plebiscite was extremely well prepared and that the plebiscite itself took place in an atmosphere of calm and in accordance with the usual democratic standards. Except for minor anomalies observed in some polling stations, which were often corrected on the spot, the Special Representative had come to the conclusion that the plebiscite of 23 October 1977 took place in a normal way and that it was an example in democracy.

966,232 votes had been cast, 706,805 voted in favour of the ratification of the treaties, 245,117 against, 14,310 were invalid ballots.

This "witnessing" mission (a euphemism for "observation") was a first: for the first time, the U.N. had sent a mission to observe an electoral process in a sovereign country, at that country's request. No debates by Member States had preceded the U.N. approval, given by the U.N. Secretary-General himself, without formal prior endorsement by the General Assembly or the Security Council, even though the

General Assembly was in session. The General Assembly was only "informed" *post facto* by the report of the mission, circulated at the request of the Permanent Representative of Panama.

The motivation of Panama in obtaining an international recognition of the democratic fairness of the plebiscite seems clear. As to the U.N., Secretary-General Kurt Waldheim consulted the U.S., the other party to the Panama Treaty, who raised no objection to Panama's request. Panama agreed to assume the costs of the U.N. mission. It appears that such factors as the Secretary-General's willingness and possibility of satisfying quickly and effectively a Member State's request, the U.S. agreement and the international aspect of the plebiscite (to ratify a bilateral treaty with international implications), overrode any other consideration, such as the question of principle, which was raised forcefully later: is the monitoring of electoral processes (plebiscites, referenda or elections) in sovereign States within the mandate of the U.N., and if so, under what conditions may such operations be authorized?

In fact, this small, discreet and successful "witnessing" operation created an informal precedent, a successful test-case, for the later, more ambitious U.N. monitoring operations which will now be reviewed.

Namibia: The Birth of a Democratic Nation

Historical Background

European traders and missionaries arrived in South West Africa in the mid-19th century. In 1884, Germany declared a protectorate over South West Africa. During World War I, South Africa invaded the territory: the last of Germany's troops surrendered in 1915.[2]

The Peace Conference rejected South Africa's request to annex South West Africa. After five years of military occupation, the territory was placed under a class "C" mandate of the League of Nations in December 1920, a compromise between claims by South Africa, New Zealand and Australia for annexation of the former German territories and President Wilson's opposition to annexation by the victors. Under Art. 22.6 of the Covenant, South West Africa would be administered under the laws of the mandatory as an integral portion of its territory, under undefined safeguards. The only obligation of South Africa was to submit a yearly report to the League's Council.

In 1925, South Africa promulgated a constitution for the territory that mandated administrative control to the white population, established a legislative assembly and an Administrator-General, with the latter exercising executive authority.

After World War II, on 14 December 1946, the U.N. General Assembly rejected South Africa's renewed claim for the incorporation of the territory as a fifth province. South Africa refused to place the territory under the new international trusteeship system. When it rose to power in 1948, the South African National Party gave whites in the territory direct representation in the Republic of South Africa's parliament and threatened to incorporate South West Africa unilaterally.

On 11 July 1950, the International Court of Justice ruled, in an Advisory Opinion, that South Africa had no obligation to conclude a trusteeship agreement with the U.N., but held also that the mandate was still in force and that South Africa had no right to unilaterally change the territory's international status. In 1960, Ethiopia and Liberia challenged South African control of South West Africa in the Court. On 18 July 1966, a divided Court ruled that these countries lacked standing to make the challenge.

Following the Court's decision, the South West Africa Peoples' Organization (SWAPO), the insurgency movement which had contested South African control of Namibia since the sixties, adopted, also in July, a policy of "armed struggle" against South Africa's occupation.

In October 1966, the General Assembly revoked South Africa's mandate and declared the territory to be the direct responsibility of the U.N. (Resol. 2145 (XXI)). In May 1967, it established the U.N. Council for South West Africa, *inter alia*,

> to administer South West Africa until independence, with the maximum participation of the people of the Territory. (Resol. 2248 (S-V))

In 1968, the General Assembly adopted the name "Namibia" for the territory. In 1969, the Security Council endorsed the resolutions of the General Assembly (Resol. 264 and 269 (1969)): it called upon South Africa to withdraw its administration from the territory. On 30 January 1970, the Security Council declared that the continued presence there of the South African authorities was illegal (Resol. 276). In an Advisory Opinion of 21 June 1971, the Court also found that the continued presence of South Africa in Namibia was illegal and that South Africa was under an obligation to withdraw its administration immediately.[3]

In 1973, the General Assembly created the post of U.N. Commissioner for Namibia.

South Africa, however, ignored the U.N. bodies' and the Court's orders and opinions: it continued administering the territory as before.

In 1975, it convened a constitutional conference in Windhoek of the leaders of the homelands set up under the Odendaal Plan. In 1964, the Plan had divided the territory into 12 regions, or homelands, with over 60% of the land remaining under the control of the whites. SWAPO was not invited to the conference. The Turnhalle group, supported by South Africa, established an interim government and agreed to aim for independence at the end of 1976.

The independence of Angola and Mozambique in 1975, following the overthrow of the Portuguese dictatorship in 1974, led to an intensification of anti-colonialist struggles in still-dependent African territories. In Angola, a Soviet-supported government had come to power, the Marxist "Popular Movement for the Liberation of Angola" (MPLA), which then had to fight, with Cuban troops' support, a civil war against the "National Union for the Total Independence of Angola" (UNITA), financed by the U.S.A. and assisted by South African forces.

American policy towards South Africa and Namibia evolved in opposite directions. The U.S., Britain and France traditionally opposed resolutions condemning South Africa. Then, in 1985, Secretary of State Henry Kissinger, fearing further Soviet and Cuban involvement in Southern Africa, favoured the independence of Namibia, hoping for the establishment of a moderate regime.[4]

This new approach resulted in the adoption by the Security Council, on 30 January 1976, of Resolution 385, which provided a basis for the ultimate settlement of the Namibian affair. The strongly worded resolution notably called for South African withdrawal from Namibia within six months, the release of all political prisoners, the abolition of all racially discriminatory and politically repressive laws and practices, an unconditional amnesty for Namibian exiles and free elections to be held under U.N. supervision for the whole of Namibia as one political entity.

On 20 December 1976, the General Assembly recognized SWAPO as the sole and authentic representative of the Namibian people and supported SWAPO's armed struggle (Resol. 31/146): this one-sided approach did not seem to be consistent with the Security Council's more constructive proposal for a settlement and free elections: how could SWAPO be recognized as the "sole and authentic representative of the Namibian people", when SWAPO leaders had not been freely elected by the Namibian people? The U.N. had not yet chosen its role: either that of an aggressive supporter of Namibia's decolonisation, an independent Namibia to be then ruled by SWAPO, or that of a benevolent, neutral supervisor of a political settlement involving monitoring of free elections by independent (U.N.) observers.

In 1977, five Western members of the Security Council – Canada, France, the Federal Republic of Germany, the United Kingdom and the United States – known as the "Western Contact Group" tried to find a settlement of the Namibian question. They attempted to persuade South Africa to agree to Namibian independence under U.N. supervision. They worked principally with South Africa, SWAPO and the front-line states, then comprising Angola, Botswana, Mozambique, Tanzania and Zambia, who supported SWAPO. A round of "proximity talks" held in New York in February 1978 produced the "Proposal for a settlement of the Namibian situation", which was accepted by South Africa conditionally on 25 April 1978 and by SWAPO on 12 July of the same year.

The Settlement Proposal and the Secretary-General's report of 29 August for its implementation formed the basis for Security Council Resolution 435, adopted on 29 September 1978.

The Settlement Proposal was a negotiated compromise. It allowed South Africa, through an Administrator-General designated by it, to administer elections, but under U.N. supervision and control exercised through a Special Representative of the Secretary-General, who would be assisted by a "United Nations Transition Assistance Group" (UNTAG). The Special Representative would have to satisfy himself at each stage of the political and electoral process as to the fairness and appropriateness of all related measures. The following principles were agreed and guaranteed: universal adult suffrage, secret ballot, freedom of parties to organize and participate in the electoral process, freedoms of speech, assembly, movement and press.

The implementation of the resolution, which established the definitive plan for Namibian independence, was however delayed for ten years, through South African obstruction, with the support of a new American foreign policy orientation under the two successive Reagan administrations, as well as by opposite objections raised by SWAPO. Brian Urquhart, an influential actor in the negotiations as U.N. Under-Secretary-General, referred to the "reluctance of both South Africa and SWAPO to agree to anything sensible", and to the South Africans' "perennial search for a new and insurmountable obstacle to progress".[5]

South Africa was trying to strengthen Namibian political parties opposed to SWAPO and to destabilize Angola, so as to force it to stop its material support for SWAPO and the African National Congress. Then the "linkage" subordinating Namibian independence to the withdrawal of Cuban troops from Angola, a new American policy adopted in 1982, was another justification for South Africa to delay the proposed U.N. settlement. The linkage condition was rejected by SWAPO and the non-aligned movement, but also by France, Canada and Germany.

Meanwhile, two important agreements were negotiated and agreed upon in 1982.

The Agreement on constitutional and electoral principles was to ensure that elections to the Constituent Assembly and the Constitution to be approved by the Assembly fully respected democratic criteria, in line with Western democratic values and practices. While the electoral provisions and fundamental freedoms restated the principles of the Settlement Proposal of 1978, the Agreement added to these a mandatory blueprint for a democratic State through a democratic Constitution: the Constitution as supreme law, separation of powers between the three branches of government, periodic and genuine elections by secret vote for the executive and legislative, – an independent judiciary – a declaration of fundamental rights etc.

This extraordinary Agreement, unprecedented in previous decolonization cases, was approved by the Contact Group and the parties to the Namibian conflict: the Secretary-General stressed in 1989 that this agreement was part of the Resolution 435 process and binding on the parties. The text of the Agreement is in Table 6.1.

In September 1982, the Frontline states, Nigeria, SWAPO and the Contact Group reached agreement on steps to ensure the U.N.'s impartiality in the process: the role of the U.N. was to change from being an active supporter of SWAPO to that of an impartial actor in the implementation of the Settlement plan. The U.N. would not provide funds for SWAPO or any other party during the transition period. The U.N. Council for Namibia and the U.N. Commissioner for Namibia would suspend all political or other public activities during that period. SWAPO would voluntarily forego the exercise of special privileges granted by the General Assembly, including participation as an official observer.[6]

Table 6.1. Principles concerning the Constituent Assembly and the Constitution for an Independent Namibia

A. Constituent Assembly

1. In accordance with United Nations Security Council resolution 435(1978), elections will be held to select a Constituent Assembly which will adopt a Constitution for an independent Namibia. The Constitution will determine the organization and powers of all levels of government.
- Every adult Namibian will be eligible, without discrimination or fear of intimidation from any source, to vote, campaign and stand for election to the Constituent Assembly.
- Voting will be by secret ballot, with provisions made for those who cannot read or write.
- The date for the beginning of the electoral campaign, the date of elections, the electoral system, the preparation of voters rolls and other aspects of electoral procedures will be promptly decided upon so as to give all political parties and interested persons, without regard to their political views, a full and fair opportunity to organize and participate in the electoral process.
- Full freedom of speech, assembly, movement and press shall be guaranteed.
- The electoral system will seek to ensure fair representation in the Constituent Assembly to different political parties which gain substantial support in the elections.
- The Constituent Assembly will formulate the Constitution for an independent Namibia in accordance with the principles in part B below and will adopt the Constitution as a whole by a two-thirds majority of its total membership.

B. Principles for a Constitution for an Independent Namibia

1. Namibia will be a unitary, sovereign and democratic State.
2. The Constitution will be the supreme law of the State. It may be amended only by a designated process involving the legislature or votes cast in a popular referendum, or both.
3. The Constitution will determine the organization and powers of all levels of government. It will provide for a system of government with three branches: an elected executive branch which will be responsible to the legislative branch; a legislative branch to be elected by universal and equal suffrage which will be responsible for the passage of all laws; and an independent judicial branch which will be responsible for the interpretation of the Constitution and for ensuring its supremacy and the authority of the law. The executive and legislative branches will be constituted by periodic and genuine elections which will be held by secret vote.
4. The electoral system will be consistent with the principles in A.1 above.
5. There will be a declaration of fundamental rights, which will include the rights to life, personal liberty and freedom of movement; to freedom of conscience; to freedom of expression, including freedom of speech and a free press; to freedom of assembly and association, including political parties and trade unions; to due process and equality before the law; to protection from arbitrary deprivation of private property or deprivation of private property without just compensation; and to freedom from racial, ethnic, religious or sexual discrimination. The declaration of rights will be consistent with the provisions of the Universal Declaration of Human Rights. Aggrieved individuals will be entitled to have the courts adjudicate and enforce these rights.
6. It will be forbidden to create criminal offences with retrospective effect or to provide for increased penalties with retrospective effect.
7. Provision will be made for the balanced structuring of the public service, the police service and the defence services and for equal access by all to recruitment of these services. The fair administration of personnel policy in relation to these services will be assured by appropriate independent bodies.
8. Provision will be made for the establishment of elected councils for local or regional administration, or both.

Source: Annex to letter dated 12 July 1982 from the Representatives of Canada, France, the Federal Republic of Germany, the United Kingdom of Great Britain and Northern Ireland and the United States of America to the Secretary-General – U.N. Doc. S/15287.

During 1987 and 1988, the combatants in the Namibian and Angolan conflicts fought to a military stalemate in southern Angola.

However, the political stalemate was broken in 1988, thanks mainly to a new American policy encouraged by the changes in the USSR, which allowed the two powers to work in unison to try to extinguish a few regional conflicts, by applying appropriate pressure on their "client" states or liberation movements.

At the same time, South Africa had finally decided to withdraw from Namibia for political, military and economic reasons. Politically, the end of the Cold War meant, for Pretoria, that anti-apartheid movements such as the African National Congress would no longer be supported by "Marxist" States bordering on South Africa. It would therefore no longer be necessary to destabilize these States, and particularly Angola. South Africa had had a few military setbacks in Angola and was unwilling to accept more casualties. The country was enduring an economic crisis, in part due to the financial costs of the occupation of Namibia and of the fighting against SWAPO and the Angolan forces. Finally, South African leaders wished their country to be less of an international "pariah" by acceding to long-term demands and pressures in favour of Namibia's independence.

Other contributing factors to a settlement were the war weariness of Angola and SWAPO, and Angolan well-founded fears of a reduction in Soviet assistance.

Between May and August 1988, the U.S. government arranged, with Soviet support, for delegations from Angola, Cuba and South Africa to meet in London, Cairo and New York. Under the mediation of the U.S., in the presence of a Soviet observer, the parties agreed to a statement of principles for a regional settlement, encompassing the Namibian situation, and solving the "linkage" claim. In a letter of 12 August 1988 to the Secretary-General, President Sam Nujoma indicated that SWAPO, although not a party to the Protocol, would observe the ceasefire started on 12 August and welcomed the fixing of 1 November as the firm date for the commencement of the implementation of Resolution 435. He asked the Secretary-General to initiate consultations with the parties concerned.

In September 1988, the Secretary-General informed the South African State President, P. W. Botha, that the system of proportional representation had been agreed on for elections in Namibia.

On 13 December, the parties agreed to and signed the Protocol of Brazzaville, committing them to two treaties: a trilateral pact among Angola, Cuba and South Africa providing for the implementation of Resolution 435 beginning on 1 April 1989, and a related bilateral treaty between Angola and Cuba providing for the phased withdrawal of Cuban troops, to be completed by mid-1991. On 20 December 1988, the Security Council established the United Nations Angola Verification Mission (UNAVEM) to verify the redeployment and phased withdrawal of Cuban troops in accordance with the agreement (Resol. 626(1988)).

Approval of the Operation

While the final outcome of the U.N. operation was a "happy end", two incidents, of a different nature but possibly related, affected the operation.

On 16 January 1989, the Security Council adopted Resolution 628 and 629, officially welcoming the signing of the agreements between Angola, Cuba and South Africa, and decided that implementation would start on 1 April. It called on South Africa to reduce the size of its police presence in Namibia. However, serious concern emerged in the Security Council about the cost and the appropriate size of the UNTAG military contingent: this "serious concern" had been initiated by the Reagan administration[7] and then shared by the other permanent members of the Council, who would have to pay most of the costs under the U.N. scale of assessments.

Against the opposition of the Organization of African Unity, the Frontline states and SWAPO, the Secretary-General then offered a compromise: although the authorized upper limit for the military force was to remain at the 7,500 number provided by Resolution 435, the initial size would be set at 4,650, thus reducing the estimated cost of the operation from approximately $700 million to $416. The final bill, on completion of the operation, came to approximately $383 million.

The Security Council approved the Secretary-General's proposals on 16 February, and the General Assembly approved the UNTAG budget on 1 March.

More than the cost and consequent size reduction of UNTAG, the time taken to come to a final decision and approval delayed the timely implementation of the operation, and in particular, the deployment of "Blue Helmets" in Namibia: this may have played a role in the most serious 1 April crisis, which could have ended the whole transition process on the first day of its implementation.

U.N. Transition Assistance Group in Namibia (UNTAG)

The Secretary-General had proposed that the ceasefire should be effective at 0400 hours GMT on 1 April: SWAPO and South Africa formally accepted the proposal on 18 and 21 March respectively.

On 31 March the Special Representative of the Secretary-General, Mr. Martti Ahtisaari, arrived in Windhoek to assume his duties in Namibia. He was then told by the South African Administrator-General (AG) that heavily armed SWAPO forces, in combat uniform, had begun moving forward and crossing from Angola into Namibia, many other being poised to follow. Military action and casualties followed.

On 1 April, the South African Foreign Minister told the Secretary-General that if UNTAG was unable to contain the new situation, it would be necessary for his Government again to deploy its military forces which had, earlier that day, been confined to base under UNTAG monitoring in accordance with the Settlement Proposal.

UNTAG was not yet effectively deployed in the territory. Apart from the military observers and monitors, few personnel, military or civilian, had arrived and their operational capability was severely hampered by the lack of vehicles and communications. Even if sufficient U.N. forces had been deployed, the Blue Helmets could not have engaged in any fighting against SWAPO, nor could they have prevented the South African forces from leaving their bases. Their presence in sufficient numbers might, however, have persuaded the SWAPO fighters to return to Angola, or to release their arms when entering Namibia.

In the circumstances, the Special Representative and the U.N. Force Commander recommended to the Secretary-General that they be authorized to accept a strictly limited and temporary suspension of the South African Defence Force confinement to base: this recommendation was accepted.

On 8 April, SWAPO's President announced that the SWAPO leadership had decided to order its forces within Namibia to stop fighting, regroup and report to Angola within 72 hours under the escort of UNTAG.

After further fighting and negotiations, a *de facto* cessation of hostilities, the confinement of SWAPO forces north of the 16th parallel and the confinement of South African forces to their bases, under UNTAG monitoring, were only effective on 13 May.

Between 300 and 400 combatants, mostly on the SWAPO side, had been killed, and mutual distrust and hostility had been reawakened.

The bloody incident had almost wrecked the whole U.N. operation: South Africa could have used it as a motive or a pretext to withdraw from the transition process.

South Africa and Western countries maintained that the SWAPO incursion was a violation of Resolution 435 and the 1988 Geneva Protocol.

SWAPO first denied that its forces had crossed the border from Angola: its leaders asserted that the fighting involved guerrillas already based in Northern Namibia who were reporting to U.N. checkpoints for confinement to bases under U.N. supervision. The Secretary-General reported to the Security Council, on 3 April, that UNTAG was of the view that SWAPO had infiltrated armed personnel and material into Namibia around the time of the ceasefire, but without offensive intent.[8]

SWAPO's responsibility in the incident appears credible: some observers believe that SWAPO had sent troops into the territory after the ceasefire in order to make its military presence a *fait accompli*, in order to increase its political prestige and influence in the future elections. Another explanation is that SWAPO, not being a party to the negotiations leading to Resolution 435 and to the Geneva Protocol, did not find itself bound by these agreements, or misunderstood its requirements. A less credible excuse is that the incursion was an initiative taken by local SWAPO chiefs, without prior approval by the SWAPO leadership.

Besides the human losses, the loss of prestige of SWAPO and the threat to the still fragile agreements, the incursion and subsequent fighting caused a six-week delay in the implementation of the operation.

UNTAG was composed of a military contingent of 4,650 troops, including 1,700 logistics and support personnel, with an undeployed reserve of 2,350. Its civilian contingent was made up of:

- 1,498 U.N. police observers;
- 1,700 registration and election supervisors, of whom 800 were recruited by 28 governments;
- 441 administrative office staff until the election period, when an additional 1,000 professionals and 200 field staff were required.[9]

In addition to UNTAG, a large number of voluntary missions and groups, representing governments as well as non-governmental organizations, monitored the process and reported to their constituents.

In order to create the political conditions for free and fair elections, UNTAG had to ensure, initiate or monitor the following:

- the South African military structure in Namibia had to be dismantled;
- the South West Africa Police had to be brought under effective monitoring;
- SWAPO forces had to be confined to base in Angola;
- discriminatory and restrictive legislation had to be repealed;
- political prisoners and detainees had to be released;
- an amnesty for returnees had to be proclaimed; and
- thousands of Namibian exiles had to be returned.

All these matters required negotiations between the U.N. Special Representative and the South African Administrator-General, and sometimes with the South African government itself. None of these issues were easily resolved.

As scheduled, the South Africa Defence Forces were reduced to 1,500 men by 24 June, under UNTAG monitoring. The remaining 1,500 were withdrawn after the certification of the elections, on 21 November.

The monitoring of the South West Africa Police, in which 2,000 members of "Koevoet", the brutal counter-insurgency unit, had been absorbed, created major problems to UNTAG: the Koevoet forces were a major part of the problem of law and order, as emphasized by UNTAG officials.

Following negotiations in New York and Windhoek, 56 discriminatory or restrictive laws were repealed in the Summer of 1989: these instruments of colonial repression and apartheid were incompatible with the holding of free elections by universal suffrage.

An Amnesty Proclamation was promulgated on 6 June, thus permitting the repatriation programme. UNHCR carried out this programme, together with other U.N. agencies. In Namibia, the Council of Churches was UNHCR's implementing partner. A massive airlift started in June. By the end of the process, 42,736 Namibians had been brought back from exile.

Monitoring the Electoral Process

Though the electoral process remained under the responsibility of the South African Administrator-General, every step in the process took place under active supervision and control of the U.N. Special Representative and UNTAG: in effect, the Special Representative had a veto right on each step, which reinforced its negotiating position.[10]

As regards registration of voters, the Administrator-General issued a draft Proclamation on 24 April which was rejected in its entirety by the Special Representative: according to the Commonwealth Observer Group, the draft seemed designed to keep Namibia in a quasi-colonial status.[11] Following intensive negotiations between the two parties, including direction from the U.N. Secretary-General from New York, the Special Representative finally gave his consent on 26 June to a much amended Proclamation, which was duly issued.

The Special Representative's consent was conditional upon the Administrator-General's agreement to an exchange of letters which defined in detail UNTAG's role in the registration process. In particular, it contained the important provision that no application for registration could be rejected without the concurrence of an UNTAG official. Provision was made for appeals and for the receipt of objections to registrations.

Registration of voters began on 3 July and was to close on 15 September. At the Special Representative's request, this was extended to 23 September, so that all eligible voters would be given an opportunity to register. In accordance with the Proclamation, anyone over the age of 18 could vote, if he or she was born in Namibia, or if they had been continuously resident there for four years, or if they were the child of a person born in Namibia.

Seventy registration centres were established, together with 110 mobile registration teams which covered 2,200 points throughout the country. Each registration was supervised by UNTAG officials and the civilian police of UNTAG was present at each location. The central register was supervised by UNTAG computer experts. 701,403 Namibians were registered on the electoral rolls.

An agreed Proclamation was then issued on the registration of political parties for the election: 10 parties registered.

At the instigation of the Special Representative and under his chairmanship, the nine then-certified political parties signed an agreement among themselves on 12 September: it established a Code of Conduct which they pledged to respect during the electoral campaign. The Code included, *inter alia*, the following points:

- An essential part of free and fair elections is freedom of political campaigning. Everyone has the right to put forward their political principles and ideas, without threat or fear, to every other person, without exception. But freedom of political campaigning also carries responsibilities, including the duty to accept every other person's freedom to campaign;
- Parties will notify UNTAG in advance of their planned meetings and other rallies;
- Intimidation is unacceptable and forbidden;
- No weapon may be brought to any political rally, meeting, march or other demonstration;

- Party members and supporters will not disrupt other parties' rallies, meetings etc.
- Party leaders undertake to honour the outcome of free and fair elections so certified by the Special Representative of the U.N.

The draft Election Proclamation published by the Administrator-General evoked major criticisms from the U.N., other observers and the public. Difficult negotiations were only concluded on 6 October.

358 polling stations were established: the total number of U.N. personnel directly involved in the supervisory process was 1,758, including 885 specialist personnel made available by the governments of 27 States. 358 UNTAG personnel, acting as ballot-box supervisors, were drawn from the military component. The remaining electoral supervisors came from UNTAG's civilian component and staff members from other U.N. organizations. In addition, 1,023 UNTAG police monitors were assigned to electoral duties.

All UNTAG election supervisory personnel were given specialist training. A voter-education programme was carried out by UNTAG, by the Administrator-General and by the political parties.

In spite of all the agreements and rules, the period preceding the election was marred by obstruction and intimidation. For instance, in June, the Special Representative expressed increasing concern about intimidation taking place in the northern part of the territory. More clearly, but privately, UNTAG officials were disturbed by the unwillingness or inability of the Administrator-General to prevent election intimidation practices by security forces opposed to SWAPO. The Commonwealth Group referred to

> obstructive tactics, and belated, grudging concessions of its Administrator-General (which) have placed innumerable and needless obstacles in the path of the Special Representative in particular, and the political process in general... every single step (besides the withdrawal of the South African troops) to be taken has encountered resistance, evasion and actual delay.

On 13 September, a senior official of SWAPO, Anton Lubowski was killed by unknown "extremists", a deliberate attempt to sabotage the electoral process.[12]

Throughout the pre-election period, UNTAG had to address repeated allegations, mostly deriving from South African security sources, of imminent invasion of the north by SWAPO forces. A few days before the election, South Africa claimed, on the basis of supposedly intercepted messages between UNTAG units, that an imminent incursion into Namibia by SWAPO forces had been verified by UNTAG military personnel. An investigation by the Special Representative of the transcript of the alleged messages showed conclusively that they were fraudulent. The South African Foreign Minister publicly withdrew the charges 48 hours later.[13]

The elections took place from 7 to 11 November. In spite of the attempts to derail the process through violence, threats or misinformation, more than 97% of the registered voters voted in conditions of peaceful determination.

The final results, announced on 14 November showed that no party had received a two-thirds majority, which would have permitted it to dominate the debates of the future Constituent Assembly, and determine, alone, its contents. Fears of a dominant, one-party system were therefore assuaged. SWAPO had received 41% of the Assembly's 72 seats, – its main opponent, the Democratic Turnhalle Alliance, had 21 seats and five of the remaining eight parties also obtained representation. Only 1.4% of ballots had been rejected as invalid.

On the same day, the Special Representative of the Secretary-General certified, in fulfilment of his responsibility under the Settlement Proposal, that the electoral process in Namibia had, at every stage, been free and fair, and that it had been conducted to his satisfaction. In his statement, Ahtisaari said, "Its youngest democracy has given the whole world a shining lesson in democracy, exemplary as to commitment, restraint and tolerance".

On 21 November 1989, the newly elected Constituent Assembly convened. The Constitution was adopted by consensus on 9 February 1990, which, as previously agreed, reflected multi-party democracy, with entrenched fundamental rights and freedoms and an independent judiciary.

One week later, Sam Nujoma was elected as the first President of the country which became independent as the Republic of Namibia on 21 March 1990.

Symbolically, in recognition of the role of the U.N. as legal authority over Namibia, the President took the oath from the U.N. Secretary-General, and not from the President of South Africa.

An Assessment

The UNTAG operation was "successful" insofar as its mandate,

> to create conditions for the holding of free and fair elections for a Constituent Assembly which would draw up a Constitution under which Namibia would proceed to independence as a free and sovereign State

was fulfilled. UNTAG managed, with the active support of influential Powers, and in spite of major hurdles, to prepare the ground for elections in a country which had never known democratic elections: the U.N. broad and complex functions included the implementation and monitoring of the ceasefire, the reduction of South African military and political presence, the repeal of discriminatory laws, amnesty, the release of political prisoners and detainees, return of refugees, registration of voters and political parties, agreement on a political Code of Conduct, monitoring of elections, certified as free and fair, and announcement of results. UNTAG insisted on establishing such electoral standards as secrecy of the ballot, reasonable speed in the counting of the ballots and accountability and openness of the process to the competing parties. The large U.N. (1 U.N. election supervisor for every 412 voters) and international presence played a dissuasive role in avoiding unfair electoral practices.

The operation was also a success insofar as the results of the elections were accepted by the political parties and the Namibian people and was followed by the peaceful gathering of the Constituent Assembly, the approval of a democratic Constitution, the peaceful election of a President and the formation of a government. Namibia then was a free and sovereign State, which became a member of the U.N., as a democratic State.

Most observers recognized that the U.N. and its presence in Namibia played a crucial role in Namibia's democratic transition to independence and thus scored a much deserved success for the Organization itself.[14]

UNTAG's task was multidimensional: it had military, police, logistical, humanitarian, electoral and administrative responsibilities: however, the main U.N. role, from New York and in Windhoek, was political.

The U.N. was not alone in observing the electoral process. UNTAG welcomed outside observers from governments, intergovernmental and non-governmental organizations: the OAU, the Frontline States, the Non-Aligned Movement, the Commonwealth and the Inter-Parliamentary Union sent observer groups. Certain governments, including the U.S.A., sent high-level observer missions during the election period. A number of NGOs also sent observers and reported on the process: these included the National Democratic Institute for International Affairs, Oxfam, the Commission on Namibia of the Lawyers Committee for Civil Rights under Law, the European Parliamentarians against Apartheid and various church groups. Because of the large presence of international observers, many complaints of intimidation and criticisms of the proposed laws were aired in public and in diplomatic forums throughout the world.[15] These groups and their constituencies generally supported the U.N. Special Representative's efforts and facilitated the resolution of conflicts, problems or misunderstandings.

At the same time, the Namibia operation could not have been implemented without the pressures and influence of the U.S.A. and the then Soviet Union on the parties (governments or liberation movements) to the conflict, and the consequent reluctant South African decision to withdraw from Namibia. Security Council resolution 435 of 1978 was only applied in 1989. Its implementation was one of the "dividends" of the end of the Cold War. Crises, such as the 1 April SWAPO incursion, were resolved through the intervention of government bodies such as the intergovernmental Joint Commission,[16] while the U.N. could only alert governments and call for help.

With strong governments' initiatives and support, the U.N. offered the usual facilities for negotiations and formalization of agreements, then played the key operational role in carrying out the terms of the various agreements.

The major innovation of the U.N. Namibia operation was not that it was a large multidisciplinary operation, with both military and civilian components, but that it was the first decolonization process which brought a democratic nation into the world.

Peace and Democracy in Central America: The Nicaragua Elections

Within the U.N. operations of the second generation, the U.N. Observer Mission to verify the electoral process in Nicaragua (ONUVEN) was an even more striking innovation in several respects: if we leave aside the discreet 1977 Panama "witnessing" operation, it was the first time that the U.N. had formally and openly monitored an electoral process in a sovereign country, a "first" which then served as a formal precedent for other similar operations, – it was the first U.N. electoral monitoring operation in the Western Hemisphere, an area protected from non-American intervention through the Monroe doctrine of the 19th century, – it was the first joint operation between the U.N. and a regional organization, the Organization of American States (OAS), the latter having already acquired considerable experience in election observation, – it was part of a regional "peace and security" plan: the Esquipulas peace plan initiated by the five Central American presidents in August 1987, – it was not due to an initiative from the superpowers, the U.S. initially showing more hesitancy or opposition than support, besides its aggressive hostility against the Sandinistas and its obvious lack of trust in their electoral commitments or promises: however, the USSR was retrenching from support for leftist governments, including the Sandinista Government and the Bush administration was facing internal opposition to continued Contra support, – ONUVEN was established by the U.N. Secretary-General himself, and not by a resolution of the General Assembly, although the General Assembly welcomed his decision – ONUVEN was not authorized by a decision of the Security Council: as the operation did not involve the use of military personnel, it was not technically considered as a peace-keeping operation, which explains that the Security Council was not required to formally authorize the operation: the Council endorsed the Secretary-General's decision *post facto*. The full support of the Secretary-General, the Peruvian Perez de Cuellar, to the regional peace plan, and his particular interest in the region, no doubt played a significant role in ensuring the success of this operation.

Background

Years of internal and external conflicts in Central America inspired peace initiatives by the Governments of Colombia, Mexico, Panama and Venezuela – known as the Contadora Group – in 1983, and then by the Presidents of Costa Rica, El Salvador, Guatemala, Honduras and Nicaragua. After preliminary consultations in Esquipulas, Guatemala, in 1986, Costa Rican President Oscar Arias Sànchez drafted a comprehensive peace plan, based on the principle of solving several interrelated problems simultaneously. The plan, for which President Arias was awarded the 1987 Nobel Peace Price, was embodied in the final declaration of a summit of the five Central American Presidents held in Guatemala in August 1987.[17]

The "Procedure for the Establishment of a Firm and Lasting Peace in Central America", known both as the Esquipulas II Agreement and the Guatemala

Procedure of 7 August 1987, dealt with issues of national reconciliation, an end to hostilities, democratization, free elections, termination of aid to irregular forces and insurrectionist movements, non-use of the territory of one State to attack other States; negotiations on security, verification and the control and limitation of weapons, refugees and displaced persons, cooperation, democracy and freedom for peace and development, international verification and follow-up, and a timetable for the fulfilment of commitments.

More precisely, in the area of democracy and electoral processes, the Presidents undertook, *inter alia*, to

> promote an authentic democratic process (in their own countries) that is pluralistic and participatory, which entails the promotion of social justice and respect for human rights (and) to invite the Organization of American States, (and) the United Nations... to send observers to verify that the electoral process has been governed by the strictest rules of equal access for all political parties to the communications media and by ample opportunities for organizing public demonstrations and any other type of political propaganda.

On 7 October 1987, the General Assembly expressed its "firmest support" for the Esquipulas Agreement (Resol. 42/1). It requested the Secretary-General to afford the fullest assistance to the Central American Governments in their effort to achieve peace, especially by responding to the specific requests made of him in the Agreement. A similar "supporting" and "requesting" Resolution was adopted by the General Assembly on 15 November 1988 (Resol. 43/24).

In a Joint Declaration of 14 February 1989 adopted at Costa del Sol, El Salvador, the five Presidents noted the announcement by the President of Nicaragua of a series of measures that his Government was prepared to undertake in order to foster a process of democratization and reconciliation in his country, among which was the holding of national elections no later than 25 February 1990. The last elections, held in November 1984, had been marred by the abstention of opposition groups, due to Sandinista harassment of some campaign rallies. International observers, in particular the representatives of the Secretary-General of the U.N. and the Secretary General of the OAS, would be invited to be present in all electoral districts during the process, in order to "verify that the electoral process is genuine". In the same Declaration, the Governments also undertook to draw up a joint plan for the voluntary demobilization, repatriation or relocation of members of the Nicaraguan resistance and their families.

On 3 March 1989, the Minister of Foreign Affairs of Nicaragua requested the Secretary-General to establish a group of international observers whose mission would be to verify that the measures announced by the Government were implemented and that the electoral process was "genuine during every stage".

As there was no formal precedent for carrying out such observation in an independent country, and as the General Assembly was not in session at the time, the Secretary-General informed its President in April (Doc. A/44/210) of the

Nicaraguan request: although in the past, the U.N. had declined invitations from Member States, this case had special factors. First, it was not a request by a single Member State, but it was supported by the other four governments of the Esquipulas peace process, – secondly, it was in line with the General Assembly's request to the Secretary-General, in its Resolution 43/24 of 15 November 1988, "to afford the fullest possible support to the Central American Governments in their efforts to achieve peace, especially by taking the measures necessary for the development and effective functioning of the essential verification machinery" – finally, it was not simply a request for a token presence on election day, which had been a feature of many other previous invitations by Member States, but for the verification of the fairness of the entire process throughout its 10-month duration and in all electoral districts.

Before deciding on the Nicaraguan request, the Secretary-General sent several missions to Nicaragua to establish contact with the Government, electoral authorities and opposition parties and to observe the debate in the Legislative Assembly on the reforms of the electoral laws and of the laws regulating the mass media. Contacts were also made with the Nicaragua resistance. Recommendations were made by the U.N. on the electoral reform process. The Secretary-General also wrote to the Secretary-General of the OAS suggesting that the mandate be carried out jointly. U.N. and OAS experts determined that Nicaraguan election laws were democratic and compared favourably with other laws in the region.

On 5 July 1989, in the absence of any objection, the Secretary-General informed the President of the General Assembly of his decision to establish the U.N. Observer Mission to verify the electoral process in Nicaragua (ONUVEN). The terms of reference of the mission were contained in an exchange of letters between the Secretary-General and the Government of Nicaragua (Doc. A/44/375). The Secretary-General's decision to create ONUVEN was subsequently endorsed both by the Security Council on 27 July (Resol. 637) and by the General Assembly on 23 October (Resol. 44/10). The General Assembly's approval was cautious: this was an "extraordinary measure" justified only by its relation to the maintenance of international peace and security. Explicitly, no precedent was being created.

On 4 August, the Sandinistas and 14 opposition parties signed an agreement guaranteeing free and fair elections to be held in February 1990. The Government agreed to suspend military conscription from 1 September until after the elections and to amend security and press restrictions. They also provided amnesty for some political prisoners.[18]

Pre-election and Election Monitoring

ONUVEN became operational on 25 August 1989. The Secretary-General appointed Mr. Elliot L. Richardson (U.S.A.) as his Personal Representative. Observers felt that the appointment of a senior American politician, diplomat, a member of the Republican party, was a clever move intended to involve more closely the U.S. government in the operation.

ONUVEN's mandate included the following tasks: verifying

- that political parties were equitably represented in the Nicaraguan Supreme Electoral Council (CSE) and its subsidiary bodies,
- that political parties enjoyed complete freedom of organization and mobilization, without hindrance or intimidation,
- that all political parties had equitable access to State television and radio,
- that the electoral rolls were properly drawn up, and informing the CSE of any complaints received or any irregularities or interference detected in the electoral process. The mission was to submit periodic reports to the Secretary-General or, through him, to the General Assembly.

ONUVEN observers were granted complete freedom of movement and access nationwide. The core group of ONUVEN observers, present in Nicaragua throughout the whole electoral process, attended all major political rallies held by the opposition parties and the party in power.They received, analyzed and followed up on hundreds of complaints submitted by political parties. Where intimidation was alleged, or in cases where candidates withdrew from the campaign, ONUVEN carried out interviews in order to obtain full information. ONUVEN monitored television programmes with news or political content, along with political party broadcasts and electioneering broadcasts by major radio stations. The same was done in the case of political information in national daily and weekly newspapers. ONUVEN also introduced the systematic use of statistically based verification methods, both during registration and voting, which replaced the one-to-one verification method conducted by UNTAG. On election day, the projection, or "quick count", was within half a point of 1% accurate by 9 p.m. This information, which remained confidential, was crucial in obtaining an agreement by both sides to restrain the reaction of their respective supporters.

On 17 October, the U.S. Senate agreed to send $9 million in aid to the Nicaraguan opposition "UNO", a coalition of parties headed by Violeta Barrios de Chamorro, the widow of a murdered newspaper editor who had led the opposition to former dictator Anastasio Somoza. The Nicaraguan delegate to the U.N. General Assembly's Third Committee condemned this decision as an interference in Nicaragua's internal affairs and a threat to its interests and its "inalienable right" to elect its authorities freely. The U.S. delegate replied that the funds provided by the U.S. National Endowment for Democracy would be handled in accordance with Nicaraguan law: 50% for the Sandinistas, and 50% for opposition parties.

Also in October, former U.S. President Jimmy Carter announced that he would bring his own group of election monitors – the Council of Freely-Elected Heads of Government – to Nicaragua for the February vote.[19]

Nicaragua's polarized electoral campaign was not immune from acts of violence and intimidation. For instance, in January 1990, the U.N. Personal Representative mentioned in a press conference unbalanced coverage in the state-owned news organizations and misuse of government property for campaigning by the Sandinistas. He cited violence and intimidation at political rallies and by rebels in the countryside as areas of particular concern.[20] The situation subsequently improved.

On election day, on 25 February 1990, 207 ONUVEN observers travelled throughout Nicaragua, assisted by a team of 34 persons stationed at the Managua headquarters and regional offices. The observers visited 2,155 polling stations located in 141 of the 143 municipalities in Nicaragua. During the elections, 86% of the registered electorate cast their vote (1,510,838 out of 1,752,088); 89% of those eligible had registered, showing the people's eagerness to vote.

The unexpected outcome was the victory of opposition candidate Violeta Chamorro over Daniel Ortega for the presidency, by 15%: the opposition UNO coalition won 52 seats in the 91-seat Assembly, while the Sandinistas took 38 and the Social Christian Party took 1. After over a decade of civil war, a change of majority and government had been peacefully achieved through an internationally monitored democratic electoral process.

The U.N., the OAS, President Carter's monitors and a large number of government and non-governmental organizations' observers had played a major role in this successful outcome: 278 organizations, mainly non-governmental, had provided 2,578 election observers. The CSE had also accredited 1,500 foreign journalists.

As reported by the Council of Freely-Elected Heads of Government,[21]

> Observer teams complemented each other. The OAS provided excellent fieldwork with observers who came to know the regions well, were trusted by both sides, and whose presence helped contain violence and resolve conflicts. Also, a large OAS team during the elections provided for comprehensive observation . . . that reassured voters and guaranteed verification of the integrity of the process and the count. The U.N. also provided good teams in the field, excellent analyses of complaints, and a quick count that provided early and accurate projections on the night of the elections. The Council delegation had more flexibility as a private group. With high visibility due to the prestige of its members and its Chairman, President Carter, it actively mediated conflicts between President Ortega, Mrs. Chamorro, and other key leaders in the country. The group also encouraged leaders from the major parties to understand the need for reconciliation after the election in order to rebuild the country and end the war.

Assessing the electoral process, ONUVEN reported that it had been "impartial and fair throughout" and that the elections had been conducted in a "highly commendable manner".

After the elections, moderation prevailed: on 22 March, UNO and Sandinista negotiators announced that they had reached agreement on a full transfer of power to the opposition, including control over the military and security forces. On 18 April, a week before Chamorro's inauguration, the Sandinista government, government-elect, rebel leaders and the Archbishop of Managua reached agreement on an immediate ceasefire and a timetable for complete disarmament.

Upon request of both the President and the President-elect of Nicaragua, the Secretary-General had assigned a small team to assure a U.N. presence in Nicaragua during the transition period. This team played a role in the various negotiations which followed the elections.

While ONUVEN itself was a relatively small operation (237 observers at maximum strength), it attracted the publicized support and the presence of many other organizations and observers. It facilitated the peaceful transfer of power in Nicaragua, it enhanced the role of the U.N. as a capable, impartial and objective monitor of free elections.

The success of the operation and of its aftermath, a peaceful transfer of power, was dependent on the political will and maturity of the political authorities and their opponents, and of their supporters.

No doubt, the world publicity given to the elections, and the elections' assigned role within the Central American peace process, were also instrumental in the success of this second operation.

Until the elections of 25 February 1990, Nicaragua never had an election in which the winners and all the losers accepted and respected the results, thus assuring a peaceful transition.

This positive trend was unfortunately reversed in the following two cases, those of Haiti and Angola: well-monitored elections were followed, in one case, by a military coup, and in the other, by the loser's recourse to renewed armed struggle, in attempts to reject the outcome of the democratic electoral process.

Haiti: A Short-lived Democratic Experiment

The U.N. monitoring of elections in Haiti was the second such operation in a sovereign country, also at the request of the country's government. However, the international element found in the Nicaragua operation, as a part of a multilateral peace process was not present in the case of Haiti, nor could it be related to any concern for the international peace and security in the region. Its only motivation was to support the efforts of the people of Haiti "to consolidate their democratic institutions in the face of the potential for destabilization": in other words, the U.N. was asked to intervene in the domestic affairs of a sovereign country in order to establish an internal democratic order in a country which had only known poverty, violence, instability and dictatorship, since it became independent in 1804.[22]

The U.N. operation in Haiti was therefore another significant "first" insofar as the U.N. was to provide electoral technical assistance and training, to observe and verify elections, and assist in maintaining public security in a small country devastated by internal conflict, without any credible justification as to a potential threat to international peace and security. The U.N. was furthermore to support democracy in a country which had never known democratic institutions nor democratic practices: a really "daunting" challenge.

Historical Background

A former Spanish, then French possession, following a slave revolt, Haiti became in 1804 the western hemisphere's second independent republic. It is now the poorest nation in the hemisphere. With a population of 6.5 million, 80% of Haitians earn less than $100 annually, 78% of them are illiterate.[23]

Throughout the 19th century, civil wars and a succession of dictators impoverished the country's economy. Of the 22 Haitian presidents who held office between 1843 and 1915, 14 were overthrown, 1 resigned, 3 were murdered, 3 died of natural causes in office, and only 1 finished his term.[24]

Haiti was occupied by the U.S. Marine Corps from 1915 to 1934. Then, military dictatorships followed, until François Duvalier was elected president in 1957. Within a year, he began ruling by decree, suppressed opposition voices and spread terror through his private militia, the "tonton macoutes". Upon his death in 1971, his son Jean-Claude assumed the presidency, and was unable to effect meaningful reforms. Following anti-government demonstrations, he left the presidency and his country in February 1986, under American and French pressures, and took refuge in France.

Before leaving Haiti, Duvalier transferred all powers of government to a six-member Council of National Government (CNG). A Constituent Assembly, elected in October 1986, prepared a new Constitution which was overwhelmingly ratified in a referendum held in March 1987. It called for:

- the establishment of an impartial, non-military Provisional Electoral Council (CEP) to supervise the forthcoming elections;
- a reduction of the executive's powers and the simultaneous restoration and expansion of the powers of the legislature and the judiciary;
- and the exclusion of individuals associated with the Duvalier regime from public office for 10 years.

In 1987, the U.N. Human Rights Commission invited the Haitian Government to consider, among other measures, the possibility of inviting international observers for the forthcoming elections (Resol. 1987/13).

The CEP was established in May 1987. Violence and assassinations preceded the presidential and legislative elections, scheduled for 29 November 1987. On election day, shootings took place at a number of polling stations, killing 34 people. In an attempt to avert further violence, the CEP cancelled the elections.

In a television appearance, General Namphy, the more powerful member of the CNG, blamed the CEP for the failure of the elections and criticized foreign observers for interfering with the electoral process. Most observers, including an international delegation sponsored by the U.S. National Democratic Institute for International Affairs, later reported that the armed forces and the police, who were responsible for the security of the elections, had tolerated and in some cases even participated in the violence. The U.S. State Department country report confirmed these findings.[25]

New elections held on 17 January 1988 resulted in the victory of Leslie F. Manigat as President. Voter turnout was reportedly below 5% and widespread voting irregularities were observed on election day.

President Manigat was overthrown on 19 June in a military coup led by General Henri Namphy. Manigat was flown out of the country.

General Namphy dissolved the National Assembly and announced that he would rule by decree. He declared himself President and assembled a 12 member government which included only one civilian. In July, Namphy suspended the 1987 Constitution.

Following a massacre by tonton macoutes at St Jean Bosco Church on 11 September, who killed at least 12 people, wounded some 70 others and set the church on fire, General Namphy was overthrown by members of the Presidential Guard and allowed to leave for the Dominican Republic. He was replaced in another military coup by another general, Prosper Avril, formerly the Chief of presidential security under Jean Claude Duvalier.

Avril promised that his regime would initiate a transition to civilian rule in Haiti. In February 1989, he partially restored the 1987 Constitution, and in March, formed a Provisional Electoral Council. He survived an abortive coup d'état early April. In September, the Electoral Council published an electoral timetable, which was criticized as too long and too complex by most political forces. According to an expert to the U.N. Commission on Human Rights,[26] General Avril's Government gave the impression of vacillating between a coalition with the Duvalier forces and one with the democratic organizations. Instability was still the rule. A cause for concern was certain statements by Avril indicating, for example, on 27 November 1989 that "the Haitian people must be able to eat before they go to the polls".

On 10 March 1990, during a nationwide protest, Avril announced his resignation, handed power over to General Herard Abraham and flew to Miami.

A week earlier, the "Group of Twelve", representing Haiti's 11 major political parties and one civic organization, had called for Avril's resignation and proposed an interim government to be led by a member of the Supreme Court and a 19-member Council of State representing 11 different sectors of Haitian society and eight provincial delegates.

On 13 March 1990, Ertha Pascal Trouillot, a Supreme Court judge, assumed the presidency. Her government's sole objective would be to lead the country to free and fair national elections. She made it clear from the beginning that she had no wish to remain in office beyond the elections.[27]

On assuming office, the interim government restored the 1987 Constitution as the fundamental law of Haiti: the Constitution provides for a president directly elected for five years, a directly elected parliament composed of a 27-member Senate and a 83-member House of Representatives, and a prime minister appointed by the president. It establishes a strict separation of powers among the executive, the legislature and the judiciary, but gives the incoming president wide powers to implement reforms during the first six months in office. In May, the interim government appointed a new Provisional Electoral Council (CEP). On 10 July, the CEP published a new election law. The first run of elections was scheduled for 16 December 1990.

Haiti's Request for U.N. Monitoring

Shortly before his downfall, General Avril had requested the U.N. to supervise the planned elections. Mrs. Pascal Trouillot, President of the Interim Government of Haiti, renewed this request. The U.N., with UNDP financing, responded by deploying a technical mission in the country in June 1990 to help establish a credible and honest electoral process through technical and practical advice, practical training measures and the exchange of experience with other developing countries. On 19 June, the Secretary-General appointed Joao Augusto de Medicis as his Personal Representative for Haiti.

On 23 June, the President of the Interim Government submitted to the Secretary-General a broader and more specific request for electoral assistance.[28] Her request was supported by the Council of State, a body specifically set up for the transition to democracy, the Provisional Electoral Council, an independent body responsible for the electoral process, and the Haitian Armed Forces, responsible for security.

Her request had two components: one was the observation and verification of the regularity of the electoral process, – the other concerned public security.

The first part of the mission would cover the entire electoral process, particularly registration of voters on the electoral rolls, registration of candidatures, freedom of expression and freedom of political parties to mobilize, respect for the equality of candidates in the electoral campaign, and independent verification of the outcome of the vote.

In addition, a visible and active international presence would dissipate voters' fears and ensure representative participation of the population. To this end, U.N. advisers with experience in security matters would assist the Coordination Committee for Electoral Security of the Haitian Armed Forces in developing and implementing electoral security plans.

When the General Assembly first met to consider Haiti's request, on 20 July, two problems arose: a constitutional problem concerning the competence of the U.N. body which should properly consider the request and a serious political problem.

Was the proposed operation an electoral monitoring operation, similar to that carried out in Nicaragua, or was it a peace-keeping operation? The Security Council is the proper body to approve the latter, while the General Assembly could authorize the former.

This point was clarified in a second letter from Mrs. Pascal Trouillot, dated 9 August: the Haitian Government did not wish for, nor was it requesting, the dispatch of "Blue Helmets" or of any peace-keeping force to ensure the security of the country, a task for which the Haitian Armed Forces were basically responsible.

In its civilian component, the U.N. Mission would therefore need a nucleus of some 50 observers, rising to a few hundred at the time of elections, – coordination with the OAS would be envisaged.

In its security component, it would need two or three advisers to give assistance to the Coordinating Committee, and a number (to be determined) of observers with solid experience in the public order field.

Political objections were raised mainly by Latin American countries, opposed to any external interference in domestic matters, with bitter memories of past U.S. military interventions, including the very recent Grenada and Panama operations. The prospect of introducing foreign military officers to Haiti (although only security specialists were actually sought) triggered the protest of such countries as Bolivia, Cuba and the Bahamas among others. This resulted in a postponement of the General Assembly debate. More generally, these countries feared that approving the Haiti request would set a precedent for groups or governments to use the U.N. to legitimize their elections.

To these two problems, many observers, analysts and national and international representatives added their concerns and doubts about the ability of a small number of international electoral and security observers to influence events in a country where people had been the victim of military domination and abuses and had never been allowed to practise democracy. Would such temporary international presence prevent the Haitian military forces from initiating another campaign of terror and, as in 1987, cause the elections to be cancelled?

U.S. Vice-President Dan Quayle visited Haiti on 9 August and bluntly warned senior Haitian military officers that unless the country held free and fair elections, the U.S. government would cut off its annual $60 million economic and humanitarian aid in 1990. Democracy, or else ... On the other hand, Washington offered $3 million to Haiti's Electoral Council to help defray electoral expenses.[29]

On 8 October, the Security Council asked the Secretary-General to respond "positively" and "on an urgent basis" to Haiti's request. In a letter to the Secretary-General, the President of the Council said that its members hoped that the Assembly would take urgent action so that assistance could be extended in time for the election, which involved among other things, the provision of advisers, observers and experts on electoral security matters, but did not include the use of any U.N. peace-keeping forces.[30]

Finally, on 10 October, the General Assembly approved Haiti's request by Resolution 45/2 (adopted without a vote) and requested the Secretary-General, in cooperation with regional organizations and Member States, to provide the "broadest possible support" to Haiti as follows:

(a) A nucleus of some fifty observers that would arrive in Haiti prior to voter registration and would leave only after the elections;

(b) Reinforcement of the nucleus at the time of elections and voter registration, bringing the total to a few hundred observers;
(c) Assistance to the Coordinating Committee for the security of the elections, to be provided by two or three advisers;
(d) Observation of the implementation of the electoral security plans by specialized staff, that is, by observers, the number of whom remains to be determined, with solid experience in the public order field...

The inclusion of security observers in the operation was not unlike that of police monitors in UNTAG, except that in Haiti, the observers would not deal with law and order in general, but would only advise the Haitian military and the police concerning the security of the electoral process.

Estimated costs should not exceed $6.5 million, according to the Fifth Committee.[31]

ONUVEH and the Elections

In line with the General Assembly resolution, the Secretary-General established the U.N. Observer Group for the Verification of the Elections in Haiti – ONUVEH. Haiti also asked the OAS and several non-governmental organizations to provide electoral observers. A system of informal cooperation was established among the groups.

The ONUVEH mission was headed by the Personal Representative of the Secretary-General for Haiti. It included three divisions: a division for electoral observation, composed of a nucleus of 40 international staff, with the addition of a further 130 observers at the time of the elections themselves, some coming from the U.N. Secretariat, some being contributed by Governments and some being volunteers from U.N. agencies and non-governmental organizations working in Haiti; a division for security observation, consisting of 64 security experts contributed by Governments, most of whom were temporarily reassigned from existing U.N. peace-keeping operations; and a division for administration, composed of 26 international staff, in charge of telecommunications, general services, finance, transport and personnel. International staff came from 36 countries.

The men and women who served with ONUVEH, all of them volunteers, arrived in Haiti immediately after the establishment of the mission. Teams of electoral observers and security observers were then deployed throughout the country. At the same time, ONUVEH established a country-wide communications network.

The first task of ONUVEH was to help create a climate conducive to the holding of democratic elections, through establishing contact with the Provisional Electoral Council, the local electoral and military authorities and explaining the purpose of the U.N. mission. A radio and television campaign was conducted by an ONUVEH information team. U.N. observers investigated registration problems and irregularities. They attended political meetings and monitored radio and television broadcasts to ensure that all candidates had equal access to the mass media.

On the eve of the first round of elections, ONUVEH reported that the electoral campaign and voter registration had taken place without violence, with only one tragic exception, and without intimidation. The Provisional Electoral Council, the executive branch and the military had shown their impartiality. The candidates allowed to run represented the whole spectrum of Haiti's social and political life.

The first round of elections was held on 16 December. Voters were asked to choose, by separate ballots, their president, legislative representatives and local officials.

When the polls closed at 6 p.m., ONUVEH electoral observer teams had visited 1,813 polling stations in all nine electoral departments, observing the voting process. The U.N. security observers accompanied their Haitian counterparts on all their rounds throughout the day. In general, irregularities were minor and resulted from lack of experience or from logistical problems. ONUVEH detected no widespread effort to disrupt the elections, to intimidate voters or to falsify the process. Over 70% of those registered voted.

As in Nicaragua, ONUVEH and OAS applied the "quick-count" process. Seventy-five ONUVEH teams and seventy-five OAS teams ended election day at 150 pre-selected sample points where, when the polls closed, they observed the counting of the ballots and noted the results of the presidential election. These results were communicated to ONUVEH headquarters where by 10 p.m. ONUVEH experts were able to project the outcome of the presidential election. The Government, the Provisional Electoral Council, the political parties and the main electoral candidates were informed. The quick-count technique was instrumental in assuring public confidence in the counting process and respect for the electoral results, and in alleviating potential tension due to delay in announcing official results. ONUVEH had reliable information at the end of election day on 16 December, information which was shared with responsible Haitian officials and could pre-empt any post-election attempt to falsify the electoral results.

This prompt announcement was particularly important as the Electoral Council only announced the winner, Jean-Bertrand Aristide, on 24 December, and only released the final results on 11 January. Aristide had won 67% of the vote, a figure corresponding closely to that of the ONUVEH projection.

ONUVEH concluded that no violence had occurred and that there was no doubt

> that the elections were conducted freely and fairly, with exemplary participation by political parties and the electorate in a historical break with a past of electoral fraud.[32]

Satisfactory conditions also prevailed during the second round of legislative elections held on 20 January 1991, albeit with a lower turn-out of voters.

In the view of the U.N., it was a combination of factors – the courageous efforts of the Government and the electoral authorities, the exemplary role of the army, the enthusiasm and determination of the Haitians, ONUVEH's assistance and the commitment of the observers to a free, fair and secure electoral process – which set the stage for Haiti's first successful democratic elections held in conditions of tranquillity and liberty.

The international delegation of the Council of Freely-Elected Heads of Government and of the National Democratic Institute for International Affairs generally agreed with the U.N. assessment:

the delegation concluded, *inter alia*, that

- The people of Haiti voted in record numbers to express their desire for democratic change. The overwhelming popular mandate given to Aristide expressed the people's desire to break with Haiti's history of authoritarian rule and economic stagnation;
- In contrast with the aborted November 1987 elections, the Government of Haiti supported the election process. The international presence contributed greatly in providing confidence to the electorate;
- The election environment was far from perfect. Several incidents of violence occurred during the pre-election period, which resulted in numerous fatalities and injuries. However, the delegation stressed as a basic theme that the election process must go forward.[33]

The newly elected President, notwithstanding a failed coup d'état in January, was inaugurated on 7 February 1991.

The Haitian military forces and civilian elites had not been converted to democracy by internationally monitored free elections: on 30 September 1991, President Aristide, the first freely elected chief executive in Haiti's history, was overthrown by the army. The military takeover began with mutinies on 29 September: at least 26 people were killed and about 200 injured on 30 September. Aristide was forced into exile.

On 7 October, the junta appointed Supreme Court Justice Joseph Nerette as unelected provisional president, then Jean-Jacques Honorat as Prime Minister. In June 1992, Marc Bazin, a former World Bank official, who had come second in the presidential elections with less than 13% of the vote, replaced Honorat.

After the Coup of 30 September 1991

The OAS and the U.N. promptly condemned the coup through several resolutions and decided to apply pressures on its leaders through economic sanctions. The possibility of a military intervention to restore democracy in Haiti was envisaged within both organizations but not retained as a realistic option.

On 5 June 1991, the General Assembly of the OAS had approved Resolution 1080, creating a new mechanism for convening Foreign Ministers in response to an irregular interruption of the democratic process in any member state.

Following the violent overthrow of Aristide, the OAS Permanent Council approved a resolution on 30 September condemning the coup and convening an *ad hoc* meeting of Foreign Ministers pursuant to Resolution 1080. The Foreign Ministers, in a resolution adopted on 3 October, reiterated the vigorous condemnation of the Permanent Council and demanded full restoration of the rule of law and of constitutional order and the immediate reinstatement of President Jean-Bertrand Aristide in the exercise of his legitimate authority. The diplomatic mission which the OAS then sent to Haiti failed to convince the rebels to restore the legitimate order.

On 8 October, the Ministers of Foreign Affairs urged the OAS Member States to freeze the assets of the Haitian State and to impose a trade embargo on Haiti, except for humanitarian aid.

Aristide asked the OAS to send a civilian mission to Haiti to support constitutional democracy: a proposal to send a permanent mission of 500 civilians and a lightly armed security force "to try to keep the two sides from fighting each other" was discussed but not approved.[34]

The U.S.A. had also strongly condemned the coup on 1 October. Its spokesman said that the U.S. Government did not recognize this junta and added that it was suspending all assistance programmes to Haiti.

At the United Nations, also on 1 October, the Secretary-General expressed "deep regret" over the recent violent events in Haiti which posed grave threats to democracy. The Security Council, after first refusing to meet on 30 September on the grounds that this was an internal affair in which it should not get involved, changed its position and agreed to hear Aristide on 3 October. The Council did not vote a resolution, allegedly deferring to the OAS to take the lead in working out a solution: in fact, it deferred to the opposition or reluctance of some of its members "to convene the Security Council every time a coup d'état has taken place"... Security Council members, in a non-binding statement of their President, still strongly condemned the "grave events" in Haiti and called for the restoration of the legitimate government.[35]

The U.N. General Assembly formally condemned, on 11 October,

> the attempted illegal replacement of the constitutional President of Haiti, the use of violence and military coercion and the violation of human rights in that country;

affirmed as unacceptable "any entity resulting from that illegal situation", demanded the immediate restoration of the legitimate government of President Aristide, and gave support to the OAS resolutions (Resol. 46/7).

During the debate preceding the vote of this resolution, reference had been made to human rights abuses committed during Aristide's seven months in office.

It had been established that Aristide, an austere Roman Catholic priest supportive of "liberation theology", had allowed, and even encouraged mob violence against the suspected tonton macoutes, the rich and the corrupt, and even against political opponents. In an inflammatory speech on 27 September, he exhorted a vast crowd to give any thief or spy "what he deserves" and indirectly condoned "necklacing".

While Aristide's economic policies had remained moderate, he had antagonized both friends and foes among the political elites. His efforts to shut down smuggling rackets operated by the army, his plans for a new civilian police force and a European-trained presidential guard aroused fear and resentment among the armed forces.

As stated by the Dominican Foreign Minister during the General Assembly debate, while many governments have been accused of some type of human rights abuses, such accusations have never been accepted as an argument for the forceable overthrow of a democratically elected government.[36]

Furthermore, the argument against Aristide's human rights record could be reversed against his opponents, whose notorious abuses before and after his tenure have been recorded and publicized by the U.N. and various human rights groups.

On 17 May 1992, the OAS Ministers of Foreign Affairs approved another resolution (3/92), as another effort to isolate Haiti's military-backed government and reinstate President Aristide. The proposed measures were, *inter alia*, to expand and intensify the monitoring of the trade embargo, and to urge member states to deny access to port facilities to any vessel that does not abide by the embargo and to ensure that air transport is not used in violation of the embargo. Even though the trade sanctions are not respected by European countries, they have crippled Haiti's economy.

On 24 November, the U.N. General Assembly again condemned "the attempted illegal replacement" of Haitian President Aristide and the ensuing human rights violations. The Secretary-General, in a report dated 3 November, had cited reports of a pattern of "gross and widespread human rights abuses" one year after the coup d'état.[37]

Following intense U.S. pressures on both Aristide and the military junta, in relation with the election of Bill Clinton to the U.S. presidency and fears of an exodus of Haitians to the U.S., and with the active intervention of the U.N. and OAS Special Representative, Dante Caputo, the Haitian Army announced on 17 January 1993 that it had agreed to: – U.N.-led negotiations aimed at reinstating democracy in Haiti, – the deployment of an international civilian observer force, – the appointment of an interim Prime Minister, to replace Marc Bazin. The announcement followed the delivery of a letter from Aristide, in which he agreed to negotiate with coup supporters, for the first time since his overthrow. This apparent breakthrough was however short-lived.

Bazin's illegal government did not lose time in organizing elections, unmonitored by international observers, on 18 and 25 January 1993. The European Community condemned these elections as "not free and fair, since the necessary preconditions, notably freedom of expression and the right to an open political dialogue, did not exist in Haiti".

Following further negotiations, in a report issued in March 1993, the U.N. Secretary-General recommended that the General Assembly establish a U.N. component of the "International Civilian Mission to Haiti". The mission's main objective would be to verify observance of human rights in accordance with the Haitian

Constitution and international human rights instruments. Special attention would be devoted to the right to life, the integrity and security of the person, personal liberty, freedom of expression and freedom of association. He stated that almost all forms of popular organization and activities were targets of repression and that many of the executions and cases of arbitrary arrests and torture were linked to efforts to suppress support for the ousted President.

A total of 260 observers would be deployed in the capitals of each Haiti's nine departments. The U.N. and the OAS would each provide half of the observers, who would be drawn primarily from France, Canada and Caribbean nations.

On 20 April, the General Assembly adopted a resolution by consensus authorizing the mission and restating its established position that President Aristide must be returned to power. The resolution also linked the easing of the OAS economic embargo and increases in technical and economic aid to an end of the political crisis.

The U.N./OAS proposal for a settlement of the crisis calls for a new consensus prime minister, a new army leadership, amnesty for the coup plotters and the eventual return of Aristide. The Army was reluctant to accept Aristide's return unless he committed himself to an amnesty.

In mid-April and again in mid-May, the Haitian military authorities remained inflexible: they rejected any foreign intervention in their country. The presence and the reporting duties of U.N. and OAS observers would undoubtedly embarrass the government and the military: hopefully they might prevent further harrassment of Aristide's supporters and generally assist in the restoration of human rights and fundamental freedoms, and in the establishment of a more peaceful political climate.

On 16 June, the Security Council decided to give the military rulers of Haiti one week to restore democratic civilian rule or face a blockade to cut off the country's oil and weapons and have Haitian's financial assets frozen worldwide.

On 2 July, General Cedras, who led the September 1991 coup, agreed to a U.N. plan under which President Aristide would return to power on 30 October 1993, some of the high military command, including General Cedras, would resign, coup leaders would be amnestied. In anticipation of an agreement, the U.S. administration announced its readiness to provide $36 million aid, to be "carefully timed to support the negotiations and respond to concrete progress toward restoring democracy". President Aristide signed the plan on 3 July. All prior negotiations had been carried out under the mediation of the Special Representative of the U.N. and the OAS, Dante Caputo and with the support and in the presence of representatives from "friendly countries", Canada, France, U.S.A. and Venezuela.

This agreement was an apparent success for the U.N. and the OAS, for democracy and, more importantly, for the Haitian people. However, its implementation would need to be monitored very closely by the Special Representative and friendly countries' representatives.[38]

Angola: From Ballots to Bullets

On 31 May 1991, the ruling Popular Movement for the Liberation of Angola (MPLA) government and the rebel National Union for the Total Independence of Angola (UNITA) signed an accord intended to end 16 years of civil war. The peace agreement (Acordos de Paz pará Angola) provided for a ceasefire, the creation of a multi-party democracy through changes in the Constitution, respect for human rights and basic freedoms, including the right of free association, – then "free and fair elections" for a new government, following voter registration conducted under the supervision of international elections observers, who would remain in Angola until they certified that the elections were free and fair and that the results had been officially announced.[39]

A former Portuguese colony on the Atlantic coast of Southwest Africa, Angola gained independence in 1975 after 14 years of guerrilla war led by three independence movements. The Marxist-Leninist, Soviet-backed MPLA, dominant around the capital of Luanda, declared Angola a People's Republic. The rival UNITA, led by Jonas Savimbi, and the National Front for the Liberation of Angola (FNLA, which had practically disappeared by 1979), waged guerrilla war against the MPLA government, with the U.S. supplying weapons and financial support, and the occasional military intervention of South African forces. With Soviet support, Cuba dispatched 20,000 troops to Angola to buttress the MPLA regime, who were progressively raised to 50,000. The USSR was the main supplier of arms to Angola. While Angola is potentially a rich country (oil, diamonds, iron ore and agricultural products), the civil war left the country with a ruined economy. Of its 10 million population, the number of war casualties has been estimated in a range of 100,000 to 350,000, 500,000 refugees have fled the country and there are approximately 600,000 internal refugees.

The new policies of Mikhail Gorbachev and the end of the Cold War led to the withdrawal of Cuban troops from Angola, the independence of Namibia, and to the negotiations between the MPLA Government of Jose Eduardo dos Santos and Jonas Savimbi, UNITA's leader under Portuguese mediation, in the presence of U.S. and Soviet observers, who put strong pressure on the Angolans to compromise. The U.S. Secretary of State, James A. Baker 3rd and the Soviet Foreign Minister, Alexander A. Bessmertnykh, whose governments had pledged to suspend military aid to both sides, witnessed the ceremony of signature of the accords, as well as the Chairman of the Organization of African Unity and the Secretary-General of the U.N. During the ceremony, Mr. Savimbi pledged that he would not go back to the bush to re-start the war.[40]

One day before the signature of the accords, in response to a request made by the Government of Angola,the Security Council had voted unanimously to entrust a new mandate to the U.N. Angola Verification Mission (UNAVEM), i.e. to verify those accords until general elections were completed in that country on 30 November 1992.

UNAVEM I had been established in 1988 to verify the redeployment and total withdrawal of Cuban troops from Angola: the last of those troops had left on 25 May 1991.

UNAVEM II would monitor the ceasefire as well as the conduct of the Angolan police. The new mission was to be composed of 350 military observers, up to 90 police observers, an air unit of three aircraft and twelve helicopters, a 14-member medical unit and a civilian support staff drawn from the U.N. Secretariat numbering approximately 80 persons, together with a similar number of locally recruited staff. Estimated costs were $132.3 million, to be borne by Member States according to the U.N. scale of assessments.[41]

UNAVEM II was originally a relatively small U.N. peace-keeping operation (ceasefire monitoring) intended to create acceptable conditions for the holding of free and fair elections.

Election-monitoring was only added to the mandate of UNAVEM II in March 1992. On the basis of observations by his Special Representative, Margaret Anstee, the Secretary-General took the initiative to recommend to the Security Council this new role as a "daunting challenge", in view of the devastated condition of the country, its lack of infrastructure as well as political and administrative instability. Additional costs were estimated at $18.8 million.

The Security Council agreed unanimously to this proposal on 24 March: UNAVEM II would now include an electoral division to assist the country in the holding of free and fair elections: this division would consist of 200 observer teams of two people each who would monitor all stages of the electoral process. The allocation of an average of only five observers in each province would however only allow for sample observation by the U.N. teams. In fact, only about 100 observers monitored the registration of voters and the political campaign: their number was raised to 200 only for the elections of 29 and 30 September.

Members of the Council urged the Angolan parties to comply scrupulously with the provisions of the Peace Accords, including demobilization of their troops without delay, formation of a unified national armed force, effective operation of joint police monitoring units, and extension of the central administration. In his report to the Council, the Secretary-General also urged the parties to renew their commitments to the realization of the elections. The U.S. delegate to the Council added that "the responsibility for the elections must properly rest not with the U.N., but with the Angolans". The Secretary-General confirmed this position:

> The Angolan elections are essentially a national, sovereign affair. The U.N. role is to observe and verify the elections, not to organize them.[42]

The Electoral Campaign and the Elections

As proposed by the U.N. Special Representative, the elections for a president and an assembly of 223 members, with constituent powers, were scheduled for 29 and

30 September 1992. Registration of voters was to take place in the period 20 May–31 July: it was extended for ten days. By then, 4,862,748 voters were registered, 13 Presidential candidates had been nominated and 24 political parties established.

The election campaign essentially opposed the two leading parties, MPLA and UNITA, in virulent verbal cross-accusations and in a tense and at times, violent, climate. The MPLA had formally abandoned Marxism-Leninism in 1990 and had moved slowly toward economic reform: it was still charged with allegations of poor management, corruption, bureaucracy and incompetence. UNITA was often perceived as brutal, tribalist, also incompetent, and as or more totalitarian than the MPLA. The leaders of both parties were convinced that they would win the elections. No significant political "third force" was able to emerge.

In July, the Secretary-General urged all parties to work together "to reduce the current brinkmanship" and to bring it into control. A few days before the election, the Security Council called on all parties to urgently complete the demobilization of the remaining Government and UNITA troops and the collection and centralized storage of weapons. It also expressed concern at the recent deterioration of the political and security situation in the country. The Secretary-General urged that all political parties pledge to respect the results of Angola's first-ever elections, as verified by the U.N. Mission.

According to the National Election Council and the U.N., about 75% of the registered voters voted on 29 and 30 September "in conditions which can generally be described as peaceful and orderly".

Peace and order were however short-lived, as the "loser", Jonas Savimbi and his party, UNITA, rejected the results of the elections, claiming that they had been rigged, and tried to gain power by force.

On the basis of the reports of 89% of the polling stations, on 7 October, MPLA's Dos Santos was ahead with 50.9% to Savimbi's 39.3%. In the parliamentary elections, MPLA also led with 55% of the votes against 33.4% for UNITA.

UNITA rejected these results and threatened to return to arms. It claimed that the elections were "stained by frauds and violations". UNITA General Arlindo Chenda Pena demanded that the elections be reviewed or annulled and said that the publication of the results should be halted "to avoid the worst".[43]

While the results of the elections should have been announced within eight days after the voting, the Angolan government was persuaded to postpone this announcement until the arrival of a U.N. *Ad Hoc* Commission created by the Security Council to support the implementation of the Accords. The Commission held urgent meetings with government, military and rebel officials. The National Election Council investigated fraud charges under U.N. observation. In several attempts to avert renewed civil war, U.N. representatives, the South African Foreign Minister R.F. Botha and the U.S. applied pressure on Savimbi to persuade him to accept the election results and not to resort to war. The U.S. urged all parties in Angola to resolve election issues peacefully: a rejection of the electoral process and a return to violence would be unacceptable to the international community and to the Angolan people who participated enthusiastically in the elections. By mid-October, it appeared that negotiations were prevailing over the strict implementation of election results. While the initial results of the presidential election showed that Dos Santos had received more than 50% of the votes, so that no run-off second round was needed, the results, officially announced on 17 October, were surprisingly 49.57% of the votes for Dos Santos and 40.07% for Savimbi. Run-off presidential elections therefore had to be organized within 30 days, under increased international supervision, thus giving some satisfaction to UNITA.

In her statement on 17 October, the U.N. Special Representative declared that the elections had been "free and fair":

> while there were certainly some irregularities in the electoral process, these appear to have been mainly due to human error and inexperience.

Most of the international observers had also contradicted UNITA's claims of fraud.

Fighting initiated by UNITA against government forces resumed on 11 October, causing thousands of deaths.

On 30 October, the Security Council strongly condemned the resumption of hostilities by UNITA and demanded that such acts cease forthwith.

On 26 November, representatives of the Government of Angola and UNITA, meeting under U.N. auspices, adopted the "Declaration of Namibe" underlining the commitment of both parties to fully accept the validity of the Peace Accords and to effectively apply a ceasefire. Two days later, UNITA resumed fighting.[44]

At the end of January 1993, representatives of the Angolan Government and UNITA met in Addis-Ababa to discuss a ceasefire in their renewed civil war.

At the same time, the U.N. Secretary-General recommended that the Security Council set a deadline of 30 April for the warring parties to make peace. For him, the Council faced three alternatives: keeping the U.N. operation going when its mandate expired at the end of January, – reducing the force to about 150 monitors in only six locations, – or shrinking the force further, and moving all personnel to the relative safety of the capital. The Secretary-General was backing the last option: he placed the blame for the continuing violence on both parties, stating that they had failed to meet their military and political commitments and to "make the necessary efforts to promote national reconciliation".

The U.N. was being blamed for having too few observers and monitors for the operation, and for having failed to insist on the disarmament of the UNITA movement before the elections.[45]

To which it is easy to reply that: first, the size of such an operation is related to its costs, which are decided upon by the Member States, and mostly by the main contributors, – secondly, neither U.N. peace-keeping forces nor election-monitoring groups have enforcement powers: they are entirely dependent on the good faith and good will of the disputing parties to abide by agreements, and can only rely on persuasion if they do not. The only recourse of the Secretary-General is then to refer the matter to the Security Council, or the General Assembly, for further advice or decision.

As fighting was spreading in Angola, the Secretary-General's pragmatic position was to seek a dialogue between the two parties, rather than being "confined to legal arguments": in other words, he did not consider that the U.N. should wholeheartedly support the winner of the internationally monitored elections, declared "free and fair" by the U.N. He believed that

> the international community should persist in trying to bring the two sides together, in helping them to reach agreements and in supporting, on the ground, implementation of whatever arrangements they agree on.

On 12 March 1993, the Security Council again condemned the violation of the peace agreements by UNITA, and set a deadline of seven weeks for the two parties to hold a meeting at the highest level.

After 40 days' discussions, the U.N.-sponsored peace talks in Abidjan between the Angolan government and UNITA broke down on 21 May, over the rejection by UNITA of the peace plan drafted by the U.S., Russia and Portugal. On 19 May, the U.S. had finally recognized the Angolan government. On 2 June, the Security Council condemned UNITA for the breakdown of the Abidjan talks and for escalating violence, while reinterating its demand that UNITA "accept unreservedly" the results of the 1992 elections and abide by the peace accords. The term of UNAVEM was extended, – the 700-person operation had been reduced to 150 since October 1990 and was to be further reduced by 25% and its role reassessed.

By mid-1993, prospects for another agreed settlement appeared slim. Both the Government and UNITA were again engaged in another bitter, and probably long, civil war.[46]

Comments

Following the initial self-determination operations monitored by the U.N. in colonial territories, the "second generation" of U.N. monitoring of electoral processes started well.

The "nation-building" of Namibia under U.N. auspices, after decades of exhortations, guerrilla war and obstruction, has finally been a success: with a few incidents and crises, internal peace was restored, the South African forces and administration withdrew, the pre-electoral and electoral processes were carried out efficiently, election results were accepted by the contending parties, the Constituent Assembly adopted a democratic Constitution, and Namibia became not only independent and sovereign, but has, so far, maintained a democratic governance.

The transition of Nicaragua from a one-party Communist state to a pluralist state through free elections has also been successful on the same counts: first, U.N. and OAS monitoring have ensured that the electoral process, registration of parties and candidates, registration of voters, political campaigning, the election and its results were carried out fairly; secondly, election results were accepted by the losers, not an easy acceptance for a government and a party who believed in their victory, and thought that they genuinely represented the "people": the defeat of the Sandinistas in elections that they administered may be regarded as attesting to their integrity and democratic credentials; thirdly, in spite of political problems and tensions, Nicaragua is still under democratic governance.

The subsequent cases of Haiti and Angola show that free elections do not guarantee to the voters a democratic future. In both cases, elections were monitored by international observers and the U.N. declared that these elections had been free and fair. In one case, democracy was overthrown by a military coup d'état, in the other, civil war was re-initiated by the loser in the elections.

There is no lack of reasons to explain the failure of the democratic experiment in these countries.

In Haiti, the long history of dictatorships, military rulers, privileged elites, misery and corruption, greed and trafficking, uncontrolled violence, did not prepare the traditional rulers to give in to the ballots. It was also difficult for the representatives of the poor, when they unexpectedly gained power, not to take revenge over two centuries of oppression.

Angola's past, with its colonial domination, its anti-colonialist struggles, followed by a Communist takeover and a civil war, with foreign support on both sides, hardly prepared its political leaders and their troops for political compromise and acceptance of electoral results, particularly when these were to maintain the existing Government and party in power.

In both cases, neither the leaders nor the population have had any preparation for the difficult art of democracy nor any democratic experience. The Haitian elites feared the loss of their privileges and did not appreciate nor accept the general evolution of most countries in the Western Hemisphere towards democracy. The Haitian military leaders held on to their power, illicit trades and profits: they had not yet learned that the army should limit its role to the defence of the country, and not interfere in internal politics.

However, the compromise agreement reached early July 1993 between Haitian army leaders and President Aristide give some hope that democracy may progressively be introduced in the country, under strong and persistent pressure from "friendly" governments, the U.N. and the OAS.

On the other hand, no peaceful solution is in view for Angola.

Whatever the final outcome of both crises, the acceptance by the U.N. of such operations raises several questions:

- Should the U.N. accept all government requests indifferently, with a risk of "overreach" and inadequate means, or should strict criteria be established and observed before U.N. bodies accept such requests? In practice, U.N. bodies decide on such requests on political grounds, and their decisions are unlikely to be limited by pre-determined technical criteria.

- Should the U.N. only accept "easy cases", where the prognosis of democratic adaptation appears favourable? However, this would defeat the whole purpose of international monitoring missions, i.e. to help undemocratic countries to at least start their democratic transition;
- Does the responsibility of the U.N. in accepting and organizing the international monitoring of elections in a particular country stop on the day when the election results are announced, or does it extend beyond this period to a longer or shorter "after-election" period? On the one hand, the mandate of the U.N. in Haiti or in Angola did not extend to the installation and maintenance of a democratic regime in either country, but only to the pre-election and election monitoring period. On the other hand, international election monitoring tends to create expectations in the country itself, in other countries, in international organizations and in public opinion that the U.N., or any other intergovernmental organization, is also responsible for the success or failure of the democratic experiment and, in the case of post-election attack against democracy, should take some action to restore it in that country.

What action? Voting resolutions condemning coups d'état are meant to shame the usurpers of democracy through the rhetorical pressure of international public opinion. These resolutions are rarely respected, unless backed at least by political pressures and economic sanctions.

International organizations also encourage negotiations, offer their good offices, mediate, with varying degrees of success.

Traditional peace-keeping forces may be sent to control a ceasefire, but only with the agreement of the opposing parties. Another intermediate type of intervention is that approved for Haiti: sending a large U.N. and OAS contingent of human rights monitors to the country, who would observe and report on the situation, and perhaps provide an element of confidence needed to create a climate more propitious to the implementation of the July 1993 agreement.

In the Haiti case, it appears that patient and insistent mediation, supported by economic sanctions voted by the U.N. and the OAS, and political pressures from influential countries, finally obtained the reluctant consent of both parties to a compromise agreement.

Should international organizations intervene with military forces in a derelict country, and enforce democracy? It is probable that such intervention would only worsen the internal political situation and that renewed fighting would follow the withdrawal of the international military intervention. The decision against a military intervention in Haiti was wise, in view of the strong opposition of Latin American and Carribean governments to past U.S. military ventures in the Hemisphere, and also in view of the local hostility created by the U.N. "enforcement" role in Somalia.

On the basis of the recent experience gained by the U.N., it appears unrealistic and counter-productive to limit strictly the purposes and duration of a U.N. election-monitoring operation. As evidenced by the Haitian case, the continued involvement and intervention of the U.N. in various forms, after the coup, proved necessary and hopefully effective. While the U.N. does not have the necessary resources to improve significantly, on a long-term basis, the political, economic and social conditions in a country, nor to eradicate the deep roots of internal conflicts, its short- or mid-term assistance and monitoring may be sufficient to prevent or resolve post-electoral conflict.

While the preparation and the holding of elections require a minimum degree of cooperation between opposing parties, discreet negotiations between those parties should be encouraged by the U.N., shortly before the elections, in order to consider the possible political consequences of electoral victory and defeat. In the interest of civil peace, a government of national union might be envisaged, with appropriate representation of the various parties, based on their electoral results.

The U.N., as well as other intergovernmental and non-governmental organizations should play a decisive role, not only in democratic training, electoral assistance, election monitoring, but also in supporting pre- and post-election political negotiations between the political leaders and other forces in the country, with a view to maintaining civil peace and achieving national reconciliation.

Such an active and possibly costly role by the U.N. requires that the organization enjoys the crucial political and financial support of its influential members, and develops and maintains the operational capacity and competence to carry out all these tasks.

Notes

1. V.Y. Ghebali, "Le développement des opérations de maintien de la paix depuis la fin de la guerre froide", in *Trimestre du Monde*, 1992/4, pp. 67–85, and Georges Abi-Saab, "La deuxième génération des opérations de maintien de la paix", ibid., pp. 87–97.
2. See *The Blue Helmets – A review of U.N. Peace-keeping*, 2nd Ed., U.N., 1990, Chap. XVII, for a detailed description of the operation, as viewed by the U.N. For the views of UNTAG participants: see Ronald Dreyer, "The U.N. and Namibia: An Overview (1946–1990)", in *International Geneva Yearbook*, Vol. V, 1991, pp. 27–38. Dreyer acted as U.N. elections supervisor. Another UNTAG participant, Gabriele Winai Ström, submitted a paper on "U.N. Intervention and Supervision – The Role of the U.N. in the Namibian Conflict", to the Atlanta Conference of the International Studies Association, 31 March – 4 Apr. 1992. Another detailed description of the operation is in *Nation Building: the U.N. and Namibia*, National Democratic Institute for International Affairs, Washington, 1990. See also *A Life in Peace and War*, by Brian Urquhart, Harper and Row, 1987, Chap. XXIII.
3. "Legal Consequences for States of the Continued Presence of South Africa in Namibia (South West Africa) notwithstanding Security Council Resolution 276 (1970)", ICJ Reports, 1971.
4. Dreyer, op.cit., pp. 30–31.
5. Ibid., pp. 33–35, –Urquhart, op.cit., pp. 309–310.
6. The "Impartiality Provisions" are contained in an "Informal Checklist", –see text in *Nation Building*, op.cit., Appendix IX.
7. *International Herald Tribune*, 21 Dec. 1988.
8. *Nation Building*, op.cit., pp. 23–25, *Blue Helmets*, op.cit., p. 363.

9. Ström, op.cit., p. 11.
10. *Blue Helmets*, op.cit., pp. 379–383.
11. "Preparing for a Free Namibia: Elections, Transition and Independence – The Report of the Commonwealth Observer Group on Namibia", Windhoek, 10 Oct. 1989, Commonwealth Secretariat, London, p. 21.
12. U.N. Doc. DH/435 of 22 June 1989 and DH/488 of 13 Sept. 1989, *International Herald Tribune*, 19 June 1989, – Commonwealth Report, op.cit., pp. xi, xii.
13. *Blue Helmets*, op.cit., p. 373.
14. See for instance, "Report of the Mission to observe the elections in Namibia", Doc. CL/146/10-R.1 of 20 Dec. 1989, Inter-Parliamentary Union, Geneva, para. 64.
15. *Nation Building*, op.cit., pp. 79–80.
16. The Joint Commission had been set up in Brazzaville in December 1988 by Angola, Cuba and South Africa, and included representatives of the U.S.A. and the USSR. See Dreyer, op.cit., p. 37.
17. *Blue Helmets*, pp. 389–392, –*U.N. Focus*, "Election Supervision, the U.N. Experience in Namibia and Nicaragua", Nov. 1990, –*Issues/45*, U.N. Association of the U.S.A., 1991, pp. 35–43, U.N. Doc. A/46/609, 19 Nov. 1991, pp. 10–14.
18. *Issues/45*, op.cit., p. 37.
19. Ibid., p. 38, –U.N. Doc. A/C.3/44/SR.42 of 14 Nov. 1989.
20. *International Herald Tribune*, 17 Jan. 1990.
21. "Observing Nicaragua's Elections, 1989–1990", The Council of Freely-Elected Heads of Government, The Carter Center of Emory University, Special Report No. 1, p. 12.
22. *Freedom in the World – Political Rights and Civil Liberties – 1991–1992*, Freedom House, 1992, pp. 233–235, –"The 1990 General Elections in Haiti, International Delegation Report", Council and National Democratic Institute for International Affairs, 1991, Chapter 2, –see also, "The World in Turmoil: Testing the U.N.'s Capacity", The Academic Council on the U.N. System, 1991–4, pp. 40–41.
23. *World Development Report 1992*, World Bank, Oxford University Press, 1992, p. 218.
24. "The 1990 General Elections in Haiti", op.cit., p. 30.
25. Ibid., p. 33, –"U.N. Assistance for Human Rights", Rädda Barnen/International Commission of Jurists, Sweden, Sept. 1988, pp. 136–137.
26. U.N. Doc. E/CN.4/1990/44 of 23 Jan. 1990, pp. 22–23.
27. "The 1990 General Elections in Haiti", op.cit., p. 35.
28. U.N. Doc. A/44/965 of 17 July 1990. For a short U.N. account of the Haiti Operation, see U.N. leaflet DPI/1120, March 1991, "U.N. Electoral Assistance to Haiti".
29. *U.N. Observer and International Report*, Sept. 1990.
30. U.N. *Press Release*, DH/741, 8 Oct. 1990.
31. U.N. *Press Release* GA/AB/43 of 10 Oct. 1990.
32. U.N. *Press Release* SG/SM/4531. See also U.N. Doc. A/45/870 of 14 Dec. 1990, "Electoral Assistance to Haiti", and Add. 1 of 22 Feb. 1991.
33. "The 1990 General Elections in Haiti", op.cit., pp. 8–9.
34. The full text of OAS Resolution 1080 and excerpts from Resolutions of 3 and 8 October are found in *Journal of Democracy*, Jan. 1992, pp. 128–130. See also, U.S. *Daily Bulletins*, Geneva, EUR212 of 1 Oct., EUR302 of 2 Oct., EUR416 of 3 Oct., EUR311 of 9 Oct., and *International Herald Tribune*, 4 Oct. 1991.
35. U.N. *Press Release* DH/986 of 1 Oct., DH/989 of 4 Oct., U.S. *Daily Bulletin* EUR514 of 4 Oct., *Le Monde*, 4 Oct. 1991. The USSR, the U.K., the U.S., France, Belgium and Austria were in favour of voting a resolution, while India, Yemen, Cuba and Ecuador were opposed, and Ivory Coast, Zimbabwe, Romania and China hesitant: *Le Monde*, 5 Oct. 1991.
36. *Le Monde*, 11 Oct. 1991, U.S. *Daily Bulletin*, EUR506 of 11 Oct. 1991, –Pamela Constable, "Haiti's Shattered Hopes" in *Journal of Democracy*, Jan. 1992, pp. 41–51.
37. U.N. *Press Release* DH/1265 of 9 Nov. 1992, and U.S. *Daily Bulletin* EUR303 of 25 Nov. 1992.

38. *International Herald Tribune*, 18 Jan. 1993, U.N. *Press Release* DH/1317 of 26 Jan. 1993, U.S. *Daily Bulletin* (Geneva), 9 and 10 Feb. 1993, *Le Monde*, 18 March 1993, –U.N. Resol. 47/20 of 20 Apr. 1993. *International Herald Tribune*, 16 June, 3–4 July 1993, *Le Monde*, 6 July 1993.
39. Excerpts from the portion of the Accords on "Fundamental Principles for the Establishment of Peace in Angola" may be found in *Journal of Democracy*, Jan. 1992, p. 134. See also *Freedom in the World* op.cit., pp. 85–87.
40. *International Herald Tribune*, 2 May, 1–2 June 1991, *Le Monde*, 2–3 June 1991.
41. Security Council Resol. 696 of 30 May 1991, –U.N. *Press Release* SC/251 of 30 May 1991.
42. U.N. *Press Release* DH/1094 of 6 March 1992, DH/1104 of 23 March, DH/1105 of 24 March 1992, U.S. *Daily Bulletin*, EUR305 of 26 March 1992, *–U.N. Observer and International Report*, June 1992.
43. U.N. *Press Releases* DH/1177 of 7 July, DH/1196 of 3 Aug., DH/1228 of 17 Sept., DH/1229 of 18 Sept., DH/1238 of 1 Oct. 1992, *Le Monde*, 29 Sept. and *International Herald Tribune*, 7 Oct. 1992.
44. U.N. *Press Releases* DH/1242 of 7 Oct., DH/1249 of 16 Oct., DH/1250 of 19 Oct., DH/1259 of 30 Oct., DH/1278 of 27 Nov. 1992, U.S. *Daily Bulletin* EUR205 of 14 Oct 1992, *Le Monde*, 16 and 20 Oct. 1992, *International Herald Tribune*, 7, 9, 13, 14, 19 Oct. 1992, *The Economist*, 5 Dec. 1992.
45. *International Herald Tribune*, 19, 28 and 29 Jan. 1993.
46. U.N. *Press Release* SG/SM/1399 of 15 Jan. 1993, U.S. *Daily Bulletin* (Geneva) of 27 Jan. and 2 June 1993, *Le Monde*, 13, 14–15 March, 4, 21, 23–24 May 1993, *–International Herald Tribune*, 24 May 1993.

CHAPTER 7

ONGOING U.N. MONITORING OPERATIONS

A contrasted and composite image emerges from the review of completed U.N. monitoring operations reviewed in the previous Chapter.

On the one hand, a series of U.N. initiatives have changed both the size and the nature of U.N. missions. One such initiative led the organization from the earlier, almost routine, small observation missions of plebiscites and referenda in dependent territories to a large, complex, and costly operation, which helped a colonial territory gain independence and create democratic institutions, through the presence of large U.N. military and civilian contingents, supported by hundreds of other international observers.

The new democratic mandate assumed by the U.N. was even more evident in the Nicaragua, Haiti and Angola operations, where the main, or only purpose of the U.N. presence was to monitor elections in these sovereign countries, in order to ensure that the electoral process was free and genuine.

On the other hand, while the monitoring role carried out by the U.N. in those countries was generally effective, the hoped-for democratic transition failed in Haiti and Angola, raising questions as to the justification for U.N. electoral interventions in general, and in particular in countries which are not yet ready for the compromises and tolerance required by democratic governance, or where a fragile ceasefire may soon be shattered by the tensions of the electoral process and by the outcome (winner/loser) of the elections.

Is the U.N. over-extending itself and creating excessive expectations? Will the organization, in spite of its democratic ambitions, be linked to democratic failures? Should its role extend to imposing, or restoring democracy by force, when the politicians and/or the military reject democracy in a particular country?

On-going operations, not yet completed, also raise such questions. Some may not even reach the stage of the electoral process, on account of the lack of co-operation of parties in implementing signed agreements. The planned referendum for Western Sahara may never be held because of Moroccan obstruction, – the Cambodian elections were held in only part of the country because of their rejection by the Khmer Rouge. The Mozambique operation is only starting, but concern has already been expressed that it may follow the unhappy Angolan precedent.

Western Sahara: Self-Determination or Annexation?

On 11 August 1988, the U.N. Secretary-General and a representative of the Organization of African Unity (OAU) presented to the parties to the conflict in Western Sahara, namely Morocco and the "Frente Polisario" proposals for its settlement. These proposals, which included a ceasefire and the holding of a referendum, under U.N. auspices, to enable the people of Western Sahara to choose between independence and integration with Morocco, were approved by the two parties on 30 August 1988.

On 27 June 1990, the Security Council, by resolution 658, endorsed the proposals and the Secretary-General's plans to implement them.

Historical Background

Western Sahara lies between Morocco and Mauritania on the northwest coast of Africa. Phosphate mines are its principal economic resource. The territory of 264,000 square kilometers is inhabited by a nomadic population of 186,000, of whom approximately 60,000 are refugees living in camps in southwestern Algeria.

A Spanish colony since 1884, the U.N. placed it in 1963 on the list of Non-Self-Governing Territories with the right to self-determination, in accordance with the 1960 Declaration on the Granting of Independence to Colonial Countries and Peoples (resolution 1514 (XV)).[1]

In December 1965, the General Assembly requested Spain to take all necessary measures for the Territory's decolonization, and in December 1966, the Assembly requested Spain to determine, in consultation with Mauritania and Morocco, the procedures for the holding of a referendum under U.N. auspices.

In 1973, the "Popular Front for the Liberation of Saguia el-Hamra and Rio de Oro" (Polisario) was founded and began an armed struggle against Spain.

In 1974, Spain announced plans for a referendum: these were rejected by the King of Morocco, who could not accept a referendum which included the option of independence . . . In September, he proposed to submit the case to arbitration by the International Court of Justice. In December, the General Assembly requested the Court to give an advisory opinion on the legal status of the Territory.

The Court concluded that the materials and information presented to it did not establish any tie of territorial sovereignty between the territory of Western Sahara and Morocco or Mauritania. The Court had

> not found legal ties of such a nature as might affect the application of resolution 1514 (XV) in the decolonization of Western Sahara and, in particular, of the

> principle of self-determination through the free and genuine expression of the will of the peoples of the Territory.[2]

Ignoring the Court judgement, Spain, Morocco and Mauritania agreed in November to partition the territory between the latter two countries. Spain withdrew from Western Sahara as a colonial power on 26 February 1976.

On 27 February, the Provisional Saharawi National Council, backed by the Polisario, proclaimed the founding of the Saharawi Arab Democratic Republic (SADR).

In October 1975, the King of Morocco sent a peaceful "Green March" of 350,000 Moroccans into the territory, as a *de facto* annexation: clashes, then serious fighting, ensued with the Polisario.

In August 1979, Mauritania renounced its part of Western Sahara, which was promptly annexed by Morocco.

In June 1981, King Hassan II announced his acceptance of a referendum in the Western Sahara.

On 11 June 1983, the OAU Summit adopted a resolution (AHG/Res.104 (XIX)), urging

> the parties to the conflict, the Kingdom of Morocco and the Polisario Front, to undertake direct negotiations with a view to bringing about a ceasefire to create the necessary conditions for a peaceful and fair referendum for self-determination of the people of Western Sahara, a referendum without any administrative or military constraints, under the auspices of the OAU and the U.N.

In November 1984, Morocco withdrew from the OAU in protest at the SADR's admission to the organization.

In October 1985, Morocco declared a unilateral ceasefire.

On 2 December 1985, the U.N. General Assembly invited the Chairman of the OAU and the Secretary-General of the U.N. to exert every effort to persuade the two parties to the conflict to negotiate the terms of a ceasefire and the modalities for the referendum (Resol. 40/50).

Between July 1985 and May 1988, the former U.N. Secretary-General, J. Perez de Cuellar, initiated a series of consultations and visits with OAU Chairmen, representatives of Morocco (including King Hassan II himself), Algeria, Mauritania, and Polisario representatives.

Fighting resumed in early 1987, while Morocco was building a defensive wall, in order to prevent Saharawi incursions from Algeria.

Approval of the U.N./OAU Settlement Plan

On 11 August 1988, he presented his peace proposal, in separate meetings, to both parties as a "compromise which will no doubt promote a just and durable solution of the Western Sahara question".

Both sides agreed to the plan "in principle" on 30 August, and, on 20 September, the Security Council, in resolution 621, noted the "agreement in principle" given by both parties to the joint U.N. and OAU proposals, and, as a first step in initiating a U.N. mission, the Council authorized the Secretary-General to appoint a Special Representative for Western Sahara.

In May 1990, the Secretary-General, in consultation with the OAU Chairman, established an Identification Commission whose mandate was to verify the eligibility to vote of the territory's people and to issue them voter registration cards.

On 27 June, the Security Council approved the Secretary-General's plan for a settlement of the Western Sahara question. According to the plan, there would be a transition period during which:

- The Special Representative of the Secretary-General would have sole and exclusive responsibility over all matters relating to the referendum, including its organization and conduct;
- He would be assisted by an integrated support group of U.N. civilian, military and civil police personnel, the U.N. Mission for the Referendum in Western Sahara, MINURSO;
- There would be a ceasefire monitored by U.N. military personnel, followed by an exchange of prisoners of war under the auspices of the International Committee of the Red Cross (ICRC);
- Morocco would undertake an appropriate, substantial and phased reduction of its troops in the Territory;
- Combatants on each side would be confined to locations specified by the Special Representative and monitored by U.N. military personnel;
- The U.N. would organize and conduct a referendum, and issue the necessary regulations, rules and instructions for that purpose (in particular, voting would be by secret ballot, with arrangements made for voters who could not read or write);
- The U.N. would monitor other aspects of the Territory's administration, especially the maintenance of law and order, to ensure the necessary conditions for the holding of a free and fair referendum;
- After proclamation of an amnesty, political prisoners would be released and all laws or regulations which, in the view of the Special Representative, could impede the holding of a free and fair referendum, would be suspended to the extent deemed necessary;
- All refugees and other Western Saharans resident outside the Territory and wishing to return would be enabled to do so by the U.N., after the latter had established their right to vote;
- Unless the Special Representative determined that circumstances dictated otherwise, the referendum would be held 24 weeks after the ceasefire came into effect and its results would be proclaimed within 72 hours; and
- Neighbouring Algeria and Mauritania would cooperate with the Special Representative in ensuring that the transitional arrangements and the results of the referendum were respected.

The civilian unit of MINURSO was expected to total approximately 275 international (U.N.) staff members, the security unit up to 300 police officers and the military unit approximately 1,600 observers.

On 29 April 1991, the Security Council finally established MINURSO, under its authority (Resol. 690). In his report of 19 April (S/22464), the Secretary-General had stressed that four conditions had to be met for MINURSO to be able to carry out its responsibilities effectively and with complete impartiality. First, MINURSO must at all times have the full support and backing of the Security Council; secondly, it must operate with the full cooperation of the two parties, particularly with regard to the comprehensive cessation of all hostile acts; thirdly, the cooperation and support of the neighbouring countries must be assured; and fourthly, the necessary financial resources must be made available by Member States in a full and timely manner.

On 17 May 1991, the General Assembly approved a $140 million budget for the first six months of MINURSO (Resol. 45/266).

The Secretary-General had appointed, in October 1988, Hector Gros Espiell (Uruguay) as his Special Representative. Upon his resignation in late 1989, Johannes Manz (Switzerland) replaced him, only to resign at the end of 1991. A third Special Representative was appointed in March 1992, Sahabzada Yaqub-Khan (Pakistan).

In June 1991, Major-General Armand Roy (Canada) was appointed as Force Commander of MINURSO's military contingent.[3]

The ceasefire was effective on 6 September 1991, and the referendum was scheduled for January 1992.

Postponed to an unspecified date in 1993, it may never be held.

The "Waiting Game" of Morocco

The parties to the conflict are the Kingdom of Morocco and a liberation movement: their inequality is evident, even if the Polisario has benefitted from the support of the U.N. and of the OAU.

Morocco has annexed Western Sahara and occupied it militarily: Morocco has deployed 130,000 well-equipped troops, backed by air power, while the Polisario has only a few thousand guerrilla fighters who have to rely on the desert and Algeria for escape and a refuge.

The Territory is considered by most Moroccans as a legitimate part of "Greater Morocco".

As a former French protectorate with close political and economic links with France, Morocco has France's support. As a conservative Arab country, a solid Cold War and Gulf War ally, a supporter of the current peace negotiations between Israel and Arab countries, the King of Morocco is a useful and friendly partner for the U.S.[4] For both countries and other Western States, the continuation of King Hassan's regime, whatever its faults, is a necessary bulwark against the wave of

Islamic fundamentalism. Hassan II's implicit blackmail argument is that if Western Sahara does not remain with Morocco, his loss of face may cost him his throne.

Besides the weakness of the support to the U.N. plan by at least two permanent members of the Security Council, the conflict in North West Africa has always been considered peripheral, of little strategic import.

The Polisario supported the U.N. referendum as its only chance to win control of Western Sahara. It could not win a "liberation" war against Moroccan power: neither the initial financial and material support received from Algeria, Libya and Cuba,[5] nor the diplomatic recognition given by 70 to 100 countries to its government-in-exile nor the support given by a weak and ineffective OAU could override King Hassan's determination.

Morocco's agreement "in principle" to the U.N. plan was given on the premise that the Western Saharans eligible to vote in the referendum would overwhelmingly decide in favour of the Territory's integration with Morocco.

To this end, Morocco challenged the initial findings of the U.N. Identification Commission, which had transmitted to the two parties in October 1990 a revised list of 70,204 names of eligible voters, based on the 1974 Spanish census list, requesting the parties to update it, taking into account the population changes in the Territory in the past 16 years.

To the U.N.'s and the Polisario Front's dismay, the Moroccans insisted on adding a second list of more than 120,000 additional potential voters. These would include nomadic Saharans who had settled in southern Morocco, northern Mauritania and southwest Algeria at the time of the census.[6] This inflated claim could only delay indefinitely an agreement by both parties on a final list of qualified voters, in view of the length of time required, and difficulties in verifying each name and identity. In December 1992, consultations with Western Sahara chieftains were cancelled due to disagreements over the powers of some of the participants. The participants – 19 of them nominated by Morocco and 19 by the Polisario – were expected to advise the U.N. Special Representative on ways and means of identifying prospective voters.[7]

In the meantime, Morocco was applying measures of repression in Western Sahara: the Polisario alleged that, on 24 September 1992, the Moroccan security forces had opened fire on Saharawi demonstrators in the town of Assa, and hundreds of Saharawis had been arrested in October in Smara and Layoune. Ignoring the planned U.N. referendum, Morocco informed the U.N. in August 1992 that a referendum on constitutional reform would be held in October across the nation, including in the disputed Western Sahara. Morocco was also encouraging the defection of Polisario leaders through pardons, job and financial rewards. Furthermore, the U.N. Secretary-General reported in December 1991 that as was "well known, a number of persons who are claimed to belong to Western Sahara have been moved into the Territory".[8]

Morocco was also actively hampering the deployment and intervention of the U.N. military and civilian contingents. By June 1992, only 349 U.N. military observers and other personnel had been allowed in Western Sahara, only to monitor the ceasefire, and under restricted conditions. A report by the U.S. Senate Foreign Relations Committee condemned the U.N. for failing to respond to ceasefire violations and threats by Moroccan forces to fire on unarmed American, Canadian, British and other officers acting as U.N. military observers. Moroccan soldiers allegedly threatened the military at gunpoint and warned that they would open fire if the U.N. persisted in patrolling certain areas. The same report also alleged that the U.N. had failed to report dozens of ceasefire violations by both sides in discussions with Morocco and the Polisario. Morocco had held up shipments of U.N. supplies, including medical supplies of the Swiss Medical Unit. An independent observer testified on 1 October 1992 to the Subcommittee on Africa Committee on Foreign Affairs, U.S. House of Representatives, that

> MINURSO officials are veritable hostages . . . There is no U.N. presence or evidence of its authority – no flags, signs, or symbols fostering confidence in the population.[9]

The movements of journalists and other visitors are also strictly controlled.[10]

In March 1992, the U.N. Secretary-General alluded to the necessity of considering "alternative courses of action" and a "new approach" to the Western Sahara question if an agreement on the existing U.N. plan had not been reached by the end of May 1992.

Ten months later, no agreement had been reached, and the Secretary-General was faced with a political impasse which only the Security Council could resolve.

In a report dated 26 January 1993, the Secretary-General requested guidance from the Council on "how best to proceed". He said it was "regrettable" that the two parties had "failed . . . to reach a relatively straightforward compromise" on the holding of a meeting of tribal chiefs at the end of November 1992. He noted that there were substantial disagreements between the parties regarding fundamental issues.

He presented the Council with three broad options: one option was to continue the talks, but "the chances for success . . . are very slim", – another (implausible) option was the immediate implementation of the settlement plan and the holding of the referendum, possibly without the cooperation of one of the parties, – a third option would be to adopt an alternative approach not based on the settlement plan.

On 2 March 1993, the Security Council urged the two parties to cooperate with the Secretary-General in his efforts to work out the modalities for the holding of a free and fair referendum of self-determination of the people in that Territory before the end of the year, at the latest.[11]

Comments

The difficulties of implementation of the U.N. plan may be related to the four conditions for success defined by the Secretary-General in his 1991 report:

1. "MINURSO must at all times have the full support and backing of the Security Council": support has been given periodically, but not as a politically important operation deserving of the constant attention of the permanent members. The Western Powers had other more compelling issues or crises to deal with, such as the Middle East peace negotiations, the civil war in former Yugoslavia, the Cambodia operation. Neither the U.S. nor France seem to have applied effective pressures on Morocco in order to allow the operation to proceed without further delay, including the deployment of U.N. contingents.
2. "MINURSO must operate with the full cooperation of the two parties, particularly with regard to the comprehensive cessation of all hostile acts": clearly Morocco has not cooperated with MINURSO, but, on the contrary, has openly hampered the planned process. Morocco, and to a more limited extent, the Polisario, have engaged in occasional fighting.
3. "The cooperation and support of the neighbouring countries must be assured": it appears that Algeria has stopped its support of the Polisario.
4. "The necessary financial resources must be made available by Member States in a full and timely manner": U.N. Members have reduced the proposed budget for the operation, but, as only part of the planned contingents was actually deployed in Western Sahara, the available financial resources have not been, so far, a constraining problem for the operation.

The real alternatives open to the Security Council may be the following:

- to continue the U.N. operation on the same premises and conditions;
- to apply effective pressure on Morocco in order to proceed with the preparation and holding of the referendum;
- to initiate new negotiations between the two parties in order to resolve promptly, by mutual agreement, the electoral lists issue;
- to encourage Morocco, as part of a settlement without referendum, to grant Western Sahara a guaranteed, well-defined, degree of political and administrative autonomy;
- to recognize that the present political and other conditions lead to the cancellation of the U.N. operation of self-determination, thus allowing Morocco to decide freely Western Sahara's fate.

Prospects for the successful continuation of the U.N. operation in Western Sahara are not promising: it is unlikely that the proposed self-determination referendum will be held before the end of 1993.

The Challenge of Cambodia

Finding a peaceful solution to the situation of Cambodia has been a concern of the U.N. since 1979, following the military intervention of Vietnam in December 1978, which removed the Khmer Rouge leadership from power, although they remained in parts of the country as the main anti-government group, waging guerrilla warfare, financed and armed by China.

The resolution voted on 14 November 1979 by the General Assembly (Resol. 34/22) did not express relief nor satisfaction at the removal of the genocidal Khmer Rouge from power: on the contrary, the Assembly "deeply regretted" the method used for this removal, i.e. "the armed intervention by outside forces in the internal affairs of Kampuchea" and called for the immediate withdrawal of all foreign forces from the country. However, as a democratic after-thought, the Assembly also

> 10. *Resolve(d)* that the people of Kampuchea should be enabled to choose democratically their own government, without outside interference, subversion or coercion;

The democratic self-determination concept was to be one of the basic tenets of the creation of the future United Nations Transitional Authority in Cambodia.

The U.N. operation in Cambodia is the most ambitious peace-keeping, national reconciliation and "nation-rebuilding" operation to be carried in a sovereign country: the U.N. Transitional Authority in Cambodia (UNTAC), with military and civilian contingents should restore civil peace, organize and run democratic elections for a constituent assembly, i.e. restore Cambodian independence and establish democratic institutions in the country. The refusal of the Khmer Rouge to apply the agreements which they had signed has however hampered the progress of the operation and initially dampened hopes that civil peace would soon be restored to Cambodia.

Historical Background

Cambodia achieved its independence from France in 1953. Its leader, Prince Norodom Sihanouk, attempted to keep Cambodia as a non-aligned country. He was overthrown in a rightist, U.S.-supported coup, and replaced by General Lon Nol in March 1970. In turn, the Lon Nol regime fell in April 1975 to the Communist Khmer Rouge. Once in power, the Khmer Rouge undertook a ruthless programme of agrarian reform, forced dogmatic indoctrination and physical elimination of the Western-oriented elites, which resulted in the deaths of an estimated 1 to 3 million Cambodians, a genocide inflicted by its leaders on their own population. Vietnam, a Soviet client State, invaded Cambodia in December 1978, ousted the Khmer Rouge, and installed the Communist government of the Kampuchean People's Revolutionary Party, under the leadership of Khmer Rouge defector Heng Samrin and Hun Sen as Prime Minister.

In 1982, three anti-Vietnamese groups formed the Coalition Government of Democratic Kampuchea to overthrow the Vietnam-supported Government. Led by Prince Sihanouk, these were the Chinese-backed Khmer Rouge, with an estimated 30,000 to 40,000 troops, the Sihanouk National Army, led by the Prince, with up to 20,000 troops, and the Khmer People's National Liberation Army, led by former

Prime Minister Son Sann, with approximately 10,000 soldiers. The coalition was in fact totally dominated by the Khmer Rouge leadership.

In mid-1988, Vietnam removed 50,000 of the estimated 120,000–140,000 troops it had stationed in Cambodia, and announced a complete withdrawal in September 1989.[12] The withdrawal was however not monitored by independent observers.

The end of the Cold War, the withdrawal of Soviet military aid to Vietnam, pressures on China to cease its political and military support to the Khmer Rouge, the interest of other Asian countries in bringing peace to that area, diplomatic efforts from Western countries, including the leadership of France, the former colonial power, as well as general war weariness helped in bringing all parties towards a political solution. Improved relations between the USSR, China and the U.S.A. reduced tensions among the major sponsors of the four Cambodian factions and gave an impetus to multilateral efforts towards a peaceful settlement.

The situation in Cambodia was first considered by the U.N. Security Council early in 1979, but the lack of agreement among the permanent members prevented the Council from taking any decision. Later in 1979, the General Assembly adopted a resolution . . . in which it called for the withdrawal of all foreign forces from Kampuchea, appealed to all States to refrain from any interference in the internal affairs of the country and resolved that the people of Kampuchea should be enabled democratically to choose their own government, without outside interference, subversion or coercion. The Assembly also requested the Secretary-General to exercise his good offices towards a peaceful solution. The Secretary-General and his Special Representative, Rafeeuddin Ahmed, maintained contacts with concerned Governments and Cambodian parties and formulated proposals.

At the initiative of France, 18 countries, including the five permanent members of the Security Council, and the Cambodian parties attended the Paris Conference on Cambodia from 30 July to 30 August 1989, the French and Indonesian Foreign Ministers acting as co-Chairmen, with the participation of the U.N. Secretary-General. No agreement was reached.

In November 1989, Australian Foreign Minister Gareth Evans proposed that Cambodia's seat in the U.N. (still fictionally occupied by the deposed Khmer Rouge Government) should be declared vacant and the country administered by the U.N. until elections could be held.

Following several meetings in 1989, the five permanent members of the Security Council met in Paris in January 1990 and agreed on the need for an enhanced U.N. role, including a transitional period between a ceasefire and elections. The five pledged to honour the results of the elections. In August, the five announced that they had agreed on a framework for a comprehensive settlement of the Cambodian conflict. On 10 September, in the Jakarta Informal Meeting, the four Cambodian parties accepted the framework, in its entirety, as the basis for settling the conflict. They also agreed to form the Supreme National Council (SNC) as the unique legitimate body and source of authority in Cambodia throughout a transitional period. On 20 September, the Security Council adopted resolution 668 endorsing the framework.

On 23 October 1991, the Agreements on a Comprehensive Political Settlement of the Cambodia Conflict were signed by the leaders of the four Cambodian parties – Prince Sihanouk, Sonn San, Prime Minister Hun Sen, and Khieu Samphan – and by the representatives of 18 other countries in the presence of the U.N. Secretary-General.

The 1991 Agreements

The main objectives of the Agreements were to restore and maintain peace in Cambodia, to promote national reconciliation and to ensure the exercise of the right to self-determination of the Cambodian people through free and fair elections. At the same time, the sovereignty, independence, territorial integrity and inviolability, neutrality and national unity of the country must be preserved[13]: more accurately, these attributes should be restored to the war-torn and divided country.

To these ends, the Agreements provide for the establishment, by the Security Council, of a U.N. Transitional Authority in Cambodia (UNTAC) with civilian and military components under the direct responsibility of the U.N. Secretary-General, who will designate a Special Representative.

The transition process commences with the entry in force of the Agreements and terminates when the constituent assembly elected through free and fair elections, organized and certified by the U.N., has approved the constitution and transformed itself into a legislative assembly, and thereafter a new government has been created.

The Agreements re-affirm that the SNC is the unique legitimate body and source of authority in which, throughout the transitional period, the sovereignty, independence and unity of Cambodia are enshrined. The SNC, presided by Prince Sihanouk, delegates to the U.N. all powers necessary to ensure the implementation of the Agreements.

Upon entry into force of the Agreements, the ceasefire will take effect, foreign forces and their weapons will be withdrawn from Cambodia, all outside military assistance to all Cambodian parties will cease, all Cambodian forces and their weapons will be regrouped, cantoned, under UNTAC supervision.

UNTAC will be responsible for the organization and conduct of the elections. In order to ensure a neutral political environment conducive to free and fair general elections, administrative agencies, bodies and offices which could directly influence the outcome of elections will be placed under direct UNTAC supervision or control, with particular reference to foreign affairs, national defence, finance, public security and information. All civil police will operate under UNTAC supervision or control. The specific authority of UNTAC in the exercise of its responsibilities in relation to the electoral process is reproduced in Table 7.1.

UNTAC will be responsible, during the transition period, for fostering an environment in which respect for human rights "shall be ensured". The U.N. will facilitate the repatriation in safety and dignity of Cambodian refugees and displaced

Table 7.1. UNTAC authority in relation to the Cambodia electoral process

In the exercise of its responsibilities in relation to the electoral process, the specific authority of UNTAC will include the following:

a) The establishment, in consultation with the Supreme National Council (SNC), of a system of laws, procedures and administrative measures necessary for the holding of a free and fair election in Cambodia, including the adoption of an electoral law and of a code of conduct regulating participation in the election in a manner consistent with respect for human rights and prohibiting coercion or financial inducement in order to influence voter preference;
b) The suspension or abrogation, in consultation with the SNC, of provisions in existing laws which could defeat the objects and purposes of this Agreement;
c) The design and implementation of a voter education programme, covering all aspects of the election, to support the election process;
d) The design and implementation of a system of voter registration, as a first phase of the electoral process, to ensure that eligible voters have the opportunity to register, and the subsequent preparation of verified voter registration lists;
e) The design and implementation of a system of registration of political parties and lists of candidates;
f) Ensuring fair access to the media, including press, television and radio, for all political parties contesting the election;
g) The adoption and implementation of measures to monitor and facilitate the participation of Cambodians in the elections, the political campaign and the balloting procedures;
h) The design and implementation of a system of balloting and polling, to ensure that registered voters have the opportunity to vote;
i) The establishment, in consultation with the SNC, of coordinated arrangements to facilitate the presence of foreign observers wishing to observe the campaign and voting;
j) Overall direction of polling and the vote count;
k) The identification and investigation of complaints of electoral irregularities, and the taking of appropriate corrective action;
l) Determining whether or not the election was free and fair and, if so, certification of the list of persons duly elected.

Source: "Agreements on a Comprehensive Political Settlement of the Cambodia Conflict – Paris, 23 October 1991", U.N., Annex 1, "UNTAC Mandate", Section D – Elections, section 3.

persons, while the release of all prisoners of war and civilian internees will be accomplished under the direction of the International Committee of the Red Cross.

The ultimate purpose of the Agreements was not only to initiate a peace process, to restore Cambodia as a sovereign, independent and neutral country, but also to establish democratic institutions in the country.

According to the agreed "Principles for a new constitution for Cambodia",[14]

> 4. The constitution will state that Cambodia will follow a system of liberal democracy, on the basis of pluralism. It will provide for periodic and genuine elections. It will provide for the right to vote and to be elected by universal and equal suffrage. It will provide for voting by secret ballot, with a requirement that electoral procedures provide a full and fair opportunity to organize and participate in the electoral process.
>
> 5. An independent judiciary will be established, empowered to enforce the rights provided under the constitution.

Approval of the United Nations Transitional Authority in Cambodia (UNTAC)

On 16 October 1991, the Security Council welcomed the election of Prince Sihanouk as the Chairman of the Supreme National Council and decided to establish a U.N. Advance Mission in Cambodia (UNAMIC) immediately after the signing of the forthcoming Paris Agreements (Resol. 717). On 31 October, the Security Council authorized the Secretary-General to designate a Special Representative for Cambodia to act on his behalf (Resol. 718). On 8 January 1992, the Council approved unanimously the Secretary-General's proposal to expand UNAMIC's mandate to include training in mine clearance and the initiation of a mine clearance programme among the Cambodian people (Resol. 728). On 9 January, the Secretary-General appointed Yasushi Akashi (Japan) as his Special Representative.

On 28 February, the Security Council authorized, again unanimously, the establishment of UNTAC as a $1.9 billion peace-keeping operation involving about 22,000 foreign personnel to oversee the country's transition to a new administration after multi-party elections (Resol. 745). UNTAC's term was not to exceed 18 months and it was vital that elections be held by May 1993 at the latest, as recommended by the Secretary-General. UNTAC was to be deployed as soon as possible. Under the direction of the Special Representative, UNTAC would consist of seven distinct components: military, electoral, human rights, civil administration, police, repatriation and rehabilitation.

The 15,900-man military component, headed by a Force Commander, would verify withdrawal and non-return of foreign forces and their arms and equipment, supervise the ceasefire, including regroupment, cantonment, disarming and demobilization, assist with mine clearance, etc.

The Council's Resolution, in part,

> 8. *Strongly urges* the Cambodian parties to agree to the complete demobilization of their military forces prior to the end of the process of registration for the elections as well as to the destruction of the weapons and ammunition deposited into UNTAC custody in excess of those, if any, which may be deemed necessary by UNTAC for the maintenance of civil order and national defence, or which may be required by the new Cambodian Government;

The electoral component would consist of 72 international personnel operating from headquarters and 126 personnel at 21 provincial and municipal centres. Under the supervision of headquarters and provincial electoral personnel, 400 U.N. Volunteers will operate from each of the 200 districts. Electoral personnel will be supplemented by 800 Cambodian teams (4,000 personnel) during the three- to four-month period of voter registration, and, for the polling process, by 1,000 international supervisors and 8,000 Cambodian polling teams (56,000 personnel).

The human rights and civil administration components would consist of some 224 specialists, assisted by 24 international support staff.

The police component would consist of some 3,600 civilian police monitors.

All UNTAC components would be assisted by an estimated 7,000 locally recruited support personnel, including some 2,500 interpreters and additional temporary staff.[15]

The financing had been authorized by the General Assembly in an initial amount of $200 million on 14 February 1992 (Resol. 46/222). Final costs may range from $1.4 to 1.7 billion.

The "Difficult" Deployment of UNTAC: The U.N. Story

All was in place for the implementation of the Paris Agreements, signed by all four Cambodian parties, and endorsed unanimously by the Security Council and the General Assembly: the U.N. had designed a comprehensive, multi-disciplinary and multi-purpose operational programme apparently based on solid political grounds, the most ambitious operation since the U.N. Operation in the Congo.

Quite rightly, the U.N. Secretary-General had affirmed that the success of UNTAC depended above all on the full cooperation at all times of the Cambodian protagonists and all other parties concerned.[16]

Not all Cambodian parties cooperated: from the beginning of the U.N. operation the Khmer Rouge (The "Democratic Kampuchea" party) deliberately obstructed the implementation of the plan by preventing the deployment of UNTAC, by military force, in the areas controlled by them, thus reneging on their formal international pledge.

The following events, as reported by the U.N., show in part the progressive deployment of UNTAC in Cambodia, excepting the Khmer Rouge areas, the development of its components' planned activities leading to elections in May 1993, – together with recurrent Khmer Rouge attacks, provocations, kidnappings and killings intended to derail the whole democratic experiment, or to try to de-legitimize its results. The U.N.'s response was limited, in New York, to rhetorical expressions of "concern" and demands of compliance issued by the Security Council, and, in the field, to negotiations with the aggressors to convince them, without recourse to self-defence, to release those U.N. peace-keepers or civilian observers they had abducted.

UNAMIC, established in November 1991, quickly met resistance from the Khmer Rouge, who refused several times to hand over military maps indicating mine fields to be swept so that the refugees in camps in Thailand could be safely repatriated. Moreover, during the first months of 1992, they tried to consolidate their position in the central province of Kompong-Thom, and especially Highway 12, leading to the northern city of Preah-Vihear. The Khmer Rouge then accused the Vietnamese forces of participating in the delayed counterattack of Phnom Penh. In February, "unknown elements" fired on a UNAMIC helicopter, wounding an Australian officer.[17]

The Secretary-General's Special Representative arrived in Phnom Penh on 22 February 1992. At the end of March, the repatriation of 375,000 Cambodian refugees from Thailand started, while 642 prisoners of war and civilian detainees had been released by the Government of Cambodia under the direction of the ICRC. In April, the Special Representative submitted a draft electoral law to the SNC, while the UNDP launched a road reconstruction programme to facilitate repatriation operations.

By May, 4,000 U.N. personnel, including some 3,600 troops were in Cambodia. At a press briefing, the Special Representative said that UNTAC had established a positive presence in Cambodia and was working well with the SNC. However, he added that the Khmer Rouge continued to deny the U.N. free access to the five regions controlled by them: on 30 May, he and General John Sanderson, the Commander of UNTAC military contingent, were forcefully prevented from driving into an area near Pailin.

In June, Mr. Akashi announced at a meeting of the SNC that, despite the Khmer Rouge "Democratic Kampuchea" Party's unwillingness to comply with the Paris Peace Accords signed in October 1991, UNTAC would proceed with the second phase of the peace plan as scheduled, on 13 June. Under phase two, UNTAC would regroup and canton selected forces of the three other parties. These troops were to be placed under the control of the U.N. peace-keeping forces, surrender their arms and wait to be demobilized. While urging maximum self-restraint, he said that if the Khmer Rouge stepped up their military activities, UNTAC "will have to bear in mind the right to self-defense of the other Cambodian parties".

On 12 June, the President of the Security Council expressed "deep concern" over "difficulties" encountered by UNTAC: ceasefire violations were still occurring in the Kompong Thom province where the National Army of the Democratic Kampuchea had recently laid new mines.[18]

On 17 June, the U.N. announced that 5,000 troops from three parties had cantoned, handing over some 5,000 weapons and more than 140,000 rounds of ammunition to UNTAC.

On 2 July, the civil administration of UNTAC entered its active phase: UNTAC had opened provincial offices throughout Cambodia and appointed Directors in 20 provinces.

On 21 July, the Security Council, in a unanimous decision, strongly deplored the continuing refusal by one of the parties to permit the necessary deployment of all components of UNTAC. The Council requested that international assistance to the rehabilitation and reconstruction of Cambodia "from now on only benefits the parties which are fulfilling their obligations".

On 14 August, the Special Representative signed the U.N. Electoral Law for Cambodia, 1992, following consultations with the SNC.

By October, the UNHCR had repatriated more than 150,000 Cambodians from camps in Thailand.[19]

The Security Council demanded, on 13 October, that Democratic Kampuchea immediately fulfil its obligations and facilitate the full deployment of UNTAC in areas under its control.

By November, the voter registration campaign had passed the 2 million mark. On 24 November, an electoral team working with UNTAC was fired on by "unidentified assailants": three people were injured. The Chief Electoral Officer, Reginald Austin, stated that the registration process would proceed, but that caution was needed.

On 30 November, the Security Council decided that UNTAC should proceed with preparations for free and fair elections to be held in April/May 1993 in all areas of Cambodia to which UNTAC had full and free access as at 31 January. The resolution (792), adopted by a vote of 14 in favour with one abstention (China), also envisaged possible economic and financial sanctions, such as the supply of oil and freezing of assets, against the Democratic Kampuchea, in view of its obstruction of implementation of the peace plan, China's abstention reflected its disagreement with the use of sanctions.

On 1 December, the Khmer Rouge kidnapped two British military observers and four naval observers, two from the Philippines, one from New Zealand and one from the U.K., on patrol in Kompong Thom province. They fired on a U.N. helicopter, while six U.N. civilian police monitors were injured in two land-mine incidents in Siem Reap province.[20]

In December, UNTAC announced that the number of Cambodian voters equipped with their registration cards for the 1993 elections was close to 4 million. The total number of political parties registered to take part had reached 20. 15,608 U.N. peace-keepers from 32 Member States were deployed in the country.

Also in December, the Khmer Rouge detained 46 Indonesian UNTAC peace-keepers, four military observers and two local staff. Such "illegal" detention was strongly condemned by the Security Council. After negotiations, the detainees were progressively released.

By 22 December, 4.2 million voters had been registered by UNTAC.

On 27 December, according to the Minister of Foreign Affairs of Vietnam, a group of Khmer Rouge attacked a fishing village in Cambodia in search of Vietnamese "so as to murder them": they killed 14 people, including 12 Vietnamese, and injured 14 others.

On 12 January 1993, two Cambodian nationals with UNTAC and a seven-year old local girl were killed and several other UNTAC personnel were injured when an "unidentified group" of about 40 people attacked a village with rockets and automatic weapons in the district capital of Siem Reap. The attackers fired at the tent used for electoral registration, burned and ransacked the houses of UNTAC police officers.

On 19 January, four UNTAC naval observers who had been detained (illegally) by a unit of the National Alliance of Democratic Kampuchea (NADK – Khmer Rouge), were released after more than 48 hours in captivity.[21]

By the end of January, the closing date for voter registration, over 4.5 million Cambodians had registered to vote. Elections to the constituent assembly would be held from 23 to 25 May 1993, as agreed in a meeting of the SNC with the U.N.

Special Representative and Marrack Goulding, the Under-Secretary-General for Peace-keeping Operations, on 28 January.

Early February, the Cambodian People's Armed Forces (CPAF – Government forces) launched a series of attacks on the NADK in several provinces held by the Khmer Rouge, in order to regain territory allegedly seized by the Khmer Rouge in violation of the U.N. ceasefire. On 2 February, Prime Minister Hun Sen ordered an end to the offensive, which he justified as their right to self-defense, and asked the U.N. to create a buffer zone, manned by U.N. peace-keepers, between the Khmer Rouge and the Government forces. Although it was understood that the Government forces and party were "frustrated by the current political and military situation", the UNTAC spokesman said that UNTAC found CPAF's offensive actions "unacceptable".

China expressed deep concern over the Cambodian government attack.

Early March, Khmer Rouge forces attacked and occupied Stung, where they looted U.N. buildings and equipment, and then withdrew.

On 10 March, Khmer Rouge guerrillas killed 38 unarmed ethnic Vietnamese civilians, including many women and children, near Siem Reap: in the words of the UNTAC spokesman, "the sole motive for the attack seems to have been to terrorize and kill".[22]

Why did the Khmer Rouge representatives sign the Paris Agreements and then refused to apply them? What are their objectives?

The Position of the Khmer Rouge

The Khmer Rouge have refused the regroupment, cantonment and demobilization of 70% of their forces, which was to take place between 13 June and 30 September 1992. They have not provided full freedom of movement to UNTAC military and civilian personnel: on the contrary, they have blocked their deployment into their zones, and harrassed, kidnapped or killed UNTAC international and Cambodian persons attached to UNTAC. Their actions, described above, imply that they have decided not to participate in the planned peace and election process, nor to cooperate with UNTAC and the other three Cambodian parties in implementing the Paris Agreements.

Their refusal to honour their signature is based on the following points.

First, they charge that UNTAC has not established enough administrative control to ensure that the Government will not subvert the elections. To ensure neutrality leading up to elections, the Khmer Rouge want a more powerful SNC to oversee the country's administration in conjunction with UNTAC. On this point, they also want "consultative committees" composed of all four factions to monitor vital government functions. The Khmer Rouge have incorporated this demand into a Thai-Japanese proposal to set up an Administrative Consultative Body attached to the SNC. The Government has rejected this demand as being outside the framework of the peace plan, which entrusts the direct control of vital government functions to UNTAC, and designed only to obstruct the Agreements' implementation.

Secondly, they claim that a substantial Vietnamese military and civilian presence remains within Cambodia in violation of the Agreements. They allege that up to one million Vietnamese were illegally settled in Cambodia during Hanoi's occupation. They demand that all ethnic Vietnamese be sent back to Vietnam to prevent them from upsetting the political balance by packing in votes for the Government's Party (CPP) as Cambodian citizens. However, they have not provided UNTAC with specific reports which could be investigated. In March 1993, UNTAC investigation teams only found three Vietnamese soldiers serving with the Government forces, who had settled down in Cambodia.[23]

According to *Le Monde* (4 March 1993), following its announcement of the "total withdrawal" of its forces in Cambodia in September 1989, Vietnam maintained a discreet military presence of 4,000 men, until July 1991, when these were also withdrawn. On the other hand, there may be from three to four thousand Vietnamese settled in Cambodia who may have acquired legally (or bought) Cambodian nationality. Some of these, called mercenaries, assist occasionally the Government forces when fighting the Khmer Rouge.

Even if all these settlers were registered voters, their numbers would not significantly influence the results of elections one way or another.

In September 1992, the Khmer Rouge demanded that Yasushi Akashi resign, a demand which he rejected. On 10 December, they boycotted a meeting of the SNC, at which the UNTAC Commander said that "So far, no presence of foreign forces has been detected in the country".

In March 1993, in another attempt to justify the refusal of the Khmer Rouge to abide by the Paris Agreements, Khieu Samphan, the faction's representative on the SNC, accused U.N. officials and the Western Powers on the Security Council of aligning themselves with Vietnam in an effort to eliminate the Khmer Rouge. He asserted that the Western nations viewed the Khmer Rouge as an obstacle to the West's "strategic and economic designs on Cambodia". He asserted that Vietnam was so weakened by the collapse of the Soviet Union that it has formed an "alliance" with the West to maintain its influence in the region.

The Khmer Rouge had informed Prince Sihanouk already in September 1992 that they would not accept the results of the planned elections.

Two attempts at finding a compromise and convincing the Khmer Rouge to comply with the Paris Agreements failed: Khieu Samphan rejected Japanese and Thai proposals in a meeting in Phnom-Penh on 29 October 1992, – as well as French and Indonesian entreaties in another meeting in Beijing on 8 November. M. Dumas, the French foreign minister said that the Khmer Rouge were "hostile to the continuation of the peace process".[24]

Initially financed by China, the Khmer Rouge and their weapons were then mainly financed by the sale of gems from the mines of Pailin and timber to Thailand: earnings were estimated at more than $5 million monthly. At the end of

December, Thailand ordered an end to cross-border trading of logging and oil with the Khmer Rouge in compliance with the sanctions voted by the Security Council on 30 November 1992.[25]

According to Western officials, the Khmer Rouge control no more than 400,000 of Cambodia's 8 million people (now estimated by UNTAC as 12 million) and about 15% of the country, mainly in the western sector adjacent to Thailand. The U.N.'s military intelligence estimates the Khmer Rouge's army to include no more than 5,000 to 10,000 troops, far from previous bloated estimates of 40,000 guerrillas. The Khmer Rouge can inflict damage but they could not re-conquer power by military force against the Government forces, estimated at about 200,000.

While this does not explain the Khmer Rouge's initial acceptance of the peace plan, their rejection of the electoral process was probably based on their justified fear that they would lose the elections to the Government's party, or even to the party of Prince Norodom Ranariddh, son of Prince Norodom Sihanouk. Rejoining the process would expose their weaknesses and would result in the sacrifice of their military forces, their main bargaining chip and instrument of threat. Hence, their harrassment of UNTAC personnel, their terror attacks against ethnic Vietnamese, their withdrawal from the peace and election process, their attempts to prevent the election by creating a climate of fear and insecurity, their excessive claims, their refusal to negotiate in good faith. Their self-imposed armed isolation could have led to a partition of Cambodia, but mainly showed their loss of significance and influence in the future of Cambodia, following the U.N.-organized and supervised elections.

The Attitude of the Cambodian Government

The logic of the peace plan was that government power would be transferred to the SNC and to UNTAC, thus neutralizing the Government in place.

This did not occur: through the non-cooperation of the Khmer Rouge, the SNC became divided and ineffective, – the UNTAC leadership was not able to assume effectively the powers assigned to it by the Agreements, except in some areas. The Government then retained all essential powers and influence through its administration, party and troops and used these, in the classical Communist tradition, to make sure that *they* would win the elections, in spite of public perceptions of ineptitude, corruption and repression, even in the absence of electoral competition by the Khmer Rouge.

U.N. officials, diplomats and human rights advocates reported in January and February 1992 that the Government had launched a new intimidation campaign of voters, by forcing them to submit their U.N.-issued voter registration cards for inspection, or by confiscating them. Widespread threats of retaliation against those who will not vote for government candidates have been circulated. There have been from 20 to 40 assassinations of opposition political organizers and numerous attacks on their offices. The main target of the escalating violence has been Funcinpec (United Front for an Independent, Neutral, Peaceful and Cooperative

Cambodia), the party led by Sihanouk's son: since November 1991, Funcinpec has suffered 18 assaults on party offices and officials, causing the death of 20 party organizers or workers. Government authorities also tore down Funcinpec's election posters and threatened party workers.

Dominique McAdams, the head of the U.N. electoral division's legal section called the collection of voter registration cards "an act of intimidation" that violates the electoral law. She identified Sok An, the chief of staff of the ruling Cambodian People's party and a top aide of Prime Minister Hun Sen, as the source of instructions to some local party and administration officials to examine registration cards.[26]

In response to these acts of intimidation and other violations of human rights, the Special Representative approved a directive early January 1993 empowering UNTAC to indict individuals and prosecute cases using the local legal system. UNTAC would review investigations of politically motivated acts of violence, ethnic killings or any other crime. Where sufficient evidence existed, UNTAC military and police officers would have powers of arrest and detention. Cases would then be sent to the courts for prosecution. The first arrest of a member of the Government party was made on 11 January, for his alleged involvement in an attack on a member of an opposition party.

However, when Akashi showed an intention to remove the Governor of Battambang province, Ung Sami, on evidence that he had been involved in a series of attacks against opposition party workers and offices, the Government threatened to end cooperation with UNTAC.[27]

UNTAC's Uneasy Position

Prior to the elections, UNTAC was criticized by all parties, The Khmer Rouge accused the U.N. of siding with the Cambodian Government, Vietnam and the Western Powers. Funcinpec felt that it was not being adequately protected by UNTAC against the political violence instigated by the Government's party. Western public opinion could not understand why UNTAC did not respond militarily, in self-defense, to the Khmer Rouge's repeated provocations, kidnappings and killings. Prince Sihanouk was apparently "exasperated" by the "immobilism" of UNTAC. UNTAC credibility and leadership were under attack: UNTAC had not been able to assert its authority over the Cambodian factions, it had not overcome the Government's obstruction of efforts to supervise the five key ministries. Akashi was accused of lacking management skills. The U.N. New York bureaucratic requirements were also being criticized, as well as the generous daily allowances granted to UNTAC personnel in addition to their salaries, and "excessive" budget allocations for the operation. The French Chief of UNTAC's Civilian Administration, Gérard Porcell, resigned in February 1993 in frustration over the U.N.'s lack of power: he said that UNTAC's absence of firmness with the Khmer Rouge was a signal to the other parties, which eschewed all cooperation.[28]

On the other hand, other observers approved the U.N. for wisely rejecting calls for military action against the Khmer Rouge, "hasty ultimatums or other emotionally satisfying denunciations", and for controlling an urge for quick results.

Akashi re-affirmed, in January 1993, that UNTAC was a typical peace-keeping operation which does not include any kind of enforcement action.

> We use our presence and persuasion to calm the situation and bring about greater cooperation between UNTAC and the Cambodian factions, and between the factions themselves.

In spite of the Khmer Rouge's non-cooperation, UNTAC has proceeded with the repatriation of refugees, the adoption of an electoral code, the registration of voters and political parties, a voter education programme and the monitoring of human rights.

On 8 March, the Security Council unanimously adopted a resolution announcing that it will recognize the Government that emerges from Cambodian elections in May. This resolution, approved by China, the former supporter and ally of the Khmer Rouge, was a clear signal to the faction's leader, Pol Pot, that the only legitimate authority in Cambodia will be that resulting from the elections. The U.S. Ambassador said:

> We are committing ourselves to supporting only the government which will emerge from the elections as the sole, legitimate authority for all of Cambodia.

and the Japanese Ambassador added:

> We do not want the Khmer Rouge interfering in the election and we do not want to see the Khmer Rouge objecting to the result of the election.[29]

The same Resolution (810) urged all Cambodian parties to cooperate fully with UNTAC and called on UNTAC to continue in its efforts to create and maintain a neutral political environment conducive to the elections. It further demanded that all Cambodian parties take necessary measures to end acts of violence, threats and intimidation committed on political or ethnic grounds.

On 6 May, the Khmer Rouge isolated themselves further by boycotting talks in Beijing in which the other Cambodian factions agreed to press ahead with the elections scheduled for 23–25 May.[30]

The Elections and Their Results

UNTAC's Electoral Component was charged with organizing and conducting the elections. To this end, it recruited some 475 U.N. Volunteers who were deployed as District Electoral Supervisors responsible for recruiting, training and supervising the Cambodian polling teams. As many as 50,000 Cambodians were recruited to man these teams. In addition, UNTAC recruited over 800 International Polling Station Officers. They were complemented by UNTAC staff and, following a three-day training course, were deployed to the polling sites.

While UNTAC was unable to create a "neutral political environment", by March 1993, its Electoral Component had successfully registered 4.7 million Cambodians as voters, over 96% of the total eligible population, including most of the 300,000 refugees repatriated from Thailand.

Despite the Khmer Rouge's campaign of threats and violence, nearly 90% of the registered voters cast ballots during the election period. The U.N. Secretary-General said that

> the spectacularly high voter turnout is eloquent testimony to the confidence that UNTAC has inspired among the people of Cambodia, as well as to their deep yearning for participatory democracy.

On completion of the voting, the head of UNTAC, Yasushi Akashi, declared that the election met "the yardstick for a realistic standard" of free and fair elections. A delegation of international observers led by Andrew Peacock, a former Australian foreign minister, confirmed this assessment: the poll was a clear expression of the will of the Cambodian people.

On 10 June, UNTAC announced the final results of the elections: Funcinpec obtained 45.47% of the total valid votes, followed by the governing Cambodian People's Party with 38.22 %. The other 18 parties shared the remaining votes. Funcinpec's victory was notable in view of the violent campaign waged by the Government against it, but it did not give the winners a parliamentary majority.

In the words of Prince Norodom Sihanouk, the Khmer Rouge had suffered "a historic defeat": they were unable to disrupt and stop the election, and the voters' registration and high turnout disproved their claim that the elections were not accepted by the Cambodian people.[31] Their miscalculations seem to show that they had lost track of new political factors in Cambodia, where the people mainly wanted to live in peace, and at the international level, where U.S. influence and the loss of their Chinese support weakened their political and military position.

Finally, they had underestimated the effect of UNTAC's presence. After months of criticisms and harrassment by the main Cambodian parties, and scorn from various international media, the U.N. mission appeared to have achieved what many observers believed to be an impossible task: organize and run the first free and fair election in Cambodian history, against heavy odds. Even though UNTAC was not able to enforce a ceasefire, disarm and demobilize the parties' military forces, nor to assume the administration of the country, as a result, to a large extent, of the Khmer Rouge's reneging of their obligations under the Paris Agreements, – even though UNTAC appeared, at times, to be more of a passive victim than an assertive peacemaker, – even though UNTAC was not able to establish and maintain a "neutral political environment", the holding of "free and fair elections" and their results were a credit to the U.N. operation's civilian and military members, to the resilience of the U.N. Secretary-General and his Special Representative and their determination to apply, inasmuch as possible, the terms of the Paris Agreements and the decisions of the Security Council.

The second electoral place obtained by the Government's party, in spite of, or perhaps because of the violence exercised against the Funcinpec, was also a relative defeat for Hun Sen and his supporters, which explains, but does not justify, his initial attempts to reject the results of the election as "unfair".

On 21 June, Prince Norodom Sihanouk announced that his son Prince Norodom Ranariddh, leader of the winning Royalist party, Funcinpec, and Hun Sen had agreed to set up a joint interim Government: Ranariddh and Hun Sen would serve as co-presidents, both in charge of the defense and interior ministries, and Son Sann as vice president. The Cambodian People's Party then formally accepted the results of the elections "in the interests of national reconciliation, peace and stability".

To a large extent, this peaceful compromise agreement was due to the efforts of Prince Norodom Sihanouk, who would preside over the interim Government's weekly meetings. Conditional financial offers to assist the Government also contributed to the agreement.

UNTAC's undertaking to finance, temporarily, the salaries of Cambodian soldiers, policemen and civil servants, unpaid for weeks, was made conditional on the Government's full cooperation with the peace process, which required the PPC's acceptance of the elections results. Pledges of approximately $880 million by foreign governments were also conditional on the formation of an interim Government and the drafting of a new Constitution.

Early July, the Constituent Assembly approved the formation and composition of the interim Government.

As a complete reversal of their earlier position, even the Khmer Rouge seemed belatedly ready to join the peace process, which they had tried to destroy. On 1 July, Khmer Rouge envoys met Prince Norodom Sihanouk and the U.N. Commander in Phnom Penh to discuss the opening of territory held by them to the newly formed Government. Khmer Rouge military commanders had also told U.N. peace-keepers that they wanted to join the new national army to be created by the new authorities.

By mid-1993, it appeared that the Cambodia operation, initially assessed as another costly U.N. debacle, had in fact fulfilled its main objectives, in spite of apparently unsurmountable obstacles:

- overall civil peace had been maintained in the country;
- national reconciliation was progressing;
- the Cambodian people had exercised its right to self-determination through free and fair elections.

Whether these achievements will be durable and whether Cambodia will become and remain a pluralist democracy can only be the object of conjecture.

It is to be hoped that the Cambodian people's first democratic victory and their need for peace will not be frustrated.[32]

Mozambique: Another Angola?

On 4 October 1992, after 14 years of civil war, Mr. Joaquim Alberto Chissano, President of the Republic of Mozambique, and Mr. Afonso Macacho Marceta Dhlakama, President of the Mozambique National Resistance (Renamo), the rebel group, signed in Rome a General Peace Agreement. The Agreement called for U.N. participation in monitoring its implementation, in providing technical assistance for general elections and in monitoring these elections.

On 16 December, the Security Council decided to establish ONUMOZ, the U.N. Operation in Mozambique (Resol. 797). In its report, the Secretary-General had warned the Council that

> in the light of recent experiences elsewhere, the recommendations in the present report may be thought to invite the international community to take a risk. I believe that the risk is worth taking; but I cannot disguise that it exists.

The renewed fighting in Angola, the serious difficulties faced by the U.N. operations in Cambodia and in Somalia could not but cast a shadow over preparations for another comprehensive U.N. operation involving national reconciliation, disarmament of combatants and free elections.

Would the former Portuguese colony follow the bloody precedent of Angola, or would different factors result in a peaceful and democratic outcome?

The similarities are striking: both Angola and Mozambique were colonized by the Portuguese, both became independent following a liberation war, both became communist one-party states, both suffered from years of civil war caused by rebel movements mainly created and supported by South Africa, as part of its strategy of destabilization of the Frontline states, both populations have suffered from deteriorating economic conditions, poverty, killings and other violations of human rights. Some of the differences are the size of the population (8.5 million in Angola, 16.1 million in Mozambique), different ethnic groups, different political leaders with different motivations, a different geographical position.

Another factor of influence will be the impact of the U.N. operation in Mozambique, the number of U.N. peace-keepers and other personnel, the duration of their presence in the country, taking into account the U.N. experience in Angola.

Historical Background

After more than two decades of fighting Portuguese colonial occupation, the Mozambique Liberation Front (Frelimo) successfully established the People's Republic of Mozambique in 1975. Samora Machel led the Marxist-Leninist one-party state until he was killed in an airplane crash in 1986. Joachim Chissano succeeded him as both president and Frelimo party leader.[33]

As a communist dictatorship, all power resided in the "vanguard party", with a powerful secret police. Frelimo's rural modernization programme often forced peasants off their traditional lands into communal villages. New revolutionary organizations and values were imposed on traditional social structures.

The rebel Mozambique National Resistance (Renamo) was reportedly sponsored by the Ian Smith regime in Rhodesia in response to Frelimo's support for the armed insurgency against white minority rule in Rhodesia, in an attempt to overthrow, or at least destabilize a marxist regime. When Rhodesia became independent as Zimbabwe in 1980, South African public and private sources provided material and financial support to Renamo's 25,000-member guerrilla force, which controlled large areas of rural territory. While it was supported by traditional tribal figures and peasants, Renamo committed atrocities against civilians, including kidnapping peasants to serve as forced labour in the guerrilla war. Deserters from both Renamo and the army took to banditry or set themselves up as warlords in local fiefdoms independent of outside control.

In 1984, the Government agreed to expel the African National Congress from its territory as a condition for withdrawal of South African support to Renamo, the Nkomati Accords, but South Africa did not respect this pledge.

By 1987, the devastating effects of war and the detente between the U.S.A. and the USSR enticed the Government to negotiate with the rebels and attempt a reconciliation.

The conflict has claimed over one million lives, displaced 4.5 million others inside the country and scattered two million others in neighbouring countries of Malawi, Tanzania, Zambia and Zimbabwe.

On 30 November 1990, President Chissano imposed a new Constitution, formally providing for universal suffrage, direct legislative and executive elections, and a powerful executive branch. It also provides for the basic freedoms, including free association, the right to strike, religious freedom, the independence of the legal system. A unicameral people's assembly was indirectly elected by provincial assemblies in 1991, but all candidates had to be approved by Frelimo.

Direct talks took place between the government and Renamo in Rome in 1990, thus recognizing the rebel group as a legitimate political force. On 1 December 1990, a limited ceasefire agreement was reached, but it broke down on Renamo's allegations of ceasefire violations. In October 1991, the outcome of new talks under Italian mediation was to reach a general peace agreement as soon as possible. The two parties agreed in principle to create a control commission, comprising representatives of both sides, of the U.N. and other parties to be decided, to supervise a peace accord. On 12 March 1992, the government and Renamo signed Protocols on Electoral Principles, followed on 16 July by a joint Declaration on guiding principles for humanitarian assistance.[34]

After 11 official meetings in Rome over 27 months, thanks to the effective mediation of Italy and Zimbabwe and other intermediaries, including several government and U.N. observers,[35] President Chissano and the President of Renamo, Afonso Dhlakama, signed on 4 October 1992 the General Peace Agreement.

Under the Agreement, the ceasefire was to come into effect not later than 15

October 1992, followed by demobilization of the two sides' forces, except for those who would serve in the new Mozambican Defence Force. An estimated 62,000 government and 20,000 Renamo soldiers were scheduled to hand in their arms to the U.N. at 49 designated assembly points.

New political parties would be formed and preparations made for the elections, to take place not later than 15 October 1993.

The U.N. was requested to undertake a major role in monitoring the implementation of the Agreement and was asked to perform specific functions in relation to the ceasefire, the elections and humanitarian assistance. The implementation of the Agreement was to be supervised by a Supervisory and Monitoring Commission (CSC) chaired by the U.N. The U.N. was also to chair two Commissions charged with the responsibility for the ceasefire and for the reintegration of demobilized military personnel.

U.N. Approval of the U.N. Operation in Mozambique (ONUMOZ)

On 13 October 1992, the Security Council welcomed the signature of the Peace Agreement, and, on the recommendation of the Secretary-General, approved the appointment of an interim Special Representative and the dispatch to Mozambique of a team of up to 25 military observers (Resol. 782).

The newly appointed interim Special Representative, Aldo Ajello (Italy), and a team of 21 military observers, drawn from existing U.N. peace-keeping missions, arrived in Mozambique on 15 October, the day the Peace Agreement entered into force, and were deployed in the country. Additional outposts were established to verify the withdrawal of foreign troops from Mozambique.

The President of the Security Council, in a statement on 27 October, expressed the Council's deep concern about reports of major violations of the ceasefire, called upon the parties to halt such violations immediately and urged them to cooperate fully with the interim Special Representative.

On 4 November, Mr. Ajello appointed the Supervisory and Monitoring Commission (CSC). CSC then appointed its three main subsidiary commissions: the Cease-fire Commission, the Commission for the Reintegration of Demobilized Military Personnel and the Joint Commission for the Formation of the Mozambican Defence Forces.

On 3 December, the Secretary-General recommended the establishment of a U.N. Operation in Mozambique (ONUMOZ) to demobilize and disarm the two sides' forces and provide assistance for democratic elections scheduled for October 1993. With the Angolan situation in mind, he recommended that "very substantial resources" be made available, especially on the military side: it would "not be possible in Mozambique to create the conditions for a successful election" unless the military situation was brought fully under control. The Peace Agreement would not be implemented unless the Mozambican parties made a determined effort in good faith to honour their commitments.

Describing the difficulties of the operation, he referred to the size of the country, the devastated state of its infrastructure, the disruption of its economy by war and drought, the limited capacity of the Government to cope with the new tasks arising from the General Peace Agreement. He emphasized the breadth of responsibilities entrusted to the U.N. under the Agreement.

On 16 December, the Security Council, taking a "worth-taking" risk, approved the Secretary-General's report and established ONUMOZ until 31 October 1993 (Resol. 797).

ONUMOZ would consist of between 7,000 and 8,000 military and civilian personnel, assigned to political, military, electoral and humanitarian functions. There would be 354 military observers, 5 infantry battalions of up to 850 personnel each, one engineer battalion and 3 logistic companies; 128 police monitors; and an electoral division of up to 148 election officers who would be helped by up to 1,200 international observers for the elections themselves.

The terms of reference of ONUMOZ's electoral component are shown in Table 7.2.

Table 7.2. Terms of reference of ONUMOZ's electoral component

The electoral mandate of ONUMOZ is to provide technical assistance and monitor the entire electoral process. Under the terms of the Agreement, legislative and presidential elections would be held simultaneously one year after the date of signature of the Agreement. This period may be extended if warranted by the prevailing circumstances.

The terms of reference of ONUMOZ's electoral component would be:

(a) to verify the impartiality of the National Elections Commission and its organs in all aspects and stages of the electoral process;

(b) to verify that political parties and alliances enjoy complete freedom of organization, movement, assembly and expression, without hindrance and intimidation;

(c) to verify that all political parties and alliances have fair access to State mass media and that there is fairness in the allocation of both the hour and duration of radio and television broadcasts;

(d) to verify that the electoral rolls are properly drawn up and that qualified voters are not denied identification and registration cards or the right to vote;

(e) to report to the electoral authorities on complaints, irregularities and interferences reported or observed, and, if necessary, to request the electoral authorities to take action to resolve and rectify them, as well as conducting its own independent investigation of irregularities;

(f) to observe all activities related to the registration of voters, the organization of the poll, the electoral campaign, the poll itself and the counting, computation and announcement of the results;

(g) to participate in the electoral education campaign;

(h) to prepare periodic reports on the evolution of the electoral process, for submission to the Secretary-General through his interim Special Representative.

The electoral component would also prepare independent reports about the conduct of the elections. It would establish a special relationship with the National Elections Commission.

In addition, the Secretary-General's interim Special Representative would coordinate technical assistance to the whole electoral process in Mozambique, which would be provided through the United Nations Development Programme, other existing mechanisms of the United Nations system, and through the bilateral channels.

Source: U.N. Department of Public Information Document "United Nations Operation in Mozambique (ONUMOZ)", January 1993, pp. 4 and 6.

Estimated costs to the U.N. for the establishment and deployment of ONUMOZ for a period of 10-and-a-half months would be approximately $332 million.

Recent Developments

The deployment of the U.N. military force, a prerequisite to the effective demobilization of the rival forces, was slow. The U.N. secretariat has had difficulties in finding countries willing to send national contingents to Mozambique.

The first part of the Italian contingent (1,300 troops) arrived in the country in March 1993. Other battalions from Bangladesh, Botswana, Uruguay and Zambia arrived in May. Troops from India, Portugal, Japan and Argentina will also participate as unarmed observers.[36]

The delay in the arrival of infantry battalions has prevented, by mid-1993, the demobilization of both parties' troops and the creation of a joint army of 24,000, an airforce of 4,000 and a navy of 2,000, each side contributing half of each force. Renamo insisted that 65% of U.N. peace-keepers be deployed before it would allow its troops to be demobilized.

In a report to the Security Council of April 1993, the Secretary-General stated that elections could not be held in October 1993, as scheduled, because of difficulties in implementing the peace agreement, although Mozambique was "enjoying relative peace".

Renamo had adopted an intransigent position: its leader, Afonso Dhlakama, had consistently failed to attend meetings organized by the Commissions monitoring the implementation of the peace agreement, complaining of lack of proper housing.

While the government has given to the U.N. its list of 29 "assembly points" for the demobilization of its forces, Renamo refused to make its list public, insisting that only the U.N. could visit its 20 assembly points.

The major difficulty facing the U.N. programme was, in mid-1993, the establishment of a uniform political authority,[37] itself dependent on the creation of relations of trust between the two parties under U.N. auspices.

Will Afonso Dhlakama be another Jonas Savimbi? Any forecast of the political, military and electoral situation in Mozambique in the next 12 months (July 1993 – July 1994) would be presumptuous.

The best chance of success for the U.N. operation is that elections do *not* take place until the two parties' forces are actually demobilized and a new joint Mozambican Defence Force is created and trained under U.N. supervision. This essential pre-requirement was recognized by the Security Council in Resolution 818 of 14 April 1993.

General Comments on U.N. Operations

The U.N. has recently accepted more and more "daunting challenges" in the name of peace, one of its originally declared objectives, and democracy, a more recent concern. While the U.N. was created essentially to maintain international peace and security, its role has extended to the restoration of civil peace within the national borders of countries, national reconciliation and the creation of democratic institutions, under the real or alleged justification that civil war or disorder, military coups and other undemocratic practices in one country may cause regional conflicts and thus endanger international peace and security. The conflicts in ex-Yugoslavia would tend to confirm this assumption.

The U.N. has taken, and is currently taking risks in accepting to organize and run multi-purpose operations with political, military, electoral and humanitarian components, as in Namibia, Angola, Cambodia and Mozambique.

The U.N. is taking risks when it intervenes in a country torn by civil war and entertains hopes for national reconciliation and democratic acceptance by the "loser" of elections, whether the loser is the challenger, as in Angola, or the ruler, as in Cambodia.

The U.N. is taking risks when it accepts a request for its election monitoring services in a country without democratic tradition or culture, where transition to democracy may only be a superficial and insincere effort by a non-elected ruler to satisfy international creditors and deceive international public opinion.

The U.N. is taking risks when it is unable to obtain the disarmament and demobilization of the opposing parties' armed forces, when its peace-keepers become helpless targets, and when it still continues to proceed with the planned and approved operation, even if some of its key premises and objectives are laid aside.

Are the risks of failure and loss of prestige assumed by the U.N. compensated by expected or assured benefits for the Organization, its member States, and more importantly, for the populations concerned?

Following the mainly symbolic and "safe" observation missions in the field of self-determination, where independence was generally the expected and evident outcome of the electoral exercise, the pro-democracy operations have entailed a significant expansion of the U.N. ambitions and capacity, with added uncertainties and difficulties.

The new "World Directorate", the Security Council, found it convenient to lead the dormant organization in those yet uncharted directions: the permanent members showed their power, exerted their influence, with their newly found agreement, to promote democratic values. China and developing countries, while remaining wary of a new, neocolonialist Western Crusade under democratic guise, still preferred an intervention (with the host country's acceptance) by the global organization where they have some say in decision-making, rather than a more direct imposition of "rich" and powerful countries on "poor" and weak ones.

In case of apparent success of a U.N. monitoring operation, in the sense of a declaration that elections have been free and fair, followed by the acceptance of electoral results by the contesting parties, the U.N. benefits by a renewed prestige, the recognition of its political flair (or that of Security Council members) and of its operational competence. The population concerned will benefit from civil peace and political stability, more respect for political and civil rights and may expect to reap the dividends of an improving economy. The Cambodian operation has shown, besides and beyond UNTAC's electoral mission, the importance of the diplomatic and political role of the U.N. in helping party leaders to come to a peaceful political agreement, instead of re-igniting civil war.

In case of a "half-success", in the sense of certified free and fair elections followed by the rejection by one or several parties of the electoral results, renewal of political unstability and/or civil war, the U.N. may either be complimented for its courageous decision to take on an uncertain challenge, or, which is more likely, it may be blamed for its unwieldy and costly intervention which raised and let down people's expectations: the population's taste for democracy and free elections may be soured and their trust in the U.N. may be affected for some time. On the positive side, the Angola fiasco may have served as a useful warning to the U.N. and U.N. member States that elections without demobilization of warring factions adds an excessive risk to such difficult and complex operations, – and that the number of U.N. military and civilian forces in any one operation must be appropriate to the size of the country and to the size of the population.

Although the U.N. Secretary-General, in his report of 18 November 1992,[38] predicted that the U.N. role in electoral assistance should diminish over time as countries develop their own expertise and institutions to support the electoral process, as a logical consequence of democratization, transition to democracy will remain a slow, hesitant and sometimes painful process, with reversals, coups and relapses.

It is therefore likely that the U.N. electoral assistance role, as well as similar functions assumed by other intergovernmental organizations and non-governmental organizations, will continue to expand in the foreseeable future, as a welcome expansion of the U.N. traditional activities.

Notes

1. This historical background (until 1988) is mainly based on a "U.N. Backgrounder, The Question of Western Sahara", dated 25 Aug. 1988.
2. U.N. General Assembly Resol. 3292 (XXIX) of 13 Dec. 1974, – Western Sahara Advisory Opinion of 16 Oct. 1975, *ICJ Report 1975*, p. 12.
3. U.N. *Press Release* DH/645 of 21 May 1990, U.N. Doc. S/21360 of 18 June 1990, "Report of the Secretary-General on the Situation concerning Western Sahara", U.N. *Press Releases* SG/SM/1201, SC/247 of 24 Apr. 1991, DH/918 of 25 June 1991, SG/A/234 of 24 March 1992. See also U.N. Doc. A/46/609 of 19 Nov. 1991, para. 24.
4. Shimon Peres of Israel visited King Hassan II in Morocco in 1986.

5. "Building on Sand: The U.N. Experience with Peacekeeping in the Western Sahara", W.J. Durch, The Henry L. Stimson Center, Washington, D.C., Prepared for presentation at the 33rd Convention of the International Studies Association, Atlanta, Georgia, 31 March – 4 April 1992, p. 3.
6. U.N. *Press Release* DH/939 of 25 July 1991, *International Herald Tribune*, 29 Feb. – 1 March 1992.
7. U.N. *Press Release* DH/1282 of 3 Dec. 1992.
8. *International Herald Tribune*, 17 and 28 Aug. 1992, *West Africa*, 26 Oct – 1 Nov. 1992, U.N. *Press Releases* DH/1213/Corr. 1 of 26 Aug. 1992, SC/264 of 31 Dec. 1991.
9. U.N. *Press Release* DH/1155 of 4 June 1992, – *The Interdependent*, Spring 1992, – *La Tribune de Genève*, 21–22 Dec. 1991, – Testimony of Jarat Chopra in Thomas J. Watson Jr. Institute for International Studies "Briefings", Nov. 1992.
10. *Le Monde*, 17 Sept. 1991, – *La Tribune de Genève*, 18, 20 Dec. 1991, – *La Liberté*, 17 Oct. 1991.
11. U.N. *Press Releases* DH/1091 of 3 March 1992, DH/1341 of 2 March 1993, – see "Report by the Secretary-General" on "The Situation concerning Western Sahara" dated 26 January 1993, Doc. S/25170, and Security Council Resol. 809(1993) of 2 March 1993.
12. Data are based on *Freedom in the World – 1991–1992*, Freedom House, 1992, p. 132, with permission – supplemented by the author's comments.
13. U.N. Doc. "Agreements on a Comprehensive Political Settlement of the Cambodian Conflict, Paris, 23 October 1991".
14. Ibid., Annex 5.
15. U.N. *Press Release* SG/272 of 28 Feb. 1992.
16. U.N. *Press Release* SG/SM/1303-CAM/2-SC/271 of 28 Feb. 1992.
17. As quoted in "The State of the United Nations: 1992", The Academic Council on the United Nations System, 1992, p. 14, – *Le Monde*, 3 Apr. 1992 and U.N. *Press Release* DH/1087 of 26 Feb. 1992.
18. U.N. *Press Releases* DH/1063 of 22 Jan. 1992, DH/1109 of 30 March 1992, DH/1112 of 2 Apr. 1992, DH/1133 of 4 May 1992, DH/1159 of 10 June 1992, DH/1161 of 12 June 1992.
19. U.N. *Press Releases* DH/1164 of 17 June 1992, DH/1173 of 30 June 1992, DH/1175 of 2 July 1992, DH/1187 of 21 July 1992, DH/1205 of 14 Aug. 1992, DH/1239 of 2 Oct. 1992.
20. U.N. *Press Releases* DH/1246 of 13 Oct. 1992, DH/1275 of 23 Nov. 1992, DH/1277 of 25 Nov. 1992, DH/1279 of 30 Nov. 1992, DH/1281 of 2 Dec. 1992.
21. U.N. *Press Releases* DH/1290 of 15 Dec. 1992, DH/1293 of 18 Dec. 1992, DH/1295 of 22 Dec. 1992, DH/1305 of 8 Jan. 1993, DH/1308 of 13 Jan. 1993, DH/1312 of 19 Jan. 1993.
22. U.N. *Press Releases* DH/1317 of 26 Jan. 1993, DH/1320 of 29 Jan. 1993, DH/1321 of 1 Feb. 1993, – *Le Monde*, 6 March 1993, *International Herald Tribune*, 3–5 Feb., 17 and 26 March 1993.
23. See Don Dickinson's article "Cambodia's evolving situation", in *International Review*, Winter 1992–1993, p. 8, – *International Herald Tribune*, 2 March 1993.
24. *Le Monde*, 5 and 29 Sept., 31 Oct. 1992, – *International Herald Tribune*, 9 Nov., 11 Dec. 1992, 2 March 1993.
25. *U.N. Observer and International Report*, Dec. 1991, – *International Herald Tribune*, 28 Dec. 1992, 2–3 Jan. 1993, *Le Monde*, 5 March 1993.
26. *International Herald Tribune*, 10 Nov. 1992, 16 Feb. 1993, *Newsweek*, 4 Jan. 1993.
27. *Far Eastern Economic Review*, 21 Jan. 1993.
28. *International Herald Tribune*, 29 Sept. 1992, 27–28 Feb. 1993, – U.N. *Press Releases* DH/1304 of 7 Jan. 1993, DH/1307 of 12 Jan. 1993, – *Le Monde*, 3 March 1993.
29. *International Herald Tribune*, 10 Nov. 1992, 4 Jan. and 10 March 1993.
30. *International Herald Tribune*, 7 May 1993.
31. *Tribune de Genève*, 8–9 May 1993, *Newsweek*, 7 June 1993, *Le Monde*, 11 June 1993.
32. *International Herald Tribune*, 29–30 May, 22 June, 2 July 1993, *Le Monde*, 23 June 1993, *Newsweek*, 28 June 1993.

33. The main part of the historical background is based on *Freedom in the World – 1991–1992*, op.cit., pp. 334–336. See also *Le Monde*, 1 Jan. 1993.
34. *International Herald Tribune*, 21 Oct. 1991, – *A Global Agenda – Issues before the 47th General Assembly of the United Nations*, U.N. Association of the U.S.A., University Press of America, 1992, p. 56. On the U.N. Operation in Mozambique (ONUMOZ), see the 7-page Doc. DPI/1326 published by the U.N. Department of Public Information in Jan. 1993.
35. *Le Monde*, 1 Jan. 1993 refers to the efforts of the Christian Community Sant Egidio, Tiny Rowlands, Director of Lonhro and Pik Botha, South African Minister of Foreign Affairs, as facilitators and organizers of meetings. Observer States at the Rome talks included France, Portugal, the U.K. and the U.S.A.
36. *The Economist*, 19 Dec. 1992, 6 Feb. 1993, *International Herald Tribune*, 23 Feb. 1993, *Newsweek*, 1 March 1993, *Le Monde*, 5 March 1993, *West Africa*, 24–30 May 1993.
37. *West África*, 5–11 Apr. 1993, U.S. *Daily Bulletin*, Geneva, 14 Apr. 1993. The "Report of the Secretary-General on the U.N. Operation in Mozambique" dated 2 April 1993 is in Doc. S/25518.
38. U.N. Doc. A/47/668, p. 20.

CHAPTER 8

ELECTION ASSISTANCE AND MONITORING BY OTHER INTERGOVERNMENTAL ORGANIZATIONS

The U.N. is not the only intergovernmental organization (IGO), nor the first one, to believe in and to promote democracy, nor in observing plebiscites, referenda and national elections. Other IGOs have had an advisory role in providing governments, on request, with technical and legal assistance on electoral matters and have assumed an operational role in monitoring national elections.

The Organization of American States (OAS), the oldest regional organization, has "democracy" inscribed in its Charter since 1985 and has been a pioneer in monitoring national elections in the Western Hemisphere.

The Commonwealth, successor to the British Empire, has also been active in supporting former British possessions in their transition to democracy: the Commonwealth has organized a number of election or referenda observer missions, mainly in Africa, but also in Asia, in British Guiana and in Gibraltar.

The Council of Europe has been, since its foundation in 1949, a "Club of democratic nations", equally opposed to the defeated fascist-nazi regimes and ideologies, and to Marxism-Leninism practised and promoted by the USSR. It has created the most advanced judicial system of protection of human rights in the world (reserved to those European countries which have ratified the European Convention on Human Rights) and is helping new democracies in Central and Eastern Europe to create the political and legal infrastructures needed to serve pluralist democracy, human rights and the rule of law. Its role in the field of promotion of democracy is advisory, and also operational: the Council's Parliamentary Assembly has sent a number of missions to observe national elections in Central and Eastern Europe.

The European Community, originally a purely economic group, has in practice always limited its membership to democratic countries. The 1992 Maastricht Treaty specifically refers to "principles of democracy". In the mid-1980s, the European Community established a linkage between democracy and its development aid policy. The Community mainly provides assistance in pre-election measures.

When adopting the "Charter of Paris for a New Europe" in 1990, the States participating in the Conference on Security and Cooperation in Europe (CSCE) committed themselves to ensure full respect for human rights and fundamental freedoms, to abide by the rule of law and to promote principles of democracy and democratic institutions, including free elections, and the protection of minorities and religious freedoms. The CSCE Office for Democratic Institutions and Human Rights has, since its creation in the same year, assumed both an advisory and an operational role in the electoral field in Central and Eastern Europe.

While the U.N. "seal of democratic approval" may apply to countries in any part of the world, regional organizations such as the OAS, the Council of Europe, the European Community or the CSCE are in principle only concerned with States members of their organization, with the exception of States which may be or become eligible for membership, provided that they belong to the same defined geographical area. Similarly, the Commonwealth may send election observer missions only in member countries, with the notable past exception of Namibia.

As for the U.N., these organizations will initiate observation missions only at the request or with the explicit consent of the governmental authorities of the state concerned, in order to respect their national sovereignty. Some of the missions are carried out by one intergovernmental organization only (for instance, a number of OAS missions are in this category), while others may be joint missions: for instance, the joint U.N./OAS operation in Nicaragua.

In most cases, the IGO operation is joined or preceded by representatives of non-governmental organizations. Government representatives may also be sent by specific countries to observe a particular electoral process with the permission or at the request of the observed country.

Election observation or monitoring by the U.N. will tend to have the highest international visibility: success or failure will be more publicized and may have positive or negative consequences for the organization's prestige, future programmes and budget, besides the more crucial consequences for the country under observation and its people.

Election monitoring by other IGOs, without U.N. participation, will tend to be less publicized, with lesser consequences for the organizations concerned in case of success or failure of the electoral process.

Some countries requesting electoral assistance and/or monitoring may prefer to call on the U.N. rather than on regional or other non-universal organizations. They may feel that the U.N. will be more impartial and detached from regional or local contingencies and pressures than a regional organization, and that its "approval" will be more significant and internationally recognized. On the other hand, observers from regional organizations may provide a more appropriate political, social, cultural and linguistic competence and understanding to an electoral assistance programme or an election observation operation than U.N. observers. Joint U.N./other IGOs missions or operations may provide benefits from both sources, provided that an effective coordination, or at least, cooperation, is ensured.

Examples of the democratic mandate of the above-mentioned IGOs and of their activities in the electoral field follow.

The Organization of American States

Founded in 1890 as the International Union of American Republics, with its Commercial Bureau in Washington, D.C., the organization is the oldest regional organization in the world. The Union became the Organization of American States (OAS) in 1948: it is a multi-purpose regional organization, providing a forum for political, economic, social and cultural cooperation among the member states of the Western Hemisphere. In 1992, there were 35 member states at the OAS and 28 permanent observers. Its regular budget for 1992 was $65,398,200, plus voluntary funds.

The organization's essential purposes are listed in Art. 2 of its Charter[1]: they refer to the strengthening of peace and security on the continent, ensuring the peaceful settlement of disputes, common action in the event of aggression, seeking the solution of political, juridical, and economic problems, promoting, by cooperative action, their economic, social, and cultural development and the limitation of conventional weapons.

In addition to these orthodox missions of international cooperation, another "essential purpose" of the OAS, incorporated in its Charter in 1985, is, in Article 2 b), "To promote and consolidate representative democracy, with due respect for the principle of nonintervention".

For Representative Democracy

In contrast with the absence of "pro-democracy" references in the U.N. Charter, the OAS Charter, as amended by the Protocol of Cartagena de Indias in 1985, takes a firm and explicit stand for representative democracy.

Besides the text in Art. 2 b), the Charter's Preamble declares, in part, that OAS states are

> Convinced that the historic mission of America is to offer to man a land of liberty . . . ;
>
> Convinced that representative democracy is an indispensable condition for the stability, peace and development of the region;
>
> Confident that the true significance of American solidarity and good neighborliness can only mean the consolidation on this continent, within the framework of democratic institutions, of a system of individual liberty and social justice based on the respect for the essential rights of man;

Other references to the effective exercise of representative democracy or to democratic principles are found in Art. 3 d) and 30.

However, the Charter also includes the traditional limits to the international action of an IGO: representative democracy cannot be imposed on any member state in view of the principle of non-intervention and of the right of every State to choose, without external intervention, its political, economic, and social system (Art. 2. b) and 3 e)).

The American Declaration of the Rights and Duties of Man, adopted in Bogota in 1948, includes political participation and voting rights in its Art. XX, on lines similar to Art. 21 of the Universal Declaration of Human Rights adopted by the U.N. General Assembly in the same year:

> Every person having legal capacity is entitled to participate in the government of his country, directly or through his representatives, and to take part in popular elections, which shall be by secret ballot, and shall be honest, periodic and free.

As the U.N. "International Covenant on Civil and Political Rights" followed the Universal Declaration in 1966, the American Convention on Human Rights followed the American Declaration in 1969. Its Art. 23 re-affirmed the citizens' right to participate in government, as well as rights to freedom of thought and expression, right of assembly, freedom of association, rights to judicial protection etc.[2]

Following actual democratization in most countries of the continent in the 1980s, OAS governing bodies confirmed their support for the promotion of democracy in several resolutions.

On 18 November 1989, the OAS General Assembly adopted a resolution (991 (XIX-0/89)) emphasizing, in part, the member countries' decision

> to support and strengthen genuinely democratic and participatory systems through full respect for all human rights, particularly the periodic holding of honest electoral processes in which the will of the people is freely expressed and respected in the election of officials, without external interference;

The General Assembly reiterated to the Secretary General the recommendation that, when a member state so requests "in the exercise of its sovereignty", missions should be organized and sent to said state to monitor the development, if possible at all stages, of each of its electoral processes.

Such missions have been sent by the Secretary General to member countries since 1958.

On 9 January 1991, the Permanent Council of the OAS recognized that for the first time in its history the democratic system of government was in effect in almost all the countries of the hemisphere, notwithstanding continuing serious problems of a socioeconomic nature (CP/RES. 556 (843/91)).

In June, the General Assembly adopted two important "pro-democracy" resolutions:

- the first one, "The Santiago Commitment to Democracy and the Renewal of the Inter-American System", adopted on 4 June, declared the OAS member states' commitment to the defense and promotion of democracy but linked its consolidation to the need to intensify the common struggle and cooperative action against extreme poverty to help reduce economic and social inequalities in the hemisphere. The Ministers of Foreign Affairs and the Heads of Delegation of the OAS member states, "as representatives of their democratically elected governments", decided to adopt efficacious, timely, and expeditious procedures to ensure the promotion and defense of representative democracy;

- the second one, entitled "Representative Democracy", adopted on 5 June, recognized that the region still faced serious political, social and economic problems that may threaten the stability of democratic governments (AG/RES. 1080 (XXI-0/91)). In consequence, the General Assembly resolved:

1. To instruct the Secretary General to call for the immediate convocation of a meeting of the Permanent Council in the event of any occurrences giving rise to the sudden or irregular interruption of the democratic political institutional process or of the legitimate exercise of power by the democratically elected government in any of the Organization's member states, in order, within the framework of the Charter, to examine the situation, decide on and convene an ad hoc meeting of the Ministers of Foreign Affairs, or a special session of the General Assembly, all of which must take place within a ten-day period.
2. To state that the purpose of the ad hoc meeting of Ministers of Foreign Affairs or the special session of the General Assembly shall be to look into the events collectively and adopt any decisions deemed appropriate, in accordance with the Charter and international law.
3. To instruct the Permanent Council to devise a set of proposals that will serve as incentives to preserve and strengthen democratic systems, based on international solidarity and cooperation, and to apprise the General Assembly thereof at its twenty-second regular session.

This resolution is significant insofar as it extends the mandate of both the Secretary General and of the Permanent Council from traditional peace and security issues, disputes between states, to the defense of democracy in one particular country. Insofar as the international defense of democracy, as well as the international defense of human rights, in one particular country requires an intervention in the internal affairs of that country, the resolution gives priority to the principles of inter-American solidarity and cooperation, close interdependence and the consolidation (or restoration) of democracy over the principle of non-intervention, and the taboo of unlimited national sovereignty.[3]

On 10 December 1991, the Permanent Council noted that the Secretary General, in compliance with resolution AG/RES. 1063 (XX-0/90), had created the Unit for the Promotion of Democracy by executive order No. 90-3. The Council adopted the Program of Support for the Promotion of Democracy, as proposed by the Secretary General. Extracts from this Program are in Table 8.1. An institutional framework was thus set up to provide sustained, concrete and, if necessary, operational, OAS support to member states requesting advice or assistance in preserving or strengthening their political institutions and democratic procedures.[4]

Table 8.1. Organization of American States Unit for the Promotion of Democracy – *Program of Support for the Promotion of Democracy*

(Excerpts)

I. OBJECTIVE

The objective of the Program of Support for the Promotion of Democracy is to respond promptly and effectively, through the Unit, to member states that request advice or assistance in preserving or strengthening their political institutions and democratic procedures.

II. AREAS OF COMPETENCE

1. The Program is the conceptual framework for the work of the Unit. Within the General Secretariat, the Unit will be the focal point for the design, coordination, and execution of activities to accomplish the stated objective, and will serve as a clearinghouse for the resources placed at its disposal, as well as the repository for pertinent information and expertise.
2. The Program has two basic areas of competence: advisory services and assistance.

A. *Advisory Services*

a. With respect to the preservation and strengthening of political institutions and democratic procedures, the advisory services conducted by the Unit under the Program may include activities in the areas of information, research, training, education, and institutional support. As appropriate, such activities could be conducted in connexion with the executive, legislative, and judicial branches of government; the electoral organs, political parties; public and private entities; the media; and the exercise of political, economic, social, and cultural rights, as may be agreed with the receiving government.

b. In order to carry out its activities, the Unit will seek the assistance and expertise of competent institutions.

c. Without prejudice to the foregoing, these activities could also include, as appropriate, assistance in the improvement of institutions; encouragement of and assistance in the development of academic and research activities on democratic values and political systems in the Americas by means that include scholarships and fellowships; the training of personnel from electoral organizations of the member states; the design of school curricula aimed at promoting and developing democratic ideals; the encouragement of exchanges among institutions and experts on issues related to the promotion of democracy, including the interrelationship between representative democracy and economic, social, and human rights.

d. In order to best and most effectively perform its advisory functions, the Unit will prepare, for the benefit of member states, an inventory of institutional and individual expertise on matters related to the objective of the Program, as well as data banks on the countries' electoral, legislative, and judicial systems, and may eventually establish its own data bank.

B. *Assistance*

In the field of assistance, the Program will call for a range of activities such as:

a. On the basis of experience gained by the Organization, and within the framework of the promotion of representative democracy, assistance in the observation of electoral processes, which, when feasible and when requested by a member state, could include assistance in preparing and conducting the elections and in observing the voting and the post-election phase

. . .

c. The formulation of criteria to guide the work of electoral observers

. . .

Source: Organization of American States Doc., Permanent Council, Doc. OEA/Ser. G, CP/RES. 572 (882/91), 10 December 1991.

The OAS Condemns Communism, Then Anti-Democratic Coups

During the 1950s, the organs of the OAS, in response to U.S. initiatives, adopted a series of resolutions urging safeguards against Communist subversion of individual states. During the Cold War and under the Monroe Doctrine, the U.S. considered that a Latin American country converted to communism was a potential threat to peace and security in the Western Hemisphere and an advance party for Soviet expansion and aggression: any government suspected of communism or socialism, even if assuming power as a result of free and fair elections was to be condemned, and, if possible, eliminated by overt or covert means, preferably with the support of the U.S.-dominated OAS.

In June 1954, the U.S. Central Intelligence Agency, in cooperation with neighboring Honduras and Nicaragua, mobilized and equipped an army of exiles to overthrow the elected leftist Guatemalan government of President Arbenz Guzman, whose regime had antagonized Washington and U.S. business interests by nationalizing the assets of U.S. companies. The U.N. Security Council considered a Brazil-Colombia-sponsored resolution referring a Guatemalan complaint to the OAS which was defeated by a Soviet veto. Following the Council debate, the OAS organized a commission of inquiry of the Inter-American Peace Committee to go to Guatemala, Honduras and Nicaragua. The government of Guatemala collapsed three days before the arrival of the OAS fact-finding group and the new anti-communist regime withdrew its predecessor's complaint to the U.N.

During the crisis, President Eisenhower said that it would be a "terrible thing if the communist dictatorship establishes an outpost on this continent".[5]

On 31 January 1962, the Final Act of the Eighth Meeting of Consultation of Ministers of Foreign Affairs was signed at Punta del Este, Uruguay. In a strongly worded anti-communist statement, the Ministers declared that the continental unity and the democratic institutions of the hemisphere were in danger. The purpose of the subversive offensive of communist Governments, their agents and the organizations which they controlled was the destruction of democratic institutions and the establishment of totalitarian dictatorships at the service of extra-continental powers. The Ministers then agreed that "the principles of communism are incompatible with the principles of the Inter-American system". They also recommended that governments of American states, whose structure or acts were incompatible with the effective exercise of representative democracy, hold free elections in their countries, as the most effective means of consulting the sovereign will of their peoples.

The Ministers decided to "exclude the present Government of Cuba from participation in the inter-American system": there is no "exclusion from membership" clause in the OAS Charter. The justification for this decision was that the present Government of Cuba had identified itself with the principles of Marxist-Leninist ideology (declared incompatible with the inter-American system), had established a political, economic, and social system based on that doctrine, and accepted military assistance from extracontinental communist powers, including even the threat of military intervention in America on the part of the Soviet Union.[6]

In 1965, U.S. marines invaded the Dominican Republic to prevent an elected leftist government from taking power. During the crisis, Washington took the position that any leftist deviation in the hemisphere, even if produced by democratic elections, constituted an attack to which the other nations of the region could respond by exercising the right of "collective self-defense". An OAS force partially replaced U.S. military contingents.[7]

The pressures and dangers of the Cold War had given priority to the rejection of communism in the region, to the detriment of the democratic process when electoral results gave the "wrong" outcome.

The incipient détente and the end of the Soviet threat, together with the democratic wave in Latin American countries, enticed the OAS to change its targets: its organs started to condemn totalitarian, military, non-communist, regimes and autocratic despots, and the overthrow of democratic governments through coups d'état.

On 23 June 1979, the Seventeenth Meeting of Consultation of Ministers of Foreign Affairs of the OAS condemned the "inhumane conduct of the dictatorial regime" governing Nicaragua and took position for the immediate and definitive replacement of the Somoza regime, the installation in Nicaragua of a democratic government, guarantee of the respect for human rights for all Nicaraguans and the holding of free elections as soon as possible.[8]

Following the cancelled Haitian elections of 29 November 1987, the Permanent Council of the OAS, in a resolution adopted on 7 December, "deplore(d) the acts of violence and disorder" and expressed its conviction that it was necessary to resume the democratic process so that the people of Haiti may express their will through free elections, without pressure or interference of any type.[9]

Following the annulled Panamanian elections of 7 May 1989, the Twenty-First Meeting of Consultation of Ministers of Foreign Affairs took to task General Noriega, on 17 May, in the following terms:

> CONSIDERING:
> That the grave events and the abuses by General Manuel Antonio Noriega in the crisis and the electoral process in Panama could unleash an escalation of violence with its attendant risks to the life and safety of persons;
> That these events have abridged the right of the Panamanian people to freely elect their legitimate authorities;
> That the outrageous abuses perpetrated against the opposition candidates and citizenry violate human, civil and political rights;
> That the crisis, which involves internal and external factors, is escalating rapidly, and could seriously endanger international peace and security;...

The Meeting then entrusted to the Ministers of Foreign Affairs of Ecuador, Guatemala and Trinidad and Tobago the urgent mission of promoting, with the assistance of the Secretary General of the OAS, conciliation formulas for arriving at a national accord that could bring about, through democratic mechanisms, a transfer of power in the shortest possible time, and with full respect for the sovereign will of the Panamanian people.[10]

While all these resolutions repeated the standard "nonintervention" formula, they all implied, and particularly the last one, a definite intervention in the internal affairs of the concerned state: respect for the "sovereign will of the people" was finally prevailing, in the regional organization, over the respect for national sovereignty.

In Suriname, the democratically elected President M. Ramsewak Shankar was deposed by a military coup on 24 December 1990. On 28 December, the Permanent Council of the OAS declared that this act of force violently disturbed the democratic institutional order of a member State, violated the right of its people to elect its governors freely, and dealt a severe setback to the democratization process in the Hemisphere. The Council categorically repudiated the coup and appealed for the reestablishment of the democratic institutional order in Suriname.[11]

In response to the military coup in Haiti of 29 September 1991, the Secretary General of the OAS requested a special meeting of the Permanent Council, in accordance with the procedures established by General Assembly resolution AG/RES. 1080 in June 1991. The Permanent Council energetically condemned the events and their authors on 30 September (Resol. CP/RES.567 (870/91)). Further action taken by OAS organs has been reviewed in Chapter 6.

The same resolution 1080 was used again to call the meeting of the Permanent Council that condemned the abortive Venezuelan coup of 3–4 February 1992.

On 5 April 1992, Peru's President Alberto Fujimori, with Army support, announced the dissolution of the Parliament and the suspension of constitutional guarantees. On 6 April, under resolution 1080, the Permanent Council called for an emergency meeting of the OAS Foreign Ministers. On 13 April, the Ministers adopted a resolution deploring the events in Lima, calling for an immediate return to the democratic order, and urging against the taking of any new measures that might aggravate the situation. In addition, the special meetings established a mission, headed jointly by the Uruguayan Minister of Foreign Affairs and the Secretary General of the OAS, that would make three visits to Lima in April and May 1992. The mission's aim was to assess the situation first-hand, and to encourage dialogue between Fujimori and the Peruvian political parties, with the participation of other democratic sectors, in order to return the country to democracy.

As noted by Eduardo Ferrero Costa,[12] the combined pressure exerted by the OAS, key foreign governments, and the international financial system proved effective: six weeks after his "autogolpe", Fujimori promised at a second ad hoc meeting of OAS Foreign Affairs Ministers, held at Nassau in the Bahamas, that he would schedule elections for a Constituent Congress to deliberate on constitutional changes while also carrying out all the legislative functions exercised by the dissolved Congress under the Constitution of 1980. Fujimori pledged that the terms of this new Congress would run for the remainder of his own period in office, ending on 28 July 1995. This pledge was embodied in the Bahamas Resolution of 18 May 1992 and may have prevented the voting of sanctions by the OAS.

Elections for the Constituent Congress were held on 22 November 1992, under the monitoring of OAS and U.S. observers. U.S. officials announced that these elections were free of any serious voter fraud and represented a significant step in the country's return to democracy.

OAS Electoral Technical Assistance and Observation

The OAS has carried out these activities since the 1960s. During the last few years, the OAS has assigned high priority to actions aimed at promoting democracy and to peacekeeping efforts, particularly in Central America. The OAS Secretary General plays a key role in approving and implementing observation missions of electoral processes. A list of Election Observation Missions carried out by the OAS is in Table 8.2.

The main characteristics of the current OAS electoral observation missions are the following:

- Most of the requests for electoral observation missions are sent directly to the Secretary General of the OAS;
- The Secretary General approves the request, without prior approval by an OAS Governing Body;
- The Secretary General informs the Permanent Council of requests received from governments for OAS participation in the observation of an electoral process;
- The Permanent Council authorizes the financing of a specific operation, through the budget of the Unit for Promotion of Democracy;
- Formal agreements are negotiated and signed by the OAS General Secretariat and the Government authorities, defining "The Privileges and Immunities of OAS Observers of the Electoral Process in (the country concerned)", and "The Relations between the Electoral Authorities of (the country concerned) and the OAS Observers in the Context of the (country's) Electoral Process";
- the OAS Secretariat makes all necessary arrangements for the missions, including the selection of participants;
- The Secretary General prepares a report on each mission and submits it to the Permanent Council.

Samples of a few electoral technical assistance and observation missions carried out by the OAS follow.

Early OAS Missions: Missions to the Dominican Republic

Following President Trujillo's assassination in May 1961,[13] President Balaguer, the new head of State started introducing democratic reforms and appealed to the OAS for assistance on electoral matters.

Table 8.2. Election Observation Missions carried out by the Organization of American States

Year	*Country*	*Type of electoral process*
1962	Dominican Republic	Presidential/general
1962	Costa Rica	Presidential/general
1963	Nicaragua	Presidential
1966	Costa Rica	Presidential/general
1966	Dominican Republic	Presidential/general
1966	Bolivia	General
1968	Ecuador	Presidential/general
1970	Dominican Republic	Presidential/general
1970	Guatemala	General
1970	Costa Rica	Presidential/general
1972	Nicaragua	National Constituent Assembly
1978	Panama	National Assembly
1978	Bolivia	General
1978	Costa Rica	General
1980	Guatemala	Municipal
1980	El Salvador	Legislative and Municipal
1981	Honduras	Presidential
1982	El Salvador	General
1984	Grenada	Parliamentary
1984	Guatemala	Presidential
1984	Panama	Presidential
1989/1990	Nicaragua	Presidential
1990	Guatemala	Presidential
1990	Dominican Republic	Presidential
1990/1991	Haiti	Presidential/general
1991	El Salvador	General
1991	Paraguay	Municipal
1991	Paraguay	Constituent Convention
1991	Suriname	General
1991	Panama	General and local
1992	Peru	Constitutional Parliament
1992	Venezuela	Municipal and gubernatorial

Source: OAS data, May 1993.

In response, the Organization dispatched a technical assistance mission composed of three members. The mission's terms of reference were to provide the Dominican Government with "technical advice on the legal, regulatory and procedural requirements for, and the technical conditions essential to, the holding of free elections". Many of the mission's recommendations were incorporated into the Dominican Republic's new electoral laws.

At the request of the Government, the mission was reactivated in June 1962 to advise the Government on the elections scheduled for December. The mission then suggested to the authorities to request outside observers for the actual balloting: the Government agreed to this suggestion. In addition to the Secretary General and seven staff members of the OAS, over 40 individuals, including diplomats, professors and lawyers, from the American continent, came to the country to observe the presidential elections.

Juan Bosch was elected president in the first democratically conducted elections after 32 years of despotism.

Three months after the elections, Bosch was overthrown in a military coup. The military leaders stayed in power until September 1963, followed by a civilian triumvirate, itself overthrown on 25 April 1965 by Colonel Caamano, with the support of leftist elements who hoped to return Bosch to power. The right challenged the legitimacy of the new government thereby leading the country towards civil war.

On 28 April, the U.S. intervened militarily in the country, causing an hostile international reaction. The U.S. force was then transformed into the (OAS) Inter-American Peace Force, still composed mainly of American troops.

The Act of Dominican Reconciliation of 9 August provided for, *inter alia*, general elections for the President and Vice-President of the Republic, members of Congress and for municipal authorities, to be held throughout the country, within a period of from six to nine months. The OAS would cooperate fully in the preparation and holding of the elections, in particular through a technical advisory commission composed of jurists and experts from the member states, and the Inter-American Commission on Human Rights, which would remain in the country throughout the electoral period.

In response to a request from the Provisional Government, the OAS sent a three-member technical assistance mission to Santo Domingo, to assess the electoral laws and preparations. At the suggestion of the mission, the Provisional Government requested the OAS Secretary General to invite distinguished individuals from the American hemisphere to oversee the elections, scheduled for 1 June 1966: 20 individuals from 13 American States observed the balloting and concluded that the elections had been "an outstanding act of democratic purity".[14]

Another OAS observer mission was dispatched to the Dominican Republic in 1970.

An OAS mission observed the presidential elections of 16 May 1990 in the Dominican Republic, which resulted in the election of Dr. Joachin Balaguer. The mission considered that the electoral process took place in a climate of tranquillity and in an orderly manner. The irregularities noted by the Mission in some of the polling stations were more the result of a certain confusion and disorganization than of premeditated and intentional acts.

Recent OAS Missions

The OAS observer mission in Nicaragua was an unprecedented undertaking for the Organization, in the words of its Secretary General.[15] The U.N. role in monitoring the Nicaragua elections has been reviewed in Chapter 6.

On 3 March 1989, in furtherance of the Agreement of Costa del Sol, signed by the five Central American presidents in El Salvador in February 1989, the Government of Nicaragua invited the Secretary General of the OAS to organize a group of international observers for the elections slated for 25 February 1990. The accord of the Nicaraguan Government with the Secretary General on the establishment of the OAS Observer Group to monitor the electoral process in Nicaragua was formally supported by the OAS General Assembly in November 1989 (AG/RES.993).

The mission of the OAS General Secretariat began with observation of the logistics of amending the electoral law. Once the negotiations conducted between the Government and the various political parties were concluded, the electoral law was amended to take into consideration many of the concerns expressed by the opposition forces in the country.

During July 1989, arrangements were made to plan for a continuous OAS presence in each of the nine voting districts in Nicaragua. The OAS observers, staff of the General Secretariat, arrived in Nicaragua in August and were deployed in the various regions. From then on, they were engaged in observing the various phases of the election process. The OAS presence was maintained until 25 April 1990, the date on which the new President of Nicaragua took office.

The OAS observer team was composed of staff of the General Secretariat and of other agencies of the system and of experts from member states. In all, there were a total of 433 OAS observers during the final days of the election period.

The OAS observers investigated specific complaints brought by the political parties and Nicaraguan citizens. Where appropriate, they referred these matters to the election authorities and other government agencies.

Observation of the whole electoral process and the number of OAS observers constituted a welcome innovation: many of the early OAS observation missions were composed of only a few "distinguished individuals", whose presence on election day was mainly symbolic.

In June 1990, the OAS General Assembly expressed its great satisfaction with the conduct of the electoral process in Nicaragua, while drawing attention to the work done by the international observers and in particular by the OAS observer group, whose presence did much to contribute to the success of those elections (AG/RES.1057).

Another OAS Mission observed the presidential elections of 11 November 1990 and 6 January 1991 in Guatemala, which resulted in the election of Jorge Serrano Elias. Again, the electoral process was considered free and fair.

The OAS Secretariat sent an observer mission to Haiti, in conjunction with the U.N. (see Chapter 6) and non-governmental organizations, to monitor the elections held in December 1990, and in January and February 1991. Following the elections, the Secretary General informed the Permanent Council that, despite certain logistical difficulties, these were free and democratic elections with a heavy turnout, thanks to the cooperation provided by the Provisional Government, the Armed Forces and the Provisional Electoral Council.[16]

At the request of the Governments concerned, the Secretary General sent the following missions:

- a mission to observe partial legislative and local elections in Panama held on 27 January 1991: the electoral process was considered normal;
- a mission of 85 OAS observers was sent to El Salvador to monitor legislative elections held on 19 March 1991: the mission concluded that the electoral process took place in conditions of tranquillity and security, – none of the political leaders raised objections to the results;
- a mission to observe the municipal elections held on 26 May 1991 in Paraguay; 47 OAS observers were present on election day;
- a mission to observe the elections to the Constitutional Convention held in Paraguay on 1 December 1991; 33 OAS observers were present on election day.[17]

The process of approval and implementation of a recent OAS observation mission is hereunder described in more detail, on the basis of the Secretary General's official report on the mission.[18]

Elections in Suriname – May 1991

On 31 January 1991, the President of Suriname invited the OAS Secretary General to observe the Surinamese electoral process in the framework of elections to be held on 25 May. The Secretary General accepted the invitation and designated an OAS staff member to coordinate an electoral observation mission to the country.

A delegation of four OAS staff members headed by the coordinator arrived in Suriname in mid-February and proceeded to set up the mission. From 18 to 20 March, the Secretary General visited Suriname and signed two formal agreements with the Government establishing the scope and purpose of the mission.

One of the formal agreements, entitled "Agreement between the Republic of Suriname and the OAS on the Relations between the Electoral Authorities of Suriname and the Observers of the OAS in the context of Suriname's Electoral Process", was signed by the Surinamese Minister for Home Affairs. This document contained provisions assuring observer receipt of credentials, access to voting records and polling stations, and otherwise facilitating the work of the mission. It also provided that the Mission inform the Surinamese Government, through its Independent Electoral Council, of any irregularities or interference observed during the electoral process.

The other formal agreement, entitled "Agreement between the Government of Suriname and the Secretary General of the OAS on the Privileges and Immunities of the Observers of the Election Process in Suriname", was signed by the Surinamese Minister for Foreign Affairs. This document was in line with Article 138 of the OAS Charter, which provides that: "The Organization of American States shall enjoy in the territory of each Member such legal capacity, privileges, and immunities as are necessary for the exercise of its functions and the accomplishment of its purposes". It pledged observer access to all of Suriname's territory and otherwise facilitated the work of the mission. To the Government, it provided assurances that the work of the Mission would be guided by the constitutional, legal, and statutory regulations in effect in Suriname.

The Surinamese electoral process encompassed the 25 May 1991 elections for National Assembly members and members for the 10 District and 62 Local Councils, and also included the subsequent election and inauguration of a new President and Vice President by the newly elected representatives.

OAS observers were present throughout the entire electoral process, which officially began on 13 February 1991 with the opening of the voter registration lists for public inspection.

Eight political organizations successfully met the requirements for participating in the elections by the 9 April deadline for their registration. The registration of candidates followed.

OAS observers attended a total of 149 political rallies during the electoral process in the nine Districts where they were held and of all the organizations contending for the elections. In contacts with political organizations and with individuals 51 complaints were received and followed up on about different aspects of the electoral process.

The elections took place on 25 May as scheduled, in an orderly and peaceful manner. The mission did not learn of any serious act of violence related to the electoral process on 25 May or at any other time during the process. The polling itself was extremely well organized and the observers had free access to polling stations, with minor exceptions which may well have been due to lack of information about the mission on the part of local officials.

Members of the mission visited 299 out of the 443 polling stations nationwide (68%) and observed no irregularities which called into doubt the validity of the process itself. Overall the elections in and of themselves were certified as free and fair. However the mission did observe several problems which affected the voter participation without calling into doubt the transparency of the elections themselves. Some confusion regarding registration formalities on the part of potential voters and electoral officials probably contributed to the national abstention rate of 31%.

In April and May, the mission was made up of 40 observers, nationals from 16 member states, and covered the entire territory of Suriname. From February to April, and from June on a core of observers stayed until Suriname's new President and Vice President were inaugurated on 16 September 1991.

The OAS mission was well received by the people of Suriname and by political organizations in general. Observers witnessed an enthusiastic campaigning and wide participation in most aspects of the electoral process.

An independent audit of the election results carried out by the mission showed no evidence of fraud in the tabulation of official results.

The mission received full cooperation from the Independent Electoral Council and was impressed by the professional manner in which election officials carried out their work during the entire electoral process.

While making allowance for the rather emphatic support given by the mission to the electoral authorities, its report gives evidence of the systematic work carried out by the observers, the adequate coverage of electoral operations and the solid basis for their assessment that the elections in Suriname had been free and fair.

A Seminar on Elections and Election Observation was held at OAS headquarters from 13 to 15 November 1991. Its participants were the highest ranking authorities of the electoral bodies of Costa Rica, Guatemala, Honduras, El Salvador, Nicaragua, Panama and Suriname, whose presentations, discussions and exchanges with OAS officials were intended as a means to analyze the process involved in organizing and observing elections in those countries, to which the OAS had sent election observation missions in recent years, and to identify opportunities for cooperation in these areas.

In the field of advisory services, the OAS will collaborate with the Association for Democracy and Development in Central America in programmes to promote democracy.

The Commonwealth

As the U.N. at the global level and the OAS at the regional level, the Commonwealth has become an active intergovernmental promoter of representative democracy and has sent many election observation missions to its member States.

Like the U.N., the Commonwealth has initially observed self-determination processes in colonial territories, then elections in sovereign member States. The first Commonwealth Election Observation Team was sent to British Guiana in 1964, and their numbers have increased in recent years.

Besides observation missions, like the U.N. and the OAS, the Commonwealth provides technical assistance in the organization and conduct of elections and, where needed, the loan or gift of materials and equipment required for the administration of polls. Constitutional experts, legal drafters and electoral advisers have been provided to governments in countries in transition to multi-party democracy.

The Commonwealth is not a typical intergovernmental organization: an offshoot of nineteenth century colonialism, the contemporary Commonwealth has no constitution or charter, no formal constitutional structure and it imposes no statutory obligations on its 50 members. It is a voluntary association of independent sovereign States, its membership adding up to a quarter of the world's nations and people. In the promotion of its fundamental values, the Commonwealth employs a strategy based on an essentially consensual approach. Its members' systems of government include monarchies, republics, parliamentary systems, presidential regimes, one-party systems and military governments. In spite of this "rich tapestry" of political governance, the Commonwealth has, since 1971, formally adopted democratic values and principles.[19]

Strengthening Democratic Institutions

In 1971, in Singapore, the Commonwealth Heads of Government adopted a "Declaration of Commonwealth Principles" which included a democratic pronouncement:

> We believe in the liberty of the individual, in equal rights for all citizens regardless of race, colour, creed or political belief, and in their inalienable right to participate by means of free and democratic political processes in framing the society in which they live. We therefore strive to promote in each of our countries those representative institutions and guarantees for personal freedom under the law that are our common heritage.

In a review of the global situation and the role the Commonwealth should play in the 1990s and beyond, Commonwealth Heads of Government agreed, at their October 1989 Meeting in Kuala Lumpur, that one area where the Commonwealth might usefully make a distinctive contribution was in the strengthening of democratic institutions in member countries. Heads of Government agreed with the Secretary-General's proposal to provide Commonwealth assistance in helping member countries to reinforce their election and other constitutional processes by mounting observer missions at the request of member governments.[20]

In the Harare Declaration of October 1991, Commonwealth Heads of Government pledged to work with renewed vigour to protect and promote the fundamental political values of the Commonwealth, including:

> democracy, democratic processes and institutions which reflect national circumstances, the rule of law and the independence of the judiciary, just and honest government.

They also agreed to strengthen the capacity of the Commonwealth to respond to requests from members for assistance in entrenching the practices of democracy, accountable administration and the rule of law.[21]

As a result of its experience in election monitoring, the Commonwealth has stressed the importance of action to create an environment conducive to the democratic process well ahead of polling day. Benchmarks were identified, including:

- a constitution that makes for a representative and accountable government;
- electoral laws that ensure proper registration of voters;
- fair nomination procedures;
- conditions that allow a secret ballot;
- adequate access to the publicly owned media for contesting parties; and
- well-trained and vigilant political party agents whose work is complemented by national and international observers.

Finally, the Commonwealth recognized that democratic structures cannot be imposed from outside but must be sustained from within, and that attention needs to be paid to the development of an endogenous democratic culture.

The Secretary-General prepared in October 1991 a set of "Guidelines for the establishment of Commonwealth groups to observe elections in member countries". Excerpts are given in Table 8.3.

In summary, the decision to establish a mission rests with the Commonwealth Secretary-General, subject to receipt of a formal request from the government concerned and assurance of support by political parties. Without executive functions, the role of the group of observers is to make an independent judgement as to whether the poll was free and fair. Its advisory (good offices) role is limited. Groups are usually small, ranging in practice from four to thirteen observers, plus supporting secretariat staff.

Like the observers in early OAS missions, Commonwealth observers are selected as "distinguished individuals" from various countries of the group: they have included a Chief Justice, senior lawyers, diplomats, senior civil servants, parliamentarians, former government ministers, senior electoral administrators and other persons of renown. Some have served in several Commonwealth missions. During their mission, observers should be independent from their government: they serve in their personal capacity.

Commonwealth Observation Missions

The first experience of the Commonwealth in observing an election was in sending a team of 12 members from seven countries to British Guiana in 1964. The team's terms of reference were brief but clear:

> To observe the British Guiana election and report to the Commonwealth Secretary of State whether
> a) the administrative arrangements were conducted in a fair and proper manner. If not, what were the deficiencies?
> b) there was freedom of expression of different points of view through broadcasting, public meetings and the press. If not, what were the restrictions?
> c) Any other matters came to the notice of the observers which, in their opinion, affected the fair and free conduct of the elections.

The group assembled in Georgetown on 30 November 1964. During the week preceding the election, scheduled for 7 December, the observers visited 34 of the 35 polling districts and over 200 of the 772 polling places. The team was favorably impressed with conduct and the results of the election. Its conclusion was that the election reflected the political conviction of the Guianese electorate.[22]

The next mission was sent to Mauritius in 1967. Elections to a new 62 member Legislative Assembly were to lead to a decision on the island's future status. In preparation for the elections, scheduled for 7 August 1967, the U.K. sent a British commission to review the country's electoral laws and a Commonwealth team, first to oversee the registration of voters, then to observe the actual ballotting. The team, composed of seven members from five countries, concluded their mission with a

Table 8.3. Guidelines for the establishment of Commonwealth Groups to observe elections in member countries – Excerpts

Introduction

...

Establishing Commonwealth Observer Groups

2. The Commonwealth Secretary-General would consider establishing an independent group of appropriate size when he receives a formal request from a Commonwealth government for the Commonwealth to observe its own country's elections. Recognizing the sensitivities and essential differences between constituting an observer mission for self-determination and decolonisation-related elections (as in Southern Rhodesia/Zimbabwe in 1980), the Secretary-General in the latter cases would need to receive an express invitation from the government concerned and be assured directly by the political parties of their support

....

3. The electoral standards and procedures to be applied should be the subject of broad agreement among the parties wishing to contest the election. While consideration would need to be given to particular local customs, circumstances and traditions, these standards and procedures would have regard in particular to those laid down in relevant international instruments and be in accordance with fundamental Commonwealth beliefs and principles. In determining whether to accede to a particular request the Secretary-General would need to take into account whether the election process as a whole in that country was in general conformity with internationally accepted norms, and that any differences were accepted by the parties.
4. Where the Commonwealth Secretary-General is asked to provide a Commonwealth observer group, consideration would have to be given as to whether, in the context of the presence of other groups which may also have been invited, the Commonwealth per se has a special role to play in the process.

Terms of reference

5. The purpose of an observer group would be to say whether in its independent judgement the poll was free and fair ... the observer group would be expected to reflect in its report and, where appropriate, bring to the attention of the appropriate authorities any matters which caused it concern. This latter function would be confined to a "good offices" role and the group would have no express or implied executive function. Its terms of reference should therefore be drawn broadly. They should reflect the fact that the group has to make a judgement as to whether, notwithstanding any particular difficulties, overall the process taken as a whole – the campaign together with registration of voters and the poll itself – has been such as to be likely to represent the wishes of the people.
6. ... the terms of reference should enable the observer group to take into account in its overall assessment the fairness of the registration process; the freedom of the parties to nominate candidates, to campaign, and to get their message across to the electorate; the freedom of parties to publish and distribute campaign literature in compliance with the general law of the land and the election law; where permits for rallies are necessary, whether these were granted or denied on a discriminatory basis; whether relevant officials were neutral as between the parties; whether the parties were permitted to satisfy themselves as to the integrity of the poll (e.g. to be represented at all times when the ballot box is unsealed; to inspect boxes as empty prior to the start of polling; to affix their own seals at relevant times and to inspect them subsequently; to be present at the count and to accompany boxes if they are transported for counting elsewhere); whether the act of voting was secret, and whether the ballot boxes, when not closed, were in full view of the presiding officials and the party polling agents; whether voting took place in an atmosphere conducive to voting without intimidation; and whether the count was properly conducted.

Composition

7. The group would be appointed by the Commonwealth Secretary-General on an ad hoc basis and

would comprise individuals of high standing and proven integrity whose considered opinions would be likely to carry weight. In determining its membership, the Secretary-General would have regard to the need for the group to be able to command the confidence and trust of all those participating in the elections. The precise size would depend on the size of the country where the poll was to be observed, both geographically and in terms of its electorate. The minimum size of a group would be three. In addition, the group would be serviced by a small team, from the Commonwealth Secretariat (augmented from outside as may be necessary) which would provide logistical support and expert advice on such matters as the relevant electoral laws and the conduct of elections generally.

Modus Operandi

8. The Secretary-General would need to be assured from the outset that the members of the group would enjoy free and open access to polling places and counting stations and that it would be free generally to pursue its mandate. The group would, where possible, arrive in the country concerned before the conclusion of the election campaign. In some circumstances it might be desirable to be present for at least a part of the registration process and/or for the nomination of candidates. The group would remain until the count was concluded and the result announced. In the ordinary course of events a group might be in a country for up to two weeks (the final week of the campaign, the days of the poll and the period of the count). In accordance with international practice it would be open to the group, should it wish to do so, to make an interim announcement of its findings to date ahead of the count commencing (as recognized international practice suggests that this can prevent a group from being criticised subsequently for having allowed the results of the count to influence its judgement as to other events). The group would act in its own independent judgement and would not be representative of governments, either individually or collectively, or of the Secretary-General. The opinions expressed would be those of its members only. Members would serve in their individual capacities. The group would be asked to send its report initially to the Commonwealth Secretary-General and to the government of the country in question, and thereafter to the leaderships of the political parties taking part in the election. The Secretary-General would then transmit copies of the report to other Commonwealth governments in the usual way.

Financial

9. Funding of observer missions should be on a pan-Commonwealth basis rather than be the responsibility of the particular government concerned...

Other Commonwealth Assistance

10. ...

Annex A

The Group is established by the Commonwealth Secretary-General at the request of the government of ..... supported by the political parties. It is to observe every relevant aspect of the organization and conduct of the elections in accordance with the law of ..... relating to elections. Its function is to ascertain whether, in its impartial judgement and in the context of that law, the elections have been free and fair.

The Group has no executive role; its function is neither to supervise nor act as a commission of inquiry but to observe the process as a whole and to form a judgement accordingly. It is to submit its report initially to the Secretary-General and to the government of ....., and thereafter to the leaderships of the political parties taking part in the election.

Source: Common wealth Secretariat Document, October 1991.

favorable assessment: they were in no doubt that the elections were conducted from start to finish in a fair and free way and that the results reflected the true wishes of the Mauritian people. The newly elected Assembly, meeting in late August opted for independence for the country before the end of the year.

Also in 1967, another Commonwealth team observed a referendum offering the population of Gibraltar a choice between continued British rule and integration with Spain. The referendum had been decided by the U.K., against the opposition of the U.N. where the anti-colonialist majority tended to ignore the free will of the people concerned. The Commonwealth team of five members had the usual terms of reference. Ninety-seven percent of the registered voters turned out to cast their ballots: 12,138 voted to retain their link with the U.K., while 44 voted to pass under Spanish sovereignty. The observers' unanimous view was that the actual conduct of the referendum fully conformed with the requirements for the free expression of choice through the medium of the secret ballot. The U.N. General Assembly rejected the holding of the referendum, and thus its results, in a resolution of 19 December 1967 (Resol. 2335 (XXII)).[23]

In February 1980, a Commonwealth Group was constituted to observe elections which led Southern Rhodesia to become independent as Zimbabwe. An integral part of the Accord reached by Commonwealth Heads of Government at Lusaka in August 1979, and the ensuing Lancaster House Agreement was the decision to hold free and fair elections in Southern Rhodesia, properly supervised under British Government authority, and with Commonwealth Observers. The territory would be brought to independence on the basis of majority rule, following the unilateral declaration of independence of 1965, U.N. condemnations and sanctions, rebellion and repression. In spite of the suspicion and mistrust of opposing parties, the tenuous ceasefire held, and the eleven Commonwealth Observers, with 52 assistants, concluded that the election was a valid and democratic expression of the wishes of the people of Zimbabwe. In spite of a certain degree of violence and fear, the system of proportional representation based on party lists diminished the electoral impact of intimidation. The observers were completely satisfied with the integrity of the conduct of the poll in all its aspects, including the security of ballot boxes and the accuracy of the count.[24]

These first missions had been sent to observe electoral processes organized in British territories, under the authority of the British Government.

Then, for the first time, a sovereign state, Uganda, asked the Commonwealth Secretary-General to send an Observer Group to observe every relevant aspect of the organization and conduct of the December 1980 elections by the Electoral Commission in accordance with the law of Uganda relating to the elections. The request of the Government of Uganda had been subsequently endorsed by all four political parties. The group was composed of nine observers, plus 36 assistants and 11 members of the Commonwealth Secretariat (at full strength). The observers described the election as turbulent and troubled, characterised by confusion, delays, and intense mistrust. They criticized both the Electoral and the Military Commission, but concluded that "surmounting all obstacles, the people of Uganda, like some great tidal wave, carried the electoral process to a worthy and valid conclusion".

Critics of the Commonwealth mission to Uganda add that the campaign was marred by acts of violence and allegations of intimidation, most of which were attributed to supporters of former President Milton Obote and directed against followers of Yoweri Museveni and his Uganda Patriotic Movement. The Commonwealth team's early departure after the vote did not enable it to assess the serious charges of fraud and manipulation raised by Museveni following the elections. Museveni withdrew from the political process and renewed the armed struggle. During the next four years, more than 100,000 people died as a result of the fighting and thousands of others became refugees or displaced persons. Finally, in 1986, Obote was overthrown and Museveni seized control of the country.

The Uganda experience raises some doubts as to whether the Commonwealth team's report was hasty and over-optimistic. The fact is that the Ugandan elections, under Commonwealth observation, did not contribute to the peaceful resolution of the internal political conflict.

To these critics, one may reply that the Observer Group's mandate was limited to observe the organization and conduct of the elections. The group had neither the mandate, nor the power, to maintain or restore civil peace after the elections.[25]

The next Commonwealth mission, sent to Namibia from 24 September to 10 October 1989, had uncharacteristic features. As an exception to the rule, the mission did not concern a Commonwealth country or territory, nor was it requested by the administering authority, South Africa. South Africa had had to withdraw from the Commonwealth on 15 March 1961, as its apartheid policy was incompatible with Commonwealth values. Secondly, its observation did not cover the elections, which took place from 7 to 11 November 1989, but reviewed the preparations for the elections, and, in practice, advised the U.N. Secretary-General's Special Representative concerning some potential problems concerning the electoral process leading to Namibia's independence.

Commonwealth governments had been concerned about Namibia for a number of years, and had, in particular, applied political pressure to hasten the decolonization of the territory. Following the adoption of Security Council Resolutions 435 in 1978 and 632 in February 1989 (see Chapter 6), the Commonwealth Committee of Foreign Ministers on Southern Africa, at their meeting in Canberra on 7–9 August 1989, drew attention to a range of anxieties about the Namibia independence process. After consultations with the U.N. Secretary-General and with Commonwealth Governments, it was agreed that there would be value in sending a Commonwealth Observer Group to Namibia charged with reporting to Commonwealth Heads of Government at their meeting in Kuala Lumpur beginning on 18 October 1989.

In the short time available, a seven-member Observer Group, supported by a small team from the Secretariat, arrived in Namibia on 24 September and, after extensive travel in the country, completed their report on 10 October.

The Group's terms of reference were to:

- observe and examine the preparations leading to free and fair elections and the emergence of a genuinely independent Namibia;
- support the United Nations in its efforts to ensure the integrity of the Settlement Plan pursuant to Security Council Resolution 435; and
- report to Commonwealth Heads of Government in Kuala Lumpur on these and related matters.

While the group's final report was properly addressed on 10 October to the Commonwealth Secretary-General, the Group's Chairman, A.R. Parsons (Australia), wrote directly to the U.N. Special Representative on 3 October to alert him to some specific problems and suggest some solutions regarding the delayed electoral law and various practical measures. In its Aide Mémoire of 10 October, the group expressed concern about the apparent lack of cooperation forthcoming from the South African Administration on key aspects of the Resolution 435 process. On 14 October, the Commonwealth Secretary-General noted in his foreword transmitting the report that the just-issued Election (Constituent Assembly) Proclamation 1989 had met the principal concerns expressed by the Commonwealth after the draft law had been published in July.

It would therefore appear that the Commonwealth Governments through the political pressure applied by their meetings and through the influence of their Observer Group's presence and report, have buttressed the position of the U.N. Special Representative in his negotiations with the South African authorities concerning the electoral code and other practical arrangements.[26]

A more orthodox Observer Group was sent to Malaysia to observe the General Elections held on 20–21 October 1990, after a two-week election campaign. The Group was composed of 12 members and eight assistants from the Secretariat. Following a briefing with the Secretary-General in London, an advance party arrived in Kuala Lumpur on 9 October. Further briefings were held with the Election Commission, the Director General of the Foreign Ministry and members of the Ministry of Home Affairs, including a Commissioner from the Royal Malaysia Police and lawyers from the Attorney General's Chambers. Forty political parties were advised of the Group's readiness to meet with them. The group did not consider that it was within their terms of reference to investigate complaints and establish the validity of the allegations made: however, they brought these to the attention of the Election Commission.

The group concluded that the nomination proceedings and the organization and conduct of polling were properly and impartially carried out and that the elections allowed the voters an opportunity to freely express their choice in accordance with Malaysian law.

Without challenging the elections and their results, the observers expressed their serious concern about the many inaccuracies and imperfections brought to their notice concerning the electoral rolls. They also expressed concern about the unequal access of the opposition parties to the mainstream media, especially television.[27]

The next group, composed of 12 Observers and nine support staff, was formed to observe the parliamentary elections in Bangladesh on 27 February 1991. The group described the election as free and fair.[28]

On 31 October 1991, another group observed the Presidential and National Assembly Elections in Zambia: 13 Observers participated in the mission together with nine Secretariat assistants. The group reported that the Zambian multi-party elections were conducted in a calm and orderly manner and gave the people of Zambia the opportunity to vote for the Presidential and National Assembly candidates of their choice. The results should therefore fully reflect the will of the Zambian people. According to the Observers, the entire election process showed that there was a basis in Zambia for the development of multi-party democracy. Finally, they concluded that the elections were free and fair.[29]

Unlike most Commonwealth Observer Groups, a group was established to observe elections to a Constitutional Commission, and not legislative elections, in Seychelles, elections which were held on 23–26 July 1992.

Following the Harare Meeting in October 1991, Seychelles President Albert René announced on 4 December 1991 that after 15 years of one-party rule, his country would be transformed from a "single-party popular democracy to a pluralistic democratic system". The first step in the transition process was to hold elections to a Constitutional Commission, to be followed by a referendum on the new constitution, then general elections. The Government of Seychelles had asked the Commonwealth for assistance with the process.

A group of seven Observers was formed, supplemented by five Secretariat assistants.

The group reported that the election "was free and fair on the day, notwithstanding some shortcomings. The secrecy of the ballot was assured".

In fact those "shortcomings" were serious and could have justified invalidating the election results, which gave a majority of 58.4% to the ruling party, Seychelles People's Progressive Front (SPPF), led by President René, with the main opposition party, the Democratic Party of Sir James Mancham, receiving 33.7% of the votes.

Among some of the criticisms in the group's report:

> The issue which loomed largest and which appeared to be of most concern to all the opposition parties was the continuing link between the state and the ruling SPPF. As in all single-party states, the 15 years of SPPF rule had brought about a well-nigh complete fusion of the party and the state. The President's statement of 4 December 1991 making Seychelles once more a multi-party state should have inaugurated the effective delinking of the party from the state. In actual fact, at the time of the election to the Constitutional Commission, it did not seem that much headway had been made to this end.
>
> ...in the 1992 budget...Seychelles Rupees 9.6 million (were allocated) to the SPPF against only SR200,000...to each of the other registered parties.
>
> ...As in many developing countries, the state in Seychelles is the main employer and this makes the community dependent on those who control it for

> their jobs, pensions, loans, education, housing and other social facilities. This has placed a disproportionate advantage in the hands of the SPPF leaders...
>
> ...The Inner and Outer Islands were not the only areas perceived to be the preserve of the SPPF. Of the institutions of the state, the army, the Police Mobile Unit (PMU, which is the paramilitary wing of the police force), and the militia were widely perceived to be particularly close to the present Government and therefore having a stake in its continuation in office.
>
> ...a State of Emergency (legislation adopted) in 1981, which remains in force, and which was a source of anxiety.

Rather than condemning the electoral process, itself the first step in a transition process, the Group chose to condone the elections, in spite of the shortcomings, and to make a series of constructive proposals for the future:

- review the Voters' Registration List;
- all the parties should adopt a voluntary Code of Conduct;
- the process of separating the institutions of the state from the ruling party should be accelerated;
- establish a free and independent media;
- law enforcement and security agencies should show discipline and exercise restraint.[30]

Three other Commonwealth Observer Missions were formed in 1992: one to observe parliamentary elections in Guyana on 5 October, – the second one to observe presidential elections in Ghana on 3 November, – and the third one, to observe the 29 December Kenyan elections.

The Commonwealth Observer Group, and other international observers, who followed the Presidential, Parliamentary and Civic elections in Kenya, faced a dilemma similar to that faced by the Commonwealth Group in the Uganda and Seychelles elections. President Daniel arap Moi obtained 36% of the votes, while his closest rival, Kenneth Matiba, received 26% – the divided opposition could, if they had united their forces, have obtained the majority vote.

Despite allegations of poor administration, incidents of rigging, malpractice and electoral irregularity, the 150-strong international election monitoring teams were prepared to accept the election results despite acknowledging that they were neither free nor fair. Besides the Commonwealth Group, other teams were from the U.S., Canada, Egypt, Scandinavian countries and Japan.

In its report,[31] the Commonwealth Observer Group was generally negative about the electoral process but still concluded that it constituted a "giant step on the road to multiparty democracy":

> These were elections which proved difficult to evaluate in terms of freeness and fairness. It was evident to us from the start that some aspects of the elections were not fair. These included:
>
> – The Registration Process

> ...lack of adequate training of registration officers, registration of young persons of doubtful age qualifications, the failure of the proper authorities to issue identity cards to the many citizens...the incidence of multiple registration, the initial boycott of the process by opposition parties and the busing of persons from certain districts to others in order to strengthen party support in some constituencies...The opposition parties have now placed (the number of persons disenfranchised as a result) at over three million persons (there were 8 million voters)...
>
> – The Nomination Process
>
> ...the nomination proceedings for parliamentary and civic elections were marred by the physical prevention of a substantial number of prospective candidates from handing in their nomination papers. The result of this unlawful interference with prospective candidates was that in the Rift Valley Province 16 Parliamentary candidates, all belonging to KANU (Kenya African National Union party, President Moi's party), were declared duly elected unopposed on nomination day.
>
> – The Intimidation
>
> ...widespread tribal disturbances, threats and harassment of party supporters, in particular supporters of the opposition parties...widespread bribery by political parties, particularly the ruling party.
>
> – State Control of the Media
>
> It is regrettable that efforts were not made early enough by the Electoral Commission to encourage the media to adopt guidelines for impartial coverage...
>
> – State or Party?
>
> ...The Kenyan experience has shown that the failure to implement a timely delinking programme spells trouble for the process of transition...

Against these negative aspects, compounded by the inexperience of the Electoral Commission, the group reported, on the positive side, that millions of enthusiastic people cast their votes in a general atmosphere of calm throughout the country. The group concluded:

> Despite the fact that the whole process cannot be given an unqualified rating as free and fair, the evolution of the process to polling day and the subsequent count was increasingly positive to a degree that we believe that the results in many instances directly reflect, however imperfectly, the expression of the will of the people.

Another Commonwealth Observer Group observed the general elections in Lesotho in March 1993.

For the record, one should also mention the Commonwealth Observer Mission to South Africa, October 1992 to January 1993, although its mandate was to contribute to a climate conducive to advancing negotiations designed to establish a non-racial democracy in a united South Africa, – and not to observe elections.

A list of all the electoral processes observed by Commonwealth Observer Groups is given in Table 8.4.

The list shows an impressive, useful and welcome increase of the Commonwealth electoral observation activities since 1989.

Table 8.4. List of Commonwealth Election Observer Groups

Year	*Country*	*Type of electoral process*
1964	British Guiana	General elections
1967	Mauritius	General elections
1967	Gibraltar	Referendum
1980	Zimbabwe	General elections
1980	Uganda	General elections
1989	Namibia	Preparations for elections
1990	Malaysia	General elections
1991	Bangladesh	Parliamentary elections
1991	Zambia	Presidential/parliamentary
1992	Seychelles	Constitution Commission
1992	Guyana	General and regional elections
1992	Ghana	Presidential elections
1993	Lesotho	General elections
(1992–1993	South Africa	Promoting negotiations towards non-racial democracy)

Source: Commonwealth Documentation and Reports.

European Organizations

The Council of Europe, the European Community and the Conference of Security and Cooperation in Europe (CSCE) have had from their creation, or have recently developed, a role in promoting democracy with particular reference to the ex-USSR and its emancipated satellites, but also in respect of developing countries. This role has been, for the Council of Europe, that of a democratic bastion and beacon during the dark years of the Soviet threat of aggression and communisation of Western Europe, then the recent role of its Parliamentary Assembly in observing elections in the former Soviet Union and its satellites, – for the European Community, mainly an economic organization, the recent linking of democracy and human rights with development aid, – for the CSCE, the expansion of its role from the "basket" of human rights to the unanimous recognition by all its member states of the ideals of democracy, political pluralism and the rule of law.

While some of these organizations have engaged in observation of elections, they have also realized that democratic elections alone cannot guarantee democracy. Their role has therefore also been to build up and strengthen democratic institutions through legal and technical assistance.

The Council of Europe

The Council of Europe was founded in 1949 as an exclusive club of European democracies, in which the objective of expanding or reaching universal membership practised by other organizations was always secondary to an insistence on strict democratic and human rights credentials.

The Preamble to the Council's Statute reaffirms the founding member states'

> devotion to the spiritual and moral values which are the common heritage of their peoples and the true source of individual freedom, political liberty and the rule of law, principles which form the basis of all genuine democracy; ...

Article 3 of the Statute prescribes that every Member of the Council must accept the principles of the rule of law and of the enjoyment by all persons within its jurisdiction of human rights and fundamental freedoms, and collaborate sincerely and effectively in the realisation of the aim of the Council as specified in Chapter I: this aim is, in part, to achieve a greater unity between its Members for the purpose of safeguarding and realising the ideals and principles which are their common heritage and the maintenance and further realisation of human rights and fundamental freedoms. European States may be invited to become members if deemed to be able and willing to fulfil these provisions. Furthermore, any Member which has seriously violated Art. 3 may be suspended from its rights of representation and requested by the Committee of Ministers to withdraw. In case of non-compliance, the Committee may decide that it has ceased to be a Member (Art. 8).

In 1950, the Convention for the Protection of Human Rights and Fundamental Freedoms was adopted: based on the Universal Declaration of Human Rights, it covered initially a more limited number of human rights, including the freedoms of thought, expression, peaceful assembly. However, it provides for a machinery of supervision including a recourse to the European Court of Human Rights. Under Art. 3 of a Protocol to the Convention adopted on 20 March 1952,

> The High Contracting Parties undertake to hold free elections at reasonable intervals by secret ballot, under conditions which will ensure the free expression of the opinion of the people in the choice of the legislature.[32]

The dictatorship of the Colonels in Greece suppressed parliamentary democracy and constitutional legality in April 1967. In January 1968, the Council's Parliamentary Assembly recommended to the Committee of Ministers the suspension of Greece from membership. Without awaiting the Committee's decision, Greece withdrew from the Council on 12 December 1969. Upon the restoration of democracy, Greece was invited on 29 November 1974 to rejoin the Council.

Portugal and Spain were only admitted to the Council of Europe as Members when democracy was restored in these countries, respectively in 1976 and 1977.[33]

In September 1980, the military took power in Turkey, dissolved the Parliament and banned the political parties. Without parliamentarians, Turkey was effectively barred, after May 1981, from the Parliamentary Assembly of the Council. In July 1982, France, Denmark, the Netherlands, Norway and Sweden lodged petitions with the European Commission of Human Rights, claiming that Turkey had contravened several provisions of the Convention. In January 1983, the Parliamentary Assembly requested Turkey not to exercise its voting rights in the Committee of Ministers. Turkey was under threat of expulsion from the Council when the military allowed its return to elected government in November 1983.[34]

The democratic changes in Central and Eastern Europe have given the Council an opportunity to contribute to the integration of these countries into the European democratic "Club".

The "European Commission for Democracy through Law" (or Venice Commission) was created in 1990 under the auspices of the Council. As a consultative body, the Commission cooperates with both member States of the Council and non-member States, particularly those of Central and Eastern Europe. Its specific field of action concerns the guarantees offered by law in the service of democracy. In priority, its work will focus on:

- the constitutional, legislative and administrative principles and technique which serve the efficiency of democratic institutions and their strengthening, as well as the principle of the rule of law;
- the public rights and freedoms, notably those that involve the participation of citizens in the life of the institutions;
- the contribution of local and regional self-government to the development of democracy.

Its main activities have consisted in assisting Central and Eastern European countries in reforming their Constitution. The Commission has also adopted a proposal for a Convention on the Protection of Minorities and has organized seminars on "legislation by Decree" and "Judicial and other control of the Administration". A series of University Seminars for Democracy will also be organized.[35]

Observation of Elections

The Hungarian Parliament, represented in the Parliamentary Assembly of the Council of Europe by a special guest delegation since July 1989 was the first in Central and Eastern Europe to invite the Assembly to observe its parliamentary elections, held on 25 March and 8 April 1990. Similar requests were addressed to the Assembly by the German Democratic Republic, Romania (for two different elections), the Czech and Slovak Federal Republic, Bulgaria (for two different elections), Albania (for two different elections), Poland, Croatia, Estonia, Lithuania, and Slovenia, between 1990 and end 1992. A list of the elections observed by ad hoc Committees of the Assembly is given in Table 8.5.

Table 8.5. List of elections observed by ad hoc Observer Committees constituted by the Parliamentary Assembly of the Council of Europe – 1990–1992

Country	Type of electoral process	Dates
German Democratic Republic	Parliamentary	18.3.1990
Hungary	Parliamentary	25.3. and 8.4.1990
Romania	Presidential/parliamentary	20.5.1990
Czech and Slovak Federal Republic	Parliamentary	8 and 9.6.1990
Bulgaria	Parliamentary	10 and 17.6.1990
Albania	Parliamentary	31.3, 7 and 14.4.1991
Bulgaria	Parliamentary/municipal	13.10.1991
Poland	Parliamentary	27.10.1991
Albania	Parliamentary	22 and 29.3.1992
Croatia	Presidential/parliamentary	2.8.1992
Estonia	Presidential/parliamentary	20.9.1992
Romania	Presidential/parliamentary	27.9.1992
Lithuania	Constitutional referendum/parliamentary	25.10 and 15.11.1992
Slovania	Presidential/parliamentary	6.12.1992

Source: Council of Europe, Parliamentary Assembly, – the ad hoc Committees Reports are in Docs. 6210, Addendum I and II, 7 May 1990, – 6279, Add. I, II, III, 21 Sept. 1990, – 6406, Add. II, 19 Apr. 1991, – 6543, Add. I and II, 14 Jan. 1992, – 6603, Add. I, 24 Apr. 1992, – 6674, Add. I, 21 Sept. 1992, – 6724, Add. I, 20 Oct. 1992, – Add. II, 20 Jan. 1993, – Add. III, 21 Jan. 1993, – Add. V, 1 Feb. 1993.

The main characteristic of the observation of elections by the Council of Europe is that a government request to the Council for such observation is directly related to a request for special guest membership or membership of the Council: one of the prerequisites for special guest membership or membership is the holding of free, fair, secret elections resulting in a genuine multi-party parliament. Election observation by the Council is therefore not simply an encouragement and a support given to a country in transition to democracy, it is an institutional and statutory requirement leading, or not, to admission to the Council of Europe.

Governments' requests are dealt with by the Bureau of the Parliamentary Assembly, not by the Council's secretariat. The Bureau sets up an ad hoc Committee to follow the elections on the basis of proposals from the Political Groups. Committees generally comprise between six to twelve members, representing the five political groups recognized in the Assembly, i.e. Socialist Group, European People's Party, European Democratic Group, Liberal, Democrat and Reformers' Group, Unified European Left, – and several nationalities. These small Committees of European parliamentarians are assisted by one or two staff members and consultants. Contacts are usually established with other observer groups, such as those missions organized by the CSCE Office for Democratic Institutions and Human Rights, and other governmental and non-governmental groups.

Ad hoc Committees' reports are submitted to the Parliamentary Assembly.

Their reports on the elections listed in Table 8.5 concluded that elections were "secret, free and fair and produced a genuine multi-party parliament" in the following cases:

- the German Democratic Republic elections of March 1990 – the first truly free elections since the elections to the Reichstag of the Weimar Republic held in November 1932;
- the Hungarian elections of March/April 1990: "total credibility" of the electoral process: Hungary is now a member of the Council;
- the Czech and Slovak elections of June 1990: the first free elections held in 44 years took place in a "proper, correct manner, marking a victory for democracy": both Republics are now members of the Council;
- the Bulgarian elections of June 1990: a "completely normal election process": Bulgaria is a Council member;
- the Polish elections of October 1991: unanimously positive conclusion of the Committee: Poland is a member;
- the Croatian elections of August 1992 were free and fair, in spite of some minor irregularities: Croatia has "special guest" status;
- the Estonian elections of September 1992 were carried out freely and fairly and in a democratic spirit, although a large proportion of the population living in Estonia did not participate in the elections at the national level; a far larger participation at the next parliamentary elections would facilitate the entry of Estonia into the Council of Europe – Estonia is a special guest member;
- the Slovenian elections of December 1992 were free and fair, and were held in a calm and politically mature atmosphere: a very high turnout (85.9%) confirmed the interest of voters as well as the democratic nature of the elections: Slovenia is also a special guest member.

Reports on other countries' elections did not always endorse their results wholeheartedly. For instance:

- The Albanian elections of March – April 1991, while not totally fair, particularly during the electoral campaign, could be regarded as free and democratic, especially if compared to the 1987 elections in which, out of 1.8 million voters, the single party obtained 100% of the votes (only one vote against . . .). The next elections, held in Albania in March 1992, "may be judged to have been reasonably free and fair in its overall conduct and outcome, in all the circumstances: it opens the way for closer relations between Albania and the Council of Europe". Albania is a special guest member of the Council and has applied for membership;
- Lithuania's achievement in holding elections (October – November 1992) in very difficult circumstances (continued Russian presence, a combined energy supply and economic crisis) was applauded, and the outcome "must be regarded as the will, freely expressed, of the people". Lithuania is also a special guest member of the Council and has applied for membership;
- The Bulgarian elections of October 1991 had been "free if not altogether fair". In spite of this partly negative assessment, the delegation was "satisfied that Bulgaria has a democratically elected and pluralistic parliament";

- The Romanian elections of May 1990 were considered as "generally free, reasonably secret and relatively fair": Romania has made "a step towards democracy" and the elections were only the beginning of the democratisation process. For the ad hoc Committee, it was obvious that the Council of Europe could not endorse the elections of 27 September 1992, in view of accusations concerning a large number of irregularities and even of serious cases of fraud made by some political parties and Romanian NGOs, as well as by various international observers. Romania is a guest member of the Council and has applied for membership.

The Committee recommended that, for future election observation missions, Council of Europe's delegations should pay at least as much attention to vote-counting operations as to the conduct of the election campaign and the actual voting.

In 1992, the Council of Europe published a "Handbook for observers of elections – Observing Local, Regional or National Elections in Emerging Democracies". The handbook is based on the assumption that their role will be strictly one of observation only, and that they will not be in the position of supervisors having the right to intervene and suggest changes. Excerpts from the handbook are reproduced in Annex A.

The European Community

The European Community is currently composed of 12 democratic Western European countries, although its founding Treaty, the Treaty of Rome signed in 1957, did not define any democratic criteria as a condition for admission. The Community's original objective was only economic, i.e. the creation of a common market, and there was no need then to specify any standards of political governance for future applicants, which were in any case all democracies. Admission of new members was based mainly on general political considerations and on the economic capacity of applicants to adapt progressively to the Community's requirements and regulations.

Problems arose with the applications of Greece, Portugal and Spain: Greece, associated with the Community since 1962, formally applied for membership only in 1975 when its democratic regime had been restored. Portugal had a commercial agreement with the Community since 1973: following the overthrow of the dictatorship in 1974, Portugal formally applied for admission in 1977. Franco's Spain applied for an association status in 1962 and only obtained a commercial agreement in 1970. Following Franco's death, the European Parliament adopted a resolution on 12 May 1976 which reiterated its desire to see Spain join the European Community "when it has evolved towards a genuinely democratic regime" and set the following conditions for its admission: individual, political and trade union freedoms should be restored, and the existence of all political parties should be legalized quickly, – a general amnesty should be granted to all political prisoners and those in exile should be permitted to return freely to their native country.

Greece became a member in 1981, Spain and Portugal in 1987.[36]

On 16 December 1991, the Community Foreign Ministers issued a "Declaration on the Guidelines on Recognition of new States in Eastern Europe and the Soviet Union" which required, *inter alia*, that these new states had constituted themselves on a democratic basis and that they respect the commitments subscribed to in the Final Act of Helsinki and in the Charter of Paris, especially with regard to the rule of law, democracy and human rights.

The Maastricht Treaty of 7 February 1992 referred specifically to the "principles of democracy": in its Preamble, the Heads of State of the "Twelve" confirmed their attachment to the principles of liberty, democracy and respect for human rights and fundamental freedoms and of the rule of law. The "European Union" to be created by the Treaty will respect the national identities of its member states, "whose systems of government are founded on the principles of democracy. It will respect fundamental rights, as guaranteed by the European Convention for the Protection of Human Rights and Fundamental Freedoms and by constitutional traditions common to the member states" (Title I, Art. F).

In June 1992, the European Commission proposed to include, among other conditions to be met by states applying for membership of the future European Union, the criteria of democracy and respect of human rights.[37]

In the mid-1980s, the European Community extended its concern for human rights and democracy to its development aid policy.

In a Declaration of Foreign Ministers of the Community on Human Rights, dated 21 July 1986, the European Council reaffirmed that respecting, promoting and safeguarding human rights is an essential part of international relations and one of the cornerstones of European cooperation as well as of relations between the Community and its Member States and other countries.

In a Resolution dated 29 June 1991, the Council and the Community's Member States linked human rights, democracy and good governance to development. The Resolution stated that respect for human rights, the rule of law and the existence of political institutions which are effective, accountable and enjoy democratic legitimacy are the basis for equitable development.

On 28 November 1991, the Council stressed its attachment to the principles of representative democracy, of the rule of law, of social justice and of respect for human rights. It acknowledged that human rights have a universal nature and it is the duty of all States to promote them. The Community and its Member States then decided to give high priority to a positive approach that stimulates respect for human rights and encourages democracy, through an open and constructive dialogue between them and the governments of developing countries. The Council proposed to give active support for:

- countries which are attempting to institute democracy and improve their human rights performance;
- the holding of elections, the setting-up of new democratic institutions and the strengthening of the rule of law;

- the strengthening of the judiciary, the administration of justice, crime prevention and the treatment of offenders;
- promoting the role of NGOs and other institutions which are necessary for a pluralist society;
- the adoption of a decentralized approach to cooperation;
- ensuring equal opportunities for all.

The Council also stressed the importance of good governance, requiring adhesion to the following general principles of government: sensible economic and social policies, democratic decision-making, adequate governmental transparency and financial accountability, creation of a market-friendly environment for development, measures to combat corruption, as well as respect for the rule of law, human rights, and freedom of the press and expression. Limitations to military spending should also be considered.

While recognizing that democratisation is a gradual process which will sometimes take a relatively long period, the Council decided that human rights clauses will be inserted in future cooperation agreements. Increased assistance may be considered for those developing countries in which substantive positive changes in human rights and democracy have taken place.

The new approach to Community aid will be applied in negotiations to extend the Lomé aid agreement with 69 African, Caribbean and Pacific countries, which expires in 1994.

In supporting countries in transition to democracy, the Community will mainly provide assistance in pre-election measures (e.g. the electoral code and register, training for polling station officials and public awareness campaigns), basic items (such as electoral and/or identity cards, election forms, voting slips, envelopes and polling station facilities) and flanking measures (including transport, technical assistance and electoral specialists).

The European Parliament has lent its support by sending observers to some elections. As an example of EC support, a group of 50 international observers has been organized by the International Commission of Jurists in Geneva, at the request of the EC Commission, to observe the constitutional referendum held on 19 August 1992 in Madagascar (see Chapter 9).

The EC has recently given a rare and commendable example of an IGO declining to observe national conditions on the grounds of unsatisfactory political and security conditions in the country.

In May 1993, the EC issued a statement saying that, in the light of the failure of Togo's political forces to reach agreement, it was not in a position to give assistance to the organization of the forthcoming elections, nor to send observers.

The Collective of the Togolese Opposition, currently in exile, said that it would not take part in the presidential and legislative elections scheduled for June and July 1993. The International Confederation of Trade Unions (ICFTU) declared that if held under the present conditions, the presidential elections would be a farce. In a message to President Eyadema, the ICFTU pointed out that many Togolese citizens, including trade union and opposition leaders, had taken refuge in neighbouring countries because of the climate of insecurity and terror in Togo.[38]

The Conference on Security and Cooperation in Europe

The Conference on Security and Cooperation in Europe (CSCE) process included from its beginning in 1973 a strong concern, demanded by the Western States, for the respect of human rights, besides the security and other cooperation issues. However, democracy was only recognized by participating countries as "the only system of government of our nations" in 1990.

The Helsinki Final Act of 1975 cautiously included among its "Declaration on Principles Guiding Relations between Participating States" the traditional principles of national sovereignty and non-intervention in internal affairs on an equal basis with the desired respect for human rights and fundamental freedoms. While political rights were mentioned, neither democracy nor free elections were included in the text of the Act. No democratic advances were achieved in the Madrid (1980–1983) or the Vienna (1986–1989) sessions, except for the decision, taken in Vienna, to convene a Conference on the Human Dimension of the CSCE in order to achieve "further progress concerning respect for all human rights and fundamental freedoms, human contacts and other issues of a related humanitarian character".[39]

The democratic breakthrough came at the Copenhagen Meeting of the Conference on the Human Dimension of the CSCE, held from 5 to 29 June 1990, when the participating States welcomed "with great satisfaction" the recent fundamental political changes in Europe, and their (very newly) common determination to build democratic societies based on free elections and the rule of law. They defined in detail the main pre-requisites for a democratic governance, as some of the "elements of justice essential to the full expression of the inherent dignity and of the equal and inalienable rights of all human beings":

- free elections that will be held at reasonable intervals by secret ballot or by equivalent free voting procedure, under conditions which ensure in practice the free expression of the opinion of the electors in the choice of their representatives;
- a form of government that is representative in character, in which the executive is accountable to the elected legislature or the electorate;
- the duty of the government and public authorities to comply with the constitution and to act in a manner consistent with law;
- a clear separation between the State and political parties; in particular, political parties will not be merged with the state;

...

To ensure that the will of the people serves as the basis of the authority of government, the participating States will

...

- permit all seats in at least one chamber of the national legislature to be freely contested in a popular vote;
- guarantee universal and equal suffrage to adult citizens;

...

- respect the right of individuals and groups to establish, in full freedom,their own political parties or other political organizations and provide such political parties and organizations with the necessary legal guarantees to enable them to compete with each other on a basis of equal treatment before the law and by the authorities;
- ensure that law and public policy work to permit political campaigning to be conducted in a fair and free atmosphere in which neither administrative action, violence nor intimidation bars the parties and the candidates from freely presenting their views and qualifications, or prevents the voters from learning and discussing them or from casting their vote free of fear of retribution;
- provide that no legal or administrative obstacle stands in the way of unimpeded access to the media on a non-discriminatory basis for all political groupings and individuals wishing to participate in the electoral process;
- ensure that candidates who obtain the necessary number of votes required by law are duly installed in office and are permitted to remain in office until their term expires or is otherwise brought to an end in a manner which is regulated by law in conformity with democratic parliamentary and constitutional procedures.

Other elements refer mainly to human rights and fundamental freedoms.

The participating States also declared that the will of people, freely and fairly expressed through periodic and genuine elections, is the basis of the authority and legitimacy of all government.

Not content with these belated, but finally unanimous, democratic proclamations, the participating States legitimised the presence of domestic and foreign observers in order to "enhance the electoral process" for States in which elections are taking place. They invited

> observers from any other CSCE participating States and any appropriate private institutions and organizations who may wish to do so to observe the course of their national election proceedings, to the extent permitted by law. They will also endeavour to facilitate similar access for election proceedings held below the national level. Such observers will undertake not to interfere in the electoral proceedings.[40]

The "enhancing" presence of observers at national election proceedings was again recommended.

At the Moscow Meeting of the Conference on the Human Dimension of the CSCE, held from 10 September to 4 October 1991, the national sovereignty barrier, as an obstacle to the promotion of human rights and democratic progress, came under frontal attack:

> The participating States emphasize(d) that issues relating to human rights, fundamental freedoms, democracy and the rule of law are of international concern, as respect for these rights and freedoms constitutes one of the foundations of the international order. They categorically and irrevocably declare that the commitments undertaken in the field of the human dimension of the CSCE are matters of direct and legitimate concern to all participating States and do not belong exclusively to the internal affairs of the State concerned.

Procedures were set up on inviting a mission of experts to provide fact-finding and advisory services to facilitate the resolution of a problem relating to the CSCE human dimension, – and establishing a mission of CSCE rapporteurs when a State fails to invite a mission of experts.

Even more important was the members' pledge, in part II of the Moscow Document that they

> will support vigorously, in accordance with the Charter of the United Nations, in case of overthrow or attempted overthrow of a legitimately elected government of a participating State by undemocratic means, the legitimate organs of that State upholding human rights, democracy and the rule of law, recognizing their common commitment to countering any attempt to curb these basic values.[41]

The ambitious "Charter of Paris for a new Europe", signed on 21 November 1991, praised "the courage of men and women, the strength of the will of the peoples and the power of the ideas of the Helsinki Final Act (which) have opened a new era of democracy, peace and unity in Europe". The CSCE Heads of State or Government undertook "to build, consolidate and strengthen democracy as the only system of government of our nations". The democratic declarations and requirements of the Copenhagen Meeting were re-affirmed in the Charter.

The CSCE Office for Democratic Institutions and Human Rights

The Charter of Paris established, for the first time, pan-European institutions for carrying out the work of the CSCE, instead of relying only on diplomatic exchanges and periodic conferences.

Among these, an "Office for free elections" was set up in Warsaw in July 1991 with the modest mandate of facilitating contacts and the exchange of information on elections within CSCE States. The Office's functions were originally:

- to compile information on the dates, procedures and official results of scheduled national elections, as well as reports of election observations, and provide these on request to governments, parliaments and interested private organizations;

- serve to facilitate contact among governments, parliaments or private organizations wishing to observe elections and competent authorities of the States in which the elections are to take place;
- organize and serve as the venue for seminars or other meetings related to election procedures and democratic institutions at the request of the participating States.

The CSCE Council of Ministers, meeting in Prague on 30–31 January 1992, decided to change the title and expand the mandate of the Office. Re-named "Office for Democratic Institutions and Human Rights" (ODIHR), in addition to its responsibilities regarding elections, the new Office is to serve as the institutional framework for sharing information on available technical assistance, expertise, and national and international programmes aimed at assisting the new democracies in building democratic institutions. The ODIHR's expanded role was mainly the result of two factors: the dramatic increase in the number of CSCE States resulting from the break-up of the former USSR and Yugoslavia, and the recognition among CSCE States that democratic elections alone cannot guarantee democracy. Democracy cannot grow without a broader fabric of democratic institutions and a deeply based respect for human rights.

The ODIHR is a small institution, composed of two seconded diplomats, five professional assistants and five support staff.

The Office has been active in its two domaines, electoral assistance and observation – "human dimension" missions.

Electoral Assistance and Observation. The ODIHR has usually organized election seminars in the new Central and Eastern European democracies prior to the holding of elections, and then coordinated the activities of international observers before and at election time, serving as a channel for invitations to these groups . All these activities are initiated at the invitation of the host government.

For instance:

- An election seminar was organized by the Office in Sofia, Bulgaria, 10–11 September 1991, bringing together Bulgarian national and regional electoral commissioners with experts from Canada, Denmark, and the U.S. The Deputy Director returned to Sofia before the 13 October national elections in order to help coordinate the activities of nearly 200 international observers, providing advice, information and logistical support to national and intergovernmental delegations.
- Before Poland's first democratic Parliamentary elections, the Office organized an election seminar, 24–27 September 1991, which concentrated on the media's role in a democratic electoral campaign. As the 27 October general elections approached, the Office served as a clearing house for information and offered its facilities and staff to a dozen observer teams, including a large team of observers from the Council of Europe.
- Albania chose a new Parliament on 22 March 1991. In the months preceding the election, the Office facilitated the delivery to Albania of electoral materials and

other election-related equipment. On request, the Office also analyzed Albania's draft election law, comparing it to CSCE and other international standards and offering practical suggestions to the law's drafters. Two weeks before the election, the Office organized a two-day election seminar. The Deputy Director assisted in the coordination of more than one hundred international election observers from the U.N., the Council of Europe and other organizations.

CSCE observers have monitored the electoral process in a number of countries, and then declared whether the contest met, or not, international standards for free, fair and democratic elections: if it did, the Office concluded, in some cases, that its assistance was no longer necessary for the next elections. In some cases, improvements were recommended for the future.

For example:

- In Estonia, a number of international observers from governmental and non-governmental institutions observed the parliamentary and the first round of the presidential elections on 20 September 1992. Although a significant segment of the population residing in Estonia – essentially Russian-speaking – could not take part in these crucial elections, no significant breaches of international standards on electoral procedures were reported by CSCE observers. A few procedural improvements were recommended.
- In Romania, the Office, which had previously co-sponsored a seminar on electoral systems (4–7 September 1992), opened a support office in Bucharest for the CSCE observers who monitored the parliamentary elections, and the first round of the presidential elections, on 27 September 1992. Most observers with previous experience in monitoring elections in Romania noted with satisfaction a considerable improvement in the way the Central Electoral Bureau ran the poll and facilitated the work of international observers. Although the elections, as a whole, were considered generally fair, the lack of an extensive explanation of the complicated voting procedures accounted for an unusually high number of invalid ballots. Also noted by most observers was the need of a legal guarantee for domestic and international monitors to get access to the results of the voting as they were collected in the Central Electoral Bureau computer system.
- in Georgia, elections to the Parliament and to the Chairmanship of the Parliament took place on 11 October 1992. Although the majority of observers considered the election technically correct and in accord with international standards, areas of concern were noted. The Office strongly recommended that participating States support civic and voter education programmes as well as promote contacts among political parties to ensure a genuine and meaningful opposition. Furthermore, the Office encouraged CSCE States to remain actively involved in the Republic of Georgia's democratic process.
- In Lithuania, at the invitation of the Government, more than 40 international observers visited the Republic to witness the first national parliamentary elections since the restoration of its independence. Observers noted only minor problems and expressed satisfaction that, in general, the 25 October 1992 elections

appeared to meet international standards for free and democratic elections. The Office then concluded that its assistance was not necessary at the February 1993 elections.

- In Slovenia, more than 30 observers from CSCE States monitored the 6 December 1992 elections. The observers unanimously declared the contest to have been consistent with international standards for free, fair and democratic elections. Present were national delegations from Poland, Turkey, Croatia, Italy and Sweden as well as from the Parliamentary Assembly of the Council of Europe. The Office's report on these elections contained a few practical suggestions for "further improving the already high standards achieved". The Office did not foresee the need to monitor future elections in the Republic of Slovenia.

These assessments were either fully supportive of the electoral performance of a particular State, or supportive of its efforts to improve its performance.

In the case of Yugoslavia, the reports of the CSCE missions sent in 1992 were very negative.

In an effort to establish the legitimacy of the newly proclaimed Federal Republic of Yugoslavia (FRY), its Government called on 27 April 1992 for elections to take place in Serbia and Montenegro on 31 May. At the direction of the Chairman of the CSCE Council of Ministers and with the agreement of the federal Foreign Ministry in Belgrade, the ODIHR sent a fact-finding mission to report on the situation prior to these elections.

The CSCE mission concluded that the preconditions for free and fair elections, as defined by CSCE provisions, did not yet exist in this new federation. The FRY was a multi-party system in form, but not in function.

All opposition parties had decided to boycott these elections. Several opposition party leaders questioned the presence of international election observers under the present circumstances because, in their view, they would only serve to validate a fundamentally undemocratic process.

The mission recommended the postponement of the elections for at least two months beyond 31 May and the immediate restructuring of media access for opposition parties. The mission also recommended that CSCE participating States not send experts to observe the 31 May elections if they took place under current conditions.

The elections took place on 31 May, without the participation of the opposition.

The next elections, held on on 20 December 1992, were appraised as neither free nor fair. All international experts who observed the election campaign came to the conclusion that the governing party's complete control of nationwide electronic media – and its abuse of this power – made a fair campaign impossible. On election day, virtually every delegation that visited polling sites in Serbia witnessed irregularities in electoral administration, especially in voter registration: these irregularities disproportionately favoured the governing party. This party successfully exploited its control of the parliament, judiciary, and electoral administration to place bureaucratic hurdles on the path of opposition candidates' registration.

Observers estimated that 5% or more of prospective voters were not allowed to participate because their names were not placed on the voter lists. Election-day problems included multiple registration and voting (including deceased citizens' names), intimidation of voters, low standards for secrecy at polling places, group voting and voting in military units organized a day prior to election-day.

The CSCE Office sent two representatives to Serbia and Montenegro to assist international observers of the federal, republican, regional, local and Serbian presidential elections. Nearly 100 observers from 20 countries travelled throughout Serbia and Montenegro on election day. Those taking part included parliamentarians, diplomats, academic experts, NGO representatives and members of the CSCE missions of long duration in Kosovo, Sandjak, and Vojvodina. The Office held several coordinating and informational meetings with the observers. It coordinated its activities with the Embassies of Sweden and the Czech and Slovak Federal Republic (the incoming and outgoing CSCE chairs), as well as with the Embassy of the United Kingdom, which represented the European Community.

On 20 December, Slobodan Milosevic, Serbia's President since 1987, was re-elected with 56.32% of votes against Milan Panic, the Prime Minister.[42]

Invited at short notice, 60 international observers drawn from CSCE participating States monitored the referendum held in the Russian Federation on 25 April 1993.

A representative from the ODIHR was present in Moscow from 23 to 27 April and established a support office to assist observers and coordinate their deployment plan. The CSCE was the only multilateral organization to be involved *in loco* in the monitoring process. The representative of the ODIHR remained in close contact with embassies of CSCE countries in Moscow and organized, with the help of the Swedish Embassy, a briefing and de-briefing for international observers and diplomatic officers of some CSCE embassies. The representative was also in touch with foreign-based NGOs taking part in the observation, as well as with Russian media.

The CSCE observers were fully aware of the limitations of their work as highlighted by their small number in comparison with the size of the territory to be covered and by the lack of transparency in the regulations supposedly applied.

In conclusion, the observers' impression was that the referendum was conducted in accordance with generally accepted standards regarding electoral procedure, free access to the media (except that television was mainly in the hands of pro-Yeltsin forces), and fair campaigning. The observers wished to emphasize their willingness not to lecture but to help and assist in strengthening the democratic process taking place in Russia. They offered some suggestions for improving the overall process:

- the need for an electoral law applying to all voting processes;
- the need for a law on access by political parties to State-run televisions during the campaign;
- greater voters' education should be instituted;
- strict secrecy of the vote should be made compulsory.[43]

"Human Dimension" Missions. CSCE commitments on the Human Dimension include provisions for human rights and fundamental freedoms, human contacts and other related issues of a humanitarian character.

In this general field, the Office has sent a few missions and organized seminars.

Its first seminar, focusing on "Tolerance" took place in Warsaw, 16–20 November 1992. It was followed by a seminar on "Migration, including refugees and displaced persons", 20–23 April 1993, and another one has discussed "Case studies on national minorities issues: positive results", also held in Warsaw.

The Office organized a seminar on "Constitutional law" for the Islamic republics of the former Soviet Union, at their request. The seminar took place in Perugia, 27–29 November 1992.

The Office co-sponsored a seminar on "Citizenship and language laws in the newly independent States of Europe" in Copenhagen, 9–10 January 1993.

Expert missions have been sent to Estonia and Moldova.

On 28 September 1992, the Republic of Estonia invited a CSCE Mission of experts to study Estonian legislation in the areas of citizenship and language, especially regarding minority rights, in relation with CSCE and universal standards. The Mission, composed of a German and a Finnish expert, together with the Office's Deputy Director, visited Estonia on 2–5 December and included nine recommendations in its report, with a view to filling gaps in the legislation and strengthening the judiciary and the administration.

On 6 January 1993, the Republic of Moldova invited a CSCE Mission of experts to investigate current legislation and implementation of minority rights and interethnic relations. Two experts, from Denmark and Italy, two assistants, from the U.K. and Denmark participated in the Mission, together with a representative from the Office. The Mission's final report includes comments and recommendations on constitutional and legal questions, the language law, citizenship law, and the law on religious freedom.[44]

Comments

Like the U.N., the regional or transregional intergovernmental organizations reviewed in this Chapter have recently assumed an important and explicit role in promoting democratic values and practices in their member States, and in particular in sending observer missions to national elections. In the latter respect, the pioneering role of the OAS is noteworthy.

Like the U.N., these "other" IGOs recognize that elections do not create a democratic state although elections constitute one of the necessary democratic processes. IGOs have therefore also provided to their member States, on request, technical assistance and training through expert advice and seminars in such fields as: constitutional and legislative reform, institution-building, independence of the judiciary, multi-partyism, support to NGOs etc.

In the specific field of the electoral process, most IGOs also realize that their observation should not be limited to sending a small team of "personalities" for a few days to the requesting country, including election day, and publishing a generally supportive report. Advanced teams should be sent, if possible, months in advance of election day in order to review the electoral legislation and regulations, the adequacy of logistics and equipment, to assess the independence of the electoral commission (if any), the qualifications and needs for training of electoral officers, preparations for the information of voters, the registration of voters and candidates, an electoral code of conduct for political parties, fair access to the media, – and negotiate changes and improvements with the authorities. Both the U.N. and the OAS agree that international observation should apply to the whole electoral process.

It is also well established that an IGO cannot, and should not, send an observer group to monitor an electoral process in a sovereign State without an invitation or explicit consent of its legitimate authorities. Following the OAS practice, legal and administrative agreements should be discussed and approved by the Government and the IGO to determine clearly:

- the mandate of the observers' group,
- the status, rights, privileges, immunities and obligations of the observers,
- the facilities provided to the observers by the State's authorities,
- the recognition by the State of the independent status of the observers.

The IGO should also ascertain that other national authorities, including the military and the police, will generally and neutrally support the electoral process, and will respect their presence and their role.

Additionally, as established by the Commonwealth, the IGO should ensure that its presence will be welcome and supported, not only by the various State authorities, but also by the main political parties contesting the election.

Contrary to the U.N., regional or transregional IGOs have generally limited their electoral involvement to "observation and advice". They have not been mandated to organize and conduct elections, like the U.N. in Cambodia.

As for Commonwealth observers, IGO observers should not interfere with national authorities' responsibilities and activities: they have no executive functions.

On the other hand, their functions are to assess and report publicly and impartially on the preparation and conduct of the electoral process, to identify strengths and weaknesses, to express satisfaction, and/or concern, or "serious concern", over electoral irregularities, to make proposals for immediate or future improvements, and finally to conclude that the observed elections have (or not) been "free and fair", and, in a more benign and tolerant formulation, that their results generally represent "the will of the people".

Like the U.N., other IGOs have difficult decisions to take: should an IGO automatically accept a government's invitation to observe its national elections, even if minimum conditions for free and fair elections are not present?

Should an IGO refuse the invitation of a country where the government and the ruling party fully control all political power and the media, where the military or militias prevent any free expression of opposition parties or personalities? Should elections be monitored by international observers in a country still in the throes of civil war or under foreign occupation, or where competing parties, with their weapons, have no intention of accepting an electoral defeat, or where the ruling government and single party, with army support, will not give in to the freely expressed "will of the people"?

Observers, and opposition leaders in some of these countries, have asserted that the presence of international observers, under such conditions, would only legitimize a flawed electoral process and support the illegitimate rulers.

On the other hand, the refusal of IGOs to send observers' missions may leave the country in isolation, and the ruling party, or the military, free to act without witnesses, without the presence of independent and qualified election observers. In the case of the Grenada elections held on 3 December 1984, both the U.N. and the Commonwealth declined the Government's invitation to send election observers, because the election would be held with foreign troops in the country. On the other hand, the OAS and a non-governmental organization, the International Human Rights Law Group, sent observers to Grenada for the election and issued reports.

In practice, it is diplomatically difficult for an IGO to refuse a member State's invitation (or request) to send an observation team: such a refusal may be considered as a public affront and may lead to criticisms of the organization's leadership. On the other hand, as shown in the case of the Togo elections in 1993, the EC was free to decline electoral assistance and observation to a non-member State dependent on EC development aid.

NGOs have generally more freedom of decision in this respect, in view of their independence from governments.

Once an IGO has agreed in principle to observe an electoral process, a number of operational decisions have to be taken on the following points, which may affect the credibility of the mission and the national and international impact of its findings and assessments:

- composition of the team: need for competence, impartiality and international representation;
- number of observers and support personnel during the various phases of the mission, in relation to the size of the country, the size of the population;
- timing of the mission;
- geographical scope of the observation;
- logistics, national and international communications
- financing
- cooperation and coordination with other observers' groups.

But the more crucial and politically sensitive decision will have to be taken by the observers' group, in principle independently, towards the end of its mission.

If an international observer group observes elections which are clearly neither free nor fair, should it publicly condemn the process and reject its results at the risk of arousing the hostility of the authorities and possibly triggering a popular rebellion by dissatisfied voters and citizens? If they support the process and accept its results, they may seem to support an undemocratic regime and undemocratic practices. If they identify the weaknesses or irregularities in the electoral process, and then conclude that the results still represent, albeit imperfectly, the will of the people, they may be accused of applying double or, at least, flexible standards: they may appear to abandon the very principles and criteria which they were supposed to use as yardsticks for determining that elections were free and fair. Should these yardsticks be applied strictly, or should they be related to the degree of political and democratic development of a particular country?

The delicate balance found in some of the Commonwealth reports between real criticisms, a "passing" grade and constructive suggestions for improvements may be justified by the need to support the difficult introduction of a dose of democracy (several political parties, instead of only one, contested the Seychelles and Kenya elections) into a country ruled by a one-man, one-party dictatorship for an extended period of time. It may be justified by the need for time in initiating and sustaining such a considerable political and social change. Another consideration is that the country may benefit from the renewed Commonwealth presence during electoral processes (observers) and its continued assistance in the transition process (technical assistance), while a public condemnation or rejection might slow down or even stall the country's democratic transition and reinforce the rulers' authoritarian trends. Generally speaking, the tone of the reports may reflect the Commonwealth culture of an essentially "consensual" approach, far from any policy of open confrontation.

On the negative side, the concern is that a Commonwealth team will hesitate to criticise publicly a member government, even in the face of blatant fraud, intimidation or other electoral irregularities. If this type of attitude is repeatedly confirmed, the professionalism, impartiality and credibility of these teams may be in question.

To these concerns and accusations, the Secretary-General of the Commonwealth has recently replied[45] that the task of international observers must be to assess not just that an election has been free from fear but also whether its outcome broadly reflects the will of the electorate, and whether any deficiencies are "subversive enough" to vitiate the electoral process, or whether their impact is only marginal. To show that democracy was progressing within the Commonwealth, he recalled that out of the eight elections which Commonwealth groups have observed in the last two-and-a-half years, incumbents have registered victories in four and oppositions have won in three. In the eighth case, a caretaker administration handed over the reins of responsibility to a popularly elected government.

This dilemma is not faced only by Commonwealth Observers' Groups: other IGOs and IGO observers have had to make similar difficult decisions in elections held in democratically immature countries.

In this regard, the conclusions of the CSCE mission to the Federal Republic of Yugoslavia, to the effect that the preconditions for free and fair elections did not yet exist in the new federation, were appropriately frank.

In view of the Council of Europe's insistence on the holding of "free, fair, secret elections resulting in a genuine multi-party parliament" as one of the prerequisites for membership, it is also appropriate that its ad hoc Election Observation Committees generally apply stricter criteria than some other IGOs. However, criticisms have been voiced recently about the Council's tolerance of the disfranchisement of large proportions of Russian-speaking population in Estonia and Latvia.[46]

All IGOs should now become more outspoken and assertive in their democratic convictions and assessments, at the small cost of losing, temporarily, the cooperation of autocratic leaders and military regimes, against the benefit of standing firmly and publicly for democratic values and practices.

Notes

1. The OAS Charter was signed in Bogota in 1948 and amended by the Protocol of Buenos Aires in 1967, and by the Protocol of Cartagena de Indias in 1985. Its amended version entered into force on 16 November 1988. The new Art. 2 b) was part of the Protocol of Cartagena, which also embodies respect for the pluralism of political, economic and social systems.
2. The Convention, called "Pact of San Jose, Costa Rica", was signed on 22 November 1969 and entered into force in 1978. See "OAS Handbook of existing rules pertaining to human rights", 1978.
3. The Secretary General's right of initiative is defined in Art. 115 of the Charter: "The Secretary General may bring to the attention of the General Assembly or the Permanent Council any matter which in his opinion might threaten the peace and security of the Hemisphere or the development of the Member States". The Permanent Council "... shall effectively assist them (Member States) in the peaceful settlement of their disputes ..." – Art. 83. See also Art. 29, 38.
4. At its Twentieth Regular Session, held in Asuncion, Paraguay, 4–9 June 1990, the General Assembly requested the Secretary General to establish within the General Secretariat a Unit for Democratic Development and to develop a program proposal (AG/RES.1063).
5. Quoted by Evan Luard in *A History of the United Nations*, Vol. 1, Macmillan, 1984, p. 295. On Guatemala, see Thomas M. Franck, *Nation against Nation*, Oxford University Press, 1985, pp. 60–62.
6. "Final Act of the Eighth Meeting of Consultation of Ministers of Foreign Affairs", Punta del Este, Uruguay, 22–31 January 1962, U.N. Doc. S/5075, 3 Feb. 1962.
7. Franck, op.cit., pp. 70–71.
8. OAS Doc. OEA/Ser.F/II.17, Doc. 40/79 rev. 2, 23 June 1979, Resolution II.
9. OAS Doc. OEA/Ser. G, CP/RES.489 (720/87), 7 Dec. 1987.
10. OAS Doc. OEA/Ser. F/II.21, Doc. 8/89 rev. 2, 17 May 1989.
11. OAS Doc. OEA/Ser. G, CP. RES.554 (841/90), 28 Dec. 1990.
12. "Peru's Presidential Coup", Eduardo Ferrero Costa, in *Journal of Democracy*, Jan. 1993, pp. 36–37. *International Herald Tribune*, 24 Nov. 1992.
13. The summary of OAS missions to the Dominican Republic in 1961, 1962, 1966 and 1970 is based on Dennis J. Amato's "Elections under International Auspices – 1948–1970", Part II, pp. 515–522 – Dissertation published by UMI.
14. See also *The Blue Helmets*, 2nd Ed., U.N., 1990, Chapter X.
15. OAS Doc. "Annual Report of the Secretary General, 1989–1990", pp. x and 4.

16. See OAS Doc. OEA/Ser. P, AG/doc. 2672/91 of 1 May 1991, "La OEA en el proceso de observacion electoral", and "Annual Report of the Secretary General, 1990–1991", p. 9.
17. See OAS Docs. OEA/Ser. G, CP/INF. 3194/91, 13 Nov. 1991, "Report of the Secretary General on the observation of the municipal elections in Paraguay" – OEA/Ser. G, CP/INF. 3256/92, 10 March 1992, "Report of the Observation Mission on the Elections to the Constitutional Convention held in the Republic of Paraguay on December 1, 1991".
18. See OAS Doc. OEA/Ser. G, CP/INF. 3192/91, 13 Nov. 1991, "Report of the Secretary General on the observation of the electoral process in Suriname".
19. "The Evolution of the Modern Commonwealth", *Commonwealth Yearbook 1991*, pp. 5–8, – "Commonwealth Notes", June 1992, – "The Commonwealth Secretariat and the Promotion of Human Rights: Present Activities and Scope for Future Action", April 1993.
20. Reference to the Communiqué of the 1989 Meeting in Kuala Lumpur is found in the "Report of the Commonwealth Observer Group on General Elections in Malaysia – 20–21 October 1990", p. 1. The text of the Declaration of Commonwealth Principles is in "The Commonwealth Secretariat . . . ", op.cit., Annex B.
21. The Harare Commonwealth Declaration is in Annex A of "The Commonwealth Secretariat . . . ", op.cit.
22. Comments on the election observation in British Guiana and in Mauritius are summarized from Amato, op.cit., pp. 554–558.
23. Amato, op.cit., pp. 559–563, and "Gibraltar Referendum, Report of the Commonwealth Team of Observers to the Commonwealth Secretary-General, – September 1967".
24. "Southern Rhodesia Elections, February 1980 – The Report of the Commonwealth Observer Group on Elections leading to Independent Zimbabwe".
25. "Uganda Elections – December 1980, The Report of the Commonwealth Observer Group", – "Election Monitoring in Africa", Larry Garber and Eric Bjornlund, pp. 5–6, in *The Evolving Role of Intergovernmental Organizations in Election Monitoring*, A Training Seminar for the Organization of African Unity, sponsored by the African American Institute and the National Democratic Institute for International Affairs.
26. "Preparing for a Free Namibia: Elections, Transition and Independence – The Report of the Commonwealth Observer Group on Namibia", Windhoek, Namibia, 10 Oct. 1989.
27. "General Elections in Malaysia – 20–21 October 1990 – The Report of the Commonwealth Observer Group".
28. "Parliamentary Elections in Bangladesh, 27 February 1991, The Report of the Commonwealth Observer Group".
29. Presidential and National Assembly Elections in Zambia – 31 October 1991, The Report of the Commonwealth Observer Group".
30. "Elections to the Constitutional Commission in Seychelles, 23–26 July 1992 – The Report of the Commonwealth Observer Group".
31. *West Africa*, 11–17 Jan. and 1–7 Feb. 1993.
32. "Statute of the Council of Europe, London, 5 May 1949", Council of Europe Doc. No. 1 – "Convention for the Protection of Human Rights and Fundamental Freedoms and Protocols to the said Convention", Rome, 4 November 1950, *European Treaty Series* 5 and 9.
33. The effective date of Greece's withdrawal was 31 December 1970. See *Institutions des relations internationales*, Cl.-A. Colliard, Dalloz, 8th Ed., 1985, p. 508.
34. *Keesings Archives*, XXIX (July 1983), p. 32290, and XXX (Aug. 1984), p. 33039.
35. Council of Europe CDL/INF(91)5, "European Commission for Democracy through Law, Annual Report of Activities for 1990" and Appendix I – 8, 9 Feb. 1991. Doc. CDL/INF(92), 1, 14 Feb. 1992, "Annual Report for Activities for 1991".
36. Cl.-A. Colliard, *Institutions des relations internationales*, Dalloz, 9th Ed., 1990, pp. 573–574. The European Parliament "Resolution on the situation in Spain" is in the *Official Journal of the European Communities*, No. C 125/25 and 26, 8 June 1976.

37. *Le Monde*, 21–22 June 1992.
38. See EC Doc. Bulletin EC 11-1991, "Democracy and Development", – Communication from the Commission to the Council and the European Parliament, "Report on the implementation of the Resolution of the Council and of the Member States meeting in the Council on Human Rights, Democracy and Development" adopted on 28 November 1991, EC Commission Doc. SEC (92) 1915 final, 21 Oct. 1992, – "Soutien de la Commission des Communautés Européennes au processus de démocratisation à Madagascar, Rapport de la Mission d'observation du référendum constitutionnel du 19 août 1992", International Commission of Jurists. On Togo, see *West Africa*, 31 May – 6 June 1993.
39. The CSCE "Final Act" was signed on 1 August 1975 in Helsinki by the 35 nations participating in the Conference. The CSCE includes all European countries plus the U.S.A. and Canada: Doc. 14 ILM 1292 (1975). The document on the CSCE Madrid Session (11 Nov. 1980–9 Sept. 1983) is in 22 ILM 1395 (1983). The CSCE "Concluding Document from the Vienna Meeting" (4 Nov. 1986–17 Jan. 1989) is in 28 ILM 527 (1989).
40. The CSCE "Document of the Copenhagen Meeting of the Conference on the Human Dimension", 29 June 1990, is in 29 ILM 1305 (1990).
41. The Moscow Meeting Document is in 30 ILM 1670 (1991). See also Thomas M. Franck, "The Emerging Right to Democratic Governance" in *American Journal of International Law*, Jan. 1992, pp. 66–69.
42. CSCE Office of Democratic Institutions and Human Rights, "1991 Activities Report", Revised 1 May 1992, – "Report on the CSCE Fact-Finding Mission Regarding May 31 (1992) Elections in the Federal Republic of Yugoslavia", 25 May 1992, – *Bulletin*, Winter 1992–1993, Vol. 1.
43. *Bulletin*, Spring 1993, Vol. 1, No. 2, pp. 25–26.
44. *Bulletin*, Winter 1992–1993, pp. 14–19.
45. "Commonwealth Information", Opening Address by the Commonwealth Secretary-General Chief Emeka Anyaoku, at the Seminar on "Buttressing Democracy –How the Commonwealth is Doing It", 17 March 1993.
46. *Le Monde*, 26 June 1993.

CHAPTER 9

ELECTION ASSISTANCE AND MONITORING BY NON-GOVERNMENTAL ORGANIZATIONS

Non-governmental organizations (NGOs) have played, and now play an increasingly important and useful role in assisting countries in their transition to democracy, and in sowing democratic seeds in still communist and other authoritarian countries.

Some small NGOs, mainly through lack of funds and lack of available competent specialists, focus exclusively on observing electoral processes, for a few days, in specific countries where they have contacts, and sometimes historical, cultural and linguistic affinities.

Other NGOs with larger ambitions and finances have engaged in comprehensive democratic development work, of which election observation is only one part.

NGOs of the latter type may send experts in political party-building, run training seminars in political development and the skills of organization, communication and constituent contacts.[1]

NGOs' specialists may be called upon to review electoral systems and monitor elections. They may evaluate electoral codes and recommend changes. They provide technical assistance for political parties and nonpartisan associations to conduct voter and civic education campaigns and to organize election monitoring programmes, such as pollwatching and independent vote counting systems.

For instance, the U.S. "National Democratic Institute for International Affairs" (NDI), since its creation in 1983, has organized more than 35 international observer delegations that have either helped deter electoral misconduct or exposed fraud where it has occurred.

NGOs have conducted workshops at the national level on legislative procedures, electoral staffing needs, constituent services and committee structures, in order to improve the machinery of governmental systems.

At the local level, NGOs have advised national and local authorities on models of city management, citizens' and local associations' participation, relations between local and national authorities, the scope and limits of local government power.

Some NGOs have promoted dialogue and established mechanisms for improving civilian-military relations, in order to facilitate the transition of the role of armed forces from political intervention to a non-political status, to integrate them into civil society, and to develop civilian expertise in military affairs.

Finally, NGOs have initiated civic education campaigns relating to basic democratic principles, ranging from an understanding of the rule of law, an awareness of the fundamental freedoms, political pluralism, majority rule, the protection of minorities, the secrecy of the ballot to the role of citizens in national and local government

Comparative Advantages of NGOs over IGOs

In view of the great demand for democratic development assistance and electoral assistance and observation, and the scarcity of funds, intergovernmental and non-governmental organizations are not in competition for "electoral markets": they often complement each other, preferably with, but more often without, systematic assessment of needs, planning of operations and coordination of activities.

As IGOs, and particularly the U.N., do not always have the operational capacity nor the financial and human resources to respond positively to all the requests, NGOs may decide, more quickly than IGOs, to start a programme or send an observation mission to countries where IGOs are not present.

Like other types of NGOs in other fields (for instance, in the humanitarian or development field), NGOs have certain "built-in" advantages:

- as private voluntary organizations, they are not subject directly to governmental or intergovernmental agencies' policies, rules and regulations; their independence from governments may allow them to respond to requests for assistance from governments or opposition groups where their own government may be unable to do so for political or other reasons; they are not (or should not be) bound by considerations of their country's national ambitions, national political, economic, social or cultural policies, national prestige;
- they should therefore be able to concentrate their activities and efforts strictly on pro-democracy programmes, with the exclusive purpose of "giving a voice to the people"; while such programmes are political by nature, their activities and assessments should not be influenced by their own national origin and culture nor should they show any bias towards particular political views and parties;
- the fact that they are created and managed by private individuals asserts, in principle, their claim to autonomy and independence from government authority, provided that they respect national legislation and regulations in the country of their establishment and in the country where they provide technical assistance and send missions;
- as non-profit organizations, funds are to be used essentially for activities and projects within the mandate and policies of the NGO, limiting administrative and fund-raising expenditures to the minimum; their relatively low-cost management style may be an attractive alternative to IGOs' larger statutory budgets;

- NGOs are usually small organizations, with flexible administrative structures, free and able to adjust more quickly to changing environments and needs than governmental and intergovernmental bureaucracies;
- NGOs are supposed to be peoples' organizations, which promote the people to people approach, support local, grassroot associations, with a more direct and personal influence on the population than governmental or intergovernmental organizations.

While such considerations may be true, to a large extent, for other types of NGOs, they do not apply as readily to NGOs in the field of democratic development and election observation for the obvious reason that such activities are fundamentally and crucially political. Democracy is a political choice, and neither international nor national actors nor observers can be neutral when a country is trying to develop democratic laws and practices against a tradition of absolutism and the resistance of the present rulers and other beneficiaries of the present governance system.

NGOs' action in this field is necessarily political. Ultimate results of their action may benefit the people, but transition to democracy requires first applying pressure and influence on governments and the military, which other governments bilaterally or through IGOs are best placed to apply. African democratization was strongly encouraged by pressures from the U.S., the U.K., France, Belgium and other countries, either bilaterally or through the Financial Institutions and the European Community, which effectively blackmailed reluctant leaders into "going democratic" or losing their subventions.

NGOs can play an open or discreet supportive role with local democratic associations and parties in countries not yet converted to democracy. During a country's transition to democracy, they have an important role to play in education, technical assistance, observation etc.

NGOs are created in one particular country and have a national legal status, even if their activities have an international scope. NGOs such as the National Democratic Institute for International Affairs, the International Foundation for Electoral Systems, the International Human Rights Law Group and others, are American NGOs, mostly funded by public U.S. funds: their programmes reflect the U.S. image and U.S. values, even if these values are now shared by a majority of nations.

The justification for U.S. public funding of most of these institutions is two-fold: one is based on the argument that people benefit from democracy, and the other one emphasizes its benefits for the U.S. national interest. As stated in the Strategy Document of the (U.S.) National Endowment for Democracy adopted in January 1992 by its Board of Directors:

> The victories of these democratic movements, most of which received vital assistance from the National Endowment for Democracy, have brought hundreds of millions of people new hope for a freer and more prosperous future. They

have also achieved extraordinary gains for the United States, not only by advancing the democratic values that Americans hold dear, but also by bringing an enormous increase in American national security.[2]

While the progress of democracy in the world is expected to increase not only American, but also international security, the American "flag" of many of the pro-democracy NGOs may create a suspicion in some countries, among some leaders and parts of the population that the U.S. NGO may not be all that independent from its government, and may in reality represent another more or less open U.S. intervention in a weak and dependent country. Can the remaining world "superpower" appear totally innocent of an unwelcome extension, under democratic pretenses, of its domination?

The remedy to these fears and suspicions is to internationalize NGO intervention in countries requesting assistance, by associating NGOs of different origins and nationalities to pro-democracy programmes, – and to have international teams of experts and observers in missions organized by an NGO. Some U.S. NGOs include non-American members in their election observation teams.

Most of the election observer missions listed by Larry Garber in 1984 in his "Guidelines for International Election Observing"[3] have been organized by U.S. NGOs: among these, AFL/CIO, Center for Strategic and International Studies, Freedom House, Washington Office on Latin America, American Conservative Union, American Security Council, America's Watch and Lawyers Committee for International Human Rights etc.

More recent ones have also been organized by other U.S. NGOs: the International Human Rights Law Group, the National Endowment for Democracy, the National Democratic Institute for International Affairs, the International Republican Institute, the Council of Freely-Elected Heads of Government, the International Foundation for Electoral Systems. The objectives and main activities of these U.S. NGOs in the field of electoral assistance and observation will be reviewed in this Chapter.

We will then review the role of the following non-U.S. NGOs, which have recently initiated more limited programmes in electoral assistance and observation: the Paris-based International Federation of Human Rights, the Geneva-based International Commission of Jurists and the Inter-Parliamentary Union.

U.S. NGOs

International Human Rights Law Group

The Law Group is a nonpartisan, public interest organization founded in 1978, based in Washington, D.C. The Law Group works to promote and protect human rights around the world through the application of international human rights law. The Law Group works principally in countries with a long history of human rights abuse, countries undergoing a transfer of power from military to civilian rule or where a crisis has prompted the government to suspend human rights protections.[4]

The Law Group concentrates on two of the major rights guaranteed in the Universal Declaration of Human Rights: the right to "a fair and public hearing by an independent and impartial tribunal" and the right to take part in government through "periodic and genuine elections".

The Law Group has pioneered responsible election observing and the linkage of human rights concerns to the election process. In 1983, the Law Group initiated its Election Observer Project to monitor the right to political participation. The Law Group believes that a truly free and fair election consists of more than secret ballots, convenient polling places, and the responsible reporting of the results; an election is a process which includes the ability of individuals to register to vote, of candidates to campaign, of newspapers to publish and radio and television stations to broadcast, of people to gather at rallies, and of individuals feeling safe when casting their votes.

Contradictory conclusions reached by observers of elections in Rhodesia (now Zimbabwe) in 1980 and El Salvador in 1984 made it clear that the practice of election monitoring lacked standards and guidelines useful to monitors and governments holding elections.

To address that need, the Law Group published Larry Garber's "Guidelines for International Election Observing" in 1984, a widely used manual, which has been translated into French and Spanish.

Since beginning its Election Observer Project until July 1990, the Law Group has organized 25 election observer missions, mostly in Latin America and the Caribbean, but also in Asia (Philippines, Korea, Mongolia, Myanmar), in the USSR, Poland, Romania and Bulgaria, and in Africa (Zimbabwe).

The Law Group has played an important role in monitoring several key elections:

- it served as a consultant to the international delegation which observed the fraudulent 1986 presidential election in the Philippines;
- it sent six missions to Korea during 1987 to meet with government officials, party leaders, human rights activists and journalists and to assess conditions related to the conduct of a free and fair election. The Law Group then led an international delegation that observed the presidential election and sponsored a six-month stay in Korea by two attorneys who reported to the Law Group on developments following the election, observed the April 1988 National Assembly elections and conducted a study of South Korea's judicial system;
- it sent an international delegation to Chile to observe the October 1988 plebiscite;
- it exposed fraud in the 1989 elections in Panama;
- it is the only human rights organization to have observed the first multi-candidate elections in more than 60 years in the Soviet Union in March 1989;

– it witnessed the historic Polish elections on June 4, 1989.

The Law Group is an NGO in consultative status (Category II) with the U.N. Economic and Social Council. Its Board of Directors includes international law experts, practitioners, journalists and others committed to the principles of international human rights law.

National Endowment for Democracy

The National Endowment for Democracy (NED) is a U.S. private nonprofit, bipartisan, organization created in 1983 to strengthen democratic institutions around the world through nongovernmental, private sector efforts. Its Board of Directors comprises leading citizens from the mainstream of American political and civic life – liberals and conservatives, Democrats and Republicans, representatives of business and labour, and others with a long international experience.[5]

The activities supported by the Endowment are guided by the six purposes set forth in the Endowment's Articles of Incorporation and the National Endowment for Democracy Act passed by the U.S. Congress P.L. 98-164). One of these purposes is "to strengthen democratic electoral processes abroad through timely measures in cooperation with indigenous democratic forces". One of the Endowment's principles is that a democratic system may take a variety of forms suited to local needs and traditions, and therefore need not follow the U.S. or any other particular model.

The Endowment is currently funding programmes in five substantive areas, one of which concerns "Democratic Governance and Political Processes". In this area, programmes are carried out through the National Democratic Institute for International Affairs (NDI) and the International Republican Institute (IRI). Both Institutes provide infrastructure support and training in areas such as party organization, grassroots membership recruitment and message development. No Endowment funds may, however, be used to finance the campaigns of candidates for public office.

The Endowment supports programmes that provide sound technical assistance in the design and administration of election systems, as well as efforts to increase voter registration and education, training poll watchers, and other programmes that stimulate participation and enhance the legitimacy of the electoral process. Technical assistance is also provided in drafting electoral law and informing the electorate about its rights and obligations. Support is given for the organization of international election observer missions.

During the early years of the Endowment's existence, the principal focus of its activities was in Latin America, where approximately 50% of its funds were spent. By the end of the 1980s, the focus began to shift to Eastern Europe and then to the Soviet Union. Now China and Africa are attracting increased funding, and the Middle East (along with the Islamic world generally) is the next challenge.

The Endowment considers that its nature, its structure and its mission give it a distinct comparative advantage[6]:

1. As an *non-governmental organization*, the Endowment can provide political assistance to democratic forces in repressive or other sensitive situations where U.S. government support, even if channelled through intermediary non-governmental organizations, would risk serious diplomatic complications. In addition, democratic groups abroad often have a strong preference for receiving assistance from a non-governmental source, believing that their credibility or even their independence would be compromised by accepting funds from a U.S. government agency. Assistance through non-governmental channels is also more cost-effective than government-to-government aid. Finally, the Endowment's autonomy gives it the flexibility to respond quickly to changes taking place in countries around the world.
2. The Endowment's *unique structure*, which includes its four constituent institutes in the fields of labor, business and party development as well as discretionary grantees active in other sectors, enables it to respond comprehensively to democratic needs. The Endowment's structure reflects an understanding that the establishment of democracy is not limited to the successful conduct of elections but involves, as already noted, the strengthening of civil society, democratic political institutions and democratic culture. Moreover, the Endowment's multi-sectoral structure enables it to provide a "full package" response to the complex needs of emerging democracies – especially important in light of the close relationship between political and economic reform – as well as targeted assistance to movements struggling to defend democratic values in closed societies.
3. The fact that the Endowment's *sole mission is the promotion of democracy* accounts for its ability over the past eight years to reach out to and work with democratic activists around the world in an authentic and unambiguous manner and on the basis of common values and a shared vision.

While in principle an independent organization, the Endowment is closely linked with the U.S. Government and Congress. Under the National Endowment for Democracy Act, the Endowment is subject to appropriate Congressional oversight and review. The Endowment keeps the U.S. Executive branch fully informed of its programmes and solicits the views of relevant U.S. officials in Washington and in U.S. embassies abroad.

The Endowment enjoys firm bipartisan support in the Congress, and receives strong support from the White House, the Department of State, the U.S. Advisory Commission on Public Diplomacy, the U.S. Information Agency (USIA), and U.S. the Agency for International Development (USAID).

One of the Endowment's six purposes is to encourage the establishment and growth of democratic development in a manner consistent both "with the broad concerns of United States national interests" and with the specific requirements of the democratic groups in other countries aided by programmes funded by the Endowment.

The quasi-totality of its resources is provided by such U.S. agencies as the USIA and USAID.[7]

Diamond[8] agrees that one reason for the Endowment's success is its operational autonomy. Although the Endowment is funded mainly from an annual congressional appropriation, its priorities and grants are decided by an independent, bipartisan board of distinguished citizens, not by the State Department or U.S. embassies abroad. The Endowment is thus allowed a greater pluralism of approaches and strategies. However, its independence is likely to be compromised and its autonomy limited with country grants from AID, as opposed to annual appropriations from Congress.

Since a March 1991 U.S. General Accounting Office report found some misuse of grant funds, improper documentation, and inadequate monitoring of the Endowment's grant recipients, NED has constructed a more comprehensive evaluation programme while strengthening auditing and instituting independent reviews of its programmes.[9]

Most of the programmes of promotion of democratic governance and political processes funded by the Endowment are implemented by the National Democratic Institute for International Affairs and the International Republican Institute.

National Democratic Institute for International Affairs

The National Democratic Institute for International Affairs (NDI) was established in 1983. By working with political parties and other institutions, NDI seeks to promote, maintain and strengthen democratic institutions in new and emerging democracies. The Institute is currently chaired by former U.S. Vice President Walter F. Mondale and is headquartered in Washington, D.C.

NDI has conducted democratic development programmes in more than 40 countries. Programmes focus on six major areas:

- Election processes: NDI provides technical assistance for political parties and nonpartisan associations to conduct voter and civic education campaigns and to organize election monitoring programmes. The Institute has organized more than 35 international observer programmes;
- The other areas include legislative training through seminars, local government models, the improvement of civil-military relations, civic and voter education programmes, and political party training.

NDI does not presume to impose solutions nor does it believe that one democratic system can be replicated elsewhere. Rather, NDI shares experiences and offers a range of options, so that leaders of new democracies can select those practices and institutions that may work best in their own political environment.[10]

NDI's Approach To International Election Assistance

NDI has recently formulated its approach to international election assistance and developed a comprehensive methodology for this assistance.[11]

NDI's approach incorporates advice on voter education programmes conducted by election officials and civic organizations, – training programmes for election officials, political parties and civic organizations, – and a field-tested methodology for monitoring such issues as media fairness, the accuracy of registration rolls and the integrity of the vote count.

NDI emphasizes the entire electoral process, before, during and after election day.

A typical international monitoring effort conducted by NDI includes:

- one or more multinational pre-election missions to assess the campaign and the election system, including an analysis of electoral laws – NDI believes that pre-election missions are as pertinent, if not more so, than the observation of the electoral process on election day itself;
- a large scale, high profile international delegation for election week led by one or more prominent international political figures;
- a post-election assessment mission;
- training programmes and the provision of technical assistance to domestic monitoring groups; and
- a staff presence in the country to work with local groups and to coordinate the project.

At the pre-election stage, NDI may send a small international delegation to meet with government and election officials, political party leaders, civic organizers, journalists and others in order to assess the country's political situation and electoral system. The mission examines the major components of the electoral process, including election-related laws, campaign practices, balloting procedures, media access and balance, public information about the mechanics of voting, ballot access, and the system used to guarantee the integrity of the counting, tabulation and announcement of results. An NDI-sponsored team may also address the system of electoral administration and assess administrative and material needs.

NDI may also organize a comprehensive observer effort, which begins with one or more multinational missions to assess the campaign environment and election preparations and to give advice to political actors or electoral authorities.

Based on information collected during the pre-election missions and from the on-site monitoring, NDI often prepares a pre-election report and distributes it to the diplomatic community, members of international observer delegations, journalists and other interested persons, both in the country and elsewhere.

Shortly before its departure from the country, the pre-election monitoring team will typically issue a public statement highlighting areas of concern. Concerning the 31 October 1991 national elections in Zambia, for instance, the joint NDI/Carter Center pre-election teams addressed their concerns about potential impediments to a free and open campaign environment, including questions about media fairness, campaign finances and a continuing state of emergency; they expressed concerns about whether all eligible individuals had received a sufficient opportunity to register to vote; and they called for safeguards in the balloting and counting processes, including protection to ensure ballot box security and to protect the secrecy of the ballot.

If media fairness is at issue, NDI may conduct an independent review of the television and radio news programmes during the weeks leading up to the election. Generally NDI will also systematically monitor election-related coverage in the domestic print media.

NDI can help to organize and train domestic nonpartisan civic organizations and political parties to conduct voter and civic education campaigns and to organize election monitoring programmes, such as pollwatching and independent counting systems. A typical voter education programme may seek to educate the public either about certain principles of democracy or about election procedures.

NDI provides assistance to domestic political parties in establishing national, regional and local party structures, developing party themes, communicating messages, use of public opinion surveys, selection of candidates, monitoring the campaign, the balloting and counting processes, the conduct of parallel vote tabulations, and, where necessary, to file reports or complaints to the authorities.

During election week, NDI will organize large, multinational delegations to observe elections, offering a balance of expertise among government leaders, election technicians, media experts, parliamentarians, political party leaders, civic leaders, democratic activists and academics, as well as drawing delegates from both established and emerging democracies.

The observer delegations will operate according to internationally accepted standards for such missions, including those developed in Garber's *Guidelines for International Election Observing*.

For each observer delegation, NDI prepares terms of reference which, based on the findings of pre-election missions and on-site monitoring, identify specific issues for the observers to address. The delegation is briefed by NDI staff upon arrival in the country. After the staff briefings, a series of meetings are arranged with political party leaders, election officials, representatives of civic organizations and others.

Before the elections, delegates are deployed throughout the country and, on election day, they visit polling sites throughout their assigned region. Using a checklist prepared by NDI staff, the delegates evaluate specific aspects of the balloting and counting procedures. NDI provides a form on which the delegate summarizes his or her election day observations.

On election day, the observer delegation will coordinate its activities with nonpartisan domestic monitoring groups, and where appropriate, implement a parallel vote tabulation.

Following the elections, the delegation reassembles for a debriefing session. Each team reports on their observations and a statement is drafted. Usually a preliminary assessment of the process will be issued within 24 to 48 hours after the polls close.

NDI's post-election monitoring involves review of complaints about specific aspects of the election process filed with the authorities, additional review of the election results, and whether the procedures for forming a new government are being met. This may require placing a staff person on the ground for several weeks after the election, or a post-election visit by a high profile team, or both.

NDI will use the information gathered by the observer delegation and during the post-election period to prepare a comprehensive report on the election process. The Institute will ensure that the report reflects a consensus of the delegation's views and observations.

The reports published by NDI serve several purposes: informing the international community regarding the fairness of the election; providing information to scholars regarding the conduct of the elections; and educating individuals in other countries that are seeking to initiate democratic election processes.

NDI's attitude towards election observation is clearly communicated to International Delegation Members. For instance, members of the International Delegation organized by NDI for the first round of the Senegalese presidential election on 21 February 1993 were advised that in observing this election, the delegation did not presume to supervise the process or otherwise interfere in Senegalese affairs: "It is the Senegalese people who will make the final judgement about the legitimacy of these elections".

The justification for the delegation's presence was:

- to demonstrate the international community's continued interest in and support for democratization in Senegal;
- to provide the international community with an objective assessment of Senegal's electoral process.

In addition, delegation members could reflect on how the development of democracy in Senegal relates to political development in their respective countries.[12]

NDI's Practice. Observation of elections is carried out either by NDI alone, or in association with another NGO: for instance, the international delegation that observed the 7 May 1989 elections in Panama was sponsored by both NDI and the National Republican Institute for International Affairs, now the International Republican Institute (IRI), – the Council of Freely-Elected Heads of Government, based at the Carter Center of Emory University, was associated with NDI in sponsoring the 1990 General Elections in Haiti.[13]

A recent example of a pre-election mission was the NDI five-member international delegation which visited Kenya from 3 to 7 February 1992 to assess the country's changing political environment and to discuss preparations for multiparty elections. Its report contained a number of important recommendations aimed at ensuring a successful, peaceful and credible democratic transition.

NDI-sponsored international delegations are usually large, they represent a broad distribution of countries and regions, albeit with a majority of U.S. nationals, and include personalities with various professional backgrounds and responsibilities.

For instance, the international delegation that observed the 20 May 1990 Romanian national elections, sponsored by both NDI and IRI, had 73 members, 42 of whom were from the U.S. Other members were nationals of countries in Western, Central and Eastern Europe, Latin America, Asia and Africa. Their professions included parliamentarians, academics, administrators, democratic NGO representatives, media specialists, logistics specialists, election specialists, diplomats, jurists, NDI and IRI staff members.

The 31 October 1991 National Elections in Zambia were monitored by both NDI and the Carter Center. The programme included three pre-election missions that assessed the campaign environment and the electoral system, a continuous on-site presence, the training of Zambian election monitors, the organization of an independent vote tabulation, and a 40-member international delegation that observed the voting and counting process. The delegation, which was led by former President Jimmy Carter and NDI President J. Brian Atwood, included political leaders and election experts from 12 countries.

Under the joint programme, the international delegations obtained changes in the election system, reviewed complaints by the political parties, monitored political developments and conducted an in-depth analysis of media coverage during the campaign period.

The NDI/Carter Center programme also focused on strengthening domestic monitoring organizations, particularly the Zambian Independent Monitoring Team and the Zambian Elections Monitoring Coordinating Committee. In organizing a nationwide pollwatching and voter education programme, these nonpartisan civic organizations received technical advice from leaders from similar groups in Bulgaria, Chile, Namibia and the Philippines.

The Zambia programme received support from the governments of Denmark, Finland, Germany, the Netherlands, Norway and Sweden. The U.S. Agency for International Development also provided assistance.[14]

NDI's reports include both a preliminary statement and a comprehensive report. Like those of IGOs and other NGOs, NDI reports usually comment on the positive and negative aspects of a particular election, they may express more or less serious "concern" and they include an overall assessment as to the acceptability of the results of the process.

For example, the 38-member multinational delegation, organized by NDI to observe the 21 February 1993 presidential election in Senegal, issued a preliminary statement on 23 February.

The statement recalled that this election was the first national election in Senegal conducted under an electoral code agreed to by all political parties. For the first time, the electoral system guaranteed the secrecy of the ballot and gave the political parties a direct role in administering the ballot and counting processes.

Except for tragic incidents in the Casamance, the pre-election period and election day were generally peaceful, the secrecy of the ballot had been respected, there had been substantial improvement in the candidates' access to broadcast media during the campaign.

Against these positive findings, the delegation also observed administrative shortcomings, procedural inconsistencies and other irregularities, such as the inability of many registered voters to obtain electoral cards before election day, instances of duplicate electoral cards, confiscated cards, the ineffectiveness of indelible ink.

While these problems were "cause for concern", the delegation received no evidence that they materially affected the election, which represented a positive step in the consolidation of Senegal's multiparty political system. The delegation then made several suggestions for future improvement.

In a similar vein, another NDI delegation had concluded that, despite serious administrative flaws, the municipal elections held on 26 May 1991 in Paraguay represented an important step in efforts to consolidate the country's nascent democracy.[15]

As noted in the previous Chapter, some international observers' reports are so diplomatically formulated, even when "serious concern" is expressed, that they have been accused of whitewashing over failings, and breaching minimum standards. NDI, as an NGO, is more free and assertive in reporting both the positive and negative points in an observed electoral process: it may declare publicly that a particular electoral process was neither free nor fair and that its results are illegitimate.

For instance, according to press reports, an NDI report on the 11 October 1992 presidential elections in Cameroon, which saw the victory of the incumbent President, Paul Biya, cast doubt and suspicion over the election process among the people of the country and in international opinion. Among other evidence of serious flaws, the NDI Interim Report, issued on 28 October contended that:

- the election was scheduled hastily by President Biya, before adoption of an election law;
- the National Commission for the Final Counting of Votes did not represent a geographic, ethnic, regional or political balance: it failed to inspire public confidence in the integrity of the tabulation process;
- voter registration was needlessly restricted;
- the election campaign was marred by the extremely partisan use of the government-controlled television and radio in favor of the incumbent President;
- "ghost" precincts reported overwhelming vote totals in favor of President Biya;
- undue delays in the release of the official results provided the opportunity for wholesale manipulation.

The Report concluded that

> widespread irregularities during the pre-election period, on election day and in the tabulation of results must seriously call into question, by any fair observer, the validity of the outcome.

> ... While several parties were responsible for election irregularities, the overwhelming weight of responsibility for this failed process lies with the government and President Biya.

NDI's Final Report added that "the delegation cannot determine the rightful winner of the election", and urged all sides to join in peaceful dialogue.

The Government replied that the NDI Report was biased and full of inaccuracies, while the local press maintained that the report truly reflected the actual election situation in Cameroon.[16]

Over the few years of its creation, NDI has developed a substantial and impressive expertise and renown in the field of international election assistance, and more generally in its democratic development work.

International Republican Institute

The International Republican Institute (IRI), founded in 1984 as the National Republican Institute for International Affairs, is the "twin" institution of NDI, set up under the auspices of the National Endowment for Democracy (NED): both IRI and NDI are "core" grantees of NED, and both have very similar principles and programmes. IRI and NDI sometimes join their efforts in election observer missions.[17]

IRI, like NDI, is a non-governmental, non-profit political development organization that supports and administers democratic education projects worldwide. Since its creation, IRI has dedicated itself to the principle that strong and independent political organizations are fundamental to pluralistic, democratic systems of government. Its primary mission is to assist political parties and other indigenous organizations in countries attempting to realize representative forms of government.

IRI generally supports democratic development in five areas: 1) Institution Building and Party Training, 2) Civic Education and Voter Awareness, 3) Support for Electoral Processes, 4) Support for Multilateral Political Organizations and 5) International Political Exchange.

IRI assistance includes financial and technical support to a wide variety of international institutions involved in campaign and election administration, constituency relations, civic education, electoral reform, grassroots education, leadership and legislative training, municipal administration, political communication processes, and public opinion research.

Similarly to NDI, IRI promotes free, fair and truly pluralistic election and campaign environments. IRI projects in this area are initiated when municipal, legislative or national elections appear to be threatened by fraud, abuse or intimidation. IRI projects never involve partisan participation in elections.

Representative projects include analyses of electoral laws, election observer missions and training seminars for election commissions and poll watchers. Typical grantees and participants include national electoral commissions and civic organizations. IRI directly administers all election observer missions, often jointly with other organizations.

In 1984, IRI began democratic development programmes in Grenada, Bolivia and Guatemala. In 1992, it remained active in the hemisphere with programmes in 15 Latin American and Caribbean countries.

Since 1986, IRI has administered election observer delegations in Albania, Bulgaria, Cambodia, Chile, Czechoslovakia, East Germany, El Salvador, Haiti, Honduras, Hong Kong, Hungary, Panama, the Philippines, Romania and Yugoslavia.

IRI is funded by grants from NED, the U.S. Agency for International Development, foundations and private contributions.

The Council of Freely-Elected Heads of Government

The Council is an informal group of 18 former and current heads of government from throughout the Western Hemisphere. Established in November 1986 at a meeting chaired by former Presidents Carter and Ford on "Reinforcing Democracy in the Americas" at the Carter Center of Emory University, Atlanta, Georgia, the Council's goal is to reinforce democracy and promote the peaceful resolution of conflict.[18]

The Council's strength is based mainly on the renown of its eminent members, the fact that they were all freely elected, and the association of U.S. and Latin American presidents or former presidents, giving the group a credible multinational and multicultural character. It is also based on the prestige, determination and courage of Jimmy Carter, whose effective dedication to human rights, democracy and peace changed his image from one of a defeated and humiliated President to that of a respected statesman and human rights activist at the international level. It was indeed difficult for heads of government in the Western Hemisphere to ignore or reject the views or demands of a group led by a former U.S. President, who could still rely on an open or discreet support from the U.S. government and embassies. At the same time, the U.S. government was not seen to be formally and directly involved or committed by the Council's initiatives or positions.

The Council's first activities focused on Latin American countries: Haiti and Argentina in 1987, Chile in 1988, Panama in 1989, Nicaragua in 1989–1990, the Dominican Republic in 1990, again in Haiti in 1990, Guyana in 1990–1992, Mexico in 1992. A few comments follow on some of these missions.

In the spring of 1987, when the government of Argentine President Raul Alfonsin faced a challenge from the military, Council Chairman Jimmy Carter and several other members issued strong statements of support for the democratic government. In October 1987, Jimmy Carter and George Price, Prime Minister of Belize and Vice-Chairman of the Council, travelled to Haiti to lend moral support to the democratic forces and to observe the voter registration process during the vital period leading up to elections on 29 November. Mr. Price then returned to Haiti as the head of an international delegation to observe the November elections, tragically cancelled in the wake of violence and bloodshed. In 1988, Jimmy Carter and Gerald Ford co-chaired the U.S. Committee to Support Free Elections in Chile, which was established to encourage the restoration of democracy in Chile and to support the work of the Chilean Movement for Free Elections.

In 1989, the Council undertook an election observation project in Panama. In March, an international delegation consisting of representatives of Council members Carlos Andres Pérez of Venezuela, Daniel Oduber of Costa Rica and Jimmy Carter travelled to Panama to observe and evaluate the laws and procedures for the presidential, legislative and municipal elections scheduled for 7 May. Former Presidents Carter and Ford then co-chaired a U.S. bipartisan and international delegation to observe the Panamanian election. An official U.S. presidential delegation and a European Community delegation were also present, as well as approximately 250 unofficial observers. On 8 May, the government proclaimed the victory of the pro-Noriega coalition, on the basis of preliminary results. In a direct confrontation with the electoral authorities, the Carter group and the U.S. delegation denounced electoral fraud and affirmed that the opposition had in fact won by a margin of three to one. On 10 May, the president of the Electoral Tribunal of Panama announced that the elections were to be annulled due to the "interference of foreign observers". Jimmy Carter denounced Noriega's actions in a press conference. Subsequently, Jimmy Carter led the delegation to Washington to brief President George Bush, and he sent reports to leaders throughout the hemisphere, urging them to convene the OAS to use its moral and diplomatic pressure to facilitate a transition toward democracy in Panama.[19]

In July 1989, the Council was asked by Haitian President Ertha-Pascal Trouillot and the country's major political parties to monitor the 16 December 1990 general elections which saw the fragile victory of Jean-Bertrand Aristide (see Chapter 6). During the elections, President Carter led a bipartisan and international delegation with George Price and former Deputy Secretary of State John Whitehead to observe the voting. The delegation was co-sponsored by the Council and by NDI. Prior to and during the elections, the Council delegation worked with the OAS and the U.N. to coordinate observation activities and to conduct a "quick-count" of the results.[20]

The expertise and influence of the Council were shown when the Guyanese government agreed to postpone presidential elections after a Council delegation concluded that the election process was seriously flawed. In January 1991, the Council accepted an invitation from President Hugh Desmond Hoyte and leaders of the opposition parties to monitor the electoral process in Guyana, leading to the presidential election scheduled for December 1991. Following several visits to registration sites, in October, a Council delegation led by former Costa Rican President Rodrigo Carazo concluded that an accurate voters' registration list could not be completed in time for the election. The delegation recommended that Parliament be recalled and the elections postponed. A Commonwealth delegation, which was also monitoring the process, reached similar conclusions after examining the list. In November, the President recalled Parliament to postpone the elections. President Carter welcomed the decision, describing it as "pragmatic, constitutional and necessary".

On 5 October 1992, the people of Guyana chose a President and a Parliament from 11 political parties. Violence broke out and there was fear that the election would be aborted and that the country would fall into ethnic conflict. This did not occur, and the election proved to be the first in nearly 30 years that was judged by all the parties and the two official groups of international observers, the Council and the Commonwealth, as free and fair. Both groups significantly contributed to public confidence in the electoral process. The Council played an active role as mediator and conciliator in the process. It maintained an office in Georgetown for 16 months. The U.N. Development Programme and the International Foundation for Electoral Systems gave critical assistance to the elections by providing technical personnel, commodities and equipment.

The violence on election day nearly caused the collapse of the election. This was averted, in part, by the presence and action of international observers, by the personal courage of the Elections Commission chairman and by the intervention of President Carter, who joined the chairman at the Commission and secured sufficient police protection of the building. The quick count conducted by the Council provided confidence in the official election results. Finally, support for free elections was given by several friendly governments, especially Canada, Great Britain and the U.S.[21]

In 1991, the Council and NDI organized a 40-member international observer delegation for the first multiparty elections held in Zambia since 1968 (see above). On 31 October, following a four-month, comprehensive observation effort, Zambians elected a new President and 150-member National Assembly.

In 1992, President Carter visited Congo, Togo, Benin, Burkina-Faso, Niger and Mali in order to discuss with government authorities the modalities of arranging for international observers to be present during forthcoming elections in these countries.[22]

International Foundation for Electoral Systems

The Foundation (IFES) was created in 1987 in Washington, D.C. with the support of the U.S. Agency for International Development to "monitor, support, and strengthen the mechanics of the election process in developing countries . . . " and to "undertake any appropriate education activities which contribute toward free, fair, and credible elections".[23]

To these ends, IFES provides technical and material assistance to countries in transition to democracy in the following areas:

- procurement of election equipment and commodities, design of election documentation, logistics planning;
- training of election officials and poll workers, in cooperation with the electoral council of the requesting country;
- citizens' education in democracy;
- election observation.

Since its creation, IFES has developed a database containing electoral information from around the world.

IFES election observer teams, like other NGO teams, engage in technical assessment of the election process in requesting nations and produce a detailed report on the election. These reports provide an in-depth study of each country's electoral process and examine the free and fair nature of the elections.

Election observer teams are generally preceded by pre-election assessment missions, which should visit the host country at least three to six months prior to the election.

IFES has adopted strict criteria for the selection of observers, based on their knowledge and experience of the electoral process, language capability, prior service on other observer missions, and host country background knowledge. IFES chooses observers on a U.S. nonpartisan basis and strives to make its teams international in composition. Individuals who have served on IFES teams include election administrators and technicians, political scientists, campaign finance specialists, regional experts, secretaries of state, former government and foreign service officers, and chairmen of electoral administrator associations in other countries.

Prior to their departures, IFES provides observers with pre-election reports and detailed briefing materials. IFES observers examine the following 10 critical elements:

- electoral commission and electoral law;
- voter registration;
- polling place procedures;
- logistics;
- voting materials;
- ballot security;
- poll worker competence;
- counting, reporting and verification of votes;
- systems management;
- voter education and motivation.

IFES has sent observers to presidential and legislative elections mainly in Latin America and the Caribbean (Argentina, Brazil, Chile, Costa Rica, El Salvador, Haiti, Grenada, Honduras, Panama, Paraguay), but also in Eastern Europe (Bulgaria, Romania), in Asia (Nepal, Taiwan), and in Tunisia.

IFES was founded on the premise that each nation requires an electoral system tailor-made to its unique culture and environment. IFES recognizes that there is no single model of democracy and utilizes international experts who reflect the diversity of electoral systems around the globe in order to assist requesting nations to strengthen their election processes.

For instance, there were three IFES observers to the 24 October 1990 elections in Pakistan, one from the U.S., one from the U.K. and one from Japan. They were part of the International Observer Delegation sponsored by NDI. The 40-member delegation included nationals of 17 countries, and was led by a former Turkish Minister of Foreign Affairs and a Polish Senator.

IFES sent an eight-member U.S. team to observe the 12 May 1991 parliamentary elections in Nepal, as part of a 65-member multinational observer delegation coordinated by the Nepal Election Observation Committee. The U.S. team was organized by IFES in cooperation with NDI and IRI. Observer teams were formed with each U.S. delegate joining two to three other international observers from 17 other countries.

Requests for IFES assistance are either channeled through U.S. embassies, or come directly from requesting countries.

As for other U.S. NGOs engaged in international electoral assistance, IFES is mainly funded by the U.S. Agency for International Development (USAID): the seed money for IFES was a five-year, $1 million grant from USAID's Office of Democratic Initiatives, approved in October 1987. Additional funding came from the National Endowment for Democracy, and a few foundations and companies. In 1991, USAID committed $1 million to IFES to enable the Foundation to provide technical electoral assistance to African countries.

Other Non-Governmental Organizations

Among the many NGOs concerned with the promotion of democracy, and for some, the observation of elections, the more limited role of three non-U.S. international NGOs will be reviewed here, two human rights organizations and the Inter-Parliamentary Union.

La Fédération Internationale des Droits de l'Homme

The Federation (International Federation of Human Rights) was founded in 1922 in Paris, France, with the aims of communicating and promoting the ideal of Human Rights, fighting against their violations and demanding their respect. Since 10 December 1948, the Federation focused its objective on the practical implementation of the Universal Declaration of Human Rights through international monitoring mechanisms.

The Federation is composed of national Leagues, Commissions or Associations of Defence of Human Rights. The Federation claims its absolute independence, at the national and international levels, in relation with political parties and governments. The Federation has consultative status with the Economic and Social Council of the U.N., UNESCO, the Council of Europe and the OAS.

Besides its work in promoting and drafting international human rights instruments, the Federation's main operational activities consist in sending inquiry missions to any country where human rights and fundamental freedoms appear to be threatened, repressed or violated, and judiciary observation missions to trials where the rights of the defendants need to be monitored, particularly when charges are of a political nature. The findings of these missions are reported to governments and international organizations in an attempt to stop repression and obtain the release of unjustly jailed persons.[24]

The Federation has extended its operational role from the monitoring of human rights and the judidiary protection of defendants in political trials to the observation of electoral processes since 1987.

In view of the limited funds of the Federation, electoral observation missions have usually been limited to a few members (one to seven) visiting the host country for a short period. Mission members are usually legally trained persons, or human rights activists, of French nationality.

A pre-election mission of two members (one judge and one agronomist) was sent to Haiti from 7 to 17 November 1987, prior to the presidential, parliamentary and local elections scheduled for 29 November and December 1987. The mission was sponsored by a French/Haitian "Collectif" composed of 13 NGOs, including the Federation and the "Fondation France-Libertés" presided by Danielle Mitterand. The Haitian authorities were informed of the arrival and of the mandate of the mission: their prior approval was not sought. The French Embassy in Haiti was also informed. These elections were cancelled and the Haitian authorities critized foreign observers for "interfering with the electoral process".

The Federation sent one French judge to observe the 5 October 1988 plebiscite in Chile. A few magistrates and lawyers were mandated by the Federation to observe the legislative and provincial elections held in Pakistan on 24 and 27 October 1990: serious irregularities and fraud were reported by the observers. Another Federation mission observed the 10 March 1991 legislative and municipal elections in El Salvador: it reported the high abstention rate (more than 50%) and the numerous irregularities, but also the emergence of a third political force and the loss of monopoly of the ruling extreme right party.

Two French delegates observed the 12 May 1991 legislative elections in Nepal for the Federation: members of the 64-member international observer group, they stayed in the country from 8 to 16 May. They agreed that the results of this fair and equitable consultation allowed the free expression of the choices of the Nepalese people.

The Federation did not observe the 1 March 1992 referendum held in Montenegro, in which a majority of the voters decided that the territory should remain part of Yugoslavia. However, it issued a public statement on 5 March, reflecting the protest of the Civic Forum of Montenegro, the democratic opposition to the government, on the following grounds:

- the date of the referendum had been fixed by the Parliament seven days before the consultation, thus preventing the opposition to campaign against the union proposal;
- the armed forces had deployed 60,000 men in order to impress the population;
- after the vote, the radio and television started collecting the names of those who did not vote, for unknown purposes.

The Federation then considered that the results of the referendum could be challenged and should be annulled.

Seven Federation delegates (four French and three Romanian) observed the presidential and legislative elections held in Romania on 27 September and 11 October 1992. These observers complained that domestic observers with their own computers were denied access to the polling stations and communication of the electoral records for two days, after these data had been recorded in the official computers, contrary to an official instruction.[25]

International Commission of Jurists

The Commission (ICJ) is an international NGO devoted to promoting throughout the world the understanding and observance of the Rule of Law and the legal protection of human rights. Its headquarters is in Geneva, Switzerland. It has national sections and affiliated legal organizations in over 50 countries. It also enjoys consultative status with the U.N. Economic and Social Council, UNESCO and the Council of Europe. Its activities include various publications; organizing congresses and seminars; conducting studies or enquiries into particular situations or subjects concerning the Rule of Law and publishing reports upon them; sending international observers to trials of major significance; intervening with governments or issuing press statements concerning violations of the Rule of Law; sponsoring proposals with the U.N. and other international organizations for improved procedures and conventions for the protection of human rights.

The Commission entered into the electoral observation field for the first time in 1992, at the request of the Commission of the European Community, in support of the democratization process in Madagascar.

Under the auspices of the International Observatory of Democracy in Madagascar, the Commission constituted a group of 50 observers from 14 countries of Europe, Latin America and Africa, to observe the constitutional referendum of 19 August 1992. Observers were mainly legally trained persons (law professors, lawyers, magistrates etc.), and also parliamentarians, journalists and delegates of NGOs specialized in human rights matters. A number of the observers were citizens of countries in transition to democracy. Several members of the group had previously observed elections in Nicaragua, Namibia, Burkina Faso or in Haiti.

The mission had been preceded by a team of experts who had assessed, in March 1992, the political and legal environment of the country as well as the situation of the media. In July, an ICJ expert had organized a seminar on the professional code of ethics of journalists in the democratization process and produced educational material on the principles and mechanisms of democracy, intended for the general population, with the assistance of local NGOs, radio and newspapers.

The Observers' group concluded that the 19 August referendum was carried out in full respect of the legal regulations. Voters' participation was high (65%). The group formulated a number of practical recommendations to improve future electoral processes.

The ICJ then sent a group of 69 observers to monitor the presidential elections held on 25 November 1992 and 10 February 1993. The group reported that, in spite of a limited number of serious irregularities, the citizens of Madagascar were allowed to express their choice freely, loyally, honestly, and therefore democratically.[26]

Inter-Parliamentary Union

The Union (IPU) is the international organization which brings together the representatives of the Parliaments of sovereign States. The IPU was the first worldwide political organization to promote the concept of peace and international arbitration. Its origins date back to 1889 when the first Inter-Parliamentary Conference for international arbitration, attended by delegates from nine countries and three continents met in Paris. As of April 1993, 124 of the 165 Legislative Assemblies established in the world's States were represented in the IPU. Its' secretariat is in Geneva.

As the focal point for worldwide parliamentary dialogue, the IPU works for peace and cooperation among peoples and for the firm establishment of representative institutions. The Union supports the efforts of the U.N., whose objectives it shares: the IPU has been granted consultative status, as a non-governmental organization, with the U.N. Economic and Social Council. Insofar as parliaments are parts of democratic government structures and decision-making processes, the nature of the IPU as an NGO could be challenged: the IPU could be described as an hybrid entity, part NGO and part intergovernmental organization.

The IPU brings together parliamentarians of different countries and ideologies – organized in National Groups established in or by their legislative assemblies – for the objective study of political, economic, social and cultural problems of international significance. While freely elected parliaments are in principle the essential basis for representative democracy, the concept of parliament is not interpreted and applied similarly in all countries. The IPU is not a club of representative democracies: its membership includes "parliaments" of China, Cuba, North Korea, Iran, Libya, Syria, Yugoslavia.

As in the U.N., the concern for universality has so far prevailed over democratic criteria, thus underlining the IPU's implicit intergovernmental nature.

As in the U.N., the democratic wave of the late 1980s has started to "democratize" the IPU.

The VIIth Inter-Parliamentary Conference on European Cooperation and Security (promoted by the IPU), held in Vienna from 1–3 July 1991,

> 31 ... unreservedly approve(d) the provisions of the Copenhagen Document on the Human Dimension (June 1990) and those of the Charter of Paris which proclaim the objective of the rule of law and of representative and pluralist democracy throughout the continent....

> 35 . . . stress(ed) the prime importance of supporting and encouraging the establishment of democratic Governments based on the will of the people and the setting up of institutions constituted through free and fair elections.

In the debate, the Swiss delegate considered that one of the IPU's essential tasks in the future should be to ensure that the notion of democracy is given clear content and contours and that misuses which serve to camouflage undemocratic conditions are exposed.[27]

The 86th Inter-Parliamentary Conference, held in Santiago from 7–12 October 1991, condemned the coup d'état perpetrated on 30 September 1991 in Haiti and re-affirmed the attachment to democracy of the world interparliamentary community, which could not accept such a takeover by force which ran counter to political developments in the world, especially in Latin America. However the conference also recalled that, while democracy is a universal principle, it was up to each country to devise its own structures to implement that principle in conformity with its respective cultural values, traditions and aspirations, thus leaving the door open to wide variations of interpretation of this "universal" democratic principle.

In the debate, a delegate from Pakistan suggested that the IPU should monitor the holding of general elections in various countries.[28]

In September 1989, the Inter-Parliamentary Council had decided to set up a mission to observe the elections scheduled for 7 to 11 November in Namibia, while at the same time the 82nd Inter-Parliamentary Conference adopted a resolution on "Support of Parliaments to the process of independence in Namibia, the holding of free and equitable general elections, and the establishment of a new Government reflecting the popular will" which contained guidelines for the work of the mission (see Chapter 6).

In a meeting with the President of the Inter-Parliamentary Council on 7 May 1992, the U.N. Secretary-General invited the IPU to play a larger role in relation to election observation in support of the U.N. and even envisaged concluding a formal agreement of cooperation to this effect.

The traditional policy of IPU regarding its presence at electoral consultations was reaffirmed by the Inter-Parliamentary Council at its 146th session when it unanimously upheld the view that "care should be taken to ensure that the Union was present in the future at electoral consultations organized by the U.N.". At the same time, the Union

> should refrain from mandating observers for legislative elections organized without special U.N. involvement, it being understood that National Groups and parliamentarians were free – and indeed encouraged – to do so on an individual basis.

A number of parliaments and political parties in a number of countries send observers to national elections. In Canada, for example, members of Parliament representing all major parties are often chosen for official observer teams together with experts from Elections Canada.

IPU's "prudent" policy may be explained mainly by a political problem, and subsidiarily by practical considerations.

The political problem is related to the membership of the IPU: observing elections would lead the IPU to pass value judgements on the nature and representativeness of parliaments, which in turn could have an incidence on their membership in the Union. In other words, it would compel the IPU to adopt an admission criterion based on democratic principles and practices, which would replace its current "open-door" policy.

The practical problems are, first the need to establish clear criteria and norms on the basis of which to evaluate the electoral process, – and secondly the need to provide important human and financial resources as a requirement for any substantive involvement of the IPU in election observation.

In April 1993, the Inter-Parliamentary Council reaffirmed that the Union should always seek to be present at national elections and referenda which are organized, supervised or verified by the U.N. and urged National Groups and Parliaments to extend support to national electoral processes by providing electoral assistance and by participating in election observer missions.

The Council also decided to send observer missions to the elections in Cambodia, El Salvador and Mozambique, elections organized with significant U.N. involvement.

The Union delegation to Cambodia was composed of five members. It visited the country from 19 to 28 May and observed voting in well over 100 polling stations in the capital and in 14 of the country's 21 provinces. The delegation agreed with the U.N. assessment that the voting had been as fair and free as could be reasonably expected and, as such, was a clear expression of the will of the Cambodian people.

The Union and its members are now openly expanding their operational role in support of democratisation by providing electoral assistance and participating in election observer missions, subject to the condition that the Union's participation should be limited to U.N.-monitored elections and closely linked with the U.N.[29]

Comments

This short description of a few NGOs, among many others, calls for a few comments.

First, U.S. NGOs appear to dwarf other NGOs through the extent of their activities in the promotion of democracy and in the electoral observation field, based on a U.S. political will and important financial resources. As stated by Diamond,[30] "democracy promotion is one of the cheapest, most cost-effective ways of advancing the national interest". U.S. Information Agency missions in 85 countries have undertaken 132 major projects for "Building Democratic Institutions". The U.S. spends about $400 million in political assistance to democratic forces and institutions, some of which are funnelled to such NGOs as NED, IFES and others.

In spite of their affirmed independence and autonomy, their links with U.S. authorities and their financial dependence on U.S. funds cannot but influence their programmes, and as stated earlier, give a U.S. label to their interventions. In order to attempt to diversify their identity, they have internationalized most of their observation teams.

Following the example of the National Endowment for Democracy, the United Kingdom has founded the "Westminster Foundation for Democracy" in March 1992. Its aims are to

> promote the development in emerging democracies of pluralist democratic institutions such as political parties, trade unions, the media, and voluntary organizations.

The new foundation is a nonpartisan, non-governmental organization which will receive most of its funding from the British government. Like its American counterpart, it gives all of its grants openly, and the Board of Governors, which includes representatives of all political parties, makes its decisions independently from the government. Its budget for April 1992 – March 1993 is £1 million.[31]

Other democratic countries should emulate the U.S. effort and follow the British example. However, their support for democracy has, so far, mainly been carried out bilaterally, by sending official government observers to host countries, or through intergovernmental organizations, rather than directly to NGOs.

The limited financial resources of such NGOs as the Paris-based International Federation of Human Rights prove its independence from governments, but also put a serious limitation on its pro-democracy programmes.

As for humanitarian assistance, where impartiality and neutrality are two cardinal principles, it would seem that the most acceptable funding for NGOs in the electoral assistance field, in addition to financing by private, non-governmental sources, is that offered by intergovernmental organizations: a recent successful example is the pro-democracy assistance provided to Madagascar by the Commission of the European Community, through the International Commission of Jurists.

The advantage of this formula is that the operational work is carried out by an independent, expert NGO whose impartial credentials are acceptable to the host country, while its financing is offered by a multinational organization, where no one country holds all the powers. For many countries, the intervention of an intergovernmental organization is more acceptable than that of a "super" or middle power, either directly or through national agencies.

This being said, the U.S. NGOs have had a pioneering role in initiating democratic development programmes and particularly in designing a systematic approach to international election assistance and a comprehensive methodology. They have set up standards and guidelines useful to international observers and to governments holding elections. Their experience and their resources have led them to promote a long-term presence of international observers and advisers in the host country, pre-election missions to assess a country's legislative, political, economic, social and cultural environment, large teams during election time, high profile international teams, independent parallel vote tabulation through quick counts, prompt assessment of the electoral process and follow-up international presence. In summary, the U.S. NGOs have introduced and developed a competent professionalism in the field of international electoral observation. Their renown has justified their influence.

In the recent past, some of the humanitarian NGOs have added to their traditional relief and welfare activities development projects, in an attempt to address the roots of poverty, ill health or famine, and not only their symptoms[32]: similarly, the extension of the programmes of a number of human rights NGOs into democratic development and electoral assistance is logical: they realize that human rights are best promoted and protected in a democratic environment.

Some of the strengths of NGOs are, or should be, their expertise, their impartiality, their search for and experiment of innovative, alternative concepts and processes, their independence from governmental authorities and their free expression. Following NDI's lead, they should leave diplomatic, ambiguous, or sometimes contradictory, reports to intergovernmental organizations or governments. They should respect established standards for international election observation, often set by themselves – they should call a fraud a fraud, and, if justified by facts, denounce an electoral process as neither free nor fair, without calling on the moot argument that it reflects the "general will of the people".

Notes

1. This list of functions is mainly summarized from "Functional Areas of Competence" of the (U.S.) National Democratic Institute for International Affairs "A Year in Review – 1990", pp. 4–5.
2. National Endowment for Democracy "Strategy Document", Jan. 1992, p. 1.
3. *Guidelines for International Election Observing*, prepared by Larry Garber, The International Human Rights Law Group, 1984, pp. 94–96.
4. The International Human Rights Law Group Doc., incl. "Fact Sheet, – Activities Report 1978–1989".
5. National Endowment for Democracy Doc.: "Statement of Principles and Objectives, Strategy Document, Annual Report 1990", –see also "Promoting Democracy", Larry Diamond, in *Foreign Policy*, No. 87, Summer 1992, pp. 38–42.
6. National Endowment for Democracy "Strategy Document", pp. 6–7.
7. 1990 revenues of the National Endowment for Democracy were grants from U.S. Government agencies ($39,027,216) out of total revenues of $39,287,170. See NED "Annual Report 1990", p. 52.
8. Diamond, op.cit., p. 38.
9. Ibid., p. 41.
10. NDI Doc., incl. "A Year in Review – 1990", –"NDI Reports".

11. This section reproduces or summarizes an NDI Doc. "NDI's Approach to International Election Assistance", March 1992.
12. Memo. from Ken Wollack, Acting President, to International Delegation Members, 6 February 1993 re: Terms of Reference and Background Information.
13. International Delegation Reports on specific observation missions are published by NDI, and its co-sponsor, if applicable.
14. "The October 31, 1991 National Elections in Zambia", NDI/Carter Center, 1992, –"NDI Reports", Fall-Winter 1991.
15. "NDI Reports", Spring 1991.
16. *West Africa*, 30 Nov–6 Dec. 1992, – *An Assessment of the October 11, 1992 Election in Cameroon*, NDI, 1993, Executive Summary and Appendix VI.
17. For instance, both IRI and NDI sponsored the international delegations which observed "The May 7, 1989 Panamanian Elections" and "The May 1990 Elections in Romania". General information on IRI is based on IRI documentation incl. "IRI News", Spring 1992.
18. See "Background on Council of Freely-Elected Heads of Government" (called "Council" hereunder) in the Carter Center of Emory University, "Special Report No. 1", Appendix 1, p. 42, which also lists the Council's original members.
19. Ibid., – see also "The 1989 Panamanian Elections – Post-Election Report", by Eva Loser, Center for Strategic and International Studies, Washington, D.C.
20. "The 1990 General Elections in Haiti, – International Delegation Report", Council and NDI.
21. "The Carter Center News", Fall 1991, p. 11, – "Observing Guyana's Electoral Process – 1990–1992", Carter Center, "Special Report No. 3".
22. "The October 31, 1991 National Elections in Zambia", NDI/Carter Center, 1992. *Le Monde*, 4 Sept. 1992.
23. IFES documentation, incl. "IFES Programs in Election Assistance", "IFES", Fall 1990, Winter 1990, Spring 1991, Summer 1991, Fall 1991.
24. Documentation of the Fédération Internationale des Droits de l'Homme (FIDH).
25. FIDH "Rapport de Mission – Haiti – Premiàre mission d'observateurs à l'occasion des élections de fin 1987". See also "The 1990 General Elections in Haiti", Council and NDI, p. 33, – "Rapport de Mission – Mission des observateurs du plébiscite du 5 octobre 1988 au Chili", – "La lettre de la FIDH", No. 370, 6 Nov. 1990, – No. 389, 26 March 1991, – No. 404, 16 July 1991, – "Communiqué – Référendum au Montenegro", 5 March 1991, – "Une déclaration de la mission d'observation de la FIDH aux élections en Roumanie", 29 Sept. 1992, – *Le Monde*, 2 Oct. 1992.
26. International Commission of Jurists (ICJ) documentation, incl. "ICJ Report on Activities 1986–1988", – "Soutien de la Commission des Communautés européennes au processus de démocratisation à Madagascar – Observatoire international de la démocratie à Madagascar, Rapport de la mission d'observation du référendum constitutionnel du 19 août 1992", – "Rapport de mission de la CIJ par M. M. Kourouma, décembre 1992 – janvier 1993", – "Second tour des présidentielles, 10 février 1993, par M. M. Kourouma.
27. IPU documentation, incl. "IPU Bulletins" 3/91, pp. 194–195, 221, –3/92, Editorial "The Union is not a Club".
28. "IPU Bulletin", 4/91, pp. 250, 258.
29. IPU Doc. CL/146/10-R.1 of 20 Dec. 1989, "Report of the Mission to observe the elections in Namibia", – and Doc. EX/213/7-R.2 of 24 Aug. 1992, "Policy and Programme of Action of the Union – Consideration of IPU involvement in the international observation of national elections". IPU Doc. CL/152/10-R.1 of 14 April 1993, CL/152/10(a)-P.1, 15 April 1993, and "Report of the Mission to observe the elections in Cambodia".
30. Diamond, op.cit., p. 46.
31. *Journal of Democracy*, July 1992, p. 163.
32. Yves Beigbeder, *The Role and Status of International Humanitarian Volunteers and Organization – The Right and Duty to Humanitarian Assistance*, M. Nijhoff, 1991, pp. 80–94.

CONCLUSION

In a recent message, the U.N. Secretary-General, Boutros Boutros-Ghali said:

> Today we are beginning to see the task of the United Nations as indivisible: the promotion of peace and security in all its aspects. And as a key part of that view of the world, we are understanding that peace, development and democracy are interrelated, indeed mutually reinforcing.[1]

He was thus justifying the pro-democracy programmes, election monitoring and technical assistance, initiated by the U.N. in recent years, in spite of the obstacles met by some of the operations, the uncertain outcomes of some of the elections, and the criticisms addressed to the management of operations, to the expenses incurred or to the concept itself of international monitoring.

Are international observers called to a country only "to sprinkle holy water on a rigged process",[2] or are they effectively helping a country's transition to democracy? Are Western countries forcing ill-prepared countries into a ritual of democracy without substance?

The U.N. and other intergovernmental organizations, as well as non-governmental organizations realize that one-time "free and fair elections" do not transform a country into a stable democracy. However, no democracy can function without periodical elections, and an imperfect process may improve over time, with the patient and tactful support of international advisers.

Democracy has taken centuries to grow in Western countries: countries in transition to democracy must be given time to evolve progressively towards people's participation in political governance, for democratic values to grow roots among the leaders and the people. Regions and countries differ in their history, culture, traditions, internal politics, values and beliefs: these differences necessarily affect their quicker or slower acceptance of democracy, as well as the type of democratic institutions and practices which they will adopt.

There is no perfect democracy, no ideal democratic model which can be immediately transplanted into willing nations. In spite of their striking differences in institutions and practices, the U.S.A., the U.K. and France, for instance, are all representative democracies. New democracies may have to re-invent democracy, starting with self-government at the local level, democratic education, the creation of voluntary associations, multipartyism, the separation between elected rulers and the military, an independent judiciary system, free media, political checks and balances. Whatever their political structure, their common requirement is the holding of genuine and periodical elections as the legitimate source of power.

It has been argued that if elections are held prematurely and fail, the effect is to slow down democratization rather than to accelerate it, and that the presence of international observers can make things worse.[3]

While the refusal of Savimbi to accept the results of the monitored Angolan elections and his recourse to arms to take power has certainly not encouraged the democratization of his country, the success of the Namibia and Nicaragua operations point in the opposite direction. In Haiti, the international pressures on the military have been legitimized by the results of the internationally monitored elections. Without the U.N. organization of elections in Cambodia, the Khmer Rouge would still believe, and make the Cambodians believe, that they represent the "people". In Madagascar, the acceptance by the outgoing President of the victory of the opposition candidate in the February 1993 presidential elections was facilitated by the discreet presence of international observers.

It is difficult to determine in each case when elections should be held, but delaying elections indefinitely until the country is "ready" allows illegitimate leaders to hold on to power and to maintain an autocratic and arbitrary regime.

While international organizations take risks in sending observers to organize, monitor and assess national elections, their absence may allow fraudulent maneuvers by the rulers and their unchallenged continuation in power.

The U.N. Secretary-General, in relation to the establishment of the U.N. Operation in Western Sahara, had laid out four conditions which had to be met for the Operation to carry out its responsibilities effectively and with complete impartiality:

1. Full support and backing of the Security Council;
2. Full cooperation of the two parties, particularly with regard to the comprehensive cessation of all hostile acts;
3. Cooperation and support of the neighboring countries;
4. Availability of the necessary financial resources to be provided by Member States.

To these basic requirements, analysts and practitioners[4] have given more detailed advice as to the conditions which should preferably be fulfilled before elections are held and an observation mission is initiated. Depending on the regional and local circumstances, these may include:

- negotiations with government authorities and armed militias on controlled disarmament and demobilization of all armed forces, possibly re-settling those demobilized or integrating them into a new integrated army and/or police force, after suitable training;
- political parties must be allowed to organize freely, under legal conditions, except for those groups who refuse to disarm;
- if appropriate, the formation of a government of national reconciliation or a power-sharing arrangement, as a transition from authoritarian rule and/or civil war to peaceful elections and a democratic government;

- a realistic timetable for elections should be devised, taking into account the repatriation of exiles and refugees, the organization and adequate functioning of political parties, the drafting or revision of electoral laws, the setting up of electoral institutions and the training of electoral officials and party leaders, democratic and electoral information and guidance intended for the general population and voters, registration of candidates and voters, material organization for the voting etc.;
- organization or, more generally, monitoring of electoral processes by international observers in close cooperation with national and local authorities, ensuring a reasonable degree of coordination and cooperation between the various observers' groups;
- follow-up presence of international observers after the announcement of the results.

It is true that real democratization may take years and that elections should not, in principle, constitute the beginning of the process. However, elections are the building block of all democratization: no elections, no democracy.

Furthermore, decisions by intergovernmental organizations, or more precisely by their member States, to organize or monitor an electoral process are usually determined by political and diplomatic contingencies, and more rarely by systematic and objective assessments and rational considerations.

In principle, non-governmental organizations engaged in such activities have more freedom in deciding whether or not to observe an election and assess its validity.

In practice, the task of most of these NGOs is not limited to a few days' observation at election time: they initiate preliminary feasibility and assessment missions, identify the problems and weaknesses, organize training, provide expertise, procure material, sometimes months before election day, observe and assess the electoral process, and continue their technical assistance for some time after elections have been held.

It would go against their very purpose and mandate to refuse such assistance on the grounds that a country may not be quite ready for elections.

Indeed, international assistance and observers are no longer needed when a country *is* ready for elections, when it has successfully implemented its transition to democracy.

International monitoring of plebiscites, referenda and national elections has acquired its legitimacy and developed its expertise: it fulfills a needed international function, on the expectation that, ideally, in the far distant future, this function will cease when all nations are democracies.

In the meantime, as expressed by Thomas M. Franck, "the international system is moving toward a clearly designated democratic entitlement, with national governance validated by international standards and systematic monitoring of compliance".[5]

In conclusion, it may be appropriate to recall the Council of Europe's warning that international observers are strangers in a foreign land, who must exercise great care and tact if their mission is to be successful and that "in all circumstances, complete impartiality is an unwavering requirement".[6]

Impartiality should also be an unwavering requirement for all international observers sent by international organizations to assist countries in their transition to democracy.

However neither "great care and tact" nor "complete impartiality" are the only "unwavering requirements" for the success of international observers' missions: other, as important requirements, include professional competence and experience, political sense, linguistic qualifications, and, above all, the essential moral and intellectual courage to formulate and publicize their assessments that an electoral process has been (or not) "free and fair": after all is said, this last point is what international election observation is all about, within the framework of democratic development.

Notes

1. The message was sent to the Conference of the Rajiv Gandhi Foundation – see U.N. *Press Release* SG/SM/4989 of 3 May 1993.
2. In the words of the Oromo Liberation Front leader, during the elections in Ethiopia in 1992, as reported by Marina Ottaway in *CSIS Africa Notes*, Feb. 1993.
3. Ottaway, op.cit.
4. Among these, Ottaway, op.cit., – L. Berat and Y. Shain, (Provisional Governments in Democratization: The "International Interim Government" Model and the Case of Namibia", in *Coexistence*, 29/1, March 1992.
5. Thomas M. Franck, "The Emerging Right to Democratic Governance", *American Journal of International Law*, Jan. 1992, p. 91.
6. See Annex A.

LIST OF ANNEXES

Annex A

Council of Europe "Handbook for observers of elections" Observing local, regional or national elections in emerging democracies

Annex B

Commonwealth Document: Code of Conduct Adhered to by Political Parties in Bangladesh Presidential Elections, February 1992 –

Annex C

Organization of American States – Electoral Observation OAS/EOS – Suriname – Form for the Observation of Electoral Rallies or Demonstrations

Annex D

Organization of American States – Election Day Observations Polling Station Opening and Voting

Annex E

Commonwealth Document: Observation Notes for Polling Station Visits – Polling Station Report

ANNEX A

Council of Europe "Handbook for observers of elections" – Observing local, regional or national elections in emerging democracies – Excerpts

Introduction

This handbook is intended for the guidance of Observers at local, regional or national elections in emerging democracies. It is assumed that their role will be strictly one of observation only, and that they will not be in the position of supervisors having the right to intervene and suggest changes.

The handbook is divided into five parts. First, it sets out general points about the Observer Team, its formation and basic duties. Secondly advice is given on the tasks to be undertaken by the Observers in the run-up period to the Poll. The third and fourth parts discuss what is required of the Observers on Polling Day and at the count. The fifth part concerns the process of reporting after the count. Finally, a concise check list of the items dealt with in parts 1–5 is provided at the end of the handbook.

The role of the Observer will be to watch what happens during the electoral process and to report publicly afterwards, hopefully being able to say in the now hallowed phrase that the elections have been free and fair and that the result represents the will of the majority of the people.

Three assumptions are made:

i) that the team of Observers has been selected from people with the necessary knowledge and skills to observe elections effectively. Ability to speak the local language is useful; otherwise arrangements must be made to engage interpreters who, of course, must not be politically committed;

ii) that the number of Observers is sufficient to cover the election adequately, bearing in mind the size of the country or district and its population;

iii) that the Observer Team is recruited and will be used at the invitation, or with the knowledge and consent, of the host country.

1. General points

The members of the *Observer Team should be briefed* upon their duties and responsibilities at the start of their assignment. This should be done by people knowledge-

Source: Council of Europe, Handbook for observers of elections, Strasbourg 1992, pp. 5–8 and 21.

able about the country or area to be observed and its peoples but independent of all political connections. If possible, the whole team should be briefed at the same time. The briefing should be designed to ensure that all the Observers have the same approach to their task. Their independence and impartiality whilst carrying out their duties must be emphasised.

As much background information as possible must be given to the Observers about the country or district to be observed, its problems, political and economic, its peoples and about earlier elections. Where particular problems or difficulties are expected, these should be explained to the Observers.

The Observers should be given information about the political parties and their orientation, their leaders and sources of support – religious, class, ethnic, and their affiliations.

The members of the team should be given advice about the climate and living conditions in the host country. Care must be taken to ensure that they are properly prepared to undertake their tasks effectively and safely, especially in difficult climates.

A general *plan of action* for the Observers should be drawn up so that the most effective use will be made of their time (The more they can observe, the better. This will add credibility to the final report.)

Meetings of the Observers should take place during the tour of duty if time and distance permit. A regular exchange of information and views will be helpful.

The *Observers must be accredited* in a way which is satisfactory to the host government. They must be provided with badges, arm bands, certificates or other means of identification. The Observers must be readily recognisable by officials, the media and the public in the host country. All necessary arrangements must be made with the host government to ensure that the Observers are in no way restricted or impeded in carrying out their duties.

In very general terms, the Observers are responsible for seeing that the elections have been conducted in accordance with the following requirements:

1.1 That the administration of the election has been fair and impartial as between all the political parties taking part.

1.2 That no unacceptable restriction has been placed on any citizen who wishes to take part in the election process either as a candidate or as a voter.

1.3 That freedom of movement, assembly, association and expression has been respected during the election campaign.

1.4 That freedom for all the parties to conduct peaceful political activity has existed throughout the election period.

1.5 That all parties have conducted their political activities within the law.

1.6 That no political parties or other groups taking part in the election have been subjected to unnecessary restriction in enjoying free and unbiased access to the press, radio and television to express their views to the public and that they have all enjoyed freedom to advertise and publish their views.

1.7 That all political parties have enjoyed equal security during the election campaign.
1.8 That all electors have been able to cast their votes freely and without fear or undue influence.
1.9 That the secrecy of the ballot has been maintained.
1.10 That the arrangements for the conduct of (a) the poll and (b) the count have followed satisfactory standards to avoid fraud and illegality and to secure a free and fair election.

It is important that the Observer should not interfere in any of the electoral processes, even if things are going wrong, though he may be able to comment at the time to those in charge.

The amount of work which a team of Observers is able to undertake in connection with any particular election will depend upon the size of the team, the geographical area to be covered and the time available. In recent examples the time available has varied from three months to as little as a few days. The work which Observers can undertake must, therefore, be carefully prescribed in order to make the best possible use of the time available. It will, however, be desirable to cover as many as possible of the points which are listed below. If time is very short, the items marked with an asterisk should be given priority. Failure to cover these points adequately due to lack of time or to a shortage of Observers may cast doubt upon the quality and accuracy of the report which will be made by the Observers after the election. It is essential that the Observers stay on duty until the whole process of polling and counting has been completed.

Every attempt should be made to verify the points made above. If time is short and it is not possible for the Observers to carry out all the verifications themselves, they will have to rely upon interviews with representatives of the political parties and of the media.

The Observer Team should meet with the media as soon as possible at the start of their work to explain their presence and outline their duties. They should urge the media to report publicly upon the presence and responsibilities of the Observers. This should be source of encouragement to the electorate, especially if any of them are concerned about the fairness of the electoral procedures.

...

Conclusion

The task to be performed by the Observer is an important one in helping a country in its transition towards democracy. He will, however, be a stranger in a foreign land and must exercise great care and tact if his mission is to be successful.

Hopefully he will have been well briefed and be aware of any particular problems or difficulties which face him. He must adopt a friendly and co-operative approach and strive to win the confidence of everyone with whom he comes into contact – officials, media and the public. From his attitude and approach he should encourage everyone to accept that he is there to help and to assist in the emergence of democracy.

The Observer may question and comment but should not give the impression of criticising or being a hindrance; nor should he be officious in making suggestions.

In some situations the Observer should be prepared for a less than friendly reception. There may be those who do not welcome, or are positively opposed to his presence. A friendly demeanour will help the Observer to secure acceptance. In all circumstances, complete impartiality is an unwavering requirement.

ANNEX B

Code of Conduct Adhered to by Political Parties in Bangladesh Presidential Elections, February 1992

Jatiya Sangsad (Parliament) Election, 1991

Code of Conduct to be Adhered to by Political Parties

The code of conduct, finalised after discussions with the representatives of 67 political parties including major ones, is aimed at maintaining a peaceful atmosphere during the election campaign and on polling day.

The Election Commission hoped that if all political parties faithfully abide by the code, they would greatly contribute to the holding of a credible election in the country. Legitimacy of a representative government elected through such an election will not be questioned.

Code of Conduct

i) Existing election laws and rules must be adhered to.
ii) All political parties and contestants will have to extend all necessary help and co-operation to the law-enforcing authorities.
iii) Everyone should be aware of not only his own rights, but should also respect the rights of others.
iv) All political parties and candidates participating in the polls will extend full co-operation to the election officials and ensure their safety and security until the polls are over.
v) Election campaigns should be so organised that a congenial and peaceful atmosphere prevails during polling.
vi) Nothing should be done that will create tension and disrupt the congenial atmosphere of the election. All parties should exercise restraint in speech and show respect to the opinions of others so that electioneering does not turn into war of words.
vii) It is expected that criticism of opponents will occur during electioneering. However, indecorous and provocative speeches/statements, taunting, ridiculing and innuendos should be avoided. Parties should be careful so that statements or comments do not cause unnecessary tension. In case a situation for

Source: "Elections to the Constitutional Commission in Seychelles – 23–26 July 1992, The Report of the Commonwealth Observer Group", 1992, Annex VI, pp. 51–52 – by permission.

the possibility of a clash arises because of a misunderstanding between contesting parties, then an Election Co-ordination Committee composed of representatives from the concerned parties shall allay tension and settle the dispute.

viii) All political parties shall be vocal against violence. No party shall give indulgence to any kind of violent activity to demonstrate party strength or to prove supremacy. All political parties will extend co-operation to the law-enforcing agencies for recovery of illegal arms. No party will take any initiative for the release of any person arrested by police with arms during election campaign or in the polling centre during voting or in the vicinity of the polling centre during polls.

ix) All parties and candidates will have equal opportunity for publicity. Meetings, processions and other campaign activities of opponents cannot be interfered with.

x) Assistance of the nearest law-enforcing agencies will have to be sought to resist and check any sort of election offence.

xi) Any attempts to influence voting through money or allurement and to hire or use any kind of transport to carry voters other than for self and family are election offences. Everyone should be aware of these offences.

xii) political parties will reach an understanding to resist attempts to procure votes by forcible occupation of polling centres or through illegal activities in the polling centres. Votes thus obtained illegally will be of no use as the Election Commission will cancel polling in such centres.

xiii) No candidate can commit covertly or overtly any contribution or grant to any institution in his constituency until election day for the purpose of election campaigning and obtaining votes.

xiv) The congenial and peaceful atmosphere for election cannot be disturbed by spreading untrue and motivated rumour or by taking recourse to conspiracy.

xv) Election camps cannot be set up within the prohibited area or close to the polling centres and no campaign shall be allowed inside the polling centres.

xvi) In addition to the election officials, only the voters are entitled to enter the polling centres: the political parties should make sure that their workers do not enter the polling centres and loiter therein. Only the polling agents will remain seated at their designated seats in the polling centre and discharge their responsibility from there.

ANNEX C

Organization of American States Electoral Observation OAS/EOS Suriname Form for the Observation of Political Rallies or Demonstrations

ORGANIZATION OF AMERICAN STATES
ELECTORAL OBSERVATION OAS/EOS
SURINAME
FORM FOR THE OBSERVATION OF POLITICAL RALLIES OR DEMONSTRATIONS

DEMONSTRATION N°

NAME OF OAS OBSERVER(S): ______________________

LOCALITY: ______________________

DISTRICT: ______________________

DATE: ________ TIME: ________ DURATION: CANCELED ☐ INTERRUPTED ☐ ________ hrs.

ACRONYM OF ORGANIZING PARTY: ______________________

POLITICAL LEVEL OF EVENT: ☐ 1. NATIONAL ☐ 2. DISTRICT ☐ 3. LOCAL

POLITICAL SPEAKERS: ______________________

EVENT AUTHORIZED BY DISTRICT OFFICIAL: ☐ YES ☐ NO ☐ N.A.

LEVEL OF POLITICAL ORGANIZATION: ☐ 1 (LOW) ☐ 2 ☐ 3 ☐ 4 ☐ 5 (HIGH)

ESTIMATED NUMBER OF ACTIVE PARTICIPANTS: ______________________

TRANSPORT USED BY NON-LOCALS: ☐ 1. PRIVATE ☐ 2. STATE OWNED

POLITICAL CLIMATE

OVERALL TONE
- ☐ 01. EMOTIONAL
- ☐ 02. AGGRESSIVE
- ☐ 03. APOLOGETIC

THEMES
- ☐ 08. NATIONAL ISSUES
- ☐ 09. REGIONAL ISSUES
- ☐ 10. ATTACKS
- ☐ 11. APOLOGIES
- ☐ 12. PROMISES

GENERAL PUBLIC REACTION
- ☐ 13. ENTHUSIASTIC
- ☐ 14. PASSIVE
- ☐ 15. APATHETIC
- ☐ 16. AGGRESSIVE

ARGUMENTS
- ☐ 04. ANALYTICAL
- ☐ 05. POLITICAL PLATFORM
- ☐ 06. CRITICAL
- ☐ 07. NONE

INCIDENTS ☐ LIGHT

SERIOUS (check only one below)
- ☐ 01. THREATS
- ☐ 02. SABOTAGE
- ☐ 03. INVOLVING THE MILITARY
- ☐ 04. VERBAL AGGRESSION
- ☐ 05. LIGHT INJURIES
- ☐ 06. SERIOUS INJURIES
- ☐ 07. DEATHS

PREVENTATIVE SECURITY FORCES ☐ PRESENT ☐ ABSENT

ADDITIONAL COMMENTS (continue on reverse) ______________________

Source: OAS "Report of the Secretary General on the Observation of the Electoral Process in Suriname – Doc. OEA/Ser. G, CP/INF. 3192/91, 13 November 1991, p. 79 – by permission.

ANNEX D

Organization of American States OAS/EOS Election Day Observations Polling Station Opening and Voting

OAS/EOS

ELECTION DAY OBSERVATIONS
POLLING STATION OPENING AND VOTING

Names of Observers: ______________________________

INSTRUCTIONS: **If the Observer has not personally witnessed the opening of the polling station she/he should ask the officials present if everything went smoothly. In the case of being told of any incidents the Observer should seek more than one source of information.**

District: ______________________ **Code:** ______________
Municipality ("RESSORT") ______________________ **Code:** ______________
Number of Polling Station: ______________________ **Location:** ______________
Time of Observation: ______________________

OPENING AND COMPOSITION OF POLLING STATION

Hour of Opening: ______________________ **Voter Capacity of Station:** ______________
Number of Electoral Officials: ______________________

Are any of these Officials obviously identified with a political organization?	☐ Yes	☐ No
If yes, which political organization? ______________________		
Were OAS Observers present for the station opening?	☐ Yes	☐ No
Were the urns empty?	☐ Yes	☐ No
Were the ballots counted and scrutinized?	☐ Yes	☐ No
Did the president of the polling station stamp the ballots with a special seal and sign them?	☐ Yes	☐ No
Was the act of opening completed?	☐ Yes	☐ No
Did all of the Officials of the polling station sign this act?	☐ Yes	☐ No
Were any poll-watchers present for the opening?	☐ Yes	☐ No
If yes, from which political organization? ______________________		

PLEASE DETAIL ANY IRREGULARITIES WITH REGARD TO THE ABOVE:

____
____
____
____
____
____
____
____
____

The voting process took place: ☐ **Without irregularities**
☐ **With irregularities**

ANNEX E

Commonwealth Document: Observation Notes for Polling Station Visits:

Observation Notes

Part A

The Observers may focus particular attention on the following aspects of the election conduct:

Political Campaign

1. The nature of access to the electronics media available to the opposition parties.
2. The procedure (if any) for the allocation of time for political broadcasts and advertisements on the radio and television.
3. The nature of access enjoyed by the political parties to the print media.
4. The tone and contents of political broadcasts, advertisements and posters put out by the political parties.
5. The conduct of political meetings.
6. The conduct of house-to-house canvassing of voters.
7. The voter education programme on the radio and television conducted by the Director of Elections.
8. Permits for public meetings.
9. Effects of curfew.
10. Access to printing facilities.
11. Access to funds and sources of funds.
12. Access to state services.

Conduct of the polls

1. The siting of polling stations.
2. The accuracy of the list of electors at the polling stations.
3. Distances travelled by voters to polling stations in rural areas.
4. The length of time voters waited to cast their votes.
5. The steps (if any) taken to ensure that the secrecy of the ballot is assured.
6. The performance of the election officers at the polling station visited.

Source: "Presidential and National Assembly Elections in Zambia – 31 October 1991 – The Report of the Commonwealth Observer Group", Annex VII – by permission.

7. The procedure followed at the opening of the poll.
8. The adequacy or otherwise of polling stations' facilities.
9. The incidence of the loss of registration card.
10. The number (if any) of persons with national identity cards but without voters' card who were not allowed to vote.
11. The procedures in place to ensure the proper security of ballot papers, ballot boxes and official seals.
12. The general electoral environment that prevailed at the polling stations visited.
13. The transportation of the ballot boxes after the close of the polls.
14. The state of readiness of polling stations.
15. Availability of adequate supplies, eg ballot papers, sealing wax, etc.
16. Security of ballot papers prior to elections.
17. Access of party agents at all critical points, including transfer of ballot boxes.

The Count

1. The process of reconciling the number of names that voted with the ballot stubs received.
2. The determination of invalid ballots which are stamped rejected.
3. The conduct of the returning officers and their counting assistants.
4. The preparation of the Declaration of the Result of the Poll.
5. Inspection of seals.

Registration

1. Likely percentage of potential voters denied registration through early closure of rolls.
2. Procedures to challenge by voters of their exclusion from the rolls.

Part B

Questions that may be put:

Before Polling Day

1. Is electoral register full and correct? People missed off? Are there names of dead people/people who have moved away included?
2. Are election officials confident about arrangements? Are political parties and local notables (priests, lawyers, etc.) satisfied?
3. Is the man in the street satisfied with arrangements? Will he vote? If not, is he afraid to do so?
4. Has the campaign been free of intimidation, etc.? Have all parties had full access to media?
5. Is advertising (posters, leaflets, etc.) free?
6. How will voters' IDs be checked? Will it be possible to vote twice?
7. How will those away from home or ill in bed be able to vote?

On the day

1. Before polling starts, are the ballot boxes empty? Are they properly sealed?
2. Are all procedures agreed beforehand being adhered to?
3. Are all parties represented at polling stations? Are they satisfied with process?
4. Are IDs being properly checked?
5. Are voters apparently voting freely? Are they enthusiastic? Do they talk freely? Do they exhibit signs of fear or intimidation?
6. Do voters understand procedures properly? If not, are they being explained fully and impartially? Are attempts being made to suggest how they should vote?
7. Is only one person at a time allowed into the voting booth? Do their ballot papers go straight into the sealed box?
8. How long are voters waiting to vote? If a long time, are some being put off?
9. Who will run the procedures on the day? Will they be ex-Party people? How were they chosen?
10. Will all parties be present at polling stations throughout voting and count?
11. Will foreign observers have free access to all stages of process?
12. Are voters being asked suspicious questions after leaving the ballot boxes?

After Voting

1. Are the boxes kept safe until opened? Are all parties/observers present at opening?
2. Does the number of used ballot papers tally with the record of those who have voted?
3. Are the papers counted properly? Are any valid ones being spoiled during counting, intentionally or not?

Polling Station Report

Name/Team:
Polling Station Visited:
Time:

	Comments (if necessary)	
ACCESS		
Were you allowed full access to the polling station?	YES	NO
OFFICIALS		
Were you received well by official?	YES	NO
Did they have any comments or complaints?	YES	NO

MOOD

Was the mood	Orderly?	——
	Tense?	——
	Violent?	——
	Excited?	——
	Happy?	——

IF YOU SPOKE TO VOTERS

– were they happy to talk?		——
– generally satisfied?		——
– did they have any complaints?		——
were any of these:	intimidation	——
	harassment	——
	unfairness	——
	confusion	——

GENERAL COMMENTS ON APPARENT FAIRNESS:

OTHER BOOKS BY YVES BEIGBEDER

La représentation du personnel à l'Organisation Mondiale de la Santé et dans les principales institutions spécialisées des Nations Unies ayant leur siège en Europe: Librairie générale de droit et de jurisprudence, Paris, 1975, 290 p.
Management Problems in United Nations Organizations: Reform or Decline?: Frances Pinter Publishers, London, 1987, 174 p.
Threats to the International Civil Service – Past Pressures and New Trends: Pinter Publishers, London, 1988, 186 p.
"Administrative and Structural Reform in the Organizations of the United Nations Family", in *International Administration – Law and Management Practices in International Organizations*, Chris de Cooker, Ed., UNITAR/Martinus Nijhoff Publishers, 1990, II.4.
The Role and Status of International Humanitarian Volunteers and Organizations – The Right and Duty to Humanitarian Assistance:
Martinus Nijhoff Publishers, Dordrecht/Boston/London, 1991, 414 p.
Le rôle international des organisations non gouvernementales: Bruylant-Brussels, L.G.D.J.-Paris, 1992, 195 p.

LIST OF ABBREVIATIONS

ASEAN	Association of South East Asian Nations
CSCE	Conference on Security and Cooperation in Europe
DOMREP	Representative of the Secretary-General in the Dominican Republic
EC	European Community
FIDH	Fédération internationale des droits de l'homme
Frelimo	Mozambique Liberation Front
Funcinpec	United Front for an Independent, Neutral, Peaceful and Cooperative Cambodia
ICFTU	International Confederation of Trade Unions
ICJ	International Commission of Jurists
ICJ	International Court of Justice
ICRC	International Committee of the Red Cross
IFES	International Foundation for Electoral Systems
IGO	Intergovernmental organization
ILO	International Labour Organisation
IMF	International Monetary Fund
IPU	Inter-Parliamentary Union
IRI	International Republican Institute
MINURSO	United Nations Mission for the Referendum in Western Sahara
MPLA	Popular Movement for the Liberation of Angola
NED	National Endowment for Democracy
NDI	National Democratic Institute for International Affairs
NGO	Non-governmental organization
OAU	Organization of African Unity
OAS	Organization of American States
ODIHR	(CSCE) Office for Democratic Institutions and Human Rights
OECD	Organization for Economic Cooperation and Development
ONUMOZ	United Nations Operation in Mozambique

ONUVEH	United Nations Observer Group for the Verification of Elections in Haiti
ONUVEN	United Nations Observer Mission to verify the electoral process in Nicaragua
Renamo	Mozambique National Resistance
SWAPO	South West Africa People's Organization
U.K.	United Kingdom
U.N.	United Nations
UNAMIC	United Nations Advanced Mission in Cambodia
UNAVEM II	United Nations Angola Verification Mission
UNCIP	United Nations Commission for India and Pakistan
UNCOK	United Nations Commission on Korea
UNCTAD	United Nations Conference on Trade and Development
UNCURK	United Nations Commission for the Unification and Rehabilitation of Korea
UNDP	United Nations Development Programme
UNHCR	United Nations High Commissioner for Refugees
UNITA	National Union for the Total Independence of Angola
UNMOGIP	United Nations Military Observer Group in India and Pakistan
UNTAC	United Nations Transitional Authority in Cambodia
UNTAG	United Nations Transition Assistance Group in Namibia
UNTCOK	United Nations Temporary Commission on Korea
UNTEA/UNSF	United Nations Temporary Executive Authority and United Nations Security Force in West New Guinea (West Irian)
U.S.A.	United States of America
USAID	United States of America Agency for International Development
USIA	United States Information Agency
USSR	Union of Soviet Socialist Republics

BIBLIOGRAPHY

General Bibliography

Abi-Saab, Georges, "La deuxième génération des opérations de maintien de la paix", in *Trimestre du Monde*, Paris, 1992/4.

Academic Council on the U.N. System, "The World in Turmoil: Testing the U.N.'s Capacity", 1991.

Academic Council on the U.N. System, "The State of the United Nations: 1992".

Ahmad, Feroz, *The Turkish Experiment in Democracy – 1950–1975*, The Royal Institute of International Affairs, C. Hurst and Co., London, 1977.

Amato, Dennis John, "Elections under International Auspices – 1948–1970", Unpublished dissertation, The Johns Hopkins University, Ph.D., 1971.

Amnesty International, *Amnesty International Report 1990.*

Asad, Mohammad, *The Principles of State and Government in Islam*, Dar Al-Andalus, Gibraltar, 1980.

Baker, Ray S. and Dodd, William E. (Eds), *The Public Papers of Woodrow Wilson, War and Peace*, Harper, New York.

Barsh, R.L., "Democratization and Development", *Human Rights Quarterly*, Feb. 1992.

Barzun, Jacques, "The Theorem of Democracy", *Society*, Transaction Publ., 1989.

Bayanov, B., Umansky, Y. and Shafir, M., *Soviet Socialist Democracy*, Progress Publ., Moscow, 1968.

Bedjaoui, Mohammed, in *Aspects du système des Nations Unies dans le cadre de l'idée d'un nouvel ordre mondial*, Pedone, Paris, 1991.

Beigbeder, Yves, *The Role and Status of International Humanitarian Volunteers and Organizations – The Right and Duty to Humanitarian Assistance*, Kluwer/Nijhoff, Dordrecht, The Netherlands, 1991.

Berat, L. and Shain, Y., "Provisional Governments in Democratization: The "International Interim Government" Model and the Case of Namibia", *Coexistence*, March 1992.

Boutros-Ghali, Boutros, *An Agenda for Peace – Preventive Diplomacy, Peacemaking and Peace-keeping*, United Nations, New York, 1992.

Bullock, Alan, *Hitler and Stalin – Parallel Lives*, HarperCollins, 1991.

Cecil, Lord Robert, *A Great Experiment*, Jonathan Cape, London, 1941.

Claude, Inis L., Jr., *Swords into Plowshares – The Problems and Progress of International Organization*, 4th Ed., Random House, New York, 1971.

Colliard, Cl.-A., *Institutions des relations internationales*, 8th Ed., Dalloz, Paris 8th ed., 1985.

Conference on Security and Cooperation in Europe (CSCE), CSCE Office of Democratic Institutions and Human Rights, "1991 Activities Report", – *Bulletin*, Winter 1992/93, – Spring 1993, – Handbook for human dimension mechanism, experts/rapporteurs and election observers, March 1993.

Constable, Pamela, "Haiti's Shattered Hopes", *Journal of Democracy*, Jan. 1992.

Costa, Eduardo Ferrero, "Peru's Presidential Coup", *Journal of Democracy*, Jan. 1993.

Cot, J.P. and Pellet, A. (Eds), *La Charte des Nations Unies – Commentaire article par article*, Economica/Bruylant, Paris/Brussels 1985.

Council of Europe, "Convention for the Protection of Human Rights and Fundamental Freedoms and Protocols to the said Convention", Rome, 4 November 1950, *European Treaty Series* 5 and 9.

Council of Europe, "European Commission for Democracy through Law, Annual Report of Activities for 1990", "– for 1991".

Council of Europe, "Statute of the Council of Europe, London, 5 May 1949", Council of Europe Doc. No. 1.

Council of Freely-Elected Heads of Government, "Background – Special Report No. 1".

Dahl, Robert A., *Polyarchy: Participation and Opposition*, Yale University Press, New Haven, CT, 1971.

Diamond, Larry, "Promoting Democracy", *Foreign Policy*, Summer 1992.

Dickinson, Don, "Cambodia's evolving situation", *International Review*, Winter 1992–1993.

Dreyer, Ronald, "The U.N. and Namibia: An Overview (1946–1990), in *International Geneva Yearbook*, Vol. V, 1991.

Duranton-Crabol, Anne-Marie, *L'Europe de l'Extrême Droite – De 1945 à nos jours*, Ed. Complexe, Brussels, 1991.

Ebenstein, William and Fogelman, E., *Today's Isms – Communism, Facism, Capitalism, Socialism*, 9th Ed., Prentice-Hall, Englewood Clifts, New Jersey, 1985.

El-Kadhafi, Moammar, *Le livre vert*, Cujas, Paris, 1976.

Esposito, John L. and Piscatori, James P., "Democratization and Islam" in *Middle East Journal*, Summer 1991, Vol. 45, No. 3.

Foley, Hamilton, *Woodrow Wilson's Case for the League of Nations*, Princeton University Press, New Jersey, 1923.

Franck, Thomas M., *Nation against Nation – What happened to the U.N. Dream and What the U.S. can do about it*, Oxford University Press, New York/Oxford 1985.

Franck, Thomas M., "The Emerging Right to Democratic Governance", *American Journal of International Law*, Vol. 86, Jan. 1992.

Freedom House, *Freedom in the World – Political Rights and Civil Liberties – 1991–1992*, Freedom House, New York 1992.

Garber, Larry, *Guidelines for International Election Observing*, The International Human Rights Law Group, Washington, D.C., 1990.

Garber, Larry and Bjornlund, Eric, "Election Monitoring in Africa", in *The Evolving Role of Intergovernmental Organizations in Election Monitoring*, A Training Seminar for the Organization of African Unity, sponsored by the African American Institute and the National Democratic Institute for International Affairs.

Gastil, Raymond D., *Freedom in the World – Political Rights and Civil Liberties – 1987–1988*, Freedom House, New York, 1988.

Ghebali, V.-Y., "Le développement des opérations de maintien de la paix de l'ONU depuis la fin de la guerre froide", in *Le Trimestre du Monde*, Paris V University, Paris, 1992/4.

Goodrich, L.M., Hambro, E. and Simons, A.P., *Charter of the United Nations*, 3rd Ed., Columbia University Press, New York, 1969.

Gordenker, Leon, *The U.N. and the Peaceful Unification of Korea – The Politics of Field Operations, 1947–1950*, Nijhoff, The Netherlands, 1959.

Harris, Richard L., *Marxism, Socialism and Democracy in Latin America*, Westview Press, Boulder, Co 1992.

Hendel, S. (Ed), *The Soviet Crucible: Soviet Government in Theory and Practice*, S. Hendel New York, 1958.

Holland, Thomas Erskine, *The Elements of Jurisprudence*, Clarendon Press, London, New York 1900.

Huntington, Samuel P., "Democracy's Third Wave", *Journal of Democracy*, 2 (Spring 1991).

International Foundation for Electoral Systems (IFES), "IFES Programs in Election Assistance".

International Human Rights Law Group, "Fact Sheet – Activities Report 1978–1989".

Inter-Parliamentary Union, *Electoral Systems – A World-Wide Comparative Study*, Geneva, 1993.

Islamic Council of Europe, *Concept of Islamic State*, London, 1979.
Jacobson, Harold K., *Networks of Interdependence – International Organizations and the Global Political System*, 2nd Ed., Knopf, New York, 1979.
James, Alan, *The Politics of Peacekeeping*, Chatto and Windus, London, 1969.
Kautsky, Karl, *The Dictatorship of the Proletariat*, The National Labour Press, Manchester 1919.
Lenin, *Lenin, Collected Works*, 5th Russian Ed., Progress Publ. Moscow.
LeRoy Bennett, A., *International Organizations*, 3rd Ed., Prentice-Hall, Englewood Clifts, N.J. 1984.
Linz, Juan J., "Comparative Study of Fascism", in *Fascism: A Reader's Guide*, Walter Laqueur Ed., Penguin Books, New York 1979.
Lowenstein, Prince Hubertus, "The Totalitarian State in Germany and the individual", in *The Annals of the American Academy of Political and Social Science*, Vol. 180, July 1935.
Luard, Evan, *A History of the United Nations*, Vol. 1, MacMillan, New York, 1984.
Mantran, Robert, *Histoire de la Turquie*, PUF, Paris, 1988.
Mayo, H.B., *An Introduction to Democratic Theory*, Oxford University Press, New York, 1960.
Miller, David Hunter, *The Drafting of the Covenant*, G.P. Putnam's Sons, New York, London 1928.
Montesquieu, *De l'esprit des lois*, Classiques Larousse. Paris, 1971
National Democratic Institute for International Affairs, Washington, D.C. "NDI's Approach to International Election Assistance", March 1992.
National Endowment for Democracy, "Strategy Document", Jan. 1992.
Neher, Clark D., "Democratization in Southeast Asia", *Asian Affairs – An American Review*, 18/3, Fall 1991.
Nietzsche, *The Will to Power*, trans. A.M. Ludovici, 1888 in 'The International Thesaurus of Quotations', by R.T. Tripp, Penguin Books, Harmondsworth, UK, 1983 p. 231
Nitti, F., *Bolshevism, Fascism and Democracy*, George Allen and Unwin, London, 1927.
Ottaway, Marina, "Should Elections Be the Criterion of Democratization in Africa?", *CSIS Africa Notes*, Feb. 1993.
Pastor, Robert A. (Ed), *Democracy in the Americas – Stopping the Pendulum*, Holmes and Meier, New York/London, 1989.
Reiss, Hans, *Kant's Political Writings*, Cambridge University Press, Cambridge 1970.
Rousseau, Ch., *Droit international public*, Sirey, Paris 1953.
Rousseau, Jean-Jacques, *The Social Contract and Discourses*, Translated and Introd. by G.D.H. Cole, Revised and Augmented by J.H. Brumfitt and John C. Hall, Dent, London, 1990.
Scott, George, *The Rise and Fall of the League of Nations*, Macmillan, New York, 1973.
Sieghart, Paul, *The Lawful Rights of Mankind*, Oxford University Press, Oxford/New York 1986.
Steinert, Marlis, *Hitler*, Fayard, Paris, 1991.
Sternhell, Zeev, "Fascist Ideology", in Laqueur, op.cit.
Strong, C.F., *Modern Political Constitutions*, Sidgwick and Jackson Ltd., London, 1963.
Tessitore, J. and Woolfson, S., *A Global Agenda – Issues before the 47th General Assembly of the U.N.*, U.N. Association of the U.S.A., University Press of America, 1992.
Tocqueville, Alexis de, *On Democracy, Revolution and Society: Selected Writings*, J. Stone and S. Mennell (Eds), University of Chicago Press, 1980.
United Nations, "Agreements on a Comprehensive Political Settlement of the Cambodian Conflict, Paris, 23 October 1991".
United Nations, *Basic Facts about the U.N., 1980.*
United Nations *Charter*. United Nations, New York, 1987
United Nations, *The Blue Helmets – A Review of U.N. Peace-keeping*, 2nd Ed., 1990.
United Nations, *Everyone's United Nations*, Ninth Ed., United Nations, New York, 1979
United Nations, "Plebiscites held since 1920 under the control or supervision of international organizations, Memorandum prepared by the Secretariat", Doc. A/C. 4/351 of 20 Feb. 1957.
United Nations, "Enhancing the effectiveness of the principle of periodic and genuine elections – Report of the Secretary-General", Doc. A/47/668 of 18 Nov. 1992.

United Nations, "Guidelines for Member States considering the formulation of requests for electoral assistance", Doc. A/47/668/Add. 1, 24 Nov. 1992.

United Nations Development Programme, *Human Development Report 1991, – 1992 – 1993*, Oxford University Press, New York-Oxford

U.N. Association of the U.S.A. *Issues/45* Lexington Books, Lexington, MA, Toronto 1991.

U.N. Association of the U.S.A., *A Global Agenda – Issues before the 47th General Assembly of the United Nations*, University Press of America, 1992.

Urquhart, Brian, *A Life in Peace and War*, Harper and Row, New York, 1987.

Walters, F.P., *A History of the League of Nations*, Oxford University Press, London, New York, Toronto 1952.

Wambaugh, Sarah, *A Monograph on Plebiscites*, Oxford University Press, New York, 1920.

Wambaugh, Sarah, *Plebiscites since the World War*, Carnegie Endowment for International Peace, Washington, D.C., 1933.

Wambaugh, Sarah, *The Saar Plebiscite*, Harvard University Press, Cambridge, MA, 1940.

World Bank, *World Development Report 1992*, Oxford University Press, New York, Oxford 1992.

Zorgbibe, Charles, *Chronologie des relations internationales depuis 1945*, Presses Universitaires de France, Paris, 1991.

Selected Observation Reports on Electoral Processes

Center for Strategic and International Studies

Loser, Eva, "The 1989 Panamanian Elections – Post-Election Report".

Commonwealth

"Gibraltar Referendum, Report of the Commonwealth Team of Observers to the Commonwealth Secretary-General, September 1967".

"Southern Rhodesia Elections, February 1980 – The Report of the Commonwealth Observer Group on Elections leading to Independent Zimbabwe".

"Uganda Elections – December 1980, The Report of the Commonwealth Observer Group".

"Preparing for a Free Namibia: Elections, Transition and Independence – The Report of the Commonwealth Observer Group on Namibia", Windhoek, 10 Oct. 1989.

"General Elections in Malaysia – 20–21 October 1990 – Report of the Commonwealth Observer Group".

"Parliamentary Elections in Bangladesh, 27 February 1991, The Report of the Commonwealth Observer Group".

"Presidential and National Assembly Elections in Zambia – 31 October 1991, The Report of the Commonwealth Observer Group".

"Elections to the Constitutional Commission in Seychelles, 23–26 July 1992 – The Report of the Commonwealth Observer Group".

Conference on Security and Cooperation in Europe (CSCE)

"Report on the CSCE Fact-Finding Mission Regarding May 31 (1992) Elections in the Federal Republic of Yugoslavia", 25 May 1992.

Council of Freely-Elected Heads of Government

"Observing Nicaragua's Elections, 1989–1990" The Carter Center of Emory University, Special Report #1, Atlanta, GA, 1990

Council of Freely-Elected Heads of Government – National Democratic Institute for International Affairs

"The 1990 General Elections in Haiti – International Delegation Report", 1991.
"The October 31, 1991 National Elections in Zambia", 1992.
"Observing Guyana's Electoral Process – 1990–1992 – Special Report No. 3.

Fédération internationale des droits de l'homme

"Rapport de Mission – Haiti – Première mission d'observateurs à l'occasion des élections de fin 1987", 1987.
– "Rapport de Mission – Mission des observateurs du plébiscite du 5 octobre 1988 au Chili", 1989.

International Commission of Jurists

"Soutien de la Commission des Communautés Européennes au processus de démocratisation à Madagascar – Observatoire international de la démocratie à Madagascar, Rapport de la mission d'observation du référendum constitutionnel du 19 août 1992", 1992.
Kourouma, M.M., "Rapport de mission de la CIJ, décembre 1992-janvier 1993", 1993.
Kourouma, M.M., "Second tour des présidentielles, 10 février 1993", 1993.

Inter-Parliamentary Union

"Report of the Mission to Observe the Elections in Namibia", 1989.
"Report of the Mission to observe the elections in Cambodia", 1993.

National Democratic Institute for International Affairs

"Nation Building: the U.N. and Namibia", 1990.
"An Assessment of the October 11, 1992 Election in Cameroon", 1993.

National Republican and National Democratic Institutes for International Affairs

"The May 7, 1989 Panamanian Elections – International Delegation Report, 1989.
"The May 1990 Elections in Romania", 1990.

Organization of American States

"Report of the Secretary General on the Observation of the Municipal Elections in Paraguay", 1991.
"Report of the Secretary General on the observation of the electoral process in Suriname", 1991.
"Report of the Observation Mission on the Elections to the Constitutional Convention held in the Republic of Paraguay on December 1, 1991", 1992.

United Nations

"U.N. Backgrounder, The Question of Western Sahara", Aug. 1988.
"U.N. Electoral Assistance to Haiti", March 1991.
"Election Supervision, the U.N. Experience in Namibia and Nicaragua", *U.N. Focus*, Nov. 1990.

INDEX

International Studies in Human Rights

20. A. Bloed and P. van Dijk (eds.): *The Human Dimension of the Helsinki Process.* The Vienna Follow-up Meeting and its Aftermath. 1991 ISBN 0-7923-1337-2
21. L.S. Sunga: *Individual Responsibility in International Law for Serious Human Rights Violations.* 1992 ISBN 0-7923-1453-0
22. S. Frankowski and D. Shelton (eds.): *Preventive Detention.* A Comparative and International Law Perspective. 1992 ISBN 0-7923-1465-4
23. M. Freeman and P. Veerman (eds.): *The Ideologies of Children's Rights.* 1992 ISBN 0-7923-1800-5
24. S. Stavros: *The Guarantees for Accused Persons Under Article 6 of the European Convention on Human Rights.* An Analysis of the Application of the Convention and a Comparison with Other Instruments. 1993 ISBN 0-7923-1897-8
25. A. Rosas and J. Helgesen (eds.): *The Strength of Diversity.* Human Rights and Pluralist Democracy. 1992 ISBN 0-7923-1987-7
26. K. Waaldijk and A. Clapham (eds.): *Homosexuality: A European Community Issue.* Essays on Lesbian and Gay Rights in European Law and Policy. 1993 ISBN 0-7923-2038-7; Pb: 0-7923-2240-1
27. Y.K. Tyagi: *The Law and Practice of the UN Human Rights Committee.* 1993 ISBN 0-7923-2040-9
28. G. van Bueren: *The International Law on the Rights of the Child.* 1993 ISBN 0-7923-2221-5
29. L.A. Rehof: *Guide to the* Travaux Préparatoires *of the United Nations Convention on the Elimination of All Forms of Discrimination against Women.* 1993 ISBN 0-7923-2222-3
30. A. Bloed, L. Leicht, M. Novak and A. Rosas (eds.): *Monitoring Human Rights in Europe.* Comparing International Procedures and Mechanisms. 1993 ISBN 0-7923-2383-1
31. A. Harding and J. Hatchard (eds.): *Preventive Detention and Security Law.* A Comparative Survey. 1993 ISBN 0-7923-2432-3
32. Y. Beigbeder: *International Monitoring of Plebiscites, Referenda and National Elections.* Self-determination and Transition to Democracy. 1994 ISBN 0-7923-2563-X

This series is designed to shed light on current legal and political aspects of process and organization in the field of human rights.

MARTINUS NIJHOFF PUBLISHERS – DORDRECHT / BOSTON / LONDON